JUDGING NEW WEALTH

JUDGING NEW WEALTH

Popular Publishing and Responses to Commerce in England, 1750–1800

JAMES RAVEN

CLARENDON PRESS · OXFORD

This book has been printed digitally and produced in a standard design
in order to ensure its continuing availability

OXFORD
UNIVERSITY PRESS

Great Clarendon Street, Oxford OX2 6DP
Oxford University Press is a department of the University of Oxford.
It furthers the University's objective of excellence in research, scholarship,
and education by publishing worldwide in

Oxford New York

Athens Auckland Bangkok Bogotá Buenos Aires Cape Town
Chennai Dar es Salaam Delhi Florence Hong Kong Istanbul Karachi
Kolkata Kuala Lumpur Madrid Melbourne Mexico City Mumbai
Nairobi Paris São Paulo Singapore Taipei Tokyo Toronto Warsaw

with associated companies in Berlin Ibadan

Oxford is a registered trade mark of Oxford University Press
in the UK and certain other countries

Published in the United States
by Oxford University Press Inc., New York

© James Raven 1992

The moral rights of the author have been asserted
Database right Oxford University Press (maker)

Reprinted 2001

ISBN 0-19-820237-7

For

Elizabeth Durkee,
Highland Park, NJ,

and

Anatole Mines,
Cambridge, England

Business disqualifies a Man for heaven more than Pleasure does.

Mrs Thrale, 14 July 1780

ACKNOWLEDGEMENTS

MANY people have answered queries and sent me references and other material. Debts are acknowledged at relevant points, but more broadly I wish to thank Anne Barbeary, Stephen Bending, Julian Hoppit, Kazuhiko Kondo, Alan Sterenberg, John Styles, and Naomi Tadmor for sharing data with me or letting me see completed work in advance of publication. Much of the following study derives from research originally conducted under the supervision of Neil McKendrick. As always, I am grateful for his generous criticism and warm encouragement.

Research has also been very nomadic. I owe much to the advice and expertise of the archivists, curators, and librarians of the following: the American Antiquarian Society, Worcester, Massachusetts; Barclays Bank, Lombard Street; Bedfordshire County Record Office, Bedford; the Beinecke Library, Yale; Berkshire County Record Office, Reading; the Bodleian Library; the British Library; the Brotherton Library, Leeds University; Cambridge University Library; Cambridgeshire Record Office, Cambridge; Cheshire Record Office, Chester; Chester City Record Office; Colchester Public Library; the Corporation of London Records Office; the Dorset County Museum and Naturalist and Archaeological Society, Dorchester; Dorset County Record Office, Dorchester; Edinburgh University Library; Essex County Record Office, Chelmsford; Essex University Library; Gloucester Public Library; the Goldsmiths' Library, London; the Guildhall Library; Hampshire County Record Office, Winchester; Hereford City Library; Herefordshire Record Office, Hereford; Hereford and Worcester Record Office, Worcester; the Holborn Local History Library; the Houghton Library, Harvard University; the Institute of Historical Research, London; Ipswich Public Library; John Rylands University Library of Manchester; Leeds City Archives; the Lewis Walpole Library, Farmington, Connecticut; the library of the Worshipful Company of Papermakers and Stationers, Stationers' Hall; the National Library of Scotland; the Newberry Library, Chicago; the New York Public Library; the

New York Society Library; Norfolk Record Office, Norwich; Nottingham Central Library; Reading University Library and Archives; the Alexander Library, Rutgers University; Shropshire Record Office, Shrewsbury; Suffolk Record Office, Bury St Edmunds branch; Suffolk Record Office, Ipswich branch; Westminster Public Library.

Research was undertaken when supported by an SSRC, then ESRC, then Ellen McArthur studentship at Clare College, Cambridge; by a studentship from the English-Speaking Union of New Brunswick; by a Peterson fellowship at the American Antiquarian Society; and by a Newberry fellowship at the Newberry Library, Chicago. I am also indebted to the Cambridge Historical Society for a grant towards several computerized bibliographical searches. The early parts of this book were written in several different places: I am especially grateful to Miss Anatole Mines for allowing her beautiful home and garden to be host to my books and students; to Miss Elizabeth Durkee and my adopted New Jersey family for their generous hospitality; and to friends and colleagues at Clare and the Cambridge Economics Faculty for their criticisms and assistance. The book was finished during my tenure of a Fellowship at Pembroke College, Cambridge. No one could have wished for a more tolerant and convivial community in which to live and write.

CONTENTS

LIST OF FIGURES

NOTES ON THE TEXT

THE term 'bookseller' was used in the eighteenth century to describe a publisher as well as a wholesale dealer or retail bookseller. Where possible, the following study makes clear the distinction between publisher and retailer, but various quotations and contemporary references require an appreciation of the broader definition of 'bookseller'.

All quotations retain the original spelling. Italics within quotes are also reproduced from the original. Where possible, quotations and references are taken from first editions published in London. Occasionally, however, a later Dublin reprint is used where this is more accessible for the reader (as, for example, when this is the edition reproduced in *Eighteenth-Century Microfilms*). Unless this is appreciated, the later dates of many Irish (and other) reprints may cause confusion where reference is given to the five-year sampling of material as described in Chapter 2.

ABBREVIATIONS

AM	*Attic Miscellany; or, Characteristic Mirror of Men and Things* (London, 1789–91)
AR	*Analytical Review; or, History of Literature Domestic and Foreign* (London, 1788–99)
B&I	*Biographical and Imperial Magazine* (London, 1789–91)
CR	*Critical Review; or, Annals of Literature* (London, 1756–90; NS, 1791–1803)
Ec.HR	*Economic History Review*
EM	*European Magazine, and London Review* (London, 1782–1825)
ER	*English Review; or, An Abstract of English and Foreign Literature* (London, 1783–96)
ESTC	*Eighteenth-Century Short Title Catalogue*
GM	*General Magazine and Impartial Review* (London, 1787–92)
LM	*London Magazine; or, Gentleman's Monthly Intelligencer* (London, 1732–83)
MR	*Monthly Review; or, Literary Journal* (London, 1749–89; NS, 1790–1825)
N&Q	*Notes and Queries*
NCBEL	*New Cambridge Bibliography of English Literature*, 5 vols. (Cambridge, 1969–77)
PEL	*Penguin English Library*
PHIBB	Project for Historical Biobliography. G. Averley, A. Flowers, *et al.*, *Eighteenth-Century British Books: A Subject Catalogue*, 4 vols. (Folkestone, 1979)
PMLA	*Papers of the Modern Languages Association*
ScM	*Scots Magazine* (Edinburgh, 1739–1804)
T&C	*Town and Country Magazine; or, Universal Repositary of Knowledge, Instruction, and Entertainment* (London, 1769–92)
THES	*Times Higher Education Supplement*
TLS	*Times Literary Supplement*
TRHS	*Transactions of the Royal Historical Society*

I

INTRODUCTION

Is 'merchant' an inglorious name?
What say the sons of letter'd fame?
Edward Young, *Imperium Pelagi*, (1730).

DESPITE renewed interest in the lives of British financiers, merchants, and industrialists, the modern study of business élites remains comparatively youthful.[1] For the late eighteenth century in particular, the unevenness in research bedevils discussion of the social aspirations of the entrepreneurs, of their influence in the community, of their landownership or investments, of their approval or vilification.[2] Contemporary observers had no such reticence. Nor were they burdened by the demands of historical accuracy. The surviving literary legacy offers vivid commentary, not only upon the likes of Boulton, Wedgwood, and Watt, but upon hundreds of lesser merchants, manufacturers, and businessmen who offended or married the gentry, clothed or robbed the poor, won or lost on the hustings, delivered justice or were brought before it.

Defoe, writing in 1728, reflected upon one of the great questions of the age:

[1] Social historians have neglected the wealthy in Britain. The challenge is set out in Hartmut Kaelble, *Historical Research on Social Mobility: Western Europe and the United States of America in the Nineteenth and Twentieth Centuries*, trans. by Ingrid Noakes (London, 1981); W. D. Rubinstein, *Men of Property: The Very Wealthy in Britain since the Industrial Revolution* (London, 1981); 'New Men of Wealth and the Purchase of Land in Nineteenth-Century England', *Past and Present*, 92 (Aug. 1981), 125–47; and (ed.), *Wealth and the Wealthy in the Modern World* (London, 1980).

[2] Foremost among comparative studies of early industrialists (focusing most recently on social classification) are François Crouzet, *The First Industrialists: The Problem of Origins* (Cambridge, 1985); J. W. Gough, *The Rise of the Entrepreneur* (London, 1969); Katrina Honeyman, *The Origins of Enterprise: Business Leadership in the Industrial Revolution* (Manchester, 1982).

Law, trade, war, navigation, improvement of stocks, loans on public funds, places of trust, and abundance of other modern advantages and private wayes of getting money ... have rais'd a great number of familyes to not onely prosperous circumstances, for that I am not speaking of, but to immense estates, vast and, till of late, unheard of summs of money amass'd in a short time and which have, in the consequence, rais'd such families to a stacion of life some thing difficult to describe and not less difficult to giv a name to.[3]

There is no doubting the social and political impact of merchants and manufacturers in London and the provincial cities, and in most selections from literature of the period it is difficult to escape references to the social repercussions of advancing commerce. The transformation of trade and manufacturing in eighteenth-century England was paralleled by a complex literary re-evaluation of business achievement.

At face value, little of the comment was original. Sudden riches and those enjoying them have been viewed with suspicion since antiquity. Landed as opposed to commercial wealth was the key to respectability in much classical philosophical and imaginative literature.[4] In medieval England *Piers Plowman* and Chaucer's *Tales* were amongst dozens of works containing satires against money-making. The avaricious merchant was condemned in commentaries ranging from the notorious *London Lickpenny* to the fifteenth-century metrical sermons on the Feast of Corpus Christi.[5] In the seventeenth century formidable stage villains from Jonson's Sir Epicure Mammon (1610) to John Wilson's Suckdry and Squeeze (1664) were supported by colourful characters from popular books of edification. Many writers attacked the fashionable dress and social aspirations of the newly-moneyed. Printed sermons and short works of divinity extended courtesy book images of the obligation to perform good works and to be

[3] Daniel Defoe, *The Compleat English Gentleman*, ed. by Karl D. Bülbring (London, 1890), p. 257. Defoe singles out Sir Josiah Child, Mr Tysson, Sir James Bateman, Sir Thomas De Vall, and Sir William Scawen as representative commercial grandees.

[4] Source selections are given in M. M. Austin and P. Vidal-Naquet, *Economic and Social History of Ancient Greece: An Introduction* (London, 1977), esp. extracts from Demosthenes, *Against Aristocrates*. Also, P. A. Brunt, *Social Conflicts in the Roman Republic* (London, 1986).

[5] Further examples are given in V. J. Scattergood, *Politics and Poetry in the Fifteenth Century* (London, 1971), and Thomas H. Bestul, *Satire and Allegory in Wynnere and Westoure* (Lincoln, Nebr., 1974). The tradition of 'conservative money-satirists' is assessed in John A. Yunck, *The Lineage of Lady Meed* (Notre Dame, Ind., 1963). Cf. Colin Wilcockson, 'A Note on Riflynge in *Piers Plowman*', *Medium Ævum*, 52/2 (1983), 302–5, for Langland's attack on the dishonesty of merchants.

satisfied with modest rates of accumulation. Gentility and Christian charity were contrasted with the behaviour of the new and suddenly rich.[6] In 1901 a magazine contributor opined that 'the complaint that "new men" and especially London tradesmen, were ousting the old Norman families was as common in the days of Edward IV, Henry VIII, and Elizabeth as it is at the present moment'.[7]

Today, indeed, sudden shifts in wealth distribution and the ostentatious use of new money remain universal triggers to social and political turmoil. In the economic development of West Africa, India, and south-east Asia, a new super-wealthy class of contractors, material suppliers, and industrialists are the focus of bitter domestic hostilities which surface in contemporary literature. Nearer home, sensationalist reports of City scandals, post-Big Bang life-styles, and the gentrification of the inner cities are but the most recent manifestations of conflict between business-led developments and traditional interests and attitudes. This book is written in a university town where old rivalries have been reshaped by money-spinning immigrants to 'silicon fen'. Local newspapers trumpet the gains in employment and civic prestige, but several members of the chip-set are also singled out and accused of inflating local property prices and engaging in politics and business activities detrimental to the interests of the town. As when the new manufacturers arrived in the Black Country in the 1750s and in Lancashire and Yorkshire in the 1780s, many of the locals, rich and poor, are not amused.

What makes late eighteenth-century England so distinctive in this respect is the apparent suddenness and depth of the animosities aroused and their long-lasting effects. Existing studies of the early eighteenth-century reception of trade suggest the development of a sympathetic, even enthusiastic portrayal of the overseas merchant on stage and in popular writing.[8] Jacob Viner concluded that 'with little need of qualification ... an outstanding aspect of literate and articulate England from the century from 1660 to 1760 was its contentment with its existing

---

[6] Richard B. Schlatter, *The Social Ideas of Religious Leaders, 1660–1688* (London, 1940); J. S. McGee, *The Godly Man in Stuart England* (New Haven, Conn., 1976).

[7] *Spectator*, 9 Feb. 1901.

[8] Notably, the verse of Gay, Young, Savage, and Thomson, and discussed in John McVeagh, *Tradefull Merchants: The Portrayal of the Capitalist in Literature* (London, 1981), chs. 2 and 3, and John Loftis, *Comedy and Society from Congreve to Fielding* (Stanford, Calif., 1959).

economic institutions and its absence of desire for significant change'.[9] The totems of 'virtue' and 'corruption' were invoked in protracted debates about landed and moneyed interests,[10] but the arguments of specific interest groups were pitched against what was otherwise general agreement about the beneficial effects of commerce upon civil government, the national economy, education, martial and maritime power, and the processes of 'civilization'. By the end of the century, however, these splendid tributes were challenged afresh by sceptical and hostile accounts of the activities of new-rich traders, manufacturers, and servants of the East India Company. From the 1760s treatises explaining the decline of empires drew new parallels to the British condition and warned of the dangers which upstart wealth might pose to manners, morality, and national vigour. Tracts and sermons pointed to the ruinous consequences of misused trading fortunes. Publications about India and Anglo-Indian wealth promoted fierce attacks on *nouveaux riches* nabobs. Dissertations were issued in defence, not in praise of business and industry. Essays which continued to champion the status of merchant and manufacturer against that of the landed gentleman adopted the voice of a conscious minority.

The new images of businessmen also had long-term effects. Quite apart from colouring nineteenth-century portrayals of industrialists, countless private memoirs were to repeat charges established by this literature.[11] At Leeds (re-examined in a later chapter), various reminiscences were recorded in an early Victorian attempt at oral history. The narrators revel in recalling the vulgar daughters and wives of manufacturers of the town, commercial heiresses 'much unvisitable', and the activities of trading families who, despite their origins, 'were in the habit of having hot dinners'.[12] Widespread suspicions of businessmen also entered

[9] Jacob Viner, 'Satire and Economics in the Augustan Age', in Henry Knight Miller, Eric Rothstein, G. S. Rousseau (eds.), *The Augustan Milieu: Essays Presented to Louis A. Landa* (Oxford, 1971), p. 90.

[10] Given particular emphasis in J. G. A. Pocock, *The Machiavellian Moment: Florentine Political Thought and the Atlantic Republican Tradition* (Princeton, NJ, 1975), chs. 13 and 14, and recently restated, Pocock, *Virtue, Commerce, and History: Essays on Political Thought and History, Chiefly in the Eighteenth Century* (Cambridge, 1985), chs. 2 and 6.

[11] The paucity of candid and detailed business autobiographies and biographies has been ascribed to social prejudice and an anxiety to downplay profit-seeking, Neil McKendrick, general introduction to R. J. Overy, *William Morris, Viscount Nuffield* (London, 1976).

[12] Leeds City Archives, the Oates MSS (1894–7).

books which were to prove extraordinarily influential in both economic thought and public policy. Many such publications were written in the second half of the eighteenth century, conveying their message to generations of readers and students. Adam Smith was certainly not excluded from the ranks of the critics. As Professor Coleman has pointed out, *The Wealth of Nations* did not just contain the odd reference to the dishonesty and humbug of certain merchants and manufacturers, but was infused with contempt for 'the sneaking arts of underling tradesmen'.[13]

The following considers how and why tradesmen, manufacturers, and the newly-wealthy came under such prolific literary attack in the second half of the eighteenth century. The subject is restricted to England, even though, of course, the contemporary appeal or representation is often described as 'British'. The book focuses on *belles-lettres*. In eighteenth-century England, nowhere was the response more telling than in what was described as 'polite literature'. In July 1774 the anxious question before the Free Debating Society of Birmingham was 'Why is Trade and Commerce in a manner become incompatible with polite literature?'[14] The following chapters try to answer that question. In so doing, attention has to be paid to the 'manner' as much as to the meaning of incompatibility between imaginative literature and trade. The circumstances of literary production and the methods of literary circulation influence not only the form but also the content of texts. This survey attempts to probe both media and message, investigating the changing context and the changing vocabulary and imagery of debate in literature ranging from novels and periodical essays to courtesy books and popular manuals. The balance of research is weighted heavily towards the reconstruction of a body of imaginative prose literature as published and distributed by the contemporary book trade and providing a basis for checking against bias and selectivity in summarizing popular literary representations. It also offers a broadly based history of the book trades within which to examine the strategies of commercial bookselling and their influence on messages conveyed in print.

For some students of recent contributions to hermeneutics and

---

[13] D. C. Coleman, 'Adam Smith, Businessmen, and the Mercantile System in England', *History of European Ideas*, 9/2 (1988), 161–70.

[14] Cited in John Money, *Experience and Identity: Birmingham and the West Midlands, 1760–1800* (Manchester, 1977), p. 116.

reception theory, the following chapters will, perhaps, seem unadventurous, giving greatest attention to analysis of the basic narrative of the books and pamphlets considered in relation to specific external social and economic circumstances. In dealing with this material, however, we must pause and absorb before progressing to further levels of interpretation. A large proportion of the texts have not been brought together and reassessed since the decades immediately following their publication. As will be suggested later, the circumstances of literary production and circulation suggest a number of issues relating to the historical and original *understanding* of texts which can be developed further (and beyond the limits of this book), but it is also important to be quite clear about the constraints imposed by the nature of the historical evidence. The study inevitably leads to a questioning of the intention of authors and the way in which texts were received and understood by contemporary readers, but only certain relationships and responses are strictly historically recoverable. The question of authorship, for example, is a central matter for investigation, but it is also one of the most frustrating and elusive. The writers of even some of the most popular and influential literature of the period cannot be identified. Studies can be made of selected authors, of attributed and surviving works, of the locality in which they wrote, and of their early supporters and readerships, but biographical details are extremely sparse. Questions of readership and reading strategies—the subject of my continuing research—can be blurred rather than clarified by the reconstruction of an imaginary reader, either as implied by the author's text or by isolated contemporary commentators. The issue is best approached from the basis of a careful accumulation of a series of case-studies of readers and their memoirs of reading.

It is, indeed, the purpose of this book not to pursue individual reading habits and certainly not to construct model readers or 'typical' popular writers, but to range widely across the existing published works, relating these to their publishing and market history and analysing their content within the framework of social, economic, and political history. Questions of authorship and readership will be discussed in the context of the theme of each chapter, although one case-study (Chapter 6) is included to suggest the value of the micro study where authorial, readership, and supplementary local evidence does survive.[15] Although satisfying to attribute anonymous works to known authors, by analysing styles, prefatory hints, or review suggestions, attribution often provides little more than a name and sex for the writer. Even the gender cannot always be taken at face value. Many a title-page 'Miss' or 'Young Lady' was nothing of the sort. Male hacks and gentlemen and clerical writers assumed many disguises.

In one sense, we are also helped by the conscious anonymity of the writing and its low level of artistic achievement. For what is obvious through the wider study is the conformity of much popular imaginative writing. Although we must remain alert to variations and eccentricities, many books and magazine items were written to broadly shared formulas. We cannot miss the simple fact that in the expanding market of late eighteenth-century England, inexpert and hack writers borrowed liberally and gratefully from recent publications. Plots and authorial verdicts were often strikingly similar. Novelists and the writers of moral essays and dramas included cross-references or direct quotation from each other's work. In an increasingly competitive book trade, writers and booksellers were not slow to repeat successes or imitate the successful.

This is certainly true of representations of trade and industry. From the mid-eighteenth century a range of stock business characters appeared in imaginative prose and miscellanies. A soon predictable fictional cast depicted the follies and crimes of traders, trading families, and *nouveaux riches*. The heroic merchant figure established by Steele and Defoe and expanded by Lillo and early century writers, was overshadowed by an army of caricatures from the vulgar petty trader to the arrogant returned nabob and parvenu estate-owner. The projector and financier, stock villains of fifty years of plays and pamphlet literature, had new rivals. By the end of the 1780s northern manufacturers were added to the gallery of rogues.

The late eighteenth-century response was also exceptionally vigorous. Sixteenth-century merchants and tradesmen certainly

---

[15] Indications of biographical sources will be footnoted however. A complementary approach entailing several local case-studies along the lines adopted in Ch. 6, is in preparation. The aim is to provide as much authorial information as possible for selected localities.

indulged in fashionable conspicuous consumption, but censure of this in the popular literature of the time was tempered by accompanying sympathetic portrayals. Indeed, apart from one or two mirthful asides about landed pretensions and the hint of arguments countered by several indignant writers,[16] there is little opposition to the generous presentation of mercantile pride and self-esteem.[17] A balance between hostile and encouraging responses to commercial achievement was maintained, more or less, over two centuries of imaginative literature. In the popular market, Deloney, Dekker, Richard Johnson, Greene, and Webster produced successive parables featuring prosperous benevolent merchants and successful, confident apprentices risen through the ranks. The Dick Whittington ballad commenced its long and successful print history in 1605.[18] Jacobean drama reexamined profit-making, produced indictments of the merchants as a class, and in a conscious attempt at moral reappraisal, reconsidered the legitimacy of business enterprise. Although John McVeagh finds powerful *individual* examples of early hostility, the ebullience of early century criticism was not sustained after the 1630s.[19] The benevolent image of the merchant rode the storm. Its next challengers, stage-led satires against the social pretensions of the financier and self-made merchant, were also narrowly based. Such portrayals gained popularity at a time when the trader increasingly intimated embarrassment with his profession and attempted to disguise his origins. In Louis B. Wright's words, 'it was not until the social eclipse of the Restoration that wealthy members of the bourgeoisie began to ape the prodigality of courtiers and attempt to hide their connections with trade'.[20]

---

[16] Including Thomas Nashe whose 1633 *Quaternio* insisted upon the idiocy of the notion that the offspring of a landed gentleman and a mercantile heiress 'are but Gentlemen of halfe bloud'.

[17] Laura Caroline Stevenson, *Praise and Paradox: Merchants and Craftsmen in Elizabethan Popular Literature* (Cambridge, 1984).

[18] Further examples are given in Louis B. Wright, *Middle-Class Culture in Elizabethan England* (Chapel Hill, NC, 1935), ch. 2, and L. C. Knights, *Drama and Society in the Age of Jonson* (London, 1937), ch. 8.

[19] Knights offers an extensive, if dated, survey, *Drama and Society*, chs. 7–10.

[20] Wright, *Middle-Class Culture*, p. 20. The caricature of the foolish or malevolent City wife had originally appeared before the Civil War, notably in Massinger's *City Madam*, first performed in 1632 (1st known edn., 1658). There is a potentially important comparison between the initial reception of the new London merchants of the early 17th cent. and the response to *nouveau riche* wealth in the late 18th cent., but no full attempt can be made without new and detailed study of the popular literature and drama of Jacobean England.

The unbalancing of this varied response occurred a generation after the financial experiments and overseas expansion of late Stuart England. While the satires of Wycherley, Congreve, and their imitators, mocking City wives, skinflint merchants, and dishonest financiers, steadily increased during the early years of the eighteenth century, so also did portrayals of the prosperous, patriotic, and benevolent man of commerce. Even the terrors of the South Sea Bubble failed to shake the foundations of the new apologetic. There were, of course, strong, if often complex, reactions against City vices and the apparent materialism and corruption of the times, but the various evocations of a Country morality did not challenge directly notions of the potential benefits to be gained from increased national prosperity.[21] By 1740 new confidence was reached in describing mercantile contributions to civic virtue and economic and political prowess. The inundation of hostile portrayals after mid-century was therefore in contrast to the many positive responses of the previous fifty years. This was compounded by the impact of the new representations.

Indeed, the key point in terms of the broad reception of new literary portrayals was that new fictional characters and motifs were developed at the same time as and even directly related to new market possibilities in the book trade. As the commercial production of polite literature soared, the force of the attack was carried to a more extensive audience than ever before. Richard Cumberland singled out mass-produced literature as the most formative influence of the age.[22] A bevy of foreign travellers and exiles gave special mention to the new-found excitement over literature and its effects within society. Frederick Wendeborn reported that 'the romances of a Richardson, a Fielding, and others, which were formerly in high repute, begin to be laid aside, as books which make the reader soon sleepy; and the rather, since almost every week new romances, in two or more little pocket volumes, are published in London, which are written with so much ease, and are so entertaining, because they correspond so

[21] A recent review of Gay's Country persuasion is given in J. A. Downie, 'Gay's Politics', in Peter Lewis and Nigel Wood (eds.), *John Gay and the Scriblerians* (London and New York, 1988–9), pp. 44–61.

[22] Richard Cumberland, *The Observer; Being a Collection of Moral, Literary, and Familiar Essays*, 4th edn., 5 vols. (London, 1791), i. 3–6.

much with the manners and the fashions of the present age'.[23]
Cumberland and many other writers further pursued the question
raised by the Birmingham Debating Society. In contrast to those
who are born with privileges and hereditary wealth, wrote
Cumberland,

the man, who is the maker of his own fortune, acts on a stage, where every
step he takes will be observed with jealousy; amongst the many thousands,
who are set to watch him, let him reflect how many hearts there are,
rankling with disappointed pride, and envying him the lot, which in their
own conceit at least their merit had a better title to: When such a man
appears, it is the common cry—*I cannot bear that upstart*—At the same time
therefore that it must be allowed more natural to excuse the proud looks of
the high, than the proud looks of the low, still it is no bad caution to beware
of giving easy faith to reports against those, whom so many unsuccessful
people are interested to decry; for though fortune can do mighty things
amongst us, and make great men in this world, she cannot make friends.[24]

Merchants, businessmen, and early industrialists, all felt the sting
of the wider offensive. Samuel Garbett bitterly recorded the treatment given to leading businessmen and manufacturers. He was
particularly resentful of the reception he received in London.
While attending the Commission on Irish Trade in 1785, he noted
that even Pitt was 'not aware of the Station Manufacturers hold in
this Kingdom'.[25] In 1788, when Dr Edmund Cartwright began
steam-engine manufacture, he 'was considered as having
deserted his *caste*'.[26] Jedediah Strutt, anxious about his own performance in polite society, tutored his son in the best methods to
counter social embarrassment.[27] W. G. Rimmer has described

---

[23] Fred. Aug. Wendeborn, *A View of England Towards the Close of the Eighteenth Century*, 2
vols. (Dublin, 1791), ii. 61. Similar comments are offered in M. d'Archenholz, *A Picture of
England: Containing a Description of the Laws, Customs and Manners of England* (Dublin, 1790),
pp. 38–47; Clare Williams (ed.), *Sophie in London*, 1786: Being the Diary of Sophie von la
Roche (London, 1933), pp. 171, 177, 216; and Reginald Nettel (ed.), *Journeys of a German*
[Carl Philip Moritz] *in England in 1782* (London, 1965), esp. pp. 42–5 (first published in
German in 1783).

[24] Cumberland, *Observer*, i. 185.

[25] 'Letters, Copies of Letters, etc. from Samuel Garbett to the Earl of Shelburne',
photocopies in Birmingham Reference Library, ii, fos. 37–8, and cited in Donald Read,
The English Provinces, c.1760–1960: A Study in Influence (London, 1964), pp. 24–5 (further
details p. 27), and J. M. Norris, 'Samuel Garbett and the Early Development of Industrial Lobbying in Great Britain', *Ec.HR* 2nd ser. 10/3 (1958), 450–60.

[26] Mary Strickland, (ed.), *A Memoir of the Life, Writings and Mechanical Inventions of
Edmund Cartwright* (London, 1843), p. 85.

[27] Cited in Roy Porter, *English Society in the Eighteenth Century* (London, 1982), p. 87.

how newcomers to the textile industry in Leeds were received with undisguised hostility.[28] Boswell was mortified to learn that he was attacked as a vulgarian despite his birth.[29] Watt complained that the gentry treated him as a slave.[30] Boulton was worried about his son's accent and wanted to avoid what his headmaster described as a 'vicious pronunciation and vulgar dialect'.[31]

Other contemporary literature provides clear indications of the increasing influence of books carrying negative images of businessmen. Towards the end of the 1780s writers anxious about what they saw as the accumulating power of print, mounted a desperate defence on behalf of the overseas merchant. Many writers isolated the novelist as the malignant force behind new representations of tradesmen. The favoured merchant was to be defined throughout the 1780s in terms of the gentlemanly ideals of benevolence, economy, and a responsible attitude towards wealth. In fact, in defending the merchant, many writers were also to redirect criticism towards the petty vulgar trader. Despite the liberal voices, but also because of their particularization of the defence, literary hostility towards tradesmen and industrialists escalated.

In examining these changes, it is clear that the social and literary historian needs to investigate more than the alterations between the extremes of portrayals and more than the balance between approving and disapproving images. The historian must also consider the changing criteria by which businessmen were judged and the values and agencies which promoted such reactions. It is easy to construct a catalogue of hostile portraits or rehearsals of old images; it is more difficult, but far more important, to recover the changing arguments and premises behind such representations and to identify the exact means by which

---

[28] W. G. Rimmer, *Marshalls of Leeds: Flax-Spinners, 1788–1886* (Cambridge, 1960), pp. 18–20.

[29] *A Series of Letters to the First Earl of Malmesbury, his Family and Friends from 1745 to 1820*, 2 vols. (London, 1870), i. 303 (Mrs Harris, 20 Apr. 1775).

[30] Cited in John Sekora, *Luxury: The Concept in Western Thought, Eden to Smollett* (Baltimore and London, 1977), p. 107. Other examples are given in Witt Bowden, *Industrial Society in England Towards the End of the Eighteenth Century* (1925) 2nd edn. (London, 1965), pp. 154–6.

[31] Revd Henry Pickering to Matthew Boulton, 5 Dec. 1779, cited in A. E. Musson and E. Robinson, *Science and Technology in the Industrial Revolution* (Manchester, 1969), p. 201. Other examples of industrialists anxious to gentrify their sons are given in D. C. Coleman, 'Gentlemen and Players', *Ec.HR* 2nd ser. 26/1 (Feb. 1973), 92–116 (pp. 105–7).

writers were able to employ particular images as convenient vehicles for protest and proposition. The need for more rigorous approaches has been underlined by the debate about the origins and significance of modern hostility to trade, aspects of which will be reassessed in the final chapter of this book. Recent populist history, anxious to trace the origins of disdain for industrial enterprise, has obscured important distinctions between the motivations for hostile words or actions against specific types of commercial or financial operators. A premiss of this book is that by the end of the eighteenth century the dominant criteria by which businessmen were judged were social and ethical, and little related to perceptions of commercial and industrial achievement. But it is, of course, necessary to ask why this should be so. Why was a business ideal which could still astonish and inspire in its own right, overwhelmed by the sensationalist charges against individual traders and manufacturers?

Three interrelated concerns are apparent in late eighteenth-century judgements upon businessmen—fears of economic ruination, social jealousies, and ethical disquiet over the pace of social change. While much was a reworking of older themes, much that was new has unexpected implications. Not the least of these is that what might appear as anti-trading sentiment was in fact part of a wider discourse designed to defend commerce and new methods of making money. For it was the *nouveaux riches*, not the professional qualities, which were highlighted. As British commerce increased, so did the fitfulness of local and credit-based economies, and with this, concern over risk-taking and the maintenance of national and personal economic success. Literature appeared increasingly preoccupied with the rise and fall of empires and the relationship between social stability and the unity of the commonwealth.[32] Much of the hostility to trade and traders can be seen in similar terms. Men of business and the effects of their extravagance and luxury presented a threat to national harmony. New stereotyping became a means of articulating fears of economic ruination, but also of promoting approved values far removed from any immediate concern with business or financial

---

[32] John Barrell, *English Literature in History, 1730–80; An Equal, Wide Survey* (London, 1983). Cf. Linda Colley, 'The Apotheosis of George III: Loyalty, Royalty and the British Nation, 1760–1820', *Past and Present*, 102 (Feb. 1984), 94–129.

issues. The businessman was made a scapegoat for a wide range of alleged social and economic ills and became a target of abuse as a means of illustrating, preserving, and extending specific moral ideals and class values.

The key added ingredient was change in literary market conditions and in the patronage and commercial posturing of the book trade. It was a period of great flux in the productive and distributive capacity of the book trades and in the preferences of reading audiences. Writers and booksellers sought for good commercial reasons to legitimize specific modes of economic and social behaviour by upwardly mobile groups. Commercial literature defined in practical terms acceptable and unacceptable methods of gaining, retaining, and deploying wealth during a period of often bewildering change and instability. A competitive literature industry led reaction against excessive consumer-spending, contributed vigorously to the definition of legitimate economic behaviour, and stimulated unprecedented attacks upon the social presumption of tradesmen. Popular fiction cultivated hostile portraits of traders and manufacturers in order to present graphic and entertaining instruction in social proprieties and financial management. Novels, occasional essays, and magazine serializations created educative stereotypes of ideal heroes in contrast to those of despised or ridiculed men of trade. An array of sensationalist tales in commercial manuals, historical miscellanies, and conduct books for adolescents and the poor, sternly warned of the dangers of fashion, trading manners, upstart riches, and the vulgarity of under-breeding. Periodical reviews, critical essays, and readers' contributions reinforced the message.

As the purchasing power of the middling ranks increased so did their support of consumer orientated, fashion, and leisure industries. During the second half of the eighteenth century, London booksellers experimented with new forms of entertaining and instructional literature and adopted bolder methods of puffing their wares to exploit the market. Resulting increases in trading insecurity forced participants in the popular market to make ever keener assessments of public taste. Everywhere the emphasis was upon attractive design and faster, higher quality production—in novels, plays, music books, prints, magazines, newspapers, pocket-books, guides, primers, children's books, and a host of new-style miscellanies. Like many other entrepreneurs in expanding consumer industries, bookseller-publishers adopted innovatory commercial techniques to supply and stimulate market demand. The self-confidence of both the authors and booksellers increased as they exercised greater power in informing opinion. Several leading London booksellers declared themselves to be arbiters of taste and propriety.

Content and quality of work, however, soon required more explicit justification in the face of mounting criticism against rapidly written and marketed books. Writers and booksellers of best-selling literature assumed with gusto their self-appointed responsibilities as guardians of public interest and morality. The identification of public nuisances could be paraded as proof of the utility of the popular press and used to deflect accusations of irresponsible commercialism and hack, even immoral, writing. To the horror of the learned and the conservative, such posturing entailed excesses of simplification and sensationalism. Nevertheless, popular literature continued to respond quickly with explanations for current vices. The search for acceptable scapegoats became urgent.

Finally, we should not overlook wider issues raised by this study. Investigation of the image of business in this period offers insights beyond the social background to business history. One obvious challenge, the approach to be adopted in recovering representative images from a 'popular' literature, necessarily involves an examination of literary production and circulation. In itself, this invites consideration of the fuller historical background to artistic developments and the generation of popular ideas. Historical bibliography is currently advancing into new terrain and in many countries histories of the book are being written by the combined efforts of historians, bibliographers, and literary scholars. Many questions relating to this are explored in detail in the first half of this book. The early chapters examine the manufacture and promotion of popular literature in the second half of the eighteenth century, and consider the effect of commercial expansion in the book trades upon literary content.

The literary representation of business, however, also impinges on a number of continuing debates about the nature of eighteenth-century society. The second part of this book considers the images presented by the literature and evaluates the perceived threats offered by *arriviste* businessmen—economic, social, and political. Three particular problems can be isolated.

The first issue turns on a question of long standing: how, why, or even whether businessmen bought their way into the landed élite in the eighteenth and nineteenth centuries. Belief in some sort of entryism was central to the historical commonplace that British society, unique amongst its European neighbours, avoided violent upheaval by assimilating an upwardly mobile class within the preserves of power and privilege.[33] Several historians were able to show how merchants, financiers, and manufacturers bought land, married into the local gentry, and pursued particular ideals of respectability.[34] Studies qualifying both the extent and motives behind land purchase have been steadily accumulating, however.[35] Research into the fortunes of early nineteenth-century manufacturers, while enhancing the notion of integration between landed and traditional commercial interests, has demonstrated the relative poverty, powerlessness, and isolation of captains of industry.[36] Most recently, we have been offered a detailed (if geographically and socially restricted) refutation of the picture of an influx of wealthy merchants and manufacturers into landed society during the eighteenth century.[37] The obvious corollary of this is that if the businessman did not actually challenge the most basic of aristocratic bastions, then why has an

[33] This has always been accommodated easily within a wide range of theories of the circulation of élites or the assimilation between classes via social mobility, Anthony Heath, *Social Mobility* (London, 1981), ch. 8.

[34] Notably, Dean Rapp, 'Social Mobility in the Eighteenth Century: The Whitbreads of Bedfordshire, 1720–1815', *Ec.HR* 2nd ser. 27/3 (1974), 380–94; R. G. Wilson, *Gentlemen Merchants: The Mercantile Community in Leeds, 1700–1830* (Manchester, 1971); and E. L. Jones, 'Industrial Capital and Landed Investment: The Arkwrights in Herefordshire, 1809–43', in E. L. Jones and G. E. Mingay (eds.), *Land, Labour and Population in the Industrial Revolution* (London, 1967), pp. 48–71.

[35] Led by G. E. Mingay, *English Landed Society in the Eighteenth Century* (London, 1963), esp. p. 47; R. G. Lang, 'Social Origins and Social Aspirations of Jacobean London Merchants', *Ec.HR* 2nd ser. 27/1 (Feb. 1974), 28–47; Nicholas Rogers, 'Money, Land and Lineage: the Big Bourgeoisie of Hanoverian London', *Social History*, 4/3 (Oct. 1979), 437–54.

[36] Rubinstein, *Men of Property*, and 'New Men of Wealth'. In certain respects this would support theories of a continued landed-commercial hegemony as offered in Perry Anderson, 'Origins of the Present Crisis', *New Left Review*, 23 (1964), 26–53, or more potently in W. D. Rubinstein, 'Wealth, Elites and the Class Structure of Modern Britain', *Past and Present*, 76 (Aug. 1977), 99–126.

[37] Lawrence Stone and Jeanne C. Fawtier Stone, *An Open Elite? England, 1540–1880* (Oxford, 1984). As a study of business entryism, the Stones' work is also restricted in that they specifically chose to consider the violated (or potentially violated) not the violators, *Open Elite*, p. 5.

illusion of business entryism persisted for so long? How and why did images of men of trade and industry diverge from reality? If, in particular, manufacturers did not storm the citadel, why have they been associated with the more aggressive activities of the great merchants? What were the elements of the business threat? How have they been conveyed?

A second issue concerns responses to the late eighteenth-century domestic economy. The effect of demand and consumption upon economic growth has been the source of lively debate since the 1950s,[38] but virtually no study has addressed the social effects of the consumer boom outside anecdotal accounts of manners and fashions. Those insisting that economic history has been too greatly dominated by supply-side questions have attempted to examine the causes of an increasing ability and willingness to consume and an entrepreneurial stimulation of home demand.[39] Recent studies of the development of leisure and fashion industries have investigated the means by which marketing techniques exploited social competition and created taste-induced consumer demand.[40] As yet, these studies have not analysed in detail the consequences of the intellectual and popular reception of a 'consumer revolution'. Indeed, histories of the upturn in commodity expenditure have frequently relied on alarmist contemporary accounts of extravagance and social emulation in order to sketch in detail missing from statistical accounts of growing home demand. Such reactions, however, have not been considered in their own right. No study has been made of their cause, contemporary significance, or the moral and legitimizing notions

---

[38] K. Berrill, 'International Trade and the Rate of Economic Growth', *Ec.HR* 2nd ser. 12/3 (1960), 351–9; N. F. R. Crafts, 'English Economic Growth in the Eighteenth Century: A Re-Examination of Deane and Cole's Estimates', *Ec.HR* 2nd ser. 29/2 (May 1976), 226–35; J. Mokyr, 'Demand vs. Supply in the Industrial Revolution', *Journal of Economic History*, 37/4 (Dec. 1977), 981–1000; and for an overview, Cole and von Tunzelmann in Roderick Floud and Donald McCloskey (eds.), *The Economic History of Britain since 1700*, 2 vols. (Cambridge, 1981), i. chs. 3 and 8.

[39] e.g. Eric L. Jones, 'Fashion Manipulators: Consumer Tastes and British Industries, 1660–1800', in Louis P. Cain and Paul J. Uselding (eds.), *Business Enterprise and Economic Change* (Kent, Ohio, 1973), pp. 198–226.

[40] Neil McKendrick, John Brewer, and J. H. Plumb, *The Birth of a Consumer Society* (London, 1982); Louise Lippincott, *Selling Art in Georgian London: The Rise of Arthur Pond* (New Haven, Conn., 1983). For further perspectives, Fernand Braudel, *Capitalism and Material Life, 1400–1800*, trans. by M. Kochan (London, 1973); and the collection of articles in *Business History Review*, 37/1–2 (1963), esp. Dwight E. Robinson, 'The Importance of Fashions in Taste to Business History: An Introductory Essay', pp. 5–36.

employed. Increased conspicuous consumption did not pass without loud and revealing moralizing.

A third (and very old) question concerns the making of a middle class. Recent studies have given particular attention to the cultural constituents of class formation. Was the middle class, which is invariably rising and never depressed, particularly pushy in the late eighteenth century? One comparison of different regions of late eighteenth- and early nineteenth-century England has offered a new analysFais of the ways in which 'middle-class farmers, manufacturers, merchants and professionals ... critical of many aspects of aristocratic privilege and power, sought to translate their increasing economic weight into a moral and cultural authority. Their claim to moral superiority was at the heart of their challenge to an earlier aristocratic hegemony'.[41] Such predominance by the middle class, however, has been questioned by recent high-profile, often polemical, charges against neo-Whiggish, economically reductive interpretations of Hanoverian Britain.[42]

If anything is clear from these two approaches it is that both cannot be entirely right. One crucial element in the explication of an 'élite hegemony' is the interpretation of contemporary publications. Here, detailed study can show the precise ways in which literary responses were consonant with action—an exercise which undermines full belief in the endurance of an aristocratic and confessional *ancien régime*. Just as the avalanche of works protesting against trade does not necessarily indicate an effective disdain for trade, so references to aristocratic standards and norms does not necessarily represent the absence of middle-class self-justification. It is not difficult to argue (and has never been so) that power within society remained with the aristocracy and the great landowners. It is undeniable that they controlled the political machine, that they were at the apex of a highly deferential society, that in certain ways the development of 'modern' class consciousness in eighteenth-century Britain has been overstated.

[41] Leonore Davidoff and Catherine Hall, *Family Fortunes: Men and Women of the English Middle-Class*, 1780–1850 (London, 1987), p. 30.

[42] J. C. D. Clark, *English Society*, 1688–1832: Ideology, Social Structure and Political Practice during the Ancien Regime (Cambridge, 1985), and *Revolution and Rebellion: State and Society in England in the Seventeenth and Eighteenth Centuries* (Cambridge, 1986). Cf. Joanna Innes, 'Jonathan Clark, Social History and England's "Ancien Regime"', *Past and Present*, 115 (May 1987), 165–200.

But this is far from saying that the aristocracy was the only, or even the most, dynamic force in society. This work will argue that a society incorporating many aristocratic ideals was becoming more bourgeois, and that it is middle-class assertiveness which dominates and explains the complex reaction to trade in the second half of the eighteenth century. In her study of attitudes to trade in sixteenth-century Britain, Laura Stevenson claims that in periods of social upheaval traditional discourse has greater psychological appeal than innovation. She shows how Elizabethan praise of bourgeois men was expressed in the rhetoric of the aristocracy.[43] The question hinges on our interpretation of the language of change. What is the actual significance of a traditional, historical vocabulary? In eighteenth-century England, as in earlier centuries, perceptions of society did not always reflect the reality of social structure. The present could also be described in terms of the past; middle-class aspirations could also be advanced in the language and allusions of imagined nobility.

---

[43] According to Stevenson, authors did not praise merchants in 'bourgeois' terms as she calls it, that is for their 'diligence', 'thrift', or financial talents, but rather praised them for their magnanimity or as being courtly or chivalric, *Praise and Paradox*, pp. 2–8, 131–58.

2

PUBLISHING PROFILES

I have lived wholly out of the World this Year, so I sent for the *Novels of the day* to instruct me how the World *goes*—and they *do* instruct me ... the little Summer at Weymouth or such Trash ... The Dialogue copied from Conversation. These little Books are mighty useful as Portraits of the *Manners*—Watteau & Sevignè began these Delineations, Hogarth & Fielding continued 'em.

Thraliana (23 Apr. 1808).

THE literary image of business has been a popular research topic in the last decade, but critical questioning of the sources has been limited in two areas in particular. Firstly, little is clear about the pedigree of the various types of literary representation said to have encouraged hostility to business in England. The history of the mature nineteenth-century response—with all its ambiguities—remains isolated, dominated by study of famous reactions to industrialism and particular *causes célèbres* and adrift from its eighteenth-century moorings. Secondly, source material has been very selective. The history of the 'luddite interpretation' of business—of the reinterpretation of the past and of the selection of particular texts for ends critical of the business world—has not yet been successfully married with study of the agency of literature in the formation of contemporary ideas and partisanship.[1] This last requires identification of texts of contemporary influence and popularity rather than of those selected from the reading lists of modern critics who have studied imaginative literature for very different reasons. At what point was the late

---

[1] Of many reviews making similar points, John Baxendale in *History Workshop*, 21 (Spring 1986), 171–4.

seventeenth- and early eighteenth-century enthusiasm for commerce dampened by doubt? How exactly was this hostility towards commerce and industry observable and influential in society? How is it possible for the historian to locate the origins, conveyance, and appeal of anti-business prejudice? Recent advances in book trade history have underpinned new attempts to explain the role of print in society. Pioneering studies have investigated the circulation of popular chapbooks and their portrayal of the extraordinary and the everyday.[2] Others have explored perceptions of commercial and industrializing Britain by considering working-class and artistic responses, and, ambitiously, the longer-term literary verdict on the merchant.[3] The depiction of the merchant in the sixteenth century has also been considered with close attention to popular writers, the economics of bookselling, and the representativeness of texts.[4] For the second half of the eighteenth century, however, there has been little examination of methods of identifying popular literary output. There is still no full study of the commercial development of the late eighteenth-century book trade. In short, we know little either about literary perceptions of trade and industry during the years of commercial and industrial expansion in the late eighteenth century, or about the means by which such opinion was established. The poverty of research on the literary response is the more telling because of the changes in the commercial orientation of the book business. We remain largely ignorant of the literary reaction to an industrializing society at the very time

---

[2] Margaret Spufford, *Small Books and Pleasant Histories: Popular Fiction and its Readership in Seventeenth-Century England* (London, 1981), and her *The Great Reclothing of Rural England: Petty Chapmen and their Wares in Seventeenth-Century England* (London, 1984); Victor Neuburg, *Popular Literature: A History and Guide* (London, 1977); and his *Chapbooks: A Guide to Reference Material*, 2nd edn. (London, 1972); Leslie Shepard, *The History of Street Literature* (London, 1973); and, for comparison, Robert Mandrou, *De la culture populaire aux XVIIe et XVIIIe siècles: La Bibliothèque bleue de Troyes* (Paris, 1964), and Roger Chartier, *The Cultural Uses of Print in Early Modern France*, trans. Lydia G. Cochrane (Princeton, NJ, 1987).

[3] Martha Vicinus, *The Industrial Muse—A Study of Nineteenth-Century Working Class Literature* (London, 1974); Francis D. Klingender, *Art and the Industrial Revolution* (1947), revised edn. (London, 1968); Ivan Melada, *The Captain of Industry in English Fiction, 1821–1871* (Albuquerque, N. Mex., 1970); Alasdair Clayre (ed.), *Nature and Industrialization: An Anthology* (Oxford, 1977); Ivanka Kovačević, *Fact into Fiction: English Literature and the Industrial Scene, 1750–1850* (Leicester, 1975); Igor Webb, *From Custom to Capital: The English Novel and the Industrial Revolution* (Ithaca, NY, 1981); Norman Russell, *The Novelist and Mammon: Literary Responses to the World of Commerce in the Nineteenth Century* (Oxford, 1986); McVeagh, *Tradefull Merchants*.

[4] Stevenson, *Praise and Paradox*.

that popular literature was transformed by more assertive and innovative bookselling. In this regard, it is worth stressing how historical appreciation of the new fiction industry of the period has been thwarted by both contemporary and modern disdain for an output that undeniably included many formula-written pot-boilers.[5] Very soon after birth, the mass fiction and popular literature trade was denounced from journal and pulpit as seditious and immoral and as debasing civilized society. In fact, of course, outrage from the critics and defensiveness from the producers only confirms how successful the commercialization of the literature actually was. Slighting reference to the artistic inferiority of the works of popular authors and commercial publisher-book-sellers, however, made them objects of embarrassment and contempt for many students of eighteenth-century literature and social history. A. S. Collins criticized the popular press of this period for what was 'unhappily, a tendency to speculate in trash', and Mrs Leavis was unable to resist apologies in her study of the popular audience.[6] As J. H. Plumb commented of earlier self-appointed guardians of public taste, 'they believed that the very act of writing for a mass audience led to coarseness and triviality and to a loss of subtlety and refinement'.[7] Perhaps the problem is best illustrated by considering the hostility which in recent years has greeted our own cultural pariah, television. Although popular television has exercised an important influence upon social attitudes in modern Britain, both the BBC and ITV neglected to preserve their most popular but low-brow recorded productions of the 1950s and 1960s. In exactly the same way, many conserving libraries and book-collectors (until recently) put little value on the bulk of popular publications of the eighteenth century. As a result, future students of television will share with present historians of commercial publishing a dependence upon unsympathetic and hostile published analysis for much of their source material.

An alternative approach derives from renewed sociological

---

[5] 'Tenth-rate pulp, artistically depraved and morally shallow', in the words of J. C. Beasley, *Novels of the* 1740s (Athens, Ga., 1982), p. 2.

[6] A. S. Collins, *Profession of Letters: A Study of the Relation of Author to Patron, Publisher and Public*, 1780–1832 (London, 1928), p. 113; Q. D. Leavis, *Fiction and the Reading Public* (London, 1932).

[7] J. H. Plumb, 'The Public, Literature and the Arts in the Eighteenth Century', in Paul Fritz and David Williams (eds.), *The Triumph of Culture: Eighteenth-Century Perspectives* (Toronto, 1972), pp. 27–48 (p. 47).

interest in the history of popular literature. Diverse studies have explored ways in which literature not merely reflects but also shapes society, and many have given new attention to the fuller corps of writers and producers.[8] Even here, however, the pursuit of 'popular' reading and writing has seldom been broadly based. The most famous essays in the sociology of literature have examined the nature of authorship and the relationship between the 'great writer' and his society, rather than the history of contemporary reaction to the literary market.[9] There are few wider studies of historical receptions of literature, despite long-standing calls for further research. Influential advocates, including Raymond Williams, have demanded an appreciation of both the selective processes by which literature is received and the particular efforts required to understand its production and influence in its original terms.[10] Historical analysis of literature as both evidence of and as a causal agent in the development of social thought, must adopt a more plebeian approach than that of the literary critic. It must develop a methodology which treats of literature as it was produced, distributed, popularized, and discussed.[11] Close analysis of the influence of eighteenth-century popular literature has remained a distant goal. Two general sets

---

[8] Peter Humm, Paul Stigant, and Peter Widdowson (eds.), *Popular Fictions: Essays in Literature and History* (London and New York, 1986).

[9] For a general survey, John Hall, *The Sociology of Literature* (London and New York, 1979) and for specific approaches, Jane Routh and Janet Wolff (eds.), *The Sociology of Literature: Theoretical Approaches* Sociological Revue Monograph, 25–26 (1977–8); Robert N. Wilson (ed.), *The Arts in Society* (Englewood Cliffs, NJ, 1964); Ruth A. Inglis, 'An Objective Approach to the Relationship between Fiction and Society', *American Sociological Review*, 3/3 (Aug. 1938), 526–33; Diana Laurenson and Alan Swingewood, *The Sociology of Literature* (London, 1972); and Leo Lowenthal, *Literature, Popular Culture and Society* (Palo Alto, Calif., 1968).

[10] Raymond Williams, *Culture* (London, 1981); *The Long Revolution*, (London, 1961), 1980 edn., ch. 2, esp. pp. 67–70; and re-evaluating the Lasswell formula 'Who says what, how, to whom, with what effect?', 'Communications as Cultural Science', in C. W. E. Bigsby (ed.), *Approaches to Popular Culture* (London, 1976), pp. 27–38.

[11] Pioneering attempts to measure contemporary popular reaction include Milton C. Albrecht, 'Does Literature Reflect Common Values?', *American Sociological Review*, 21/4 (Aug. 1956), 722–9; Lee Benson, 'An Approach to the Scientific Study of Past Public Opinion' *Public Opinion Quarterly*, 31/4 (Winter 1967), 522–67; and Louis Galambos, *The Public Image of Big Business in America, 1880–1940* (Baltimore and London, 1975). The superior sources for the publication and demand for literature in France during this period have enabled the advanced work seen in Henri-Jean Martin, Louis Desgraves, Alfred Morin, *et al.*, *Histoire et Civilisation du Livre*, 8 parts (Paris, 1966–75); in G. Bollème *et al.*, (eds.), *Livre et société dans la France du XVIIIᵉ siècle*, Civilisations et Sociétés, 1; Paris, 1965; and in many contributions to *Revue française d'histoire de Livres* (Bordeaux, 1971–).

of problems are clear: questions relating to the full extent of the production and circulation of literature, and questions of its interpretation in terms of its contemporary reception. These issues are not wholly separable, however, and the underlying premiss of this book is that an attempt to provide a picture of a complete literary market-place puts us in a better position to judge the equivalence between texts in terms of their influence and historical significance. From the perspective of contemporary readers, the eighteenth-century fiction industry extended well beyond the lives and works of those fêted in later literary studies. Edward Kimber, Eliza Haywood, Charlotte Lennox, Frances Brooke, and Sarah Fielding all rivalled the contemporary popularity of Fielding and Richardson. For many readers, fashionable but now long-forgotten booksellers and commercial librarians like the Noble brothers and Thomas Hookham were far more important literary figures than the Rivingtons, the Dillys, or the other great publishers immortalized by Gibbon and Dr Johnson.

The way in which readers went about their reading is a fascinating, if enigmatic subject, and one which will be assisted by projects in progress at many centres researching the book and popular culture. Aspects of the actual processes of text comprehension will be attempted at appropriate places in the following chapters, but it is worth giving a brief general survey of the problems. The reader was a complex filter—not merely a mesh which caught some of the text in interesting or eccentric ways, but a processor partly constructed and reshaped by previous reading and reading experience. External factors also affected the way a reader read as well as the circumstances in which reading took place and the ends to which it was directed. As a recent commentary has insisted of the popular text, 'if a piece of popular fiction is both difficult to read and not subject to the conventional criteria of 'literary merit', then how to read its 'meanings' has to be extracted more deliberately from the ideological, social and political matrix that encloses and, in large measure, produces it'.[12] Historians of popular literature do not share the advantage of sociologists researching contemporary reading habits and the readers' understanding of texts. As Janice Radway has insisted, readers are not just passive receptacles for texts, but are cultural

---

[12] Humm, *et al.*, *Popular Fictions*, p. 5.

consumers who are actively reinterpreting and redefining messages. Radway, however, is able to explore the exact stages and
nuances of reader responses by interviewing living book buyers
and borrowers.[13] The historian has only a few accounts of
reading or representations of reading practice offered by contemporary prints and writings. The reception of particular texts can
be identified only haphazardly from contemporary commentaries and personal memoirs. Such sources are relatively few
in number, correspond to a relatively small proportion of reprinted and popular texts, and, above all, cannot give answers to some
of the most significant questions.

Ultimately, the historian of eighteenth-century literature is left
primarily with the published text itself as a starting-point for
interpretation and judgements concerning value and equivalence. This underpins the strategy adopted here that problems of
selection of evidence and textual equivalence are best resolved by
the reconstruction of full publishing profiles. An historically
rigorous examination of social images created and conveyed by
particular types of literature requires estimates of total literary
output in order to provide historically consistent selections of
texts.

In this respect, studies of popular literature of the period have
been most handicapped by bewilderment over the timing and
dimensions of the upturn in publication. Despite the welter of
literary attention, until quite recent times the history of popular
fiction has been frustrated by ignorance of the number of new
titles and new editions of novels, magazine and periodical tales,
part-issues, and associated literature.[14] Many studies of historical
'images' in imaginative literature relied upon well-known texts
and works selected only because of their literary merit. Concentration on such lions inevitably unbalanced the wider history of
eighteenth-century literature. For the historian, it invited what

[13] Janice A. Radway, *Reading the Romance: Women, Patriarchy and Popular Literature* (Chapel Hill, NC, 1984).

[14] Titles from the leading children's book publisher of the period are listed in S. Roscoe, *John Newbery and his Successors, 1740–1814: A Bibliography* (Wormley, Herts., 1973). Magazine serializations have been catalogued by Robert D. Mayo, *The English Novel in the Magazines, 1740–1815* (Evanston, Ill., 1962) and Edward W. Pitcher, 'Robert Mayo's "The English Novel in the Magazines, 1740–1815"': New Facts', *Library*, 5th ser., 31 (1976), 20–30, and 'More Emendations and Facts', *Library*, 6th ser. 2 (1980), 326–32. Imaginative educative works are included in Robin Alston, *A Bibliography of the English Language from the Invention of Printing to the Year 1800* (Ilkley, 1974).

has been described as 'cultropomorphic distortion' or the selection of a very few works as representative of the whole.[15] Other
studies left the safe harbours of 'great texts' to swim bravely in
uncharted seas of 'minor fiction' or 'popular literature'. A pleth-
ora of studies of the development of certain 'characters' within
late eighteenth-century English literature set out with almost no
aids to navigation. Many foundered on the rocks of selection or
were inundated by the unsorted materials to which they were
exposed and sank without trace.[16]

The studies in later chapters are therefore based on an attempt
to consult as much as possible of the surviving and accessible
imaginative prose literature of the period, setting this within a
reconstructed profile of the total output of such literature in the
second half of the eighteenth century. The bibliographical base
for this had to be constructed from scratch and its sources will be
described below. The size of this problem forces, for the present,
inevitable restrictions on the type of literature examined. It is
hoped that this will prove less a retreat from grappling with the
total dimensions of popular publishing of the period, than a step
towards that goal by the consolidation by strict and careful process of a very large part of a massive evidential base.

Greatest attention in this study will be given to imaginative
prose publications, both because such books constituted the
fastest growing sector of the popular book trade and also because
they attracted most notoriety in their reflection of and commentary upon contemporary social attitudes. Poetry and
drama—which included the publication of playbooks to be read
in the home—must not be neglected in any fuller exploration of
the relationship between print and popular culture in the late
eighteenth century, and both forms are reviewed in later chapters

[15] Robert Darnton, 'Reading, Writing, and Publishing in Eighteenth-Century France:
A Case Study in the Sociology of Literature', *Daedalus*, 100/1 (Winter 1971), 214–56 (p. 214).

[16] Of many early brave attempts, Lois Hall Galbraith, *The Established Clergy as Depicted in
English Prose Fiction from 1740 to 1800* (Philadelphia, 1950); Kenneth Chester Slagle, *The
English Country Squire as Depicted in English Prose Fiction from 1740 to 1800* (Philadelphia, 1938);
Mary Muriel Tarr, *Catholicism in Gothic Fiction: A Study of the Nature and Function of Catholic
Materials in Gothic Fiction in England, 1762–1820* (Washington, DC, 1946); Harold Francis
Watson, *The Sailor in English Fiction and Drama, 1550–1800* (New York, 1931). There are many
similar studies, notably the massive volumes of Myron F. Brightfield, *Victorian England in its
Novels*, 4 vols. (Los Angeles, 1968). A rare early study attempting historical investigation into
the literary stereotype is Harm Reijnderd Sientjo van der Veen, *Jewish Characters in
Eighteenth-Century English Fiction and Drama* (Groningen, 1935).

where they are of direct concern to the themes, authors, publishers, or readers under discussion. This book is based, however, on an attempt at a thoroughgoing appraisal of the burgeoning fiction industry of the period and will be led by that form in its examination of the changing representation of business and personal wealth. The hope must be that other products of the book trade, reluctantly omitted from a study which has already taken many years to complete, will be examined in other research projects. The philosophy behind the book is that it is better to aim at a mastery of one (and the most important) range of popular publishing than to drown, like many predecessors, in oceans of unordered materials.

The analysis offered in later chapters is based on a continuing project to recover all fiction published and reprinted in Britain and Ireland from 1750 to 1800. A full bibliographical survey of both extant and non-surviving fiction printed in the first two decades of this period has now been separately published and listings for the final decades are in preparation.[17] The imaginative literature considered comprises novels, short stories, collected works, collections of tales, serialized and magazine fiction, moral tales, children's literature, jest-books, and miscellanies ranging from imaginary voyages to fictional biography. These, the sources for this study, were the type of publication sold by the fashionable booksellers or to be found on the shelves of the new circulating libraries. They are not chapbooks from the pedlar's tray or market stall, nor are they the learned or expensive tomes of great private or subscription libraries.

The second constraint forced by the huge scale of the surviving material is the adoption of periodic sampling. It quickly became apparent that the project would become unmanageable if detailed consultation were to be attempted for all the literature recovered—although it is hoped that the full descriptive checklist of prose fiction of the period will provide the basis for subsequent studies by others. As will be made clear below, this limitation is not as severe as it might at first seem. The most popular, most reprinted works are the most likely to appear and reappear in the seasons of literature read in detail for this study. Formula writing and the close similarity of much hack and unreprinted

---

[17] James Raven, *British Fiction, 1750–1770: A Chronological Check-List of Prose Fiction Printed in Britain and Ireland* (London and Newark, NJ, 1987).

work offers a further check against unrepresentativeness. The strategy has therefore been to concentrate upon five-yearly cohorts of all extant and available material from 1750, 1755, 1760, 1765, 1770, 1775, 1780, 1785, 1790, and 1795.[18] The ribs of this five-yearly sampling are not designed to show through in later discussion. Analysis is led by theme, not by a chronological progress through the sample years. Reprinted works within the years often originate from years between or before the period, while discussion of authors and elaboration upon developments in the booktrade is necessarily superimposed. Moreover, the difficulty in reconstructing the manner in which texts were received should not tempt a slavish adherence to the counting of titles and typologies now that this is enabled by new bibliographical groundwork. Quantitative *mentalités* can induce blindness. As Roger Chartier has warned, 'the ways in which an individual or a group appropriates an intellectual theme or a cultural form are more important than the statistical distribution of that theme or form'.[19] Nevertheless, it is important at the outset to give a survey of the bibliographical foundations.

BOOK TRADE RESEARCH

The problem remains that study of many aspects of the production of popular literature is either in its infancy or is restricted to its earlier, less aggressively commercial history. Analysis of the chapbook, of subscription lists, of booksellers' trade sales, and of the production and distribution of popular ephemera is largely wanting for the second half of the eighteenth century.[20] The patchiness and often highly localized nature of the evidence

---

[18] Details of consultation rates from the original project are given in J. R. Raven, 'English Popular Literature and the Image of Business, 1760–1790', Ph.D. thesis (University of Cambridge, 1985), pp. 138–9.

[19] Roger Chartier, *Cultural History: Between Practices and Representations*, trans. Lydia G. Cochrane (Cambridge, 1988), p. 35.

[20] Margaret Spufford's detailed examinations of the circulation and impact of the chapbook end as the 18th cent. begins. Detailed study of copyright transaction is restricted to the first two-thirds of the century, Terry Belanger, 'Booksellers' Trade Sales, 1718–1768', *Library*, 5th ser. 30/4 (Dec. 1975), 281–302, his 'Booksellers' Sales of Copyright: Aspects of the London Book Trade, 1718–1768', Ph.D. thesis (Columbia University, 1970), and Cyprian Blagden, 'Booksellers' Trade Sales, 1718–1768', *Library*, 5th ser. 5/4 (Mar. 1951), 243–57.

creates great difficulties in researching the means for the circulation of the books and of the relationship between literary output
and the changing commercial base of the trade. Distinguished
studies have explored the 'widening circle' of middle-class
literacy, the relish for reading, and the circulation of literature
during the eighteenth century.[21] Collins's original depiction of a
growing reading public has been enriched by renewed investigation of the publishing and retail of books and magazines.[22] Other
surveys, however, have shown how much remains to be understood about the promotion and sale of print in this period.[23]
There has been meagre consideration of the changing commercial techniques of booksellers in promoting specific types of
work.[24] In the study of serializations and part-number publications, the pioneering work of R. M. Wiles for the first half of the
century has now been carried beyond 1750, but the attention
given the later period has focused upon the serialization of fiction
rather than upon the avalanche of new part-number publications

[21] An excellent summary is presented in Roy McKeen Wiles, 'The Relish for Reading
in Provincial England Two Centuries Ago', in Paul J. Korshin (ed.), *The Widening Circle:
Essays on the Circulation of Literature in Eighteenth-Century Europe* (Philadelphia, 1976), pp. 87–115.
The best introductions to the 18th cent. book trade proper are Graham Pollard, the 3rd
and 4th Sandars Lectures of 1959, reprinted as 'The English Market for Printed Books', in
Publishing History, 4 (1978), 8–48 (pp. 25–48); Terry Belanger, 'From Bookseller to Publisher:
Changes in the London Book Trade, 1750–1850', in Richard G. Landon (ed.), *Book Selling
and Book Buying: Aspects of the Nineteenth-Century British and North American Book Trade* (Chicago,
1978), pp. 7–16; Pat Rogers, *Grub Street: Studies in a Subculture* (London, 1972); John Feather,
'British Publishing in the Eighteenth Century', *Library*, 6th ser. 8/1 (Mar. 1986), 32–46;
Isabel Rivers (ed.), *Books and their Readers in Eighteenth-Century England* (Leicester, 1982); and
Robin Myers and Michael Harris (eds.), *Sale and Distribution of Books from 1700* (Oxford,
1982), with annual volumes thereafter.

[22] A. S. Collins, *Authorship in the Days of Johnson: Being a Study of the Relation Between Author,
Patron, Publisher and Public, 1726–1780* (London, 1927), and *Profession of Letters*; questioned by
Richard D. Altick, *The English Common Reader: A Social History of the Mass Reading Public,
1800–1900* (Cambridge, 1957), and given modified support by R. M. Wiles, 'Middle-Class
Literacy in Eighteenth-Century England: Fresh Evidence', in R. F. Brissenden (ed.),
Studies in the Eighteenth Century (Canberra, 1968). Of contemporary supportive texts, James
Lackington's *Memoirs of the Forty-Five First Years* (1791 edn.), pp. 247–56, has been given most
attention, James Raven, 'Selling One's Life: Lackington, Eighteenth-Century Booksellers
and the Design of Autobiography', in O. M. Brack, Jr. (ed.), *Writers, Books, and Trade: An
Eighteenth-Century Miscellany for William B. Todd* (New York, 1992).

[23] J. H. Plumb, 'The Commercialization of Leisure in Eighteenth-Century England', in
McKendrick, Brewer, and Plumb, *Consumer Society*, pp. 265–85.

[24] Discussion is offered by Josephine Grieder, *Translations of French Sentimental Prose
Fiction in Late Eighteenth-Century England: A History of a Literary Vogue* (Durham, NC, 1975),
pp. 16–42, and James Raven, *The Commercialization of the Book, 1745–1814* (Cambridge, forthcoming).

for the popular market.[25] The Topsy-like research into the rise of
the novel and of serialized and part-numbered literature has yet
to include detailed examination of the mechanics of the growth of
the fiction industry. Its influence has been fully described only in
terms of choleric critical responses.[26]

A more accurate indication of the success of certain books or
genres must be provided by reappraisal of the total output of
literature. The influence of Paternoster Row or Leadenhall Street
can best be measured by recovering the range of literature first
offered to the public. The basic building-block for this is a full
examination of the contemporary production of widely read and
commercially regulated literature, the books stocked by the local
circulating library or puffed in the columns of the local newspaper. As will be shown, many images conveyed by print were
greatly conditioned by the demands of the market-place. Particular arguments and legitimizing notions were developed according
to the commercial profile of publication. Even 'trash' had its 'nor-
mative vocabulary', and the study of popular literature requires
new respect for the packaging, promotion, and influence of the
output of the commercial booksellers. The difficulty of such an
undertaking is clear. Given the paucity of publishing records of
the period, very basic bibliographical work is necessary to recon-
struct eighteenth-century literary production and to suggest the
means by which imaginative literature reflected but also reinforced and created particular assumptions and prejudices
amongst its readership. The most authoritative and general social
histories of the novel remain those by J. M. S. Tompkins and Ian
Watt, but neither of these pioneering studies, nor their progeny,
were able to draw upon any secure survey of the breadth of range
or total output of the literature.[27] Apart from magazine serials,

[25] R. M. Wiles, *Serial Publication in England before* 1750 (Cambridge, 1957); Mayo, *English Novel in the Magazines*.

[26] John Tinnon Taylor, *Early Opposition to the English Novel: The Popular Reaction from 1780 to 1830* (New York, 1943), and F. W. Gallaway, 'The Conservative Attitude Towards Fiction, 1770–1830', *PMLA*, 55 (1940), 1041–59.

[27] Joyce Marjorie Sanxter Tompkins, *The Popular Novel in England*, 1770–1800 (London, 1932), and her *Polite Marriage . . . Eighteenth-Century Essays* (Cambridge, 1938); Ian Watt, *The Rise of the Novel* (London, 1957). Also, Leavis, *Fiction and the Reading Public*; and B. G. MacCarthy, *The Later Women Novelists*, 1744–1818 (Oxford, 1947); Diana Spearman, *The Novel and Society* (London, 1966); Robert Palfrey Utter and Gwendolyn Bridges Needham, *Pamela's Daughters* (London, 1937); H. Winifred Husbands, 'The Lesser Novel, 1770–1800', MA thesis (London, 1922).

much imaginative literature has received no attention at all. Performance rather than the publication of plays has gained most
attention from historians of drama.[28] Missing also from accounts
of the literature of the period is almost any assessment of the huge
output of popular guide books, conduct books, historical miscellanies, and ephemeral *Collections*. Even more obscure is the late
century deluge of verse romances and satirical odes. No comprehensive description of books of poetry and verse has been
attempted for the period after 1750.[29] The *Eighteenth-Century Short
Title Catalogue*, still under construction, is an extremely important
and welcome resource, but it provides no certain means of
isolating particular genres of literature, and remains, self-
evidently, restricted to surviving works. Much foundation work is
still necessary. Periodical review notices, end-page advertisement
lists, and booksellers' announcements in newspapers all suggest
that a proportion of popular and fashionable publications has not
survived. Much fictional material, ranging from biographies to
the colourful narratives of imaginary voyages, is even more elusive than the hundreds of now very rare two- or three-volume
novels of the period.[30]

---

[28] For theatrical performance, G. W. Stone (ed.), *The London Stage, 1660–1800: Part IV,
1747–76*, 3 vols. (Carbondale, Ill., 1962) and C. B. Hogan (ed.), *Part V, 1776–1800* (Carbondale, Ill., 1968).

[29] Some guidance to the publication of separate poetical works is offered by *NCBEL*, iii.
374–429, but nothing approaches the comprehensiveness of the essential work for the first
half of the century, D. F. Foxon, *English Verse, 1701–1750: A Catalogue of Separately Printed
Poems with Notes on Contemporary Collected Editions*, 2 vols. (Cambridge, 1975).

[30] Model catalogue check-lists of fiction have been produced for the first half of the
century: W. H. McBurney, *A Check List of English Prose Fiction, 1700–1739* (Cambridge, Mass.,
1960); J. C. Beasley, *A Check List of Prose Fiction Published in England, 1740–1749* (Charlot-
tesville, Va., 1972); and the earlier A. Esdaile, *A List of English Tales and Prose Romances
Printed Before 1740* (New York, 1912). These are preceded by Charles C. Mish, *English Prose
Fiction, 1600–1700: A Chronological Checklist* (Charlottesville, Va., 1967); Sterg O'Dell, *A
Chronological List of Prose Fiction in English, 1475–1640* (Cambridge, Mass., 1954); and Paul A.
Scanlon, 'A Checklist of Prose Romances in English, 1474–1603', *Library*, 5th ser. 23/2
(June 1978), 143–52. A recent check-list of fiction for the second half of the 18th cent.,
Leonard Orr, *A Catalogue Checklist of English Prose Fiction, 1750–1800* (Troy, NY, 1979) is
inaccurate and incomplete (see J. C. Beasley, *Literary Research Newsletter*, 5/3 (Summer
1980), 140–47). Godfrey F. Singer, *The Epistolary Novel: Its Origin, Development, Decline and
Residuary Influence* (Philadelphia, 1933), relies on defective bibliographical evidence. Frank
Gees Black, *The Epistolary Novel in the Late Eighteenth Century: A Descriptive and Bibliographical
Study* (Eugene, Oreg., 1940), a survey of epistolary novels, is similarly flawed and based
upon a mixture of British and American imprints, providing eccentric estimates of pub-
lished output. Travel tales are considered in Philip B. Gove, *The Imaginary Voyage in Prose
Fiction* (New York, 1941) and Percy G. Adams, *Travellers and Travel-liars* (Los Angeles, 1962).

PUBLICATION ANALYSIS

In 1700 a handful of separate volumes of prose fiction were published by about a dozen London booksellers. By 1750 over forty works of fiction, some part-issues, some belonging more to the world of chapbooks than to the six-shilling two-volume novel, were published or reprinted in the year. Of these, more than thirty were printed in London and almost all the remainder in Dublin. Twenty years later, nearly one hundred different works were advertised as novels and the number of fiction publishers in London, Edinburgh, and Dublin had tripled. By 1800 some ninety new novels were published annually. At the same date, total annual novel publication, including reprints, amounted to well over 150 titles.

The production and sale of much popular literature was of course no new phenomenon. Like the middle classes, reading publics have risen with singular ease in histories of early modern Britain. In any survey of Elizabethan printing, the range of books offered is always surprising.[31] By the side of the chapbooks and fables were sold conduct books and moral primers which have much in common with their eighteenth-century equivalents. In the middle of the next century, William London's *Catalogue of the Most Vendible Books in England* reveals not only a wide variety of publications, but many of the specialisms later associated with particular eighteenth-century booksellers. Nevertheless, the size of the early market was small and readership more homogeneous than in later days of white-letter quality tomes for the gentleman and black-letter chapbooks and tracts for the rest. A *Jack of Newbury* or a *Fair Rosamond* was read by the full social range of the literate, and read aloud to many more. It is difficult to imagine, for example, any eighteenth-century commentator contending, as Henry Peachum did in *The Compleat Gentleman* of 1622, that he would not 'binde you from reading all other bookes, since there is no booke so bad euen Sir Beuis himself, Owleglass or Nashes herring, but some commoditie may be gotten by it'.[32] Beyond specialist scholarship and the few training manuals produced, no bookseller could define the social tastes of a popular audience with the accuracy of later centuries. For all the power accrued by

[31] The standard introduction remains Wright, *Middle-Class Culture*.
[32] Peachum, cited in Wright, *Middle-Class Culture*, p. 102.

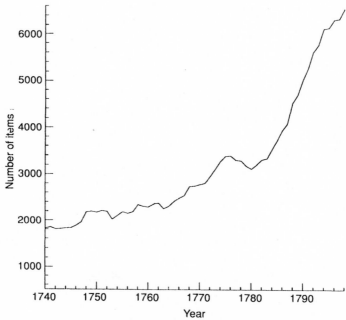

Fig. 1. *ESTC* Publication Totals, 1740–1800 (five-year moving average)
Source: ESTC estimates, including locally printed ephemera, handbills, and ballads, as well as multiple editions. Other items recorded include hymnals, atlases, song-books, slip-songs and ballads, appeal cases, advertisements, sale catalogues, petitions, parliamentary cases, miscellaneous printed lists (including society membership, customs duties, and various rates), rule-sheets, type-specimens, handbills, proclamations, and 'oddities which defy classification'. I am grateful to Michael Crump for providing the raw publication totals.

trade publishers by the mid-seventeenth century, London could boast no equivalent of the commercially alert and financially successful band of booksellers who had virtually relaunched the trade by the end of the next century. This came in two phases. In the age of Tonson and Curll the book trade explored new readerships and exploited new forms of publication, notably part-issues and advanced styles of newspapers. More vigorous commercial expansion in the book trade dates from the late 1760s, with a surge in the output and diversity of pocket-books, primers, multi-volume novels, fashionable miscellanies, and cheap reprints of classic novels.

Figs. 1, 2, and 3 indicate the upturn in publication in the final third of the century, charting, respectively, estimates of the total

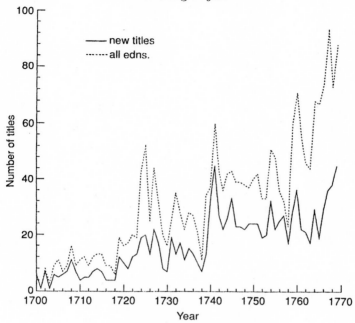

FIG. 2. Publication of Novels, 1700–1770
Source: Raven, *British Fiction*, p. 9, with full notes on compilation, pp. 5–7, 43–6.

annual publication rates from 1740, the annual publication of new novels from 1700 until 1769, and the annual publication of new novels and fiction serializations in magazines over the full century. Reclaiming the dimensions of this growth in the book trade is a task still embarrassed by the unevenness of late eighteenth-century bibliographical evidence and research. Fig. 1 was compiled using a five-year moving average of the total annual publications in *ESTC*. Fig. 2 combines new research for 1750–69 with considered use of existing checklisting 1700–49, and Fig. 3 combines existing research on magazines and early novel production with the most recent findings from the continuing project, 1770–1800.

The broader basis for Figs. 2 and 3 is a chronological index of imaginative literature, constructed from existing check-lists, library catalogues, and a range of contemporary material including reviews and publishers' advertisements in newspapers, trade catalogues, and their own books. The full resource file can

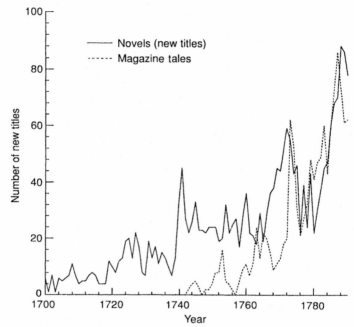

FIG. 3. Novels and Magazine Tales, 1700–1790
Sources: Mayo, *English Novel in the Magazines*; Pitcher, 'New Facts'; Raven, *British Fiction*.

fairly claim unprecedented coverage, but this should not disguise its provisional nature—nor the meagreness of the past catalogues for the second half of the eighteenth century which it supplants. Contemporary newspaper advertisements continue to provide evidence of non-surviving and unreviewed works and editions, of exact dates of publication, and of named contributing retailers. Particular attention is paid to reprinted works, whether first published within the period or before it. In such a study the calculation of survival rates is of obvious importance. Original newspaper and booksellers' advertisements have been used to record titles without surviving copies and to estimate the total output of literature. For many lost works surviving reviews have also indicated the category of work as well as its price and publisher. Occasionally, such notices also outline a plot or even quote selected passages.

The three figures should be used with caution. In particular, although Fig. 1 uses a five-year moving average to minimize erratic fluctuations, the foundation annual totals include works attributed generally to one decade—'*c*.1750' and '*c*.1760', for example. The impressive growth-rates of the second half of the century are clear, however, paralleling the expansion in jobbing and provincial printing in both volume and geographical location.[33] What is also clear is the watershed of the early 1780s. The average annual rate of growth for the years between 1740 and 1800 was 2.06 per cent. From 1740 to 1780 the growth rate was 1.58 per cent, but from 1780 to the end of the century this rate more than doubled to 3.37 per cent, a take-off in publication totals reflecting the expansion of the country distribution network, increased institutional demand, and new productivity based on financial and organizational innovation.

There are, however, many obvious deficiencies in such statistical presentations and the figures are provided only to indicate trends in publication. No counting exercise, however thorough its use of surviving contemporary sources, can follow a wholly consistent and satisfactory definition of what a novel was. It should also be noted that totals for calendar years (as given) do not correspond to the bookselling year or 'season', which generally extended from November to June. Similarly, simple tallies of titles and of their subsequent editions, do not take account of variations in the size of editions.

Increased output, however, was the result of an increase in titles and the number of editions rather than in edition sizes. Large editions were commercially dangerous and technically difficult. Philip Gaskell argues that an edition of 1,500 was the most economical: 'it was almost impossible to get the real unit cost of a substantial book below 90 per cent of the unit cost for an edition of 1,500 copies, however many were printed, and unless the interest charges were very small, the real unit cost began to rise again shortly after the edition quantity exceeded 2,000 copies'.[34] Both the uncertainties of the market and the particular costs and overheads of presswork encouraged multiple issues of small editions, rather than the printing of large ones. For a commercial (that is, a non-subscription) novel, the number of copies in

---

[33] Cf. the findings of C. J. Mitchell, 'The Spread and Fluctuation of Eighteenth-Century Printing', *Studies on Voltaire and the Eighteenth Century*, 230 (1985), 305–21, and his 'Provincial Printing in Eighteenth-Century Britain', *Publishing History*, 21 (1987), 5–24.

[34] Philip Gaskell, *A New Introduction to Bibliography*, 2nd edn. (Oxford, 1974), 160–3.

each edition appears have been about 800. Patricia Hernlund shows that 90 per cent of 514 books published by William Strahan between 1738 and 1785 were in editions of less than 2,000 copies.[35] Even Smollett's *History* numbered only 1,000 copies in its first edition.[36] Lowndes informed Miss Burney that 500 was a common edition size for a novel.[37] Editions of over 1,000 copies were contemplated only for the most celebrated authors or books. The first edition of Burney's *Cecilia* (1783) was of 2,000 copies. This compares to the 6,500 copies of the three editions together of *Joseph Andrews* (1742) or the 8,000 copies of the two first issues of Fielding's *Amelia* in 1751. After the initial success of Smollett's *History* in a small edition, some 13,000 copies of the second numbered-parts edition were sold during the first fourteen weeks. Sterne's *Tristram Shandy* was first printed in an edition of no more than 500 copies, but subsequent volumes enjoyed editions of at least 4,000 copies.[38]

At this point it should be added that one potential method of assessing the popularity of works in the eighteenth century is by analysis of the sale of copyrights between publishers. Evidence does survive of the flourishing sales of book-shares, most conducted at the exclusive marts of the trade associations. For the century as a whole, three long runs of the printed catalogues for the auction of book-shares have survived. Two of these, those of Aaron Ward and son covering the period 1718–52, and those of John Osborn and the Longmans for the period 1718–68, have been the subject of careful study.[39] Interpretation of copyright exchanges, however, is overwhelmed by difficulties. A full understanding of these transactions would require knowledge of the rate of devaluation of elderly works and the distribution of the proportion of shares in a book amongst other publishers (value may have been affected by the going rates for establishing monopolies). Account would also have to be taken of the history of the

[35] Patricia Hernlund, 'Strahan's Ledgers: Standard Charges for Printing, 1738–1785', *Studies in Bibliography*, 20 (1967), 89–III.

[36] BL, Add. MSS, 38, 730, fo. 135.

[37] A. R. Ellis (ed.), *Early Diary of Frances Burney, 1768–1778*, 2 vols. (London, 1889), ii. 307.

[38] Altick, *English Common Reader*, p. 50; Wilbur L. Cross, *The History of Henry Fielding*, 3 vols. (New Haven, Conn., 1918), i. 316, 352, 355, ii. 304; Wiles, *Serial Publication*, pp. 5–6; Kenneth Monkman, 'The Bibliography of the Early Editions of Tristram Shandy', *Library*, 5th ser. 25/1 (Mar. 1970), II–39 (pp. 14, 27, 29). The first edition of the first two volumes of *Tristram Shandy* may have been of only 200 copies.

[39] Belanger, 'Booksellers' Trade Sales' (and the Wards set also by Blagden, 'Bookseller's Trade Sales').

pirating of particular works, the frequency in the trading of copyright shares, and the possible benevolent (or malevolent) motives of publishers. Much of this information is simply unavailable, and given the evidence of very large numbers of lots for sale at each mart, the paucity of surviving copyright exchange receipts makes analysis virtually valueless. The task was beyond the contemporary bookman Mortimer, who abandoned his attempt to calculate ownership of shares because they were so greatly divided and exchanging hands so rapidly.[40]

In contrast, other contemporary sources can contribute to a checklisting of publications. In the absence of publishers' records, surviving prospectuses and newspaper advertisements have been used to supplement study of the range and composition of books and magazines, and to shed new light upon the marketing techniques of literary entrepreneurs. The hyperbole of the newspaper advertisements and handbills of the eighteenth century arrests the attention of the most despairing researcher. Indeed, the flamboyance and finesse of the advertising can still mesmerize its readers and tempt them either to take puffs at face value or to compile a partial catalogue of sensationalist billings and designs. Advertisements, for example, cannot be used as the sole evidence for edition listings or dating: it was a basic ploy of the advertising publisher to boast of perhaps fourth or fifth editions which were in fact reissues of the second or even first. It appears, for example, that James Lackington issued a 'seventh' edition of his infamous *Memoirs* in succession to the 'third'.

For all such qualifications, the trend is clear. Figs. 1 and 2 suggest the advancing levels of book trade activity from the 1740s—both in total publication and in the specialist production of new novels. These annual totals of new novels and of reprints represent a large increase upon previously accepted tallies.[41] The

---

[40] Preface, *The Universal Director* (London, 1763).

[41] A much fuller description of trends, 1750–70, is given in Raven, *British Fiction*. For the last decade alone, research has revealed four times the number of new self-styled novels given by an *ESTC* survey restricted to BL holdings, M. J. Crump, 'Stranger than Fiction', in M. Crump and M. Harris (eds.), *Searching the Eighteenth Century* (London, 1984), p. 62. Search expression submitted as 'novel #' in title, i.e. with # as any character. The *ESTC* weakness here is the result of the (then) data-base limitations and the required specificity of the search expression tw; there is no descriptive category for the novel. In 1925 Miss Husbands estimated that of the 1,341 minor novels reviewed 1770–1800, only 621 were in the British Museum, *N&Q*, 148: 386.

1740s and 1760s were particularly productive decades for new and for reprinted fiction, while novel publication reached unprecedented levels in the late 1780s—as seen in the longer perspective offered by Fig. 3. New novel titles are nearly three times more numerous in 1790 than in 1750, and estimated total novel production, including all reprints, increased by a factor of four during the same period. The 'prolific scribblerian year' of 1771–2, as the *Critical Review* called it,[42] was a high point of novel production before a short-term, volatile, but marked decline between 1776 and 1781. After 1790 publication totals continue to climb steeply, although more at the rate of the early 1760s than of 1780–88. At the 1788 peak of annual production shown here, the number of new novels was more than ten times that of the average of annual totals of the first two decades of the century.

An upsurge of new works in the late 1760s was also followed by a wave of reprints, sustaining public interest in the publication of *belles-lettres*. Similarly, the mid-period decline in novel production was accompanied by a decline in the publication of new novels. The number of new novels as a proportion of annual novel output falls between the early 1760s and 1790. Nevertheless, reissues of classics—including the Harrison monthly reprints—maintained novel output (by title-count) at just above pre-1760 levels, while the number of editions and probably the size of the popular reprinted edition actually increased. Such estimates are certainly confirmed by the outcries against a contagion of fiction in the early 1770s and again towards the end of the 1780s. Almost half of the estimated total of 1780 novels were reprints of works published two or more years previously—the great majority being reissues of works by Richardson, Fielding, Smollett, and Sterne. In 1790 reprints of works first published over two years previously were nearly four times the number of such reprints in 1760, but still only a third of the total number of novels and their editions published during the year. The precariousness of the market is reflected in the sharp falls in output before the recovery and then surge in production of the 1780s. The decline and volatility in novel production was in part caused by the effect upon the book trade of general economic difficulties. The fortunes of commercial publishing followed closely the short-term economic troughs of the

[42] Cited in Tompkins, *Popular Novel*, p. 13.

period.[43] For the fiction industry, the slumps of the late 1770s were also exacerbated by review-led reactions against deluges of ill-written and rapidly outdated 'sentimental' novels.[44]

There can be no question about the commercial risks involved in such bookselling. Financial margins were tight and unpredictable. As booksellers became more independent from trade associations, high overheads could not easily be shared and increased competition tempted larger outlays in production. Heavy investment was usually required before the sale of work achieved the necessary return, and only marginal profits accrued from most published runs. Works spurned by the public, or printed, like the first issue of Fielding's *Amelia*, in excessively large editions, required a decade or more to clear. The thrust of the business in the second half of the century was therefore to produce fast-selling, quickly printed publications. Earlier in the century, public subscription had been a method of assessing demand and sharing costs. It was especially useful insurance against heavy losses on large, technically difficult, or unusual undertakings. Subscription collection, however, was usually too lengthy a process for publishing fashionable, competitive productions. In the pursuit of market-based profit, booksellers were also unable to avoid further expenditure on advertisements and gimmicks. Safety nets were scarce. Erosion of both copyright control and strict co-operative publishing encouraged freer, more adventurous, but also more unpredictable marketing.

The serialization of fiction in part-numbers and within magazines and miscellanies advanced in both quantity and production quality during the second half of the century.[45] Fig. 3 shows how trends in full novel publication compare to available data for the issue of serialized magazine tales.[46] Again, great caution is

[43] For the difficult years of the early 1760s and 1776–80, Ian Maxted's figures for book trade bankruptcies, *The London Book Trades, 1775–1800* (London, 1977), table 14, p. xxxiii. For comparative bankruptcy rates, T. S. Ashton, *Economic Fluctuations in England, 1700–1800* (Oxford, 1959), esp. pp. 124–32, 150–66; Julian Hoppit, *Risk and Failure in English Business, 1700–1800* (Cambridge, 1987), p. 45, fig. 1.

[44] Tompkins, *Popular Novel*, esp. pp. 13–19.

[45] Mayo, 'A Catalogue of Magazine Serials and Novelettes, 1740–1815', *English Novel in the Magazines*, pp. 431–652, including 'Index of Catalogue References', and 'Chronological Index'; Melvin R. Watson, *Magazine Serials and the Essay Tradition, 1746–1820* (Baton Rouge, La., 1956), pp. 107–51, 'Register of Essay Serials'; and Michael Harris, 'Periodicals and the Book Trade', in Robin Myers and M. Harris (eds.), *The Development of the English Book Trade, 1700–1899* (Oxford, 1981), pp. 36–65.

[46] Totals are based on Mayo, *English Novel in the Magazines*, and Pitcher, 'New Facts'.

required in interpreting the publication totals of magazine serializations. While the dating of serials usually provides no difficulties, there were enormous variations in both the format and the length of magazine tales, including the size of part-issues or extracts and the regularity of their appearance. What is quite clear, however, is the increase in the number of magazine pages devoted to fiction during the period. The development of serial issues closely follows that of novel production, with striking similarities after 1775. In part, this is owing to the common origins of both types of publication, most being serials appearing in magazines and journals printed in the Row or Fleet Street. The proliferation of magazines and journals—many extremely short-lived—was particularly noticeable during the 1780s. In January 1787, at the peak of new novel publication, the *Busy Body*, *Country Magazine*, and *Humorists Magazine* were all launched.

During the same period, the production of moral tales for the young also increased greatly. John and Francis Newbery's children's titles numbered some 47 between 1751 and 1760, 111 between 1761 and 1770, and 218 between 1791 and 1800.[47] The publication of moral tales by title and as a proportion of the estimated annual publication of imaginative literature (excluding serials and chapbooks) rose dramatically towards the end of the period. Survival of early children's literature, however, is rare compared to later works. The reviewing of such publications before the 1780s was also extremely irregular and end-page advertisements fail to date and list separate editions.

Finally, across all categories, the most basic examination of 'useful and entertaining' literature from this period reveals the increasing emphasis given to modish production styles. Publishers competed with each other in adopting house-designs, typographical and ornamental decorations, and other refinements to the physical presentation of the text. The promotional value of this was coupled to commercial necessity. As D. F. McKenzie suggests: 'defining a public is, for a serious author, a social and cultural act; for the bookseller it may be primarily a commercial one ... The edition quantity and the speed with which a book is produced, are, at base, decisions about the relatively volatile or stable nature of the reading and/or buying public (running the

---

[47] Figures as given by Noblett (for datable editions only), cited in Plumb, 'New World of Children', *Birth of a Consumer Society*, p. 306 n. 86.

gamut from news sheet to classical text)'.[48] The upturn in the fortunes of the popular literature business was the result of the aggressive promotion of fashionable 'twelves' (publications in duodecimo format), of higher quality work, and of new subject-matter. During the second half of the eighteenth century, production trends in imaginative literature were clearly away from chapbook-like miscellany volumes and towards highly finished, modish works. Such books were also to introduce readers to new and caustic criticism of the business and manners of the times.

---

[48] D. F. McKenzie, 'Typography and Meaning: The Case of William Congreve', in Giles Barber and Bernhard Fabian (eds.), *Buch und Buchhandel in Europa im achtzehnten Jahrhundert*, Proceedings of the Fifth Wolfenbüttel Symposium, Nov. 1977, (Hamburg, 1981), pp. 81–126 (p. 103).

3

BOOKSELLERS AND MARKETS

Our patient Fathers trifling themes laid by,
And roll'd o'er labour'd works th'attentive eye;
Page after page, the much-enduring men
Explor'd the deeps and shallows of the pen;

. . . .

Our nicer palates lighter labours seek,
Cloy'd with a Folio-number once a week;
Bibles with cuts and comments thus go down,
E'en light Voltaire is number'd through the town;

. . . . . .

See yonder, rang'd in more frequented rows,
An humbler band of Duodecimos;
While undistinguish'd trifles swell the scene,
The last new Play, and fritter'd Magazine.

George Crabbe, *The Library* (London, 1781).

THE advances and volatility of English publication rates in the
second half of the eighteenth century reflected changes in the
commercial orientation of the book trades. The nature of business
techniques and copyright protection were all transformed. Despite a virtual technological standstill in printing methods, the
traditional basis of the book trade was remodelled. In the previous
fifty years publishing syndicates had maintained copyright protection and underwritten expensive works. Such associations,
sharing expenses, profits, and trade books, had supplanted earlier
co-operative publishing practices. In turn, however, the new
associations were undermined by individual operators entering
the book trades and eager to nurture new audiences. The near
monopoly of the London closed copyright auctions, still central to
the mid-century trade, was shattered by the 1790s.

Literature, like other fashion and leisure wares, was taken up by entrepreneurs with a sharp eye to the market. As with the manufacture of new household goods and consumables, the success of many products of the press was determined by customer identification, metropolitan trend-setting, and the exploitation of a country market.[1] At the same time, the weakening of the share book system increased the risk for all business participants. Although booksellers' associations continued jointly to issue works, fresh vulnerability and rivalries were introduced into the trade. Growing demand and the consequent heightening of competition within the trade forged new connections between publishing, bookselling, and the commercial loan of books. It encouraged a greater range of works available to the public, an increased piracy of works, and revision to the format of publications. Above all, and what will be of major concern here, competition forced greater attention to advertising, book design, the saleable value of the contents and message of a work, and methods of attracting and retaining new readerships.

The engine-room of the literature industry of the second half of the eighteenth century was Paternoster Row.[2] Its bookshops, most conducting wholesaling operations with agent booksellers, competed with those of nearby St Paul's Churchyard, ancient home of stationers, Fleet Street, and Ludgate Hill. Many new retailers and small-scale specialist booksellers opened in the West End, vying for a new calibre of customer. Most wholesale and new publishing businesses, however, remained close to Stationer's Hall and centred upon Paternoster Row and the area to the immediate west and north of St Paul's Churchyard. Many of their products were tailored for specific audiences and to promote emulative buying. At both ends of town, and in business extended to the provinces, the trade was enlivened by a succession of new promotional and marketing strategies. These depended upon a diverse band of skilled workers from printers, typefounders, and binders to publisher-booksellers, specialist

---

[1] For comparable developments, Adolph I. Klein, Dwight E. Robinson, Fritz Redlich, and Herman Freudenberger, 'Fashion: Its Sense of History—Its Selling Power', and continuation articles, *Business History Review*, 37/1–2 (1963), 1–48.

[2] New research only confirms the reflections of C. H. Timperley, *Encyclopaedia of Literary and Typographical Anecdote* (London, 1842), p. 838, that Paternoster Row was transformed in the early 1770s from a centre of old bookselling to the hub of a new novel and periodical industry. Perhaps the most evocative descriptions of the Row at the end of the 18th cent. are given in Thomas Rees and John Britton, *Reminiscences of Literary London* (London, 1896).

wholesalers and retailers, commercial librarians, and itinerant pedlars.

There is, however, no easy way to generalize about very complicated changes apparently moving in different directions. The number of independent publishers and jobbing printing businesses trebled in the final third of the century, but most London booksellers continued to co-operate informally and to order each other's books for individual customers. Provincial printing advanced with astonishing speed, but the metropolis remained more than ever the centre of the expanding trade. A radial distribution network developed in tandem with late century advances in transportation and provincial credit facilities. Wholesale, publishing, and retailing functions continued in various combinations, but by the end of the century many craftsmen, including many binders, engravers, and stationers, operated from their own shops rather than as contracted labourers. Both apprentice registration figures[3] and surviving receipts for copyright shares hint at the diversification of the trade. The potential for profits mushroomed, but competitive and ambitious publishing also brought heavy risks and spectacular failures. The adventurousness of these years is amply demonstrated in the career of George Kearsley, who was apprenticed in 1753, arrested for publishing number 45 of the *North Briton* in 1763 and sent to the Tower, bankrupted and forced to flee to France in 1764, reopened in Ludgate Street in 1765, twice bankrupted in 1784, and died in 1790.[4]

Again like many other expanding consumer industries, London booksellers—and their Dublin, Edinburgh, and provincial rivals and partners—employed innovatory commercial skills to supply and encourage new tastes. Public interest was stimulated by the attempts at comprehensive critical reviewing and by the publication of readers' contributions to the magazines.[5] Newspaper advertisements puffed 'latest' books by those said to be the

---

[3] From the listings of D. F. McKenzie, *Stationers' Company Apprentices, 1701–1800* (Oxford Bibliographical Society Publications, 1978), esp. the 'family business' entries for Bew, p. 35, Harrison, p. 161, Kearsley, pp. 200–1, and Lane, pp. 207–8.

[4] Similarly, the misfortunes of 'Ingenious Coote' and Stanley Crowder, Terry Belanger, 'A Directory of the London Book Trade, 1766', *Publishing History*, 1 (1977), 7–48 (pp. 34–5).

[5] Alvin Sullivan (ed.), *British Literary Magazines: The Augustan Age and the Age of Johnson, 1698–1788* (Westport, Conn., and London, 1983); Derek Roper, *Reviewing Before the 'Edinburgh', 1788–1802* (London, 1978); C. Lennart Carlson, *The First Magazine: A History of the*

most skilful or up-to-date authors. No educated or polite or fashionable reader could afford to be without the new works, and yet, assured the advertisements, everyone could easily afford to buy them.

The subject of these publications ranges from exotic fantasies to sober domestic moralities. Some of the liveliest works were taken from stage productions; others, from attempts to imitate Richardson, Fielding, or Sterne. Comic fiction included dozens of bawdy or suggestive skits, from the 1759 *Juvenile Adventures of Miss Kitty F——r*, to the 1785 *Ghost of Moll King; or, A Night at Derry's*, and the 1790 *Memoirs of Maria, a Persian Slave*. Stories from the London streets and exposés of political intrigue were accompanied by genteel novels set in fashionable salons or rural retreats. The picaresque ramble novel remained popular throughout the century, and many works pursued topical and personal targets. Garrick was mimicked in Kimber's *David Ranger*. Richardson's letter-moralities were parodied in Kidgell's *Card*. Shebbeare penned imaginative political satires, making him, at one point, a fellow prisoner with his rival-in-letters, Dr Smollett. At the same time, the bookshops of the Row and the West End stocked dozens of reprints, serializations, and extracts of Marmontel's tales, Mrs Rowe's moralities, and a succession of insistently didactic two- and three-volume novels.

Although much fiction was written as objective 'history', many tales also adopted various forms of narration in the first person. This might be in the style of memoirs or from the perspective of imaginary correspondent or observer. The guise might be human or otherwise. The 'spy' novel was particularly popular at mid-century and still produced in numbers in the 1790s. The most reprinted and imitated spy novel was Charles Johnston's *Chrysal; or, The Adventures of a Guinea*. It was published in the same 1759–60 season as Sterne's *Tristram Shandy*, easily the most celebrated and influential of the fictional 'memoirs' of the period. In other 'adventures', the spies included dogs, flies, a sedan chair, a pin-cushion, and a corkscrew. Like many such narrators, Eliza Haywood's 1755 *Invisible Spy* reports scandal within respectable covers. The *Invisible Spy* was reprinted eight times by the end of

Gentleman's Magazine (Providence, RI, 1938); and Albert Pailler, *Edward Cave et le Gentleman's Magazine, 1731–1754*, 2 vols. (Lille and Paris, 1975), esp. i. 350, ii. 659–67 (*Appendix of Tables*, VI).

the century, as was Francis Coventry's popular spy novel of 1751, *Pompey the Little; or, The Adventures of a Lap-Dog.*

Another favoured variation on the narrative history was the novel in letters.[6] The form was dominated in its early years by the productions of Samuel Richardson, but after his death many writers continued to turn to social *reportage* in letters, including the Minifie sisters, Maria Cooper, Jean Marishall, Phoebe Gibbes, and John Langhorne. Translations from French epistolary fiction boosted the popularity of the genre still further. Most prominent was the work of Françoise Grafigny, Marie Jeanne Riccoboni, Jeanne Marie le Prince de Beaumont, and Pierre Henri Treyssac de Vergy. One of the leading translators, Mrs Frances Brooke, also wrote her own successful letter novels. The increasing popularity of the form is marked. New epistolary novels made up no more than a tenth of new fiction published in any one year between 1750 and 1760. By the late 1760s, however, almost a third of new titles were written in letters. In addition, many of the most reprinted novels of this decade were also in letters.[7] Although more thoroughgoing bibliographical work has yet to be done, letter novels of the 1790s, while representing a diminishing proportion of overall novel output, still averaged over a dozen new titles a year.[8]

The influence of the booksellers upon both the technical and literary composition of such works should certainly not be under-estimated. Much of what has been written about the birth of a new consumerism in eighteenth-century Britain could be applied to the book business. As the *Monthly Review* wearily put it, 'we seem to live in an age when retailers of every kind of ware aspire to be the original manufacturers, and particularly in literature'.[9] London was the centre for production and inspiration. For all the recent emphasis upon the growth of the provincial trade, in book publi-cation London booksellers dominated the market. The product was centrally produced to be distributed to the provinces.[10] Locally printed books were still very rare by 1800. Writers and

---

[6] Its early history is discussed in Robert A. Day, *Told in Letters: Epistolary Fiction before Richardson* (Ann Arbor, Mich., 1966), Godfrey Frank Singer, *The Epistolary Novel: Its Origins, Development, Decline and Residuary Influence* (Philadelphia, 1933), and Black, *Epistolary Novel.*

[7] Raven, *British Fiction*, p. 12.   [8] Black, *Epistolary Novel*, pp. 2, 174.

[9] *MR* 34: 480 (June 1766).

[10] The dominance of London works is made clear in Raven, *British Fiction*, table 1, figs. 2 and 3, and 'The Publication of Fiction in Britain and Ireland, 1750–1770', *Publishing History*, 24 (1988), 31–47.

readers in the country looked to London models, to London fashions, to London reviews, and to London booksellers. An obvious additional feature of the commercialization of the book trades, however, was that many products offered their own explanation of the changes. Many writers, compilers, manufacturers, and promoters were eager to comment upon material alterations in publication. Many booksellers acted as editors or compilers of extracted or commissioned material; many drafted strong messages to be included in advertising; many promoted particular ideals for young writers to follow; and a few even wrote for their own press.

This example of another eighteenth-century industry undergoing distinctive changes as it responded to and encouraged a growth in domestic demand adds a further dimension to the quite separate 'technological determinist' approach to the history of the modern book. The work (most notably) of Walter J. Ong, Elizabeth Eisenstein, and Alvin Kernan, has demonstrated the dynamic of both print and the printing press as an independent causative force, bestriding local cultural environments.[11] It is now also apparent that in late eighteenth-century England many of the leading booksellers were extremely active in determining the kind of literature produced and the way in which it was presented. The impact of print in 'fixing' certain ideas and introducing particular notions of standardization and authority will be discussed in later chapters.

Despite robust Victorian reminiscences and book trade dictionaries, the great majority of the printers, wholesale or retail booksellers, and commercial librarians of the period remain shadowy figures. What at least is clear is that the great majority of booksellers remained small-scale operators and that the real innovations and gambles in book production, selling, and promotion were carried out by about twenty leading book trade operators. Most appear in standard book trade histories, but little detail is provided. Leading the field were wealthy establishments, operating sophisticated wholesaling or agency networks, and including the firms of Millar, Cadell, Longman, the Rivingtons, and

[11] Walter J. Ong, *The Presence of the Word* (New Haven, Conn., 1967), and *Interfaces of the Word: Studies in the Evolution of Consciousness and Culture* (Ithaca, NY, and London, 1977); Elizabeth Eisenstein, *The Printing Press as an Agent of Change* (Cambridge, 1979); Alvin Kernan, *Printing Technology, Letters and Samuel Johnson* (Princeton, NJ, 1987); and reviewed by Michael Warner, 'Literary Studies and the History of the Book', *Book*, 12 (July 1987), 3–9.

the Robinsons.[12] Brasher, often simpler, but not necessarily smaller, businesses were headed by the Noble brothers, Bell, Cooke, Harrison, Lackington, Lane, and Hogg.[13] Their operations, in a growing middle-income market, were rivalled by those of Bew, Dodsley, Hookham, Kearsley, and Vernor.[14] The full compass of bookselling was completed by dozens of short-lived or general businesses whose histories have yet to be unravelled from surviving civic and newspaper records.[15]

The most successful traders of literature shared two characteristics with certain other entrepreneurs of the time: the creation of personal fortunes and their contemporary vilification as vulgar 'mushrooms' who got rich quick. Two of the best known book trade experimenters, Lane and Lackington, ended their days very wealthy men. At his death in 1814 Lane left, according to a marginal note in his own will, a fortune of 'something under £17,500'.[16] By the 1790s, Lackington, the remainder-merchant, claimed an annual turnover of 100,000 volumes and a profit of

---

[12] Thomas Cadell I (1742–1802), apprentice to Andrew Millar, his partner from 1765 and successor in 1767, partnered by William Strahan, 1780–4, and by Andrew Strahan, 1785–93, trading as Thomas Cadell to 1793, and as Cadell and Davies, 1793–1819; Thomas Longman II (1731–97), trading in Paternoster Row, 1755–92; John Rivington I (1720–92), trading at St Paul's Churchyard, 1756–68, with Francis Rivington I (1745–1822), and with Charles Rivington III (1754–1831). Francis and Charles traded jointly, 1792–1810; James Rivington (b. 1724) was the publisher of Smollett's *History*. George Robinson I (1737–1801), traded in Paternoster Row from 1764, with George II, John, and James, from 1785, George II and James, 1794–1801.

[13] Francis Noble (d. 1792), trading from 1745 at St Martin's Court, from 1752 at Covent Garden, and opposite Gray's Inn Gate, Holborn, 1760–90; John Noble, publishing with his brother, but also independently, to 1778; John Bell (1745–1831), trading in the Strand, 1768–1801; John Cooke (1731–1810) moved to Paternoster Row, 1766, and was trading until 1792; James Harrison II, trading Paternoster Row, 1776–98; James Lackington (1746–1815), opened in Featherstone St., 1774, trading Chiswell St. from 1775 and at the 'Temple of the Muses' book emporium in Finsbury Square, 1793–8; William Lane (c. 1745–1814), trading in Leadenhall St. from at least 1775, adopting the Minerva trademark, 1790; Alexander Hogg, trading Paternoster Row, 1778–1819.

[14] John Bew (d. 1795), trading in Paternoster Row, 1774–95, dealing mainly in tracts and periodicals but also selling prints; James Dodsley (1724–97), younger brother of Robert (d. 1764) and trading Pall Mall, 1759–97; Thomas Hookham, trading Hanover Square, 1767–75, Hanover St., 1775–9, New Bond St., 1787–93, and later in Old Bond St.; George Kearsley I, trading Ludgate St., 1758–73, and Fleet St., 1773–97; Thomas Vernor (d. 1793), trading from 1766 at many addresses including Ludgate, Bishopsgate St., Birchin Lane, and the Poultry.

[15] Further comment is given in James Raven, 'The Noble Brothers and Popular Publishing, 1737–89', *Library*, 6th ser. 12/4 (Dec. 1990), 293–345.

[16] Dorothy Blakey, *The Minerva Press*, 1790–1810 (London, 1939), p. 23, and Hilda Hamlyn, 'Eighteenth-Century Circulating Libraries in England', *Library*, 5th ser. 1 (1947), 197–218 (pp. 221–2).

£4,000–5,000. He retired to Gloucestershire in 1798. In 1793
Thomas Cadell relinquished the trade with 'an ample fortune'.
James Dodsley, Thomas Longman II, and Charles Dilly each
left over £60,000.[17] Alexander Hogg gained handsome profits
from sixpenny numbers of 'miserable' and 'woeful' execution, as
did Andrew Donaldson, the breaker of *de facto* copyright.[18]
George Robinson, whom William West called 'King of Booksellers', took up a fashionable villa at Streatham. John Cooke
retired to a country estate with a 'handsome' and 'immense'
fortune.[19] Eldest or only sons of successful booksellers also
emulated their commercial cousins, the heirs to new manufacturing fortunes. They went county, did their best to obliterate
their trading origins, and contributed directly to the destruction
of bookselling records.

Certain of these booksellers have received modern attention.
Dorothy Blakey's study of William Lane has recently been
supplemented by brief reconsiderations of John Newbery and
James Lackington.[20] Of the printers, William Strahan has been
well served owing to his prestigious commissions and the unique
riches of his business records.[21] Morison's account of John Bell
provided welcome bibliographical and typographical detail,
even though it could now be supported by new evidence of Bell's

[17] Lackington, *Memoirs* (1793 edn.), p. 261; *Gentleman's Magazine* (1802), pt. ii, pp. 1173–222;
Theodore Besterman (ed.) *The Publishing Firm of Cadell and Davies: Select Correspondence and
Accounts*, 1793–1836 (London, 1938), pp. viii–ix; John Nichols, *Literary Anecdotes of the
Eighteenth Century*, 9 vols. (London, 1812–15), vi. 438, 442; E. Marston, *Sketches of Booksellers of
Other Days* (London, 1901), pp. 85–6; Philip Wallis, *At the Sign of the Ship: Notes on the House of
Longman*, 1724–1974 (London, 1974), p. 14; William Granger, *New Wonderful Museum and
Entertaining Magazine*, 6: 3135, cited in Belanger, 'Directory', p. 48.

[18] Rees and Britton, *Reminiscences*, p. 29; Henry Curwen, *A History of Booksellers, the Old
and the New* (London, 1874), p. 77.

[19] William West, *Fifty Years Recollections of an Old Bookseller* (London, 1837), pp. 92–3;
Nichols, *Literary Anecdotes*, iii. 445–9; Rees and Britton, *Reminiscences*, p. 26; Altick, *English
Common Reader*, p. 55.

[20] Blakey, *Minerva Press*; William Noblett, 'John Newbery, Publisher Extraordinary',
History Today, 22 (Apr. 1972), 265–71; Roscoe, *John Newbery*; Richard G. Landon, 'Small
Profits do Great Things: James Lackington and Eighteenth-Century Bookselling', *Studies
in Eighteenth-Century Culture*, 5 (1976), 387–99; Raven, 'Selling One's Life'.

[21] J. A. Cochrane, *Dr. Johnson's Printer: The Life of William Strahan* (London, 1964);
Hernlund, 'Strahan's Ledgers', and her 'William Strahan's Ledgers II: Charges for Paper,
1738–1785', *Studies in Bibliography*, 22 (1969), 179–95; and Robert D. Harlan, 'William
Strahan: Eighteenth-Century Printer and Publisher', Ph.D. thesis (University of Michi-
gan, 1960). Since this book was written, the long-awaited study of the business records of
William Bowyer and Son, printers of London, 1699–1777, has been published, Keith
Maslen and John Lancaster (eds.), *The Bowyer Ledgers* (London and New York, 1991).

extraordinary—if erratic—commercial flair.[22] Where other publishing careers have been discussed, attention is paid to the publication of the great works of the century rather than to the popular twelves and octavos which contributed to the fortunes of some booksellers, to the over-extension and ruination of others. Lowndes and Cadell are mostly remembered for their publication of Smith, Gibbon, and Hume,[23] while Bew, Vernor, Hookham, and the Nobles, who relied almost entirely on popular productions with quick turnovers, have been long forgotten. The commercial enterprise of Hogg, Cooke, and Harrison has not attracted the historian. Also neglected is Robinson, who in 1780 boasted the largest wholesale trade in London and was a leading copyright trader.[24] Long-servers, like George Kearsley, whose career spans from 1758 to 1813, are noted only for celebrated political contributions or their charitable work. Only the early nineteenth-century printer-author Charles Timperley, reluctantly acknowledged (in a footnote) the work of the popular press of the day:

However it may be customary to kick the ladder down when we find we no longer want it, these sort of publications must be confessed to have greatly contributed to lay the foundation of that literary taste and thirst for knowledge which now pervades all classes.[25]

In these labours, the proprietors of book publishing, retailing, and lending concerns had to be opportunist to succeed. Many of the successful literary entrepreneurs, notably Hookham, the Nobles, and Lane, built up their empires from the mutually supportive businesses of publisher, bookseller, and librarian. Other booksellers had to diversify to survive. John Bell profited handsomely in his early years from his innovatory library series and newspapers.[26] Many traders offered other services to help insure against financial hardship or to draw attention to their stationery, books, publications, or printing and binding operations. Many bookshops exchanged old books for new, sold ink, vellum, paper

---

[22] Stanley Morison, *A Memoir of John Bell, 1745–1831* (Cambridge, privately printed, 1930).

[23] Even in Nichols, *Literary Anecdotes*, vi. 441–2, and H. R. Plomer, G. H. Bushnell, E. R. McC. Dix (eds.), *A Dictionary of the Printers and Booksellers who were at work in England, Scotland, and Ireland from 1726 to 1775* (Oxford, 1932).

[24] Curwen, *History of Booksellers*, p. 69.   [25] Timperley, *Encyclopaedia*, p. 838.

[26] Morison, *John Bell*, pp. 1–4.

hangings, household wares, musical instruments, and lottery tickets, or served as a clearing-house for local information and services. For well over a decade Hookham acted as ticket-broker for the Hanover Square and St James's Park assemblies and concerts.[27] The librarian, Harrod, and the country bookseller, Sprange, supplemented the printed word with patent medicines, artists' materials, and a variety of consumer wares.[28] John Newbery's continued retail of pills and medicines to supplement his income is well known, but many other book traders advertised potions and medical gadgetry as part of their stock.[29] Henry Jackson supported his press and circulating library in Oxford Street by the sale of 'incomparable water for the eye' which, as he assured his customers, was 'of the same efficacy for Horses and Dogs'.[30]

In this expanding but volatile market-place, the larger booksellers strove to avoid a price war. In the 1770s most novels were issued bound at three shillings a volume and in paper wrappers at two shillings and sixpence. During the next thirty years the average price differential between sewed and bound works remained at sixpence a volume. Certainly, there was intense competition between rival firms, but there also appears to have been a common recognition that given the precarious nature of the book market, a war fought by price reduction would bring most operators to their knees. The result of this was renewed efforts to enlarge the market for these set-price works. Operators concentrated on advertising and sales techniques, a greater range of publications, and revisions to the design of books and magazines. The changing market-place influenced the format and typography of books, it affected the content of literature, and it encouraged new lines in domestic moralities and useful pocket miscellanies. Popular imaginative literature was to be both an instructor

---

[27] Advertisements, *Public Advertiser*, 1770–5.

[28] *The English Provincial Printer*, 1700–1800 (British Library Board, 1983), and also, *Lockett's Address*, reproduced in *Factotum*, Occasional Paper 3 (1983), p. II.

[29] Charles Welsh, *A Bookseller of the Last Century* (London and New York, 1885), esp. pp. 106–10; and Noblett, 'John Newbery', p. 269. Booksellers had been associated with the sale of patent medicines since the mid-17th cent., as described in John Alden, 'Pills and Publishing: Some Notes on the English Book Trade, 1660–1715', *Library*, 5th ser. 7/1 (Mar. 1952), 21–37; Robert Munter, *The History of the Irish Newspaper*, 1685–1760 (Cambridge, 1967), pp. 51–2.

[30] *Public Advertiser*, 19 Aug. 1780.

in the fashionable and marketed as a fashionable commodity. At the same time, the author, no longer wholly dependent upon private patronage and public subscription, was dispatched to an increasingly commercial market with all that entailed for financial prospects and artistic integrity. The 'pulse of the public' as Fanny Burney described it to her bookseller, was to be taken regularly by anxious producers and sellers of literature.[31]

Pocket-books were especially profitable publishing ventures in the new market. As publishers begged to assure customers, pocket-books could be read at the hairdressers, in the carriage, by the billiards table, or at the racecourse. This frequently invited contempt. As the *Monthly Review* said of *The Man of Failing*, 'vulgar amours, vulgarly related; and fit only to lie in the corner of the powdering room, for the hairdresser's amusement, while he is waiting for his master'.[32] Most books, however, were presented as entertaining and morally and practically instructive, and publishers sought to satisfy with design as well as with content. In a detailed review, the *Biographical and Imperial Magazine* lauded Cadell's six-volume *Historical Pocket Library* as 'useful, moral, elegant'.[33] Pocket-books were advertised as 'very portable and convenient for the pocket' and later series were guaranteed to be of size uniform with the 'practical' and 'pocketable' first issues. Individual firms specialized and competed in vade-mecums, diaries and pocket-book almanacs, advisers, and technical compendia and ready reckoners for the gentleman, merchant, tradesman, clerk, architect, builder, surgeon, or navigator. Even *Harris's Lists of Covent-Garden Ladies*, annual jamborees of erotic writing and brazenly advertised on the front pages of daily newspapers, were beautifully packaged by Ranger of Fleet Street in the modish style of the twelves. Publishers gave their own names to many pocket-books or miscellanies, advertising their exclusive features. Useful pocket cookery books, gardening books, prayerbooks, and hymn-books vied with pocket biographies, who's whos, and histories of England, of the world, and (a singular publishing success) of Freemasonry. Many pocket-books claimed to provide essential knowledge or specialist learning 'made easy'. One of the earliest and a model for later series, was Newbery's

[31] BL, Egerton MSS, 3,695 fo. 8, Fanny Burney to Thomas Lowndes, Jan. 1778.
[32] *MR*, NS, 3: 90 (Sept. 1790).
[33] *B&I*, 3 (Jan. 1790), 51-3.

1746 *Circle of the Sciences*. This was in seven volumes comprising *Grammar Made Easy*, *Arithmetic Made Easy*, *Rhetoric Made Easy*, *Poetry Made Easy*, *Logic Made Easy*, *Geography Made Easy*, and *Chronology Made Easy*. Also sold were primers and pocket-books 'for the meanest abilities'. Home law-books for the landlord or glebe-holding 'squarson' were accompanied from the 1770s by a prodigious array of useful pocket guidebooks for tourists and books promoting hobbies or accomplishments ranging from embroidery to butterfly collecting.

Separately issued imaginative literature underwent the same design changes. The slim 'novels' of the 1760s, many difficult to distinguish from crude 'lives' or sensationalist Grub Street satires, declined steadily in popularity through the 1770s. By 1790 the multi-volume novel was quite distinct from the cheaper, one-volume, and often roughly produced fictional biography or trial story. The new novel was issued in a recognizable format varying between publishers only in house style and according to yearly fashions. Greater variation in the number of volumes to each novel was clear from the late 1770s. Only children's works and ephemeral trial stories, *risqué* biographies, almanacs, and other miscellanies continued to be generally issued in single-volume form. The resurgence of the fiction industry in the 1780s was led by multi-volume duo-decimos together with the 'library edition' reprints.

For reprints in particular, it was financially attractive as well as a sound promotional ploy to issue works as part-numbers. A practice already popularized by 1750, the 'strange madness' of issuing the Bible in instalments was condemned as making 'three penny-worth of the Gospel' 'easy and familiar to Porters, Carmen, and Chimney-Sweepers'.[34] Commercial insecurity and competitiveness together explain the frequency of part-issues in the final third of the century. Serious but populist enterprises such as Smollett's *History of England* were published in sixpenny part-issues soon after the first date of issue. Smollett himself put the weekly circulation of parts of his *History* at 10,000.[35] Collections of tales included

[34] 'Against Publishing Books Piece-meal', *Gentleman's Magazine*, 4 (1734), 489; Altick, *English Common Reader*, p. 55; Wiles, 'Relish for Reading', pp. 98–9. Also, the chronological index of serials in R. S. Crane and F. B. Kaye, *A Census of British Newspapers and Periodicals*, 1660–1800 (Chapel Hill, NC, 1927), pp. 179–201. The earliest part-issue appears to be Joseph Moxon's *Mechanick Exercises*, monthly parts, 1677–80.

[35] Lewis Mansfield Knapp, *Tobias Smollett, Doctor of Men and Manners* (Princeton, NJ, 1949), p. 187.

the *Beauties of Sterne* and *Beauties of Fielding*, and such hybrids as Harrison's *Novelist's Magazine*, published in weekly numbers over nine years in the 1780s and reprinting English and Continental fiction.

Such activity rested on new market possibilities. An essential feature of trade expansion was a great improvement in the distribution of books by means of the country bookshop network. Larger and swifter mail routes down the new turnpikes were used to great advantage by the London booksellers, for whom the newspapers were also a vital advertising medium for publications which could be ordered through agent booksellers.[36] Demand for new twelves, especially fiction, was also stimulated by the popularizing role of the circulating libraries. Many were comparatively costly to join, but all assisted middle-class access to new books. Most readers of new fiction were not library-owners, but library-goers. A large audience read the latest literature only as borrowed from circulating libraries. By the end of the century commercial libraries were ten times more numerous than private library societies.[37] At least one hundred and twelve rental libraries in London and two hundred and sixty-eight in the provinces were established before 1800.[38] Lending libraries opened during this period were of many types. They included private proprietary and subscription libraries, parochial book clubs, and commercial circulating ventures.[39] Contemporary responses to the different library institutions were also various. It was the

---

[36] R. M. Wiles, *Freshest Advices: Early Provincial Newspapers in England* (Columbus, Ohio, 1965); Michael Harris, *London Newspapers in the Age of Walpole: A Study of the Origins of the Modern English Press* (London, 1987), pp. 19–48; G. A. Cranfield, *The Development of the Provincial Newspaper, 1700–1760* (Oxford, 1962); Munter, *History of the Irish Newspaper*; John Feather, *The Provincial Book-Trade in Eighteenth-Century England* (Cambridge, 1985).

[37] Paul Kaufman, 'The Community Library: A Chapter in English Social History', *Transactions of the American Philosophical Society*, NS 57/7 (1967), 1–65. Hamlyn, 'Circulating Libraries', p. 198, estimated the number of individual London book-lenders calling their establishments libraries, at 19 for 1770–80, and 26 for 1790–1800.

[38] Kaufman, 'Community Library', p. 53, with the provincial list of Hamlyn, 'Circulating Libraries', p. 198, and the full appendix 1 in her MA thesis (London, 1948).

[39] Large private proprietary subscription libraries, from the founding of the library in Liverpool in 1758, numbered some one hundred by the end of the century. The major foundations were Manchester in 1765, Sheffield in 1771, Bristol in 1774, Hull in 1775, Birmingham in 1779, and Newcastle in 1784. Other book clubs are discussed in Thomas Kelly, *Early Public Libraries: A History of Public Libraries in Great Britain before 1850* (London, 1966); John Minto, *A History of the Public Library Movement in Great Britain and Ireland* (London, 1932), appendix II, p. 258; Kaufman, 'English Book Clubs and their Role in Social History', *Libri*, 14 (1964), 1–31.

raging popularity of the circulating library which fuelled charges of the corrupting and subversive influences of the 'evergreen tree of diabolical knowledge'.[40] By contrast, the London Library Society with its respectable subscribers' committee, vowed to stock only important works in science and literature too expensive or difficult for individuals to buy, 'as well as every other publication of Taste and Entertainment which has no tendency to mislead the judgment or corrupt the heart'.[41]

In examining the market for literature, however, the historical debate over readership has not been conclusive, even before more recent insistence on questioning the evidence we have for understanding habits of reading and methods of textual appropriation.[42] The commercial products of the booksellers, however, do provide rare comments on readerships, and the dimensions of the upsurge in output already discussed do offer us something. One could call on the contemporary observer Moritz for support in such reasoning: 'German authors are hardly read outside learned circles except by a few of the middle class. Yet the common people of England read their English authors! You can tell it, among other things, from the number of editions of their works'.[43] Content and presentation of the literature also provides very general indications of intended audiences. The shorter, cheaper tales, imitating the polite novel, may not all have been meant for the leisured classes, but unlike the chapman's twenty-four-page black-letter histories, they were fashionably packaged and at least aimed at a more socially specific audience. Sympathetically, and often in the first person, various of these smaller productions told of the adventures of women servants and men of humble occupation. By contrast, the more finely printed novels include obvious appeals to a young, female, and leisured audience. Domestic heroes and heroines condemn, praise, or are surrounded by the very latest fashion products.

[40] The much-quoted remark of Sir Anthony Absolute in R. B. Sheridan, *The Rivals*, Act I, Scene ii, a scene largely devoted to a satiric denunciation of circulating libraries and the novel industry.

[41] *A Catalogue of the Books of the London Library* (London, 1786). The same manifesto declared, 'the young of both sexes too frequently suffer from a deprivation of morals as well as taste from the indiscriminate reading of common circulating libraries'.

[42] Helen Sard Hughes, 'The Middle-Class Reader and the English Novel', *Journal of English and Germanic Philology*, 25 (1926), 362–78; Watt, *Rise of the Novel*; debate summarized in Wiles, 'Relish for Reading', and his 'Middle-Class Literacy'.

[43] Nettel, *A German in England*, p. 42.

Besides content references and popularity estimates based on edition counting, works published by subscription can offer some specific indications of support. Published subscriber-lists often provide the sex, address, and in many cases, the profession of supporters. The lists, however, must be treated with caution. There is no control to determine their accuracy, and by the late eighteenth century subscription was associated with some of the least popular works. Many subscription lists were no more than an exercise in aristocratic name-dropping—a commercial embellishment intended to give a work respectability and social cachet. But the lists are not completely useless. They can reveal much about the support for specific writers. They also demonstrate clearly that whatever the actual nature of readerships, there was no reluctance on the part of noblemen, gentlemen, clerics, professional men, or college dons to be associated publicly with promoting a novel.[44] Although the great majority of subscribers gave London or home counties addresses, the lists also confirm a very wide geographical distribution of support throughout the period.

The great question remains, however, as to whether the undoubted increase in the publication, sale, and circulation of literature represented a major increase in *new* readers or only that those already reading books were buying or borrowing more. All the evidence points to the latter. If readership was a 'widening circle', stimulating and supported by the prodigious growth in newspapers and circulating libraries, then it was restricted by literacy rates and even more by levels of household income. In addition, there were increasingly specific social associations with different forms of publication. Literacy levels, which in England in 1750 may have been about 50 per cent sign-literacy for

---

[44] P. J. Wallis and F. J. G. Robinson, 'The Potential Uses of Book Subscription Lists', in A. Jeffreys (ed.), *The Art of the Librarian* (Newcastle upon Tyne, 1973), pp. 133–9; P. J. Wallis, 'Book Subscription Lists', *Library*, 5th ser. 29/3 (Sept. 1974), 255–86; F. J. G. Robinson and P. J. Wallis, *Book Subscription Lists: A Revised Guide* (Newcastle upon Tyne, 1975), and 1st supplement (1976) by C. Wadham, 2nd supplement (1977), and 3rd supplement (1980) by L. Menhennet; R. C. Alston, F. J. G. Robinson, and C. Wadham, *A Check-List of Eighteenth-Century Books Containing Lists of Subscribers* (Newcastle upon Tyne, 1983); W. A. Speck, 'Politicians, Peers and Publication by Subscription, 1700–1750', in Rivers, *Books and their Readers*, pp. 47–68; Pat Rogers, 'Book Subscriptions Among the Augustans', *TLS* 15 Dec. 1972, 1539–40; and his 'Pope and his Subscribers', *Publishing History*, 3 (1978), 7–36.

labourers and servants and 40 per cent for all women,[45] were one obvious determinant of the reading—though not aural—audience for the penny chapbook and sixpenny tale. In fact, of course, the readership of novels was not homogeneous. Political satires, accounts of Society scandals, fabulous travels, and smoking-room pornography, all had their own separate but not exclusive following. Many works were indeed designed to appeal to overlapping interest groups. London booksellers courted provincial readerships, and these were also encouraged by writers setting fiction in familiar parts of the country. At the very end of this period, a few local writers were publishing books in their own country town.

Readership was constrained more by the price of books than by standards of literacy. Novels were still cheaper than weighty religious, economic, or classical works, with even Pope's popular translation of the *Iliad* costing six guineas or twenty-five *Robinson Crusoes*.[46] At mid-century, however, even unbound, sewed novels were usually priced at two shillings a volume, with most works in sets of two volumes or more. Bound and decorated sets might cost over a guinea. Many booksellers made particular appeals to those, such as young, married, middle-class women, enjoying new levels of disposable income. An increasing number of women did have the leisure, ability, and inclination to support the Nobles and their like, but even the commercial circulating libraries, of which there were at least twenty in London by 1770,[47] were affordable only by those of substantial means. In the 1750s London circulating libraries were charging subscribers from between fifteen shillings and one guinea annually, and although this charge was reduced in the early 1760s, it was soon re-imposed. In 1760 two shillings could buy a stone of beef or a pair of shoes.

The literature considered in this study was written and published principally for the middle classes. The cultural consequences of an expansion in the middling groups in English society (especially provincial society) has been explored in much recent

[45] Discussion is led by R. S. Schofield, 'The Measurement of Literacy in Pre-Industrial England', in Jack Goody (ed.), *Literacy in Traditional Societies* (Cambridge, 1968), pp. 311–25; and David Cressy, *Literacy and the Social Order: Reading and Writing in Tudor and Stuart England* (Cambridge, 1980).

[46] Per Gedin, *Literature in the Market Place*, trans. by George Bisset (London, 1977), p. 15.

[47] Hamlyn, 'Circulating Libraries'; Devendra P. Varma, *The Evergreen Tree of Diabolical Knowledge* (Washington, DC, 1972).

writing.[48] There was, however, in addition to the extraordinary financial gulf between the very richest and poorest in society, also a wide variation in income between those of the 'middling sort'. Walter Gale, the schoolteacher, enjoyed a professional fee of £12 a year, with only £18 from the rental of a house and garden as additional income.[49] Many other men regarded as educated and socially superior to manual workmen, such as curates, were also offered official stipends as low as £20 a year. Successful petty tradesmen, on the other hand, such as Dent, the shopkeeper of Kirkby Stephen, boasted handsome profits from an annual turnover approaching £1,000.[50] It has been suggested that 150,000 households enjoyed an income of between £50 and £400 per annum in 1780, which was 15 per cent of all households in 1750 and 25 per cent in 1780.[51] This lower threshold of £50 may well have been the minimum annual income for anyone wanting to buy books.

In emphasizing the activity of booksellers in promoting and marketing the new literature, this study might appear to neglect one remaining contributor to the growth of the book trades —the writer. The authors, are, however, best treated on an individual basis and will be introduced wherever relevant in later discussion. The popularity of particular authors in the first half of this period has also been considered elsewhere.[52] In fact, many authors and compilers remain as obscure as their publishers. Only a minority of contributors can be given biographical details. London was home for the majority of writers during this period, although country towns such as Reading, Colchester, Birmingham, and Ipswich, all boasted famous local novelists or authors of moral essays. Many provincial writers, however, have left little record of their lives and careers. Miss Smythies of Colchester was famed in

---

[48] Notably, Peter Borsay, 'The English Urban Renaissance: The Development of Provincial Urban Culture, *c.*1680 – *c.*1760', *Social History*, 2/5 (May 1977), 581–603; Plumb, 'Public, Literature and the Arts', and 'Commercialization of Leisure'; and Angus McInnes, 'The Emergence of a Leisure Town: Shrewsbury, 1660–1760', *Past and Present*, 120 (Aug. 1988), 52–87.

[49] R. W. Blencowe (ed.), 'Extracts from the Journal of Walter Gale, Schoolmaster at Mayfield, 1750', *Sussex Archaeological Collections*, 9 (1857), 182–207 (p. 184).

[50] T. S. Willan, *An Eighteenth-Century Shopkeeper: Abraham Dent of Kirkby Stephen* (Manchester, 1970).

[51] D. E. C. Eversley, 'The Home Market and Economic Growth in England, 1750–1780', in Jones and Mingay, *Land, Labour and Population*, pp. 206–59.

[52] Raven, *British Fiction*, pp. 14–25.

the 1750s for her popular imitations of the Richardson novel. Mrs Woodfin published her first novel, *Northern Memoirs*, in 1756 and completed a further four works of fiction during the next ten years. Like dozens of their contemporaries, both writers have vanished without trace. Miss Smythies is not even included in the recent and most thoroughgoing of guides to women writers of the century.[53]

One thing is certain: authors of popular twelves usually received paltry remuneration for their work. From the scant evidence of bookselling accounts and memoirs, it seems that many booksellers could not afford to give authors more. As it was, full copyright was usually surrendered to the bookseller as a condition of the sale of the manuscript. If the larger, successful publisher did remain the Barabbas of the trade, then it was an accepted role: there was very little discussion of authorial right before the middle of the eighteenth century.[54] Of the popular novelists of the 1780s and 1790s, only Smith and Burney gained significant if still modest purses from their later novels. Burney, however, had received only twenty guineas from Thomas Lowndes for her first but best-selling work, *Evelina*, and Lowndes was neither poor nor uncharitable.[55] One of the very few surviving records to mention Mrs Woodfin is a receipt, dated January 1764, for the five guineas and five guineas in books paid by Lowndes in return for all rights to her latest novel, *Marianne Middleton*.[56] Successful drama could be more rewarding. Certain 1770 copyright sales to playwrights of £150, were matched by similar sales of up to £400 by 1790.[57] The most lucrative, but extraordinary copyright receipts for prose were the £4,500 achieved by Robertson for his *Charles V*, and, for fiction, Fielding's £700 for *Tom Jones* and £1,000 for *Amelia*.[58] This, however, was wealth far beyond the reach of the vast majority of writers of the period.

[53] For nearly all the female authors mentioned here, Janet Todd (ed.), *A Dictionary of British and American Women Writers, 1660–1800* (London, 1984) is an invaluable guide. Also, MacCarthy, *Later Women Novelists*. Smythies is considered in F. G. Black, 'A Lady Novelist of Colchester', *Essex Review*, 64 (1935), 180-5.

[54] James Hepburn, *The Author's Empty Purse and the Rise of the Literary Agent* (London, 1968).

[55] BL, Egerton MSS (Barrett Collection, VI), 3,695, fo. 9, Lowndes to the anonymous author, 11 Nov. 1777.

[56] BL, Add. MSS, 38,728, fo. 212, Woodfin to Lowndes, 14 Jan. 1764.

[57] Collins, *Profession of Letters*, pp. 84-5.

[58] Collins, *Authorship*, p. 34.

Despite this, many turned to writing for financial support. It is probable that then, as now, the spectacular earnings of an exclusive literary élite provided a glittering goal for needy but well-educated gentlefolk. Newspapers and hack essayists helped fuel rumours of the sums amassed by Pope, Robertson, Smollett, and others. For those starting out, or with a particular plea of poverty to make, a subscription scheme was a usual resort. Unfortunately, it is not always clear how certain schemes were organized or how great were the returns. Booksellers, of course, were never slow to announce their benevolent intentions, on the grounds, presumably, that charity was good for business. Critics in the periodicals were also inclined to leniency when reviewing subscription works by destitute or deserving authors.

It is, of course, most likely that many prefaces claiming affliction or desolation were invented. They were written—and left in or embellished by the bookseller—to encourage the acceptance of the manuscript, to invite sympathy from the reviewers, or to boost sales, whether by subscription or over the shop-counter. A suspiciously large number of books were adorned with prefaces or advertisements claiming that the work had been undertaken to save a husband or relative from the debtors' prison. Many 'first works by a young lady' were almost certainly the latest production of a mature male hack. On the other hand, there were many examples of genuine distress. Sarah Fielding supported herself by writing to the end of her life. Mrs Sheridan, Charlotte Lennox, Mrs Gomersall, and, in the early years, Mrs Smith, were all writing to keep families out of debt or gaol. Of the bookseller's role in this, one other toiling writer concluded that

the fate of the living Author, in these abused and hard times, depends much upon the caprice of this tasteless confectioner. The causes of salvation and damnation to authors, are various—arising, in a great measure, from the petulancy of this set of men, and the jealousies and distractions which subsist among them.[59]

Whether their excuses for writing were genuine or not, and whether they were writing from pleasure or necessity, authors were the very last participants to benefit from the eighteenth-century book bonanza.

---

[59] Samuel Paterson, *Joineriana: Or the Book of Scraps*, 2 vols. (London, 1772), i. 53–4.

4

PROMOTION AND DEFENCE

The manufacturers of novels, in one respect, resemble the
bakers of gingerbread; for their ingredients are the same, and
the chief difference lies in the manner of disposing the decorations.

Critical Review, 34: 350 (Nov. 1767).

The Editor very justly remarks, that 'the generation of novels
has sprung up like Hydras, and are, in general, equally nox-
ious to mankind. With a smiling face', says he, 'they often
plant a dagger, and convey a subtle poison in a sweetened
potion'.

European Magazine, 17: 344 (May 1790).

THE promotion of the publications of Augustan Grub Street often
seems sober by comparison with the brash and ingenious literary
entrepreneurship of the next fifty years. Early century part-
numbers, pocket-books, and other literary wonders sired a new
tribe of popular twelves. The titles of these were often little more
than a string of superlatives. Books by 'a Constellation of Geniuses'
or a 'Congress of Solomons' were puffed by spurious review
extracts and readers' reports. They were supported by novel
promises of 'real new work', prior inspection, money-back guar-
antees, and assurances of part-number completion with an 'over-
plus' delivered gratis. Library series or sets of works featured in
advertising campaigns planned and revised according to estimates
of the progress of sales and the operations of rivals. Ingenious
marketing strategies are documented in hundreds of surviving
newspaper advertisements, handbills, and book insertions.
Bonuses were offered for the outright purchase of serialized works.
Special discounts were advertised for special publications, special
customers, special retailers, and special occasions. Publishers and

booksellers offered superior bindings, labelling, paper, presswork, and illustrations at never-again prices.[1]

Fashion was the keynote. Samuel Richardson reported that a young lady from a country town complained that 'in this foolish town, we are obliged to read every foolish book that fashion renders prevalent in conversation'.[2] 'The booksellers, those pimps of literature', mused one contributor to the *Critical Review*,

take care every winter to procure a sufficient quantity of tales, memoirs and romances for the entertainment of their customers, many of whom, not capable of distinguishing between good and bad, are mighty well satisfied with whatever is provided for them: as their female readers in particular have most voracious appetites, and are not over delicate in the choice of their food, every thing that is new will go down.[3]

In the production of commercial literature after mid-century, quality of writing was certainly not always a primary concern. By presenting books as attractive and fashionable consumer products, many booksellers achieved a swift turnover of quickly forgotten, hurriedly produced sheets. Indeed, many of the works published in this period were associated more with their bookseller-publishers than with their authors. Very often, authorship remained unannounced.

Even more disturbing to eighteenth-century critics were what were considered to be the immoral effects of the print deluge issuing from the bookshops and new circulating libraries. Many novels and serials offered well-tried formulas of plot and characterization. Rapidly written tales abound with distressed heroes and heroines, assorted orphans, cripples, dowagers, and stepmothers. There are several examples of writers unwittingly changing the occupation, nationality, and even name of a character during the course of the narrative. The consequences of lechery and deceit are depicted in spectacularly implausible denouements. Some novels are little more than disjointed exchanges of letters or short stories. As such, they were dismissed in a few contemptuous words by the growing number of publishing critics.

[1] While indebted to the pioneering work of Richard Altick, I cannot agree with his conclusion that the 18th-cent. bookseller was not interested in enlarging his trade, and (with the 'great exception' of Lackington) was 'content merely to serve customers who came to his door', *English Common Reader*, p. 57.

[2] Letter to Bishop Hildersley [1761], cited in John Carroll, ed., *Selected Letters of Samuel Richardson* (Oxford, 1964), p. 341.

[3] *CR* 16: 449 (Dec. 1763).

In a phrase typical of scores of other fiction notices, a contemporary reviewer regarded his subject as 'a puny, miserable reptile that has here crawl'd into existence, happily formed to elude all attack by its utter insignificance'.[4]

It often needs restating, therefore, that the production and sale of much of this popular literature has to be understood in terms of a major fashion business. Print not only stimulated the fashion-booms of consumer products spreading across the nation in the time of Boulton and Wedgwood, but was itself used to sustain consumer interest in the literary product and to refashion the sales techniques of publishing and bookselling.[5] Mass production of these publications was ridiculed and condemned by those applying critical standards quite foreign to the modest origins and intentions of the new works. What was at least clear was that a novel-producing industry had arrived in London, from where its wares were circulated to the country with unprecedented speed and publicity.

In fact, in a trade where so many individual operators pursued adventurous marketing policies, many of their promotional ploys were based on a printing technology that had remained fundamentally unchanged for two hundred years. The only major exception to the unaltered state of the printing process—and it is an important one in terms of book design and composition—came with developments first in imported and then in native typeface production from the early eighteenth century. What made the second half of the century so different was the scale and competitiveness of new production and selling strategies. Most traders in Paternoster Row and rival bookselling locations had to offer up-to-the-minute selections of new books if they were to survive. Many works were even post-dated to make them seem new. Some were not dated at all so that they could always be claimed as 'of the season'.[6] Under new stewardship and in increasingly competitive conditions many puffing and customer-tempting devices reached new levels of sophistication. Additional customer services and special offers were pursued with unprecedented vigour: the creation of special audience interests and the

---

[4] *CR* 4: 95 (July 1757), notice of *The Fair Citizen*.

[5] This question is examined in detail in my forthcoming work, *The Commercialization of the Book in Britain, 1745–1814*.

[6] A favoured technique of the Nobles, Raven, 'Noble Brothers', p. 303.

production of ranges of works specifically designed for new readerships; the promotion of reader-participation; the use of new literary resources including critical reviewing and newspaper advertising (especially in the provinces); the encouragement of book-buying for the sake of fashion; and the creation of novel schemes to compel readers to maintain their custom.

Fashionable book-buying was encouraged in many ways. The day of the encyclopaedia salesman arrived. The bookseller, Knight, concluded of part-numbers that 'the system upon which they are sold is essentially that of forcing a sale'.[7] The same system operated across many types of literature by the end of the eighteenth century and in many forms. From the late 1760s booksellers experimented in new typographical layout and promoted their own house designs—a development which has received almost no attention.[8] Many of the pocket-books were issued in a series or in a bookseller's own exclusive style. Large numbers were designed to be collected as self-contained libraries. Finely engraved cards were sent as receipt tokens for books purchased in part or whole.[9] The aesthetics of attraction determined some of the most important modifications in design and content. To give just one example, Harrison's compact *Novelist's Magazine* was not only economic on paper and printing costs, but its double-column layout and small print enabled certain letters of the reprinted epistolary novels to be displayed for the first time complete on single pages. The magazine also offered fine copper-plate illustrations to favourite novels.

By this date, booksellers were also realizing the commercial potential in encouraging readers to participate in the industry. Advertisement for manuscripts and the lure of the vanity-press could bring quick profits, but the promotion of letter-pages in the magazines and the publication of amateur poetry was also good audience investment. Such inclusions reaffirmed that this was the public's own and controllable literature industry. As Robinson put it, addressing his female audience in an advertisement for the *Lady's Magazine*:

---

[7] Charles Knight, *The Old Printer and the Modern Press* (London, 1854), p. 216.

[8] Some suggestions are made in Nicholas Barker, 'Typography and the Meaning of Words: The Revolution in the Layout of Books in the Eighteenth Century', in Barber and Fabian, *Buch und Buchhandel*, pp. 127–65.

[9] One (early) collection is in the Tonson papers, BL Add. MSS, 28,275, fos. 200–17.

To the Sex this work is dedicated, from the Sex the Stores in our
Repositary are furnished; and when they are not only our Patronesses
but likewise our only Correspondents; we have nothing to fear, but
every Thing to hope.[10]

Bew and the Robinsons interleaved their magazines and miscellanies with homespun versions of lovesick Phoebes and unrespon-
sive swains. Kearsley's three-shilling *The Picture Gallery* contained
two hundred paintings by 'British Ladies'. The meagre remuneration for all but a handful of successful authors did not deter an
army of young contributors—or prevent the leading London and
Dublin booksellers from requesting still more manuscripts. Lane,
advertising for manuscripts, gave an assurance that 'Authors may
depend their literary Productions will appear with Corrections,
Beauty, Taste, and Style, at the Shrine of Public Approbation'.[11]

Such commercialization of literature, with new pressures of
production and selling, certainly affected the writers' art. Some
consequences are obvious. The part-number or magazine
serialization of new, and especially of commissioned, fiction
worked to heighten tension at the close of each episode—a technique to become infamous in the next two centuries. Similarly,
story-lines or the contents of guides or advice books had to be cut
or well padded to fit a prearranged format or number of volumes.
Market awareness and bookselling rivalry, however, encouraged
even more detailed consideration of design and content. Publishers vied to issue books that, as Dr Johnson put it, 'you may
carry to the fire, and hold reading in your hand'.[12] The public was
allured by the captivating appearance of works and the regular
features within. Booksellers frequently aimed to promote their
work with a distinctive message. As the historian of one later
American firm has commented, popular publishers 'were more
interested in causes than in stylistic elegance and preferred the
wholesome or homespun elements, even if it meant accepting
certain crudities in writing'.[13]

For the bookseller involved with fewer subscription schemes
and greater gambling on the market-place, the identification and
satisfaction of public tastes became increasingly critical. As the
periodical reviewers were quick to point out, this could easily lead

[10] *Public Advertiser*, 1 Feb. 1780.   [11] *Diary, or, Woodfall's Register*, 12 Oct. 1791.
[12] George Birkbeck Hill (ed.), *Johnsonian Miscellanies*, 2 vols. (Oxford, 1897), ii. 2.
[13] Raymond L. Kilgour, *Lee and Shepherd: Publishers for the People* (Boston, 1965), p. 279.

to a debasement of literary values. In 1761 Oliver Goldsmith created his satirical commercial bookseller, Mr Fudge, to consider the changes in the popular book trade. 'Others may pretend to direct the vulgar', said Mr Fudge, 'but that is not my way: I always let the vulgar direct me; wherever popular clamour arises, I always echo the million'.[14] The stereotyping of ideas and characters evident in so much popular fiction derived from the need to curry public favour by extending successful formulas. If publications proudly addressed up-to-the-minute issues in society, they also used familiar language and imagery to explain and evaluate social change.

Some of the most successful commercial booksellers headed retail and wholesale businesses built upon cheaply bought and amateurish contributions which were turned to financial profit. Clear, bold publishing themes were combined with typographical elegance and established design patterns to disguise the poverty of the author's style and the unoriginality of the writing or editor's compilation. Novice authors were able to draw upon a wide range of model works, readers' comments, and critical advice. Throughout this period, the *Critical Review* and *Monthly Review* pursued the policy of noticing all works. Even the most junior hacks might expect a pronouncement upon their work. Usually this was in terms of the counsel conveyed and the ideal purpose of fiction. As a result, all contributors to the book trade, authors and publishers, became both extremely conscious of the expectations of the readership and preoccupied by the discussion of forms and objectives. Novels, in particular, were said by their publishers to be useful conduct books. As such, they might defend the writers and sellers of fiction against charges of irresponsible and unhealthy social influence.

The testimony of dozens of autobiographies and private journals of these years suggests that the readers of both fiction and more serious literature were conscious that they should be reading for improvement.[15] The presses of London, Dublin, and

---

[14] *Citizen of the World*, letter li.

[15] Of many examples, the Revd William Temple, marooned in Cornwall, pursued rigorous improving reading which included much light, fashionable literature, Lewis Bettany (ed.), *Diaries of William Johnston Temple* 1780–1796 (Oxford, 1929), esp. 11–18, 52–3, 58. Similarly, O. F. Christie (ed.), *The Diary of the Revd. William Jones*, 1777–1821, Curate and Vicar of Broxbourne and the Hamlet of Hoddesdon 1781–1821 (London, 1929); Austin Dobson (ed.), *Diary and Letters of Madame D'Arblay* (1778–1840): *As edited by her niece*

Edinburgh responded eagerly, proclaiming the instructional value of their publications. This, it was argued, was all the more effective for being sweetened by the entertaining qualities of popular fiction. Critics were not slow to adjudicate. Readers and reviewers commented keenly upon the purpose of the novel, offering opinions on what was and was not acceptable within the expanding fiction industry. In turn, publishers and writers of popular literature answered criticisms. Stereotyped characterization in their fiction purported to be realistic and probable, born of the need for the novel to defy its critics, to be more than simple entertainment, and to act as an instructor in morality.

The periodical reviewer—a new and distinctive force in the book business—was an eager recruit to the swelling army of opponents to the commercial novel. Adopting the guise of spokesman for the public, he exerted increasing pressure upon writers to conform to critical ideas of content and presentation. The reviewer became the leading arbiter in colourful disputes over the worth of Grub Street fiction and its influence upon young, impressionable minds. Novel and miscellany prefaces clearly reveal the growing influence of the notices in periodical magazines and reviews. As a precaution against the savagery of reviewers, many pot-boilers were styled 'the first literary attempt of a young lady', even though many were actually none of these things.[16] Especially notable by the 1780s were the long deferential novel prefaces, pleading for leniency from the critics and often providing a catalogue of extenuating circumstances for the unworthy effort which followed. Even the assured Mrs Parsons declared that

the Author of the following Memoirs submits them to the public eye with trembling anxiety. A first effort might, perhaps, be entitled to some indulgence, did not the presumption of writing after a BURNEY, a SMITH, a REEVE, a BENNETT, and many other excellent female novelists, subject the Author of MISS MEREDITH to the imputation of Vanity.[17]

'As the first literary productions are by some treated with irony', pleaded Miss Ballin's preface to *The Statue Room*, 'how can I

Charlotte Barrett, 6 vols. (London, 1904–5), iii. 53, 70–1, 110, 205, 238, 460, iv. 24, 234, 359, 407–8; Katherine C. Balderston (ed.), *Thraliana: The Diary of Mrs Hester Lynch Thrale (Later Mrs Piozzi)*, 1776–1809, 2 vols. (Oxford, 1942), i. 328–9, 446–8.

[16] James Raven, 'A Sociology of Writing in Britain, 1750–69' *Eighteenth-Century Life* (forthcoming); Blakey, *Minerva Press*, pp. 50–2.

[17] Mrs [Eliza] Parsons, *The History of Miss Meredith*, 2 vols. (London, 1790), vol. i, p. v.

expect, for such an attempt as mine, to escape the lash—
Impossible!'[18] Unfortunately, the critics agreed with her.[19] In
the same 1790 season another novel, *Gabrielle de Vergy*, armed
itself with modesty:

> The author embraces this opportunity of expressing his reverence for
> that respectable tribunal of criticism, the Critical Review, and hopes
> he was profited by the gentle correction he received from that Review
> ... while he kisses the rod, he at the same time exults in the praise
> administered with it, and cannot forbear transcribing that praise.[20]

By 1790 most reviewers insisted that the age was one of unprecedented corruption and that a contributory evil was the mush-
rooming of illicit literature and circulating libraries. 'Every con-
siderate reader, must surely pity the lot of the monthly
journalist, who has to wade through the heap of trash voided by
circulating libraries', urged a reviewer of *Laura; or, Original Letters*:
'we are weary of bestowing critical baptism on these dead-born
monsters of the teeming brain'.[21] The verdict upon the 1782
Ways and Means—'one of those literary *bugs*, or insects, naturally
springing from the rottenness of a corrupt age'[22]—stands as
representative of hundreds of periodical notices. By the end of
this period the attack was well established:

> Novels spring into existence like insects on the banks of the Nile; and, if
> we may be indulged in another comparison, cover the shelves of our
> circulating libraries, as locusts crowd the fields of Asia. Their great and
> growing number is a serious evil: for, in general, they exhibit delusive
> views of human life; and while they amuse, frequently poison the
> mind.[23]

Censure of fiction was frequently transferred to its sellers and
producers. Cooke and his son Charles, like Lane and Dodsley
and the rest, were denounced as *nouveaux riches* profiteers and
charged with perverting good taste and social order by their
production of cheap volumes for the fashionable and the lower
orders. Lane, the 'chicken-butcher' or 'scribbling poulterer', was
lampooned as parading in splendid carriages with footmen

---

[18] Rosetta Ballin, *The Statue Room: An Historical Tale*, 2 vols. (London, 1790), vol. i, p. xi.

[19] *CR* 69: 477 (Apr. 1790); *T&C* 22: 221 (May 1790); *GM* 4: 114 (Mar. 1790).

[20] *Gabrielle de Vergy; An Historic Tale* (London, 1790), pp. iv–v.

[21] *B&I* 4: 192–3 (Sept. 1790).   [22] *CR* 54: 77 (July 1782).

[23] *MR*, NS, 2: 334 (July 1790).

brandishing gold-headed canes.[24] Lackington, with typical assurance, hurled mock-Shakespeare at those who accused him of
dunghill origins.[25] His carriage was emblazoned with his motto
'Small Gains Do Great Things'.[26]

In the face of such attacks, both writers and booksellers sought
more explicit justification for the content of their publications.
The result was to introduce greater melodrama and stereotyping
in fiction in the cause of public usefulness. Identifiable social
nuisances were to be set up and exposed. Direct and stern prefaces or addresses were to be included where necessary. Moral
responsibility and general utility were made the selling points.
One particular target of criticism could also be turned to advantage. In the fashionable literature business, taste was closely
associated with innovation. 'Change' was a powerful tool for the
late eighteenth-century literary entrepreneur. The very fear of
the influence of mass literature was used by the skilled bookman.
Popular works, it was argued, could set standards of the good and
the polite and the bookseller could teach discrimination as well as
enlightenment. Literature was marketed as an antidote to prevailing irresponsible fashions, while fashion itself remained the
leading commercial ploy of the controlling booksellers. As
Schücking was to point out, literary taste can derive from more
than an appreciation of language and ideas—it can be generated
by crude but insistent trumpeting, by a variety of manipulative
commercial actions which have nothing to do with the intellectual quality of the product.[27]

All this produced powerful and energetic booksellers, re-
sponding to and also creating the wants of a leisured reading class.
Where most authors and contributors to best-selling literature
remained poor, powerless, and prolific, the successful London
bookseller selected, promoted, and suppressed. The public may
not always have been given what it wanted: it was given what it
was said to want. Nor did the bookseller follow taste as much as he

---

[24] Blakey, *Minerva Press*, p. 6. Lane's father was a poultryman. G. H. Powell (ed.),
Reminiscences and Table-Talk of Samuel Rogers (London, 1903), p. 108.

[25] e.g. his quotation from 'Shakespeare's "Cromwell"', *Memoirs*, 1791 edn., p. 6. His
source appears to be *The Life and Death of Thomas, Lord Cromwell: By Mr. Shakespear* (London,
Tonson, 1734), pp. 3–4.

[26] Nichols, *Literary Anecdotes*, iii. 646.

[27] Levin L. Schücking, *The Sociology of Literary Taste*, 2nd edn., trans. by Brian
Battershaw (London, 1966).

professed: the most successful businessmen in the book trade kept a discreet pace ahead of the fashionable. In the words of one reviewer, most booksellers' wares were no more than 'an insidious attempt at the purses of the public'.[28] Or as another contemporary commentator put it, 'a fashionable writer makes a fashionable book, and creates a number of fashionable readers—readers, who pay more attention to the fashion of the writer, than to the fashion of the book'.[29]

In surveying the place of the reviewer in this commercial world of the novel, it would be wrong to suggest that booksellers and authors responded only to an entirely negative critical reaction. Stark and repeated contrasts between the dismissive and the occasional encouraging critical notices brought a conspicuous reaction from writers. In later studies of the reviews the smoke-screen of denunciations has obscured both the actual critical response to fiction and its effect upon writers.[30] Many critical evaluations also considered the exemplary means of presenting heroes and villains and the validity of particular plots or narrative styles. In practice, realism, probability, and the moral utility of a work were regarded by reviewers as paramount. In the final third of the century, emphasis upon the need for imaginative literature to be instructional increased dramatically in both favourable and unfavourable reviews.

The didactic merits of a work were declared by critics to be greatest where narratives conformed to reality. The critical ideals of realism, however, envisaged very particular representations of individual action, economic activity, and professional and social status. With accuracy upheld as an indication of excellence, reviewers' standards of improbability and realism assumed a crucial mediating role between readership and literature. Mounting critical concern with authenticity is obvious through the notices of the 1770s and 1780s until by 1790 very few reviews of fiction fail to comment upon the degree of realism achieved. In the 1790 reviews, the improbability of a plot or characterization was frequently derided. Typically, of *Edmund; or, the Child of the Castle,* the

---

[28] *B&I* 3: 113 (Feb. 1790), reviewing *Confidential Letters of Albert.*

[29] Paterson, *Joineriana,* i. 41. The development of publishing methods, Schücking wrote, 'could be one of the most interesting, though not the most edifying, chapters in a history of literary taste', *Literary Taste,* p. 54. His unhappiness about this is shared by almost every early commentator on the 18th-cent. book trade.

[30] Mayo was critical of this failing, *Novel in the Magazines,* p. 198.

Critical Review acknowledged that rarity was pleasing, but 'when
what is uncommon is absurd, and when what is unsuspected is
highly improbable, disgust takes the place of pleasure; and it is a
Reviewer only, steeled by frequent practice to inflexible perseverance, who does not throw aside the work with contempt'.[31]
This concern was certainly foremost in the one surviving and
detailed record of an author's anticipation of and then reflection
upon the reaction to her work. After the publication of *Evelina* in
1778, and of *Cecilia* in 1782, Fanny Burney was extremely anxious
as to whether her characters would entertain and instruct by
being accepted as both realistic and common types of contemporary society.[32] Mrs Thrale praised *Evelina*, believing that 'the
great beauty of it is that it reflects back all our own ideas and
observations; for everybody must have met with some thing similar to almost all the incidents'.[33] Burney recorded that her
mentor, 'Daddy' Crisp, held *Cecilia* to be 'a noble piece of
morality! the variety—the contrast of the different characters
quite new and unhackneyed, and yet perfectly in nature'.[34] Edmund Burke wrote to Burney of the same work: 'there are none at
all—that will not find themselves better informed concerning
human nature, and their stock of observation enriched, by
reading your *Cecilia*'.[35] Similar verdicts attested to the authenticity and moral purpose of works, which, as will be detailed
below, contained gross libels against tradesmen, caricaturing vulgarity and the parvenu.

Readers expressed great faith in the verdicts and portrayals
within fiction.[36] Such trust in realism within the literature was
built up over the last three decades of the century; prefaces
pledged allegiance to it, and reviewers continued to define it. A
long *Monthly Review* notice of 1790 stands as a typical outline for an
ideal composition:

The story of a novel should be formed of a variety of interesting incidents; a knowledge of the world, and of mankind, are essential requisites
in the writer; the characters should be always natural; the personages
should talk, think, and act, as becomes their respective ages, situations,
and characters; the sentiments should be moral, chaste, and delicate; the

---

[31] *CR* 70: 454 (Oct. 1790).
[32] Dobson, *Diary of Madame D'Arblay*, i. 37, 41–3, 72, ii. 68–75, 80–1, 199–201.
[33] Ibid. i. 98.   [34] Ibid. ii. 70 (25 Feb. 1782).   [35] Ibid. ii. 93 (29 July 1782).
[36] Note the verdict of Mrs Thrale, above, p. 19.

language should be easy, correct, and elegant, free from affectation, and unobscured by pedantry; and the narrative should be as little interrupted as possible by digressions and episodes of every kind: yet if an author chuses to indulge, occasionally, in moral reflections, in the view of blending instruction with amusement, we would not wish, altogether, to frustrate so good a design.[37]

Use of allegedly ancient manuscripts, haphazard insertion of histories, travels, and memoirs, and the abuse of the epistolary form, were all denounced where these were adjudged to transgress naturalism and probability.[38] The critics' definition of realism, however, could appear incongruous. The model conduct expected was often tortuously defined. Plots which appeared comparably absurd were given very different critical verdicts. Bicknell's *Doncaster Races* appalled the critics, yet a work by Thomson of the same year with an equally contrived and incredible plot, received praise for its design.[39] Mrs Radcliffe's spectacularly implausible *Sicilian Romance* was favourably received by both the *Monthly Review* and the *Critical Review*.[40] Somewhat unexpectedly, the *Critical Review* of March 1791, assessing the past season's offering of *Memoirs of Maria, a Persian Slave*, accepted the extraordinary story-line, commenting that 'there are many circumstances which lead us to think that these Memoirs are genuine ... The little improbabilities which appear may arise from our ignorance of eastern customs'.[41] The *Critical Review* suggested that the translated *Gabrielle de Vergy* should have retained the original episode in which the hero innocently consumed the heart of his lover.

Most notices, however, offered explanations for their apparently fluctuating concepts of the realistic. A strict moral purpose and the effectiveness of the message remained the overriding consideration for the critics. The whole attention of the notices was directed towards the effect of a work upon readers and especially upon the young. The *English Review* could excuse Thomson's

---

[37] *MR*, NS, 3: 400 (Dec. 1790).

[38] Of many examples, the contemptuous reviews of *de Montmorency*, one of many novels of 1790 purporting to be based upon a rediscovered ancient document, *CR* 69: 356–7 (Mar. 1790), and *MR*, NS, 3: 402 (Dec. 1790).

[39] *ER* 15: 465 (June 1790); *CR* 68: 75 (July 1789); and on Revd James Thomson's *Denial; or, The Happy Retreat*, 3 vols. (London, 1790), *ER* 16: 387 (Nov. 1790); and approval of the extraordinary *Louisa* in *CR* 70: 96 (July 1790).

[40] *MR*, NS, 3: 91 (Sept. 1790); and *CR*, NS, 1: 350 (Mar. 1791).

[41] *CR*, NS, 1: 349 (Mar. 1791).

extraordinary plot in *The Denial* because the author 'appears every where anxiously concerned for the proper direction of youth'.[42] Improbabilities might be accepted if the parable was sufficiently luminous, the characters exemplary (either as models or warnings), and the moral judged to be beneficial to society.

Good moral intention was not all: the parable had also to be effectively communicated. Exemplary writing must not be overlooked by those readers who most required the advice. Narrative therefore had to be direct and lively, incorporating where appropriate pathos, humour, and the cautionary episode. Jane Timbury's attempt was written off by the *Monthly Review*:

In the Philanthropic Rambler, a dead gravity is preserved throughout; which, instead of enticing the novel reader into an approbation of moral conduct, may make even a moral reader yawn.[43]

The inculcation of moral truth became the set goal, and, in commentaries such as that by the *Monthly Review*, there was implicit belief in both the existence and the creation of a 'moral reader'. As Cumberland asserted in the mid-1780s: 'to administer moral precepts through a pleasing vehicle seems now the general study of our Essayists, Dramatists and Novelists',[44] and as Clara Reeve argued in her dissertation of 1785:

If you wish in a Novel to inculcate some moral truth, to hide a jewel under so thin a veil that its brilliancy may be easily discerned, there should always be a reference to the manners and the time in which it is written; there should be the greatest probability, carried thro' the whole allegory, that your reason may not be shocked, while your imagination is pleased. If Novels were properly regulated with this design always in view, they might become really useful to society. A moral lesson otherwise dry and tedious in itself, might be communicated in a pleasing dress: as a pill has its desired effect, tho' wrapped in a gold or silver leaf.[45]

---

[42] *ER* 16: 387 (Nov. 1790).   [43] *MR*, NS, 5: 225 (June 1791).

[44] *Observer* (no. 1), i. 5.

[45] Clara Reeve, *The Progress of Romance, Through Times, Countries, and Manners, with Remarks on the Good and Bad Effects of it . . . in a Course of Evening Conversations*, 2 vols. (Colchester, 1785), ii. 92, quoting *The Trial; or, The History of Charles Horton, Esq.* Marilyn Butler concludes that 'there was too much moral-essay writing, and too much portentous criticism, for them [the popular novelists] to hide their heads successfully in the sand. They knew that their heroes and heroines were supposed to offer a moral pattern. The outcome of the action, since it would be just, would betray a sense of values. No bid for irresponsibility, no plea that their stories merely set out to entertain, could absolve them from the burden of their implicit meaning', *Jane Austen and the War of Ideas* (Oxford, 1975), pp. 29–30.

No preface from the 1790 works admitted to entertainment as the single motive for publication. Dedications linked books 'intended to expose vice and inculcate virtue' with the excellence of the patronage.[46] Tales for children, notably *Sandford and Merton*, boasted long explanatory introductions,[47] and authors included passages illustrating the reprehensible activity of reading novels. Most famously, the downfall of the 'Young Lady of Bristol' was caused by perusing books of a ruinous tendency, the author adding, 'I doubt not that almost so many girls have been seduced by books as by men ... our sense of virtue and honor were read away'.[48]

Given the continuing influence of the *Spectator*, *Tatler*, and *Guardian*, the continuing emphasis upon didacticism within the novel and associated literature is not surprising.[49] The magazine short story, and then also the essay serial perpetuated Steele and Addison's drive for reform and their satiric assaults upon the immoral self-interested man. The *Town and Country Magazine*, founded in 1769, and the *Lady's Magazine*, founded in 1770, were committed to supplying their readers with morally instructive entertainment, while the *Universal Museum* had declared in its own defence that

They [the editors] have always endeavoured to paint vice in the most frightful, and virtue in the most amiable colours; to represent the former in the cavern of despair groaning under the enormous load of accumulated crimes; and the latter, to use the expression of Seneca, as reposing on beds of Roses.[50]

While echoing the moralistic language and intentions of the early eighteenth century, popular fiction writers of this period adopted a didactic technique conditioned by competition, defensiveness, and the active interference of critics and editors. Together, they contributed to the evolution of exaggerated set-piece caricatures in popular novels. Such episodes escaped criticism as socially

---

[46] Dedication of *Letters Between Clara and Antonia*, 2 vols. (London, 1780), p. vii.

[47] Thomas Day, *The History of Sandford and Merton*, 3 vols. (London, 1783–9). Another example is William Beloe's *Incidents of a Youthful Life; or, The True History of William Langley* (London, 1790).

[48] *Memoirs of an Unfortunate Young Lady, which appeared in No's IV, V, and VI of the 'Citizen' just published in 'The Bristol Mercury'* (Bristol, 1790), pp. 9–10.

[49] Watson, *Magazine Serials*, pp. 15–16, for reprintings of Addison and Steele during the century; and MacCarthy, *Later Women Novelists*, ch. 5, 'The Didactic Novel'.

[50] *Universal Museum and Complete Magazine of Knowledge and Pleasure*, 2 (1766), preface.

harmful when they were sufficiently black and white to be deemed effective cautionary satire. Stereotyping, when 'realistic', was condoned as central to the instructional purpose of the novel or short story. By 1789 one widely acclaimed writer prefaced her work with the complaint that 'the perpetual sameness of character and event which pervades the generality of novels, has in some measure, rendered them a drug in the market of literature'.[51]

Authors responded eagerly to the cause of 'earnest morality', particularly when this appeared a fail-safe escape from critical censure.[52] Obsequious prefaces reassured reviewers of the extent of their power, and within the novels and tales, recognizable stock characters and situations gained both credibility and popularity. Critical notices reinforced the acceptability of particular characterizations or arguments. Many were cross-referenced with past and present fictional equivalents. Such encouragement cut through contradictory fulminations against improbability and unrealism, emphasizing further those caricatures deemed legitimate and laudable. Opposing values were boldly contrasted. The triumph of approved virtues embodied in hero or heroine was usually achieved only after prolonged trials against one or more adversaries. These came in various combinations of temptors and undesirables. The common technique was to register approval of a particular moral value by highlighting the folly of contrary action. The form and consequences of particular vices could be illustrated by a stock satiric character. It was here, therefore, that distinctive stereotypes, condoned as realistic and authentic, were given full rein. Stock characters were predominantly temptors or wrongdoers of varying degrees of malignity. Danger to young virtue abounded in society, it was argued, and the fictional gallery of rogues had to be much larger and less impressionistically drawn than the portraiture of moral excellence. The key point here, however, is that in illustration of specific social concerns, portrayal of the social status or profession of the villains was not indiscriminate.

Critical encouragement was given to the merciless depiction of the upstart, the underbred, and the man of commerce, extravagance, and the ton. The myth of the outcast group reinforced the approved and allegedly traditional images and codes of morality

[51] Mrs Rudd, *Belle Widows* [*sic*], 2 vols. (London, 1789), preface, vol. i, p. vii.
[52] MacCarthy, *Later Women Novelists*, p. 40.

which legitimized social position and material fortune. Writing sustained a conservative morality which was not based on absolutes or philosophical principles, but was gauged according to the minutiae of accepted—and changing—social decorum.[53] Similarly, the development of fictional characters presumed an appreciation of pre-existing values in order to elicit the required reader-response. This was particularly true where plot or characters commented upon social status, occupation, and the holding and deployment of wealth. Satire upon the transgressors of *politesse* was fêted by the reviewers. By the 1780s authors and critics had clearly tired of the narrow range of situations within which to illustrate the overall moral by the merits of the virtuous. This, coupled with the small opportunity that they presented for humour, made many critics pall at the excellence of popular heroines, and applaud new satires in which social propriety could be characterized by representations of the evil and comic vulgar. In Gorgy's *Victorina*, the *Critical Review* found 'a total want of probability, a hasty denouement, and characters, if we except the lively Marotte, so good and so insipid, for unmixed, unallayed goodness is generally uninteresting'.[54] Mrs Smith's 1790 heroine was credited with weakening *Ethelinde* : 'like Richardson's Grandison, she is far too excellent: far above the standard of nature'.[55] The result of this was that, as another reviewer put it, 'Of the characters, Ethelinde herself, though amiable and interesting, is of less importance than some others'.[56]

New imaginative literature was claiming to present an instructional, useful, and realistic portrayal of society. The 1780s had ushered in new confidence in the novel, despite the death-knell sounded by critics and commentators and the near halving of new titles between 1770 and 1780. Much of the new confidence was grounded in the very conviction of the instructive or even propagandist worth of fiction. The preface to Holcroft's *Alwyn*, published in 1780, championed the cause, distinguishing the novel from the romance:

---

[53] The goal continued to be practical virtue, not metaphorical truth: Tompkins, *Popular Novel*, p. 73; Watson, *Magazine Serials*, pp. 2–5; and Joanna Clare Dales, 'The Novel as Domestic Conduct-Book—Richardson to Jane Austen', Ph.D. thesis (Cambridge, 1970).

[54] *CR* 69: 713 (June 1790).   [55] *MR*, NS, 2: 162 (June 1790).

[56] *CR*, NS, 3: 57 (Sept. 1791).

Modern writers use the word Romance, to signify a fictitious history of detached and independent adventures ... A Novel is another kind of work. Unity of design is its character. In a Romance, if the incidents be well marked and related with spirit, the intention is answered; and adventures pass before the view for no other purpose than to amuse by their peculiarity, without, perhaps, affecting the main story, if there should be one. But in a Novel, a combination of incidents, entertaining in themselves, are made to form a whole; and an unnecessary circumstance becomes a blemish, by detaching from the simplicity which is requisite to exhibit that whole to advantage.[57]

Other authors argued that it was too late to curb the growing novel readership and that therefore the only moral corrective was a properly educative form of the novel.[58] The result was a series of direct and socially specific moral melodramas.

In the popular fiction and moral primers of the period lessons were usually illustrated first by the fictional portraits themselves, and then by the fates allotted to the malefactors. Although the plot of the great majority of the novels and serializations was resolved (after a long series of trials) by the nuptials of the virtuous, writers rarely neglected the fate of villains. The well-deserved death with its sliding scale of horrific accidents and diseases was a staple of popular literature.

The explicitness of the fate consigned to fictional wrongdoers reached new extremes of theatricality in works at the end of the period. Some flavour of this should be given before considering the underlying purpose of the portrayals. In the sample years of this study, the fiction of 1785 and 1790 produced far more dramatic fates than in 1775 or 1780, also furnishing a greater range of evil characters to receive their just rewards. Lord des Lunettes, the only well-developed 1780 precursor of the fashionable aristocratic fiends of later in the decade, escapes merely with ridicule and a

---

[57] Thomas Holcroft, *Alwyn: or The Gentleman Comedian*, 2 vols. (London, 1780), vol. i, pp. vi–vii.

[58] Prefaces urging this include, in 1780, 'An Introductory Letter, from a Father to his Chidren' in *Fatal Obedience; or, The History of Mr. Freeland*, 2 vols. (London, 1780), the 'Advertisement' by the author of *How She Lost Him; or, The History of Miss Wyndham*, 2 vols. (Dublin, 1780), and 'An Address to the Reader' by John Seally in *Moral Tales, After the Eastern Manner* (London, 1780), which declares that the tales were 'an antidote against the poison of immorality, too much prevailing in these days of dissipation and folly' (p. ii). In 1790, such prefaces included those of *Gabrielle de Vergy* (London, 1790), and of Thomson's *Denial*.

restless conscience.[59] Only the most wicked of the 1780 women, those who might lead others to capital crimes, suffer the more exquisite torments.[60] Compared to earlier years, the nasty ends within the 1790 novels were related more distinctly to the moral worth of the recipient. Sir William Turner, who has followed the heroine of *Louisa; or, The Reward of an Affectionate Daughter* across half of Europe in order to seduce her, at least becomes 'sensible of his past errors' before his leg is amputated and he dies 'in dreadful agonies'.[61] Mr Evelyn, adulterer and misogynist of *Raynsford Park*, is extinguished, 'emaciated and dispirited'.[62] Mrs Smith's Davenant is finally glimpsed in the extremis of dissipation with a 'bloated figure and inflamed countenance'. His partner in debauchery, Lord Danesforte, is reduced to 'a walking skeleton' until he 'unrepentingly was gone where all his crimes were registered'.[63] Having ruined Emma Montague in *The History of Miss Meredith* and leaving her to die of remorse in a European convent, Sir George Oldham's required death, as a fall from a horse, is at least unusually swift.

Few fallen or vulgar women were allowed to expire so easily. Arabella Burrell, flirt, gambler, and adulteress, dies from a slow and painful consumption.[64] The upstart Lady Roseville, one of the more sustained and sinister creations of the 1790 season, loses both fortune and reputation by the time of her arrival at a London sponging-house, with 'her complexion of dead white, sprinkled with a sort of dew, and tinged with purple spots; her face swelled, and all her features distended; a white froth bubbling out of her parched and livid mouth; and her large eyes, red and glassy, were rolling from side to side'.[65] Fanny Elwood, the manufacturer's daughter who had set her cap at Mrs Gomersall's hero, Charles Montgomery, is revealed as mistress and child-bearer to virtually every male character of *The Citizen*, and receives an amalgam of the year's fictional penalties. She finally dies 'in a

[59] *Letters Between Clara and Antonia*, ii. 259.

[60] Notably, Lady Ann Fostess, the malevolent force of Margaret Minifie's *The Count de Poland*, 4 vols. (London, 1780).

[61] *Louisa; or, The Reward of an Affectionate Daughter*, 2 vols. (London, 1790), ii. 174.

[62] Jane and Elizabeth Purbeck, *Raynsford Park: A Novel*, 4 vols. (London, 1790), iv. 144.

[63] Charlotte Smith, *Ethelinde; or, The Recluse of the Lake*, 2nd edn., 5 vols. (London, 1790), v. 322, 335.

[64] Alexander Bicknell, *Doncaster Races; or, The History of Miss Maitland*, 2 vols. (London, 1790), ii. 249–54, 259 (Burrell is styled Mrs Clayton at the time of her death).

[65] Elizabeth Hervey, *Louisa: A Novel*, 3 vols. (London, 1790), ii. 146.

state of insensibility and intoxication too horrid to be described'.[66] One hundred years later, from the same town in which the Elwood fable was written and which it featured, various of the lives of manufacturing daughters were recalled with the same sense of divine justice.[67]

Plainly, transgressors of correct behaviour were allotted ghoulish ends to enhance the instructional utility of the novel. In characterization and plot design, existing assumptions and new developments were reciprocal forces. A foolish or vicious type could be shown merely by his or her attitude to a particular issue—that issue could be further illustrated (often for future reference) by the performance of the evil and the virtuous. In part, this was assured by the popularity of the letter form in novels. Epistolary works did not allow direct authorial comment except through obviously approved heroines or heroes, while the demands of the elegant style expected from genteel narrators precluded sarcastic or unduly slanderous descriptions of villains. Thus knavery had to appear all the more black, while the few lively, even playful heroines of the narrative novels (such as Mrs Parsons's Miss Meredith) provided the most satirical and chastening accounts of the evil and the vulgar. Nevertheless, this does not explain why so many of the unstable and vulgar coquettes of these novels were deliberately depicted as the daughters and sisters of trade.

It is clear from the full range of imaginative literature that from the mid-1780s attacks on the vulgarity of traders greatly intensified. The comparison between the 1780 sample year and that of 1790 is suggestive. By 1780 there had developed hints of satire *against* the anti-trade prejudice. In the much reprinted *Count de Poland*, the vulgar Lady Ann Fostess, has to attend to 'those dirty trades-people from morning to night',[68] yet she is shown to derive from the social order which she denounces. This and similar ironic asides in works of these years are not presented as a fully unwarranted Margaret Hale-style condemnation of 'shoppy people',[69] but they do prefigure the early nineteenth-century

---

[66] Mrs A. Gomersall, *The Citizen*, 2 vols. (London, 1790), ii. 209–10.

[67] Leeds City Archives, Oates MSS, Mrs Buckle's Memoir: 'some of the daughters were pleasant women; others were much stuck up, especially the second daughter who died early'.

[68] Minifie, *Count de Poland*, ii. 185.

[69] Elizabeth Gaskell, *North and South*, 1855, *PEL* edn. (London, 1970), p. 50.

literary attacks upon an unthinking criticism of the *nouveaux riches*.[70] What is even more striking, however, is the temporary eclipse of this trend during the late 1780s.[71] The works of 1790 with their full array of characterizations of petty traders, businessmen, and grand merchants and nabobs, relaunched a bitter attack upon 'these sons and daughters of sudden opulence'.[72] The light humour once reserved for the burlesque upon the squire and continuing in the satires and stereotyping of the vulgarity of the families of trade, now hardened into a castigation of the pretensions of successful businessmen.[73] Mrs Charlotte Lennox's *Euphemia* relates in a series of flashbacks the distressing scenes of the heroine's late impoverishment (which has forced her to emigrate to America) and the final illness of her mother:

The privacy my mother so earnestly desired was not like to be interrupted in a neighbourhood chiefly composed of families grown wealthy by the successful arts of trade, and had chosen this retreat for their summer residence, who had no idea of any merit but riches, and allowed no claims to respect, but what were derived from the ostentatious display of them ... Our situation afforded us many opportunities of observing how fortune and nature were at strife, when the lavish gifts bestowed by the one, could not efface the despicable stamp impressed by the other. The Indian plunderer, raised from the condition of a link-boy to princely affluence, in the midst of his blaze of grandeur, looked like a robber going in mock state to execution; and the forestalling trader enjoyed his clumsy magnificence with the same aspect as when he had over-reached a less cunning dealer in a bargain ... money, which, as she said, cost them nothing to acquire, but what they valued as nothing, consequently, was expended so lavishly, as raised the prices of necessaries; and this grievance was severely felt by their less opulent neighbours'.[74]

Mrs Lennox sought to impress readers by detailing even more painful consequences of such monsters settling in a local neighbourhood. Here were the same 'summer residences' of comic

---

[70] As epitomized by Jane Austen's creation of Mrs Elton, *Emma*, 1816, *PEL* edn. (London, 1966), esp. ch. 36, pp. 309–10.

[71] There are survivals of ironic reversals in 1790 but they are isolated and minor intrusions into the plots—the most extended being the characterization of Mr Ware, businessman and benevolent MP, who apologises to guests for his inferiority, in Frances Brooke, *The History of Charles Mandeville*, 2 vols. (London, 1790), esp. i. 63.

[72] Charlotte Lennox, *Euphemia*, 4 vols. (London, 1790), i. 124.

[73] With the notable exception of the merchant proper, although even his exemption was not universally sustained.

[74] Lennox, *Euphemia*, i. 122–4.

scenes mocking parvenu bad taste,[75] but now stripped of amusing allusion. As the illness of Euphemia's mother worsens, her desire for milk and church services increases. Once in church, the invalid cannot obtain a pew. As her friend Mrs Benson laments, the pews 'are almost all taken up with the worshippers of Mammon, to whom, as they have erected an altar in their own houses, they might as well perform their devotions at home, and let Christians have access to the house of God'. As for milk, none could be procured for the dying woman 'although the cows were milked under her window'. This was because 'the brokers, the soap-boilers, and the rope-makers ladies numerous servants could not drink their tea without cream'.[76]

Other works of this year paralleled such animosity towards the successful trader or servant of a trading company.[77] The disruption commercial grandees brought to a local community was stressed throughout, their selfish and vindictive irresponsibility confirming the iniquity of their personal wealth. The offspring and dependants of businessmen were also pilloried with new severity. The literary offensive was directed against business family life, depicting spendthrift wives, an absence of patriarchal control, and the reckless follies of the young.

In reviewing these novels, the first part of this book has tried to amplify certain consequences of the replacement of private patrons by booksellers and a wider public as leading promoters of new literature. The publishing industry brought out unprecedentedly popular publications, and with them, innovative trading methods. Formula-writing was nurtured in a commercial environment from which the booksellers—'the common pests of useful letters'[78]—emerged more powerful than ever despite greater burdens and risks. The market-place certainly increased in volatility. The public was made increasingly aware of its power. In the bookselling business there developed clearer distinctions as well as rivalries between different wholesalers, independent publishers, and retailers. The commercial advantage of combination was largely lost. The trade was no longer the closed company of established families but was invigorated, as in so many other

---

[75] Below, Ch. 10.   [76] Lennox, *Euphemia*, i. 125, 124.

[77] Notably, *Arley; or, The Faithless Wife*, 2 vols. (London, 1790); *The Fair Cambrians*, 3 vols. (London, 1790); William Combe, *The Devil Upon Two Sticks in England*, 4 vols. (London, 1790).

[78] Paterson, *Joineriana*, i. 38.

expanding industries of the period, by enterprising 'mushroom' men made outrageous by their new commercial techniques.

What needs to be determined are the external causes of the targeting of the newly wealthy as subjects for stereotyping and moral instruction. It must be asked why the scapegoats of these works became predominantly *nouveaux riches* and businessmen, and also what caused the heightened concern over conspicuous consumption, manners, and social propriety. What was the threat perceived and how exactly was it stimulated? Three interlocking and negative reactions—against luxury and fashion, against vulgarity, and against sudden elevation in social station—combined to condemn the newly-moneyed and the successful businessman and his family. The specific means by which wealth was gained was hardly discussed, but the mis-use or non-use of a fortune became as much the target of popular attack as the rate of its accumulation. Familiar language and imagery boasted of the continuity of tradition, but the application of such notions as 'luxury' and 'vulgarity' was radically changed. Fashion and free-spending were vigorously attacked and the family of the suddenly opulent was obvious quarry as the carrier of the disease of extravagance and the 'rage of fashion'. The businessman was isolated as guilty of superfluous luxury and fashionable consumption, as the exemplar of a new vulgarity, and as the upstart threatening social and economic stability. His activities were used to illustrate the unacceptable aspects of luxury, to enhance a plea for greater virtue in commercial dealings, and to indicate standards of the polite and the limits beyond which social elevation and personal expenditure threatened the community. Each of these motives will be considered in relation to the reaction against men of trade and business. Popular literature was acting both as a directory of model conduct and as a purveyor of modish opinion. The tension arising between these two roles and its influence in the development of concepts of the gentleman, of vulgarity, and of the dangers of commerce and the commercial upstart clearly demands further exploration.

5

MERCHANTS, GENTILITY AND CHRISTIAN CONDUCT

> For Modes of Faith, let graceless zealots fight;
> His can't be wrong whose life is in the right:
> In Faith and Hope the world will disagree,
> But all Mankind's concern is Charity.
>
> Alexander Pope, *Essay on Man* (1733–4).

During the second half of the eighteenth century a very particular reinterpretation of 'taste' and 'vulgarity' supported literary attacks on men of trade. At the same time, many writers sought to protect the long-standing civic reputation of the merchant. The resulting contrast between the images of merchant citizen and of vulgar *nouveau riche* is important. Distinctions made between the two types throw into relief the ethical values by which businessmen were judged. In each case, the terms of judgement subtly moved from those of the early decades of the century when fervent advocates catalogued the economic, maritime, and political benefits of trade, and men of equal passion fulminated against new-fangled forms of engrossing and usury.

Superficially, the lauding of the merchant was a rehearsal of earlier heroic portrayals, just as the attack on the newly-rich manufacturer had echoes of the assaults upon the financier or projector of a hundred years earlier. The merchant, grand and good, continued to be featured off-stage as the father or uncle or guardian of countless fictional heroines and heroes. The merchant was still most commonly depicted as he who 'by his trading claspeth the island to the continent, and one country to another'.[1]

---

[1] Thomas Fuller, *The Holy State* (Cambridge, 1642), p. 113, a description enthusiastically repeated thereafter (cf. Brooke's inclusion, below, p. 87–8).

What is obvious, however, is a broader moral intention to much of the writing and characterization. In many didactic works of popular fiction and drama the merchant was advanced from incidental player to central character. In turn, imaginative portrayals of tradesmen called upon a whole repertoire of encoded statements about social ethics and custom derived from two centuries or more of morality literature. This heritage must be examined in order to understand both local perceptions of the merchant and the contrasting vulgarity charges levelled against the entrepreneur. The following reviews works informing the wider moral critique of the businessman and underpinning the analyses offered by the literature of the sampled years and discussed in subsequent chapters.

In contradiction to recent accounts of eighteenth-century business portrayal,[2] it is not difficult to show how an enthusiastic image of trade was sustained after mid-century. In the wake of Steele and Defoe, a distinguished lobby of poets, novelists, playwrights and essayists lauded the achievements of commerce and contributed to a grandiose apology for the achievements of the merchant. Edward Young's merchants who vied 'with purple monarchs'[3] were replenished in imaginative literature by the creations of Thomson, Lillo, Brooke, and many other writers. Authoritative and sophisticated support was provided by popular historians such as Thomas Mortimer, and students of early economic theory from Josiah Tucker to Malachy Postlethwayt. Gibbon, revealing his descent from a City family, declared that

Our most respectable families have not disdained the counting-house, or even the shop; their names are enrolled in the Livery and Companies of London; and in England, as well in the Italian commonwealths, heralds have been compelled to declare that gentility is not degraded by the exercise of trade.[4]

Eminent clerics from Bishop Sprat to Archbishop Secker insisted that gentlemen should not despise commerce.[5]

It is important not to let imaginative writing attacking particular

[2] Notably McVeagh, *Tradefull Merchants*, ch. 4.

[3] Edward Young (1683–1765), *Imperium Pelagi: A Naval Lyric* (London, 1730).

[4] M. M. Reese (ed.), *Gibbon's Autobiography* (London, 1970), p. 5 (begun 1788 and first published posthumously, 1796).

[5] Thomas Sprat, *The History of the Royal-Society of London* (London, 1667), p. 408. Josiah Tucker, of course, was also dean of Gloucester, 1758–99. Isaac Barrow frequently discussed the benefits of trade, as did a long list of eminent 17th cent. Nonconformist clerics, including Richard Baxter, Thomas Brooks, Edward Bury, Samuel Shaw, and Richard

businessmen disguise the continuing congratulation offered to merchants. In 1795 a novel published by William Lane's popular Minerva Press could still be dedicated 'to that very respectable body of men, the Merchants and Traders of the British Empire' and depict 'that ease and respect, that so respectable a character as the "British Merchant" can never fail to incite in the bosom of every man, who feels as he ought for the dignity and happiness of his country'.[6] From Lillo to the end of the century, the image of trade presented by its defenders in fiction and drama remained an Utopian one. Lillo's *The Merchant*, a reworking of the ballad of George Barnwell and first produced and published in 1731, was reprinted at least two dozen times by the end of the century. Merchant Trueman is portrayed as a typical progenitor of British wealth and civilization. As he says to Thorowgood, 'I have observ'd those countries where trade is promoted and encouraged, do not make discoveries to destroy, but to improve mankind by love and friendship; to tame the fierce and polish the savage; to teach them the advantage of honest traffick'.[7] In addition, the trader was also the navigator, the explorer, and the champion of civil liberty, a characterization repeated in dozens of plays and novels. Asmodeus in *The Devil Upon Two Sticks* applauds the skill and integrity of the great merchant:

his own private advantage may be truly considered as a public benefit— By the commercial exertions of such men, the public wealth is augmented, general industry is rewarded and growing manufactures encouraged; and they become as it were the chief springs of that grand commercial machine which disperses through all the channels of individual industry and ingenuity, so much benefit to general society, and tends so effectively to increase the national prosperity. The British merchant sitting in his accompting-house, and arranging the concerns of his extensive commerce, is an object, whether we consider him in a political or philosophical view, of the first respect and consideration ... How superior is such a man, in the eye of reason and of Heaven, to the Noble of a thousand years, who has received the hereditary possessions without a single effort of his own and enjoys them, even in the most favourable

Steele, author of *The Trades-man's Calling* (1684). Some Anglican clergy, like John Goodman, did have doubts about the effect of trade on religion, but even they accepted in full the public advantages of trade to civilization, exploration, and national enrichment.

[6] Thomas Bolas, *The English Merchant; Or, the Fatal Effects of Speculation in the Funds*, 2 vols. (London 1795), vol. i, p. i; vol. ii, p. 272.

[7] George Lillo (1699–1739), *The London Merchant or the History of George Barnwell* (London, 1731), Act III, Scene i.

description under the influence of hereditary pride, elegant passion, or refined luxury![8]

Reviewers were also quick to acknowledge nice discrimination between the various types of fictional character associated with trade. New versions of the prince merchant were approved by critics anxious to identify literary ancestry even in works said to be grudgingly reviewed. Lofty idealism was upheld and accounts continued in popular literature of the merchant's role in promoting civilization and protecting civil liberties. Even in the 1770s stalwart merchants were introduced in the classical guise of early century fathers of commerce. In *The Birmingham Counterfeit*, 'Tiberius Mercator', 'a flourishing and wealthy merchant of London', recovers from financial difficulties and retires to his estate to be 'respected by the great and good'.[9]

Many fictional portraits were written by those allied to the commercial world by marriage or direct experience. Such writers often lived in counties adjoining the capital, basing their representations upon merchants of the City of London. For all the care taken to distinguish between merchant, financier, and petty trader, little account was taken of their day-to-day occupations. Even where heroines are married to responsible and flourishing merchants, notably in Mrs Bennett's well-received and reprinted *Juvenile Indiscretions* of 1786, few specific business details were given. The reader is fortunate if there is more than a distinction made between the East and West Indies. Beyond vignettes of individual philanthropy and virtue, there is sparse description of how the benefits of mercantile fortunes are actually transferred to the citizenry. As charges based on ostentatious fortune making and social climbing became more insistent and specific, defences became more abstract and moralizing. Consequently, such defensiveness served—often deliberately—to isolate further the newly-arrived businessman as a convenient scapegoat to bear all the common charges. Commentators from Dr Johnson to Henry Mackenzie urged a true understanding of commercial values and sought to distinguish between the legitimate horror of ill-used new wealth and the true course to be pursued by the archetypal British merchant. Several detailed

---

[8] Combe, *Devil Upon Two Sticks in England*, i. 175–7.
[9] *The Birmingham Counterfeit; or, The Invisible Spectator*, 2 vols. (London, 1772), ii. 279.

fictional portraits of merchants were designed to contrast sharply and surprisingly with the supporting cameos of degenerate petty traders.

Inevitably, attacks on specific business types created a more general prejudice. It also appears (as will be detailed in later chapters) that accusations of luxury, non-productivity, and social irresponsibility buttressed long-established critiques. As a result, the new fictional portraits of individually virtuous merchants were often presented as if the reader would be surprised by the truth. Henry Brooke's *The Fool of Quality*, published in stages between 1766 and 1770 and reprinted in 1777 and 1792, anticipates having to confirm the merchant's good qualities to the readership. Indeed, the assumption that a book's audience was in some ways already hostile to trade reinforced the didactic intent of the plot. Brooke's novel was structured around an outburst of mistrust between two contrasting brothers.[10] One personified the landed country gentleman; the other, the city merchant. The keynote is struck as one brother recalls their original confrontation:

'My lord,' he rejoined, 'I do not wish to betray you into any mistaken or unmerited complaisance. I am but a trader, a citizen of the lower order'.

I now let myself blush with shame and disappointment; I resented being deceived by the dignity of his appearance; and I was more particularly picqued by the sarcastical kind of smile with which he closed his declaration.[11]

Thenceforth, however, every laurel was awarded to the benevolent man of commerce, culminating in the reconciliation of the two brothers.[12] Any prejudice against commercial activity was severely rebuked:

The merchant above all, is extensive, considerable, and respectable by his occupation. It is he who furnishes every comfort, convenience, and elegance of life; who carries off every redundance, who fills up every want, who ties country to country, clime to clime, and brings the remotest regions to neighbourhood and converse; who makes men to be literally the lord of the creation, and gives him an interest in whatever is done upon earth; who furnishes to each the product of all lands, and the

---

[10] Henry Brooke, *The Fool of Quality; or, The History of Henry, Earl of Moreland*, 2nd edn., 5 vols. (London, 1767), i. 98–113. The book went through many pirated editions. Of the official issues, John Wesley's 1784 adaptation is particularly notable.

[11] Ibid. i. 101.   [12] Ibid. v. 72–4.

labours of all nations; and thus knits into one family and weaves into one web the affinity and brotherhood of all mankind.[13]

The paired contrast and the design of confounding expectations were repeated in many novels, notably in the 1773 *Jonathan Splitfig* and the anonymous *Trip to Weymouth* of 1790. The *Trip* was a tongue-in-cheek picaresque and 'autobiographical' novel of the rambling travels of Mr Joseph Treadlight.[14] It featured an encounter between the hero and one Charles Danby, a wealthy merchant obviously inspired by the *Fool of Quality*. 'My father though possessed of a considerable fortune, had form'd the resolution of bringing up his children to the knowledge of trade or genteel profession', explains Danby. Virtually retelling the plot of Brooke, Danby recalls the contrasting responses which he and his brother had made to their father's plan. Charles Danby learned his trade under a most worthy merchant family of Flemings, while Edward Danby indulged 'a taste for every species of dissipation'. As Ned loses his inheritance, Charles, who takes up a partnership in the Netherlands, amasses a new fortune and purchases a country estate. In retirement, Charles conforms to the expected responsibilities of his wealth and becomes an acceptable merchant gentleman: 'I ever live at my ease, in perfect charity with the world—my table is ever open to such as will favour it with their presence—as is my purse to those whom I have reason to think stand in need of it'.[15]

Other deliberately enlightening portrayals were set against more general contrasting characters or situations. In 1770, Mrs Woodfin's Sir William Traffick has 'raised himself, by Industry and Frugality, to be one of the greatest men of the City', but 'was besides this an honest man, and had a Heart replete with every Virtue'.[16] In *Munster Village* of 1778, the Earl 'has received every advantage education could bestow on him', but his guardian-aunt proposes that he study commerce and set up as a merchant. 'With great modesty and deference for her opinion, he submitted to her whether the confined maxims of a trader were not destructive of

---

[13] Ibid. i. 104.

[14] *The Memoirs of Jonathan Splitfig* (London, 1773); *The Trip to Weymouth*, 2 vols. (London, 1790). Defoe has a similar and extended dialogue in BL, Add. MSS, 32,555, fos. 17–22, written *c*.1728 and 1st printed, Karl Bülbring (ed.), *The Compleat English Gentleman* (London, 1890), pp. 43–57.

[15] *Trip to Weymouth*, i. 44–6, 48, 73–4.

[16] Mrs Woodfin, *The History of Sally Sable*, 2 vols. (London, 1770), i. 24.

the social virtues; if they did not tend to destroy those refined feelings of the soul that distinguish man from man?' His aunt responds by assuring him that no career is more respectable than that of a merchant. She reminds him of the trading connections of great English families like the Townshends and forbids him from taking up as either lawyer or soldier. The confrontation bears striking resemblance to many similar tales of the 1780s, which also anticipate an automatic mistrust of the merchant. All such works show how, despite the early protestations, the commercial career can improve the worthy man and ensure the further protection of the public welfare.[17]

In such writing, therefore, there is clear evidence for the expectation of general anti-trade prejudice. As it affects the image of the merchant, however, it provokes more apologetics than attacks. The beginnings of this defensive undertow were evident in the first half of the century, and were part of a continued justification for what was seen to be a relatively new and dynamic social group. 'The name of merchant never degrades the gentleman', insists Lillo's Thorowgood in the very first scene of *The Merchant*. 'We merchants', pleaded Steele's Mr Sealand in *The Conscious Lovers* of 1722, 'are a species of gentry that have grown into the world this last century, and are as honourable, and almost as useful, as you landed folks that have always thought yourselves as much above us'.[18]

This underlines the fundamental point that the popular literature of the period carries no sustained attack upon the basic capitalistic spirit. The merits of pure trade are unquestioned. Fears of materialism, decadence, and corruption arise from specific alarms over social upheaval and financial insolvency and even here it is the moral character of those spending in excess which determines the nature and consequences of extravagance:

Can it be any disgrace to be concerned in trade?—What would become of this kingdom was it not for its trade?—What makes us now the envy and dread of foreigners but our commerce? ... Search the earliest records of

---

[17] If a man of education assumes business he will be an appropriate companion for a gentleman concludes a work of 1767, [Jean Marishall], *The History of Alicia Montague*, 2 vols. (London, 1767), i. 7. The work also contends that an educated woman can also embark on a business career with profit for society. One of the finest examples actually comes at the end of the century, in the response given to the retort, 'But his father is only a merchant', in the children's book, *The Fortunate Lottery Ticket*, of 1797. After several pages of laboured instruction, the child recants: 'I will never despise trade again' (p. 28).

[18] Steele, *Conscious Lovers*, Act IV, Scene ii.

time; and bring them to the present period and you will find tis trade, tis traffic only, has been the rise of, and still continues every flourishing state; and, when that has failed, their grandeur has declined, and all their affluence will soon subside.[19]

The corollary of this, however, especially given the increasing defensiveness of the defendants of trade, was that many of those writers featuring the English merchant as the pivot of their narrative or drama came not so much to illustrate British commercial achievement as to represent an ethical ideal of citizenship. Many portrayals were attempts to define the ideals of the gentleman in the context of a commercial society. The merchant was increasingly judged by social criteria, not by his business endeavours. At the same time, the virtues of gentility could also be demonstrated by the negative portrayal of worthless business types and the perversion of true commerce. The merchant illustrated in detail the proper ends for wealth and taught moral lessons about charity and economy in his own community.[20] By 1790 several works from that season's output contained descriptions of the gentleman entering commerce, but significantly in all of them the gentleman merchant, personifying integrity, charity, and other social virtues, suffers ruination at the hands of vulgar *nouveaux riches* traders. His rescue is usually contrived by inherited or windfall wealth: few writers appear confident of ascribing any recovery to renewed business interests.[21]

Much of this heightened social interest derived from the defensive sections about trade and traders in early century guide books, essays, and devotional readers. After the serial contributions of Addison and Steele, the single most influential guide to the relationship between trade and gentility was Defoe's *Complete English Tradesman*.[22] Defoe's work was intended to lay down maxims for the instruction of the tradesman, with sections for the apprentice

[19] *The Distrest Wife; or, The History of Eliza Wyndham*, 2 vols. (London, Cooke, 1768), i. 124–5.

[20] Of many examples, Mr Traffic Worthy, the merchant of *Louisa* published in London in 1760.

[21] Perhaps the best example from the 1790 season is *The Slave of Passion*, in which this parable dominates the work from first to last. It is also notable for including manufacturing as an acceptable occupation, as the provider of local employment.

[22] Daniel Defoe, *The Complete English Tradesman, In Familiar Letters; Directing him in all the several Parts and Progressions of Trade . . . Calculated for the Instruction of our Inland Tradesmen, and especially of Young Beginners*, 2 vols. (London, 1726–7).

on bookkeeping, letter-writing, and 'trading stile'. Defoe distinguishes between the merchant engaged in foreign trade and the tradesman as inland retailer and wholesaler. Although the same person could be both merchant and trader, the distinction is clearly an important marker on the route to greater specification of the word 'merchant'. Letter xxii is entitled 'Of the Dignity of Trade in England more than in other Countries', and supports three arguments: that 'our tradesmen are not, as in other countries, the meanest of our people', that 'some of the greatest and best, and most flourishing families of gentry only, but even nobility, have been rais'd from trade, owe their beginning, their wealth, and their estates to trade', and that 'those families are not at all ashamed of their original, and indeed have no occasion to be ashamed of it'. Tradesmen in England, Defoe boasted, are not 'depreciated as they are abroad', or, as he feels he must add, 'as some of our Gentry would pretend to do in England'. Listing an impressive battery of both current and historical examples, he insists that 'trade is so far here from being inconsistent with a Gentleman, that in short trade in England makes Gentlemen, and has peopled this nation with Gentlemen'.[23] Capping what was probably the high point in the social acclaim for trade, Defoe went on to commend tradesmen for painting their arms on the doors of their coaches, something which was to become a favourite satire of the second half of the century and certainly not one defended even within a generation of Defoe's death.

The authority to which Steele and Defoe and their successors appealed was a complex and ancient one—and one certainly much older than Whiggish apologetics for trade flourishing in Restoration England. For many, the disparagement of trade had not only been unbecoming, but also un-British and unbiblical. Addison repeated a familiar view when he observed 'many a younger brother of a great family who had rather see their children starve like gentlemen than thrive in a trade and profession that is beneath their quality. This humour fills several parts of Europe with pride and beggary'.[24] From the sixteenth to the eighteenth century a distinctive respect for the merchant was upheld by the conduct book and reinforced by sermons and

---

[23] Ibid. i. 370–1, 379, 376. 'An Estate's a pond', he writes, 'but a Trade's a spring', ibid. i. 375.

[24] *Spectator*, 1711, no. 108.

religious essays. Henry Peacham's *The Compleat Gentleman*, first published in 1622, offered various sections of cautions and recommendations. Although his real concern was to illustrate the superiority of gentry and nobility over all other ranks, he was keen to insist upon a fair assessment of merchants:

> the exercise of Merchandise hath beene (I confesse) accounted base and much derogating from Nobilitie, except it be exercised and undertaken by a generall Estate, or Deputies thereof. Aristotle therefore saith, That the Thebans and Lacedaemonians had a Law, that none should bee esteemed and held capable of Honor in their Commonwealth except that they had ten years given over Trading and merchandise: and Valerius Maximus reporteth that among other things the Romans had to disparage Tarquinius Driscus withall, and make him odious to the people, was that he was a Merchants sonne. Saint Chrysostome upon that place of Mathew, 'Hee cast out the buyers and sellers out of the Temple' gathereth that Merchants hardly and seldom please God.[25]

A reservoir of flexible definitions of the gentleman had been created from countless conduct and courtesy manuals. Charity, liberality, and other totems of social arbitration, were bound inextricably with the history of manners. By 1700 these definitions of gentility also had to accommodate the virtues of trade. Educational courtesy books, increasingly popular from the early sixteenth century, included many sections of advice about social behaviour and attitudes to wealth. Printed contrasts between the English courtier and the country gentleman boasted a pedigree reaching back to the early sixteenth century, while 'moral instructions from a father to a son' had been published since Caxton.[26] Courtesy books ranged from books of parental advice and polite conduct to guides to political management. One other type of publication, books of civility, was in one sense more ambitious than the later popular books of etiquette, often attempting encyclopaedic coverage of general rules of good taste applicable to all social groups. A code of ethics was set out by the courtesy book,

---

[25] Henry Peacham, *The Compleat Gentleman* (London, 1622), p. 11.

[26] The *Disticha Catonis ad Filium* had been popular throughout medieval Europe, and *The Precepts of Cato* was published in English in 1560, W. Lee Ustick, 'Advice to a Son: A Type of Seventeenth-Century Conduct Book', *Studies in Philology*, 29/3 (July 1932), 409–41. There were also many medieval collections of aphorisms, father to son. Much of the research for this section was made possible by a visiting fellowship at the Newberry Library, Chicago, 1986. The finest bibliography remains Virgil B. Heltzel, *A Check List of Courtesy Books in the Newberry Library* (Chicago, 1942).

relying not only upon external evidence, but also upon an internal referential tradition, one book summarizing or citing from another. Models of moral excellence were drawn widely, with authority invariably taken from classical authors or from Scripture, rather than from contemporary example. As one particularly influential work pronounced, 'althoughe we fynde not in the holy Scriptures the expres definicion of a Gentelmanne, or what sorte of manne he ought for to be, dyscrybed by hys pares, yet if a man be vertuous ... ther are then to be found in the holy scriptures of such gentlemenne great plenti, and many examples of their worthy dedes'.[27]

Despite avid antiquarian interest, historical consideration of printed conduct books remains patchy.[28] At least one social analyst sees this as a consequence of the political and social prevalences of our time.[29] Certain interpretations are also misleading. Literary definitions of the 'gentleman' dating from Victorian times are often isolated from their historical context and used in justification of a British civilizing ideal upheld from Kampala to Kathmandu. From this has flowed a substantial secondary stream of works investigating the concept of the gentleman in both Victorian education and imaginative literature.[30] More recently, a very different approach has appeared. Until the 1830s, it is suggested, 'no body of theory and counsel existed in print to sanction and smooth the "rise" of any "middle class" '.[31] This, however, is both to underestimate the output of works in the seventeenth

---

[27] H. Braham, *The Institucion of a Gentleman* (London, 1555), pp. [25–6].

[28] In addition to Heltzel, the foundation studies are A. Smythe-Palmer, *The Ideal of a Gentleman* (London, 1908); Ruth Kelso, 'The Doctrine of the English Gentleman in the Sixteenth Century', *University of Illinois Studies in Language and Literature*, 14/1–2 (Feb.–May 1929), 1–288; H. Mews, 'Middle-class Conduct Books of the Seventeenth Century', Ph.D. thesis (London, 1934); and John Edward Mason, *Gentlefolk in the Making: Studies in the History of English Courtesy Literature, 1531–1774* (Philadelphia, 1935). A stimulating study was offered by W. Lee Ustick, 'Changing Ideals of Aristocratic Character and Conduct in Seventeenth-Century England', *Modern Philology*, 30/2 (Nov. 1932), 147–66; and more recently Felicity Heal has considered the idea of gentility as it affects notions of the host, 'The Idea of Hospitality in Early Modern England', *Past and Present*, 102 (Feb. 1984), 66–93.

[29] 'Ceremony and etiquette have a relatively low place in the valuations of bourgeois societies. Accordingly there is a lack of systematic studies of such phenomena', Norbert Elias, *The Court Society*, trans. by Edmund Jephcott (London, 1983), p. 29.

[30] J. A. Mangan, *Athleticism in the Victorian and Edwardian Public School* (Cambridge, 1981); Brian Simon and Ian Bradley (eds.), *The Victorian Public School: Studies in the Development of an Educational Institution* (Dublin, 1975); Robin Gilmour, *The Idea of the Gentleman in the Victorian Novel* (London, 1981).

[31] Clark, *English Society*, p. 105.

century and to misread the guidance offered. It is claimed that such literature, in presenting aristocratic models of civility and virtuous conduct, offered no description or assurance of middle-class betterment. But how is it expected that courtesy literature might do this? The whole point of the gentlemanly ideal was its exclusivity and that the fact of being a gentleman was never to be openly acknowledged but rather recognized by behaviour. To explain how one became the gentleman, instead of what being one was all about, defeated the object of the chase.

There is a parallel here with what Jon Klancher regards, from a very different perspective, as the progressive distancing of the middle-class reader from accepted notions of class purpose and identity. Social pleasure, like status, must be achieved without overt effort. The more obvious the mechanics, the more elusive the satisfaction or even the achievement. In fact, what Klancher identifies (from the *New Monthly Magazine*) as a 'paradoxical lack of fit between a social subject and his pleasures',[32] can almost certainly be found in literature of a century or more before the Romantic period of which he writes. The 'old' social index was dissolving, or rather metamorphosing, by at least the late seventeenth century.

In further contradiction of an *ancien régime* view of an unreconstructed and dominant aristocratic code, specialist conduct books were not just a product of the late eighteenth century. Although the publication of etiquette books certainly soared from about the late 1770s, books like Adam Petrie's guide to deportment had been available for fifty years or more. Petrie, like many others, advised on the correct manner of walking, of offering greetings, of expressing gratitude, and of performing a whole range of social skills.[33] Antoine de Courtin's *Rules of Civility; Or, the Maxims of Genteel Behaviour* was translated from the French twelfth edition in 1703 and provided twenty-four separate sections of practical advice on politeness. This included compliments, conversation, salutation, how to conduct oneself in church, what to observe on a journey, how to comment on a play, and how to enter the house of a great person. Moreover, later manuals of

---

[32] Jon P. Klancher, *The Making of English Reading Audiences, 1790–1832* (Madison, Wis., 1987), p. 64.
[33] Adam Petrie, *Rules of Good Deportment or of Good Breeding For the Use of Youth* (Edinburgh, 1720).

politesse existed in addition to a venerable body of very wide-ranging conduct literature, not in supercession of it. Many influential fifteenth-century works included highly specific advice on social behaviour and anticipated the extremely popular mid- and late seventeenth-century books on good manners and conversation.[34] In 1630 Richard Brathwait, concluding that 'a Gentleman is a Man of himselfe, without the addition of either Tayler, Millener, Seamster or Haberdasher', presented a catalogue of moral qualities he possessed.[35] The full work, *The English Gentleman: Containing Sundry excellent Rules or exquisite Observations, tending to Direction of every Gentleman, of selecter ranke and qualitie,* was a handbook on 'gentilizing' divided into eight sections: youth, recreation, disposition, acquaintance, education, moderation, vocation, perfection. It has details on how to behave, how to speak, and how to dress as the complete gentleman. This is not a passive aristocratic code of honour, but a narrow, specific exploration of the avenue to gentility. It threatens even to expose as a sham the exclusiveness of the gentle caste.

Indeed, the central question for many of these books concerned the relationship between birth and behaviour. What was a gentleman and could a tradesman become one? The conclusion of most conduct books from the sixteenth and seventeenth centuries was that in order to qualify as a gentleman it was necessary but not sufficient to be of good breeding. Without the supplementary virtues, birth could not carry all. For if, in the age of Sir Thomas Smith, the association of gentility with gentle birth was paramount,[36] others, including William Harrison, had equivocated. In his dissertation in the first edition of Holinshed's *Chronicles* in 1577, Harrison averred that 'Gentlemen be those whome their race and bloode doth make noble and knowne'.[37] The second edition, issued ten years later, included a significant

---

[34] *The Babees Book (c.*1475) and John Russell's *Book of Nurture.* The *Facetus* advice works had been circulated throughout medieval Europe. Clark relies, it seems, on J. E. Mason's troublesome definition of 'books of civility' as offering 'rules of universal good taste' and as supposedly being replaced by more precise etiquette manuals at the end of the 18th cent.

[35] Richard Brathwait, *The English Gentleman* (London, 1630), p. 457.

[36] Sir Thomas Smith, *The Commonwealth of England* (1612). Ruth Kelso staunchly defends this rigid interpretation of gentility, while arguing that new emphasis was given to the role of personal worth, 'Sixteenth-Century Definitions of the Gentleman in England', *Journal of English and Germanic Philology,* 24 (1935), 370–82.

[37] William Harrison, 'An Historicall Description of the Islande of Britayne', in Raphaell Holinshed, *Chronicles of England, Scotlande and Irelande,* 2 vols. (London, 1577), i. 105.

change: 'Gentlemen be those whome their race and bloud, or at least their vertues doo make noble and knowne'.[38] Robert Burton, scorning those who boasted of wealth or lineage, went a little further: 'how much better is it to say with him, *Ego meis maioribus virtute praeluxi*, to boast himself of his vertues, then of his birth?'[39] It was Braham's intention to 'describe such a man as may be wortheleye called master, not leaving undeclared the blindness of those which thincke theimselves Gentlemen, onely because their fathers & auctoures did descend of noble houses'.[40] At some point, however, it is also clear that the balance of opinion in conduct books inclined to the view that it was no longer necessary to be of good birth to become the gentleman. In contradiction of recent claims, the theoretical pattern of the aristocratic code *did* make concessions to the reality of social mobility. Certainly, by the nineteenth century, Thomas Tegg's guidebook was designed to make the reader 'a gentleman, according to the usual English requirements for the character; that is, he must possess wit, money, and manners'.[41] Birth seems to have disappeared as a requirement of gentility, and it was only later that the avalanche of Victorian gentility definitions obliterated the earlier literary response.[42]

The starting-point for works questioning birth right alone was the definition of 'nobility' and the Wykehamite challenge that 'Manners maketh Man'. Even if it did not form the majority view, a large number of sixteenth- and seventeenth-century works from *Of Gentylnes and Nobylyte*, printed by John Rastell in about 1525, to Henry Peacham's *Compleat Gentleman* of 1622, concluded that gentility could not be assured by lineage.[43] Sir Thomas Elyot's *Boke Named the Governour*, first published in 1531, and generally regarded as the first English treatise on education and polite conduct,

[38] Harrison, 'Description of England', bk. ii, ch. 5, in Raphaell Holinshed, *Chronicles of England, Scotland and Ireland*, 2nd edn. 2 vols. (London, 1587), i. 162, reprinted as *Holinshed's Chronicles of England, Scotland and Ireland*, 6 vols. (London, 1807–8), i. 273.

[39] Robert Burton, *Anatomy of Melancholy* (London, 1621), p. 392.

[40] Braham, *Institucion of a Gentleman*, p.[11].

[41] Thomas Tegg, *A Present for an Apprentice*, 2nd edn. (London, 1848).

[42] Typically, by 1846 R. T. Hampson (relying heavily on selections from Holinshed) was pointing out that the word *gentle* 'in strict propriety ... belongs to none who is not descended from one of the Germanic conquerors (in medieval Latin *gentiles*) of the Roman provinces; and, by consequence, in England it should be restricted solely to the descendants of the Saxons', *Origines Patriciae* (London, 1846), p. 348.

[43] *Of Gentylnes and Nobylyte: A Dyaloge Betwen the Marchant the Knyght and the Plowman Dysputyng who is a Very Gentylman* (London, c.1525); Peacham, *Compleat Gentleman*.

reached nine editions by 1600. Elyot defines nobility as 'the prayse and surname of vertue', its essence explained as placability, affability, mercy, benevolence, beneficence, and liberality.[44] In turn, 'nobility' was related to gentility in a dozen or more works which used Elyot as the starting point for discussion and elaboration. The most famous of these, Braham's *Institucion of a Gentleman* of 1555, upholds the essential qualities of hospitality and simplicity, frequently advancing nostalgic notions of past golden ages of true gentility. More particularly, four orders are discussed, the gentle gentle or nobly born man of good behaviour, the gentle ungentle or nobly born man of bad behaviour, the ungentle gentle or base-born man of noble character, and the ungentle ungentle or the baseborn vulgar. Of these groups, the author is particularly interested in the ungentle gentle, 'of whiche sorte of gentlemen we have nowe in Englande very many, whereby it should appeare that vertue florisheth emong us'. Although 'these gentlemen are nowe called upstartes, a terme lately invented', they are to be honoured and not to be confused with rich and avaricious 'handycraft men' who, having purchased estates, demand to be called knights and esquires. These should be regarded as the 'worshypful unworthye, for that they have crept into ye degree of worship without worthines, neyther broughte thereunto by val-iencye ne vertue ... these be the righte upstartes'. The author is especially anxious to defend honourable self-made men. 'Up-starte', he writes, is 'a terme lately invented by such as pondered not ye groundes of honest meanes of rising or comyng to pro-mocion ... I speake not thys in defence of all new rysen men, but onely of suche as worthynes hath broughte unto honor'.[45]

The problem with caste, certainly recognized by Smith, was that the pedigree of gentility had to have some sort of origin. If gentility was conferred on distant ancestors, it had to be explained why they had been singled out for divine approval. The Herald's Office was not God-given. The question was further stimulated by searching debates about what professions might be followed by the younger sons of gentlemen, and whether they might also qualify as gentry. In the mid-seventeenth century, Thomas Fuller offered five maxims for the edification of the younger son, con-cluding that

[44] Mason stresses the importance of Elyot, *Gentlefolk*, p. 23.
[45] Braham, *Institucion of a Gentleman*, pp. [28], [29], [40], [43], [29], [31].

he gaineth more wealth if betaking himself to merchandise. Whence often riseth to the greatest annual honour in the kingdome. Many families in England though not first raised from the City, yet thence have been so restored and enriched that it may seem to amount to an originall raising.[46]

Sir Thomas Elyot, who warned of overemphasizing lineage, believed that 'in the begynnynge ... undoubtedly they gave the one and the other [degree and condition] to him, at whose vertue they meruayled, and by whose labour and industrie they re-ceiued a commune benefyte'.[47] From at least the time of Elyot there continued to be a long discussion over the historical idea of the gentleman, still eagerly pursued at the end of the nineteenth century.[48] 'How ridiculous it is', continued Fuller, 'when many men brag that their families are more ancient than the Moon'.[49] 'For all must begin somewhere', wrote Defoe, 'and would be traced to some less Degree in their Original than will suit with the Vanity of the Day ... the tallest Tree has its Root in the Dirt'.[50]

Certain writers, by alluding specifically to the means and re-sponsibilities of self-improvement, almost undermined the myth and mystery of gentility.[51] He who was not born to nobility might yet achieve it by social performance. This was made clear by *The English Theophrastus: or, The Manners of the Age* by Abel Boyer, published in 1695, with an enlarged second edition in 1706. The work is littered with short items of advice given under different general themes. Possibly the advice was presented as it was so that some of it could be learned by rote. Boyer also highlights what is supposed to be the most notable omission in such literature:

We are surpris'd every Day, to see some Men, that are come from the Scum of the people, raise themselves to great Fortunes and Honours; and we commonly mention this with Scorn and Reproach; as if all the

---

[46] Fuller, *Holy State*, p. 48.

[47] Sir Thomas Elyot, *The Boke Named the Governour* (London, 1534), p. 103.

[48] A wide selection of contributions is given in Smythe-Palmer, *Ideal of a Gentleman*, ch. 1.

[49] Fuller, *Holy State*, p. 49.

[50] Defoe, in *The Compleat English Gentleman*, p. 13 (fo. 4).

[51] William Ramesey, *The Gentlemans Companion; or, A Companion of True Nobility, and Gentility* (London, 1672); Obadiah Walker, *Of Education especially of Young Gentlemen* (Oxford, 1673); Jean Gailhard, *The Compleat Gentleman; or, Directions for the Education of Youth as to their Breeding at Home and Travelling Abroad* (London, 1678); Humphrey Brooke, *The Durable Legacy* (London, 1681).

Great Families in the World had not as mean a Beginning, if we would but take pains to trace them back to their Originals.[52]

Similarly, the gentle condition was not always depicted as irreversible. In 1665 Edward Waterhaus's voluminous *Gentleman's Monitor* announced 'a sober inspection into the vertues, vices and ordinary means of the rise and decay of men and families'. The collapse of various individuals or lineages was ascribed to moral fatigue. Needless luxury was condemned and frugality and thrift emphasized as the means to improvement and recovery. Indeed, the insistence upon thrift and the contrast between the extravagance of an ungentle city and the wholesome, prudent gentleness of the country was an important, wide-ranging ingredient in popular writing.[53]

Above all, the connection between medieval ideas of knighthood and chivalry and later ideals of courtesy should not be overemphasized. *The Gentlemans Companion*, written by William Ramesey and published in 1672, opened with the chapter, 'What Gentility is'. It stressed that one must not rely on noble birth:

What wise man thinks the worse of Tully for being an Up-start, or Iphicrates, and Marius, for their Mean birth, or of Agathocles, King of Sicily, for being a Porters Son. So Telephanes, King of Lydia, was but the Son of a Carter; Valentinian, the Emperor, of a Rope-maker, Primislaus, King of Bohemia, of a Cow-herd; And Tamberlain the great is by most reputed only the Son of a shepherd, as he was himself, nay, and David the King, a man after God's own heart, was no other.[54]

Ramesey also provided an important reminder that it was possible to write without shame of 'Mean birth' or of being 'an Up-start'. In an early eighteenth-century basic guide to polite behaviour, originally penned by Morvan de Bellegarde, the reader is warned not 'to despise Celidan who counterfeits Quality, before Gerontes, who is only an upstart Tradesman, and who would be thought Noble'. Likewise, 'Philemon upbraids Sofias with the meaness of his Birth, when every body knows that Philemon's Father is a Retailer of Cloth in a Town not an hundred Miles from London'.[55]

[52] Abel Boyer, *English Theophrastus; or, The Manners of the Age*, 2nd edn. (London, 1706), p. 292.
[53] For fuller discussion, see Chs. 8 and 9 below.
[54] Ramesey, *Gentlemans Companion*, p. 5.
[55] Jean Baptiste Morvan de Bellegarde, *Reflexions upon Ridicule* (London, 1706), pp. 46, 69.

Far from relying on a Renaissance aristocratic code, seventeenth- and eighteenth-century conduct books, however generalized and theoretical their advice, are anxious to avoid anachronism. The most obvious 'tradition' entering English conduct books of the sixteenth century was a classical one. Humanist moral philosophy was grafted on a Thomistic hierarchical stock. The ideal of the aristocracy was informed most notably by the Aristotelian concept of the Magnanimous Man, and a stoicism derived largely from Seneca and Epictetus. *The Moral Philosophie of the Stoicks* was first published in London in 1598. In fact, Epictetus, first translated into English in 1567, and Seneca, with a first English edition in 1614,[56] promoted two divergent though not inconsistent ideals, that of stoic tolerance and that of a sympathetic awareness and response to the needs of all men. Of the two, Epictetus' ideal of endurance has been given more attention—possibly because of its apparent fathering of that favourite conceit of modern Britain, the gentleman's stiff upper lip. It was the Senecan ideal, however, which was most quoted in early modern books of courtesy and conduct. Benevolence and helpfulness towards others became the touchstone of works from Brathwait to Allestree.[57]

What is also clear is that Brathwait's popular model for the gentleman, so heavily influenced by notions of benevolence, was opposed to that view of the 'compleat gentleman' sponsored by Elyot and Ascham and reaching a final version in Peacham. Elyot's original commitment, while severely practical, was based on moral philosophy stressing strength of character and service to the state. The concept of virtue was deliberately vague. According to Brathwait, however, 'Vertue the greatest Signall and Symbol of Gentry: is rather expressed by goodnesse of Person than greatnesse of Place'.[58] Useful activity is the key, not governorship. The Renaissance Court gentleman of Elyot has been replaced by the notion that the gentleman should be less concerned with cultured living and more inclined to charitable

---

[56] *The Manuell of Epictetus: Translated out of Greeke into French, and now into English*, trans. by James Sanford (London, 1567); *The Workes of Lucius Annæus Seneca, Morrall and Naturall*, trans. by Thomas Lodge (London, 1614). The full works of Epictetus were first available in translation in Elizabeth Carter's edition of 1752, W. A. Oldfather, *Contributions Towards a Bibliography of Epictetus* (Urbana, 1927).

[57] An account is given by Ustick, 'Changing Ideals'.

[58] Brathwait, *English Gentleman*, Epistle Dedicatory.

ministrations and an awareness of his relationship to his fellow man.[59]

One other contrast between Peacham and Brathwait—that of their authorities—is crucial to understanding the backdrop for the later gentlemen and tradesmen moralities. Brathwait's appeal to Christian tradition heightened the Senecan emphasis on benevolence and service to one's neighbours. In the margins to *The English Gentleman*, Brathwait mixed specific Christian and classical references. For the next two hundred years, writers of conduct literature laid claim to an avowedly venerable literary and philosophical inheritance, and it is clear that the literature of social manners, especially as it relates to the portrayal of new wealth, cannot be viewed in secular isolation. This was particularly true by the seventeenth century, when Aristotelian ideals were superceded, and stoic ideals buttressed, by the ideal of the good Christian. A Thomistic emphasis upon hierarchy and an Aristotelian consciousness of superiority and commitment to courage and the self always risked collision with the Christian embrace of service and humility. Most of the seventeenth- and eighteenth-century conduct books, and certainly some of those most frequently reprinted, were originally penned as instruments of practical religion and addressed broad ethical problems rather than narrow questions of social behaviour. The enormous influence of two works attributed to Richard Allestree, *The Whole Duty of Man* and *The Gentleman's Calling*, cannot be understood without appreciating the range of their religious commitment and the especial appeal of biblical allusion and authority.[60] Allestree's *Gentleman's Calling* (1660) stressed, with much biblical citation, the benefits of the stewardship of riches and the dangers of sloth and of dissipating one's stock. In addition, Allestree enumerated the advantages of being a gentleman in order to prove that a gentleman had a 'calling'. These advantages comprised time, in which to do good works, authority, to be used properly, education and wealth, each to be 'rightly husbanded', and finally, reputation, to be used to set a good example to the poor and to keep down 'the levelling principle'.

[59] This was not, of course, a new argument. Most notably, Caxton's *Book of Chivalry* instructed knights to be lovers of the common good, to place the welfare of all before the welfare of the individual.

[60] First published by Timothy Garthwait, the books became a stock-in-trade of all booksellers for a century or more.

This notion of a 'calling' was, of course, to be the linchpin of the Weber–Tawney thesis of the Protestant work ethic. 'Gentlemen', argued Allestree, 'are distinguished from the Vulgar, not only by empty Names and airy Titles, but by real Donatives, distributed to them by God, as so many distinct Advantages, fertile and prolifical Abilities, towards the bringing him in his expected Harvest of Honour and Glory'.[61] Such a 'calling' admitted not only the idea of occupation and livelihood, but also of an impulse, a summons from God, a direction towards particular duties and responsibilities. Its enactment led to that state of grace and obedience into which the Christian was truly 'called'. It was also clear that the idea of 'everyone in his calling' was linked to political assurances of the severalty of degrees:

God, in his Wisdom, discerning, that Equality of Conditions would breed Confusion in the World has ordered several States, design'd some to Poverty, others to Riches, only annexing to the Rich the Care of the Poor; yet that rather as an Advantage, than a Burden, a Seed of more Wealth both Temporal and Eternal.[62]

It was this that enabled both Locke and Swift to compare trade with a calling.[63] Here also was the corner-stone of both Puritan and Anglican justifications of temporal order and authority. Social distinctions and the 'several callings' comprised part of that reasonable order established by God, and one necessary to provide the incentive to industry and trade. Philip Ayres's *Vox Clamantis* of 1684 preached sobriety, temperance, and charity to the poor, but also included a chapter entitled 'Cautions to gentlemen to take care to preserve their Estates by wise management of them'. It advised that they compute often their incomes and disbursements, that they stayed only briefly in the City, and that they maintained old-fashioned country hospitality. In all of this, the levelling fear was sharply focused. The whole of his little work, Ayres concluded, was

to prevent this growing mischief that the wealth of the Nation be not transferred from the ancient Nobility and Gentry in England, to the Commonalty, and to Mechanicks and Mean Spirited Men (who have

[61] Allestree, *Gentleman's Calling*, 1717 edn., p. 10.   [62] Ibid. 62.
[63] In fact, Locke's position is often seriously misrepresented. To attribute to him the belief that trade 'was wholly inconsistent with a gentleman's calling', is to cite the author very much out of context. Locke freely acknowledges that gentlemen will encourage

acquired a great dexterity in getting and gathering together Riches) ... that watching an opportunity, they make not a fresh attempt to overthrow Monarchy once again in this Nation, and reduce us to a Commonwealth, for then farewell all the ancient Nobility and Gentry of England.[64]

Various influential writers, however, were concerned more to stress the impulsive, elective concept of calling to illustrate the moral imperative behind the state of gentility. Although Allestree—quite unexceptionally—believed that in 'the present age' charity was sacrificed between covetousness and luxury, charity remained the pivotal indicator and duty of the calling. This ethical gentlemanliness, which continued to inform such popular works as Clement Ellis's *Gentile Sinner* of 1660 and Isaac Barrow's *Of Industry* of 1686, gave particular prominence to charity and good works. Both were highlighted by William Darrell, the Jesuit, in his *Gentleman Instructed* of 1704. Published as a religious dialogue, it proved an extremely influential model for succeeding conduct books, mixing practical advice with unmistakable assurance about the religious foundation for the state of gentility. This sense of duty has, in fact, been underplayed in the Weber–Tawney interpretation of 'calling'. At least one of its supporters has to admit that clerics contrasted the sense of duty with working for money only. The work ethic had its social responsibilities.[65] George Wheler's *Protestant Monastery* of 1698 provides a guide to Christian practice, stressing the various duties of hospitality and obligations to society. It also provided the pattern for a succession of new conduct books reinforcing the Christian emphasis upon traditional ideals of piety, benevolence, and hospitality.[66]

As charity became the mark of gentility, 'loving the brethren' served as the catalyst to salvation across all hues of Christian belief. Where Nonconformists laid more stress on spiritual charity—on the proselytizing and spiritual power of prayer—Anglicans insisted on the possibility of charity benefiting all men, thereby

younger sons to enter trade, and implicitly supporting this, pleads for appropriate education to be available for each type of son according to his future calling or career, *Some Thoughts Concerning Education* (London, 1693), pp. 194, 241.

[64] *Vox Clamantis: Or an Essay for the Honour, Happiness and Prosperity of the English Society ... By P. A. Gent* (London, 1684), p. 109.

[65] Richard B. Schlatter, *The Social Ideas of Religious Leaders, 1660–88* (London, 1940), pp. 124–46.

[66] The 17th cent. works are discussed in Heal, 'The Idea of Hospitality'.

widening the Puritan notions of 'brethren'. Good works became the essence of the Latitudinarian Church and although Anglican writers repeatedly protested that they did not hold that the performance of good works ensured salvation, it is certainly true that their overwhelming emphasis on social charity did give the appearance of neglecting saving grace. Moreover, moral reformation was regularly presented as exhibiting practical, outward manifestations and benefits. Many stressed that the careful performance of charity might ward off natural catastrophe, an argument particularly evident in the outpouring of literature after the Lisbon earthquake of 1755. A decade later, Smollett mythologized the aftermath of the earlier London earthquake: 'the streets no longer resounded with execrations, or the noise of licentiousness; and the hand of charity was liberally opened'.[67] For many it was very much a prudential charity, that was represented as the spiritual benefit of alms-giving and community service. As Brathwait had warned:

For beleeve it (as assuredly you shall finde it) that your sumptuous Banquetting, your midnight revelling, your unseasonable rioting, your phantasticke attiring, your formall courting shall witnesse against you in the day of revenge ... Returne therefore before the evill day come: distribute to the Necessitie of the Saints, become good Dispensers of what you have received, that yee may gaine yourselves grace in the high Court of Heaven.[68]

Seventy years later, the extremely popular handbook by William Darrell was advising similarly, if in more contemporary terms: 'What you lay out on the Poor, is not spent, but put to Interest; God is Security for the Reimbursement, so that the Payment is infallible'.[69]

Some of the most influential elaborations of these propositions appeared in sermons—not only those delivered from the pulpit, but those printed and circulated for reading at home. These were such a staple of the eighteenth-century book trade that there survive numerous announcements by booksellers pleading that the market was saturated and that no new collections could be accepted for publication. Sermons on charity were certainly no

---

[67] Tobias Smollett, *The History of England*, new edn., 4 vols. (London, 1830), iii. 51.

[68] Brathwait, *English Gentleman*, p. 67, taking Amos 6: 11 as the text.

[69] William Darrell, *A Gentleman Instructed in the Conduct of a Virtuous and Happy Life* (London, 1704), p. 158. The work reached a 9th edn. in 1727.

longer confined to Quinquagesima or the opening of a local hospital or almshouse. Addresses on benevolence and the social responsibilities of wealth and status streamed from the press. The sermons of the great writers, Tillotson, Butler, Secker, and Wesley, acted as models for lesser writers and those delivering directly from the pulpit. The printed sermon, like the conduct book and exemplary tale, became a common literary property. In particular, *The Whole Duty of Man* figured prominently in that community of printed texts raided weekly by desperate or complacent clerics. The production of ready-made sermons (dispatched if preferred under brown paper wrapping) was the first major success for the highly commercial bookseller John Trusler.

The secular orientation of many sermons belies the homiletic and oratorical tradition from which they derived. From the contributions of Tillotson at the end of the seventeenth century to those of his Latitudinarian successors, many clerical writers were enthused more by the demands of justifying contemporary social order and ethical proprieties than by the *mysterium tremendum et fascinans* of their inheritance.[70] In addition to the sermons, devotional handbooks proliferated throughout the seventeenth and eighteenth centuries, itemizing aspects of practical godliness. To the Anglican communion in particular, the duties of the Second Table were portrayed as the outward manifestations of obedience and the moral order within society.[71] As James Downey has described it, 'the Church seemed almost to become a society for the reformation of manners, a place where kindred spirits met to have their sensibilities tuned to a finer pitch'.[72] Many, probably most, clerics came to believe that their chief task was to explain and justify morality. 'The most beauteous, and elected Branch of Brotherly-kindness', announced Bishop Warburton, 'is Friend-

---

[70] In buttressing the Established position, Warburton's *The Alliance Between Church and State* (London, 1736) gained formidable popularity. A broad discussion is offered by R. W. Greaves, 'The Working of the Alliance', in G. V. Bennett and J. D. Walsh (eds.), *Essays in Modern English Church History* (London, 1966), pp. 163–80.

[71] During the 17th cent. the popular distinction between the two tables of the Decalogue, the first concerning man's relation with God and the second with man's relation to his fellow men, became a key device in catechisms and summaries of doctrine, J. Sears McGee, *The Godly Man in Stuart England: Anglicans, Puritans and the Two Tables, 1620–1670* (New Haven, Conn., 1976).

[72] James Downey, *The Eighteenth Century Pulpit* (Oxford, 1969), p. 10.

ship, whose natural Root and Origin is Similitude of Manners'.[73] Ethical preaching conquered all and the metaphysical orations of Andrewes and Donne were consigned to the upper shelves of college and diocesan libraries.[74] Addison and Steele certainly reflected the Tillotsonian emphasis upon religion as a sanction for morality. At the core of their periodical writing and of so much sermon literature of the period is an optimistic, enlightened philosophy, flaunting assurance in a sophisticated society in which it was inappropriate to descend to medieval spectres of sin and damnation to transmit the teachings of the Church. Countless early eighteenth-century sermons and works of divinity pronounce with rediscovered Aristotelian fervour that reason embodies the pre-eminent faculty of appeal. Tillotson's 'His Commandments are Not Grievous', apparently by far the most popular sermon in eighteenth-century England,[75] in many ways shared in that search for the rational determinants of revealed religion as famously elucidated by Clarke, Butler, and Berkeley. The last two in particular came to be fundamentally concerned with the way in which man lived his life on earth and the moral laws erected to determine his behaviour.

By the end of the 1740s, protests gathered against this pragmatic 'no hell to ears polite' sermonizing. Opposition, when it came, however, did little to undermine the social imperative of new religious writing. Even Revivalism and early Methodism, reacting in part to preaching aimed at refining and secularizing the social order, confirmed rather than opposed aspects of moral teaching which encouraged examination of manners and social responsibilities. For John Wesley, by far the most prolific religious writer of the century,[76] good works represented the earthly evidence of sanctification and the outward manifestation of faith. In his determination to stress the reality of original sin, Wesley's teachings became increasingly obsessed with human actions rather than their profession of faith. Many of his addresses are

---

[73] William Warburton, *Faith working by Charity to Christian Edification: A Sermon* (London, 1738), p. 20.

[74] Ernest Mossner argued that 'ethical theory, by and large, was the chief intellectual pursuit of the eighteenth century, colouring even its historiography and its science', *Bishop Butler and the Age of Reason: A Study in the History of Thought* (New York, 1936), p. 105.

[75] Downey, *Eighteenth Century Pulpit*, p. 13.

[76] He wrote in whole or in collaboration nearly four hundred books and tracts.

concerned with minutiae of social conduct ranging from dress to conversation.[77]

In fact, the doctrinal ancestry of this preoccupation is not hard to uncover. The performance of good works became for many the obvious measure of inner conviction and love and of rewards and punishments. As Warburton explained in one of his many Charity sermons:

the Doctrines of Christianity will lead a Light to good Works, whereby they may be better understood. And this with great Reason. There are two ways of estimating moral Actions, either by the Merit of the Performer, or by the Benefit of their Effects.[78]

Similarly, as Richard Crossinge began his work entirely devoted to charity, 'Among all the Duties which are recommended to our Practice in the holy Scriptures, there is not any one that is mention'd with so much Praise, or enjoin'd with so much Earnestness, as the Duty of Charity'.[79] The Augustan sermon or religious guidebook remained primarily attentive to the moral state of the full, interconnected society, rather than of the individual in isolation; morality and immorality might be determined by their effects upon social harmony and the respective duties of rich and poor. In this, the moral order envisaged in earlier Puritan emphasis on piety and godly preaching, contrasted with a more conservative stress upon the ease of salvation and the performance of Christian 'well-doing'. The importance of conviction was not entirely abandoned, however. To regard life as a sojourn between this world and the world to come, and one threatened by temptation, is also to interpret all social actions as bearing upon the possibility of redemption and eternal life. It was this which had impelled many radical Nonconformists to insist upon the primacy of spiritual charity, and was in turn rejuvenated by that Berkeleian emphasis on 'inward and sincere piety' which (however unintended) was to be so influential in Methodist revivalism.[80] As expressed by

[77] W. L. Doughty, *John Wesley, Preacher* (London, 1955), pp. 87–102; John Walsh, 'Origins of the Evangelical Revival', in Bennett and Walsh, *English Church History*, pp. 132–62.

[78] William Warburton, *A Sermon Preached at the Abbey-Church at Bath, for Promoting the Charity and Subscription Towards the General Hospital or Infirmary in that City* (London, 1742), p. 9.

[79] Richard Crossinge, *A Practical Discourse Concerning the Great Duty of Charity* (London, 1722), p. 1. He goes on to quote (as so many do) St Paul, I Cor. 10: 24, 'Let no man seek his own; but every man another's wealth.'

[80] Although as Walsh points out, very few of the Revivalists were reared within the doctrinal framework of Puritanism.

Berkeley in hundreds of sermons (only ten of which now survive), civil manners were not sufficient to Christian morality. 'If you are minded duly to put in practice this Evangelical vertue of Charity', he warned, civility and complaisance had to be accompanied by 'an inward, sincere disinterested affection that takes root in the heart and shews it self in acts of kindness and benevolence'.[81] Charity, worship, obedience, mercy, and justice were testimony to a saving faith. Although it was emphasized that this did not represent the meritorious election to God's grace, the concern to evaluate good works resulted in detailed, practical prescriptions for the conduct of a godly life. Good works could again be triumphantly shown as the reflection of an inner conviction and commitment.

It is worth quoting at length from one of Warburton's appeals to charitable works:

The first founders of the Churches, let the occasion be what it would, whatever Discipline they established, whatever Doctrine they inforced, whatever vice or Heresy they stigmatized, or whatever grace or virtue they recommended, Charity was the thing still present with them, and always in their care. Charity, the bond of perfectness, the end of the Commandment; that etherial principle, which, like the elastic fluid of the Philosophers, animates, connects, and ennobles the whole system of intelligent nature ...

Benevolence [is] advanced from particular to general; it now riseth still higher, from Private to Public. And thus, having a Community for its object, it wins and truly deserves its name: Self-love being now absorbed in the noblest of all social passions, The Love of Country; which the Roman Patriot [Cicero], in a philosophic analysis of its generation and constituent paths, rightly defines to be that which 'includes all social affections'.[82]

Others also seemed unable to resist earnest social lecturing. When Secker, Archbishop of Canterbury from 1758, bemoaned the replacement of mystery by utilitarian, prudential ethics, his emphasis on a morality above reason, and on a literal interpreta-

[81] 'On Charity' (1715), BL, Add. MSS, 39,306, fos. 25–75, and printed, A. A. Luce and T. E. Jessop (eds.), *The Works of George Berkeley, Bishop of Cloyne*, 9 vols. (London, 1948–57), vii. 28.

[82] *The Works of the Rt. Revd. William Warburton*, 7 vols. (London, 1788), v. 43, 46, 'The Love of God and Man'.

tion of Scriptural truth, still led him to a Pauline concern with collective, social evil and didactic preaching about the necessity of daily tasks and duties.[83] The abiding interest remained in the incentive to moral behaviour. It was indeed the potential effectiveness of the Methodists in this matter that explains the reluctant admiration for the Revivalists by such die-hard conservatives as Dr Johnson and Secker himself. The bullish insistence by Whitefield and Wesley that reason was not enough, served to highlight the necessity for charity, good works, and social example by dramatic words and colourful use of Scriptural authority.

Even more revealing in this context, is the most repeated charge against Whitefield's firebrand populism, that the new preaching amounted to little more than salvation by faith alone and certainly not by conduct. Anti-Whitefield tracts repeat again and again the necessary duty of charity. In popular plays and novels, Fielding's Thwackum, Foote's Shift, Pottinger's Squintum, and Graves's Wildgoose all exhibited—with varying degrees of sympathy—the consequences of Methodists practising outward piety, but ignoring the charitable duties. When Smollett the historian rounds on the 'delusion of a superstition styled Methodism', his leading charge is that they, together with another fanatical sect, the Hutchinsonians, 'denied the merits of good works'.[84]

So it was to be that in the representation of the merchant in the second half of the eighteenth century, practical moral imperatives triumphed in the broad apologetics for trade. Ethical justifications of the merchant's social role proved a striking fall-back in times when that prejudice identified by Defoe, 'even in England', was focused upon certain types of trader and manufacturer. Moral certainty could also delight in vagueness. 'There is no term, in our language more common than that of Gentleman; and, whenever it is heard, all agree in the general idea of a man some way elevated above the vulgar. Yet perhaps no two living are precisely agreed respecting the qualities they think requisite for constituting this character'.[85] Charity, benevolence, humility,

---

[83] Beilby Porteus and George Stinton (eds.), *Sermons on Several Subjects by Thomas Secker*, 7 vols. (London, 1770–71), esp. vol. iii, sermons vii–xi, on the duties of rich and poor.

[84] Henry Fielding, *The History of Tom Jones, A Foundling*, 6 vols. (London, 1749); Samuel Foote, *The Minor; A Comedy* (London, 1760); Israel Pottinger, *The Methodist; A Comedy* (London, 1761); Richard Graves, *The Spiritual Quixote; or, The Summer's Ramble of Mr Geoffry Wildgoose*, 3 vols. (London; 1773). Smollett, *History of England*, iv. 459.

[85] Brooke, *Fool of Quality*, ii. 134.

and service to the community became the leading qualities displayed by mercantile heroes in plays, periodical essays, and imaginative prose and poetry. Caricatures of merchants—as will be shown in greater detail in the next chapter—were moulded into stereotypes of Christian gentlemen, an ideal type in the commercial confessional state. 'By the middle of the eighteenth century', writes Pocock, 'the historically problematic individual, who could neither return to ancient virtue nor find means of completely replacing it, had made his appearance'.[86]

Part of that struggle is to be found in the anxious redefinition of the worth of commerce. The dichotomy between the gentleman and trade, popularized most dramatically in the dozens of merchant gentleman, brother to brother, or uncle to nephew cameos, worked to support the grand historical apologies for commerce and the new enquiries into the science of trade. But just as gentlemen were urged to recognize the importance of trade, so the brother or uncle merchant was presented in no less a role than that of a model for social, ethical, and religious virtue. He was judged by those moral criteria by which the condition of gentility had for so long been sanctioned and applauded, and the occupation of merchant was justified by a bourgeois ideal of gentlemanliness, based upon ideas of responsibility and service. Virtue was 'not confin'd to Place or Condition', gentility could 'sparkle in sackcloth',[87] and Edmund Burke could offer the example of the merchant as a safeguard to society:

To be amongst rich traders, who from their success are presumed to have sharp and vigorous understandings, and to possess the virtues of diligence, order, constancy, and regularity, and to have cultivated an habitual regard to commutative justice—These are the circumstances of men who form what I should call a natural aristocracy, without which there is no nation.[88]

No aristocratic code of an élite, of a 'calling' based entirely on governorship, would have done. Trade would have continued to be viewed as separate from a calling—and indeed might have

---

[86] J. G. A. Pocock, *Virtue, Commerce and History: Essays on Political Thought and History, Chiefly in the Eighteenth Century* (Cambridge, 1985), p. 71.

[87] Darrell, *Gentleman Instructed*, pp. 9, 12.

[88] Edmund Burke, *An Appeal from the New to the Old Whigs in Consequence of some late Discussions in Parliament, relative to the Reflections on the French Revolution* (London, 1791), p. 130.

required justification in terms which really did analyse the commercial benefits of a trader's occupation rather than of his social merits and Christian responsibilities to the community.

In Foote's popular and much-reprinted play *The Minor*, Sir William Wealthy, Gent., and his brother, Sir Richard Wealthy, merchant, debate the value of their calling or trade. When Richard Wealthy attempts to marry his landed nephew, Sir George Wealthy, to a merchant's daughter, and, furious with his nephew's reaction, defends his trade, the dialogue takes a familiar course:

Sir Richard Wealthy: You derive every acre of your boasted patrimony, from your great uncle, a soap-boiler!

Sir George Wealthy: Infamous aspersion!

Sir Richard Wealthy: It was his bags, the fruits of honest industry, that preserv'd your lazy, beggarly nobility. His wealth repair'd your tottering hall, from the ruins of which, even the rats had run.

Sir George Wealthy: Better our name had perish'd! insupportable! soap-boiler, uncle!

Sir Richard Wealthy: Traduce a trader, in a country of commerce! It is treason against the community.[89]

---

[89] Foote, *The Minor*, p. 63.

6

DEFENDING TRADE IN THE PROVINCES: THE GENTLEMAN MERCHANT AND MRS GOMERSALL OF LEEDS

The best writers on the maritime power and commerce of this country, concur with me in maintaining, that there is a manifest deficit in the education of British youth of high rank and fortune, and of the sons of our opulent citizens, by neglecting to instruct them in this very important branch of knowledge, the commercial art.

Thomas Mortimer, *The Elements of Commerce, Politics and Finance* (1772).

TENSIONS between the defence of the gentleman merchant and the increasing condemnation of *nouveaux riches* traders, as suggested by the five-yearly sampling of the literature, were especially acute in those parts of the country immediately experiencing changes in local industry. London continued to offer the literary models and also the most realistic publishing opportunities for provincial writers. Those writing in towns most affected by new enterprise or new immigration, were forced, consciously or not, to balance the expected typologies and instructional ideals from available popular literature with descriptions and interpretations derived from first-hand impressions of their subjects.

Anna Gomersall of Leeds was one of about fifty women writers contributing to the stock of popular literature sold during the 1780s and 1790s by London and country booksellers. When first published, Mrs Gomersall was acclaimed as a penetrating critic of contemporary society, but public acquaintance with her work vanished during the nineteenth century. Her writing, in the words of her 1789 press advertisements, was 'occasioned by her

Husband having been a Sharer in the late very extensive Commercial Calamities'. Mrs Gomersall's noble but unrealistic aim was to attract sufficient public subscription to her books 'as may enable her husband again to enter into business'.[1]

The town of Leeds in these years presents an exceptional opportunity for study of attitudes to business and businessmen. Knowledge of the mercantile community and of new manufacturing in Georgian Leeds is especially fine.[2] The development of the eighteenth-century provincial book trade is still poorly understood, but recent research projects, led by the *ESTC*, have offered new bibliographical approaches to the history of Yorkshire bookselling.[3] Leeds boasted a lively intellectual community during Mrs Gomersall's residence. Joseph Priestley had been incumbent at the Mill Hill Chapel between 1763 and 1777, and Dr Hey's medical dissertations had won national recognition. Despite claims to the contrary, the townspeople and the leading citizens of Leeds at this period were not poor patrons of the arts in comparison to the inhabitants of other large towns in Yorkshire.[4] The now neglected Benjamin Wilson became one of the most sought-after painters of his day.[5] To great acclaim, Tate Wilkinson opened the first Leeds theatre in the Hunslet Road in 1771. For the next thirty years this theatre was the focus of a touring circuit which introduced the very latest plays and actors to the Yorkshire public.

[1] *Leeds Mercury*, 20 Jan. 1789.

[2] Pat Hudson, *The Genesis of Industrial Capitalism: A Study of the West Riding Wool Textile Industry, c.*1750–1800 (Cambridge, 1986); M. J. Dickenson, 'The West Riding Woollen and Worsted Industries, 1689–1770', Ph.D. thesis (Nottingham, 1974); and R. G. Wilson, *Gentleman Merchants: The Merchant Community in Leeds, 1700–1830* (Manchester, 1971), 'The Fortunes of a Leeds Merchant House, 1780–1820', *Business History*, 9 (1967), 70–86, 'Three Brothers: A Study of the Fortunes of a Landed Family in the Mid-Eighteenth Century', *Bradford Textile Society Journal* (1964–65), 111–21 and 'The Denisons and Milneses: Eighteenth-Century Merchant Landowners', in J. T. Ward and R. G. Wilson (eds.), *Land and Industry: The Landed Estate and the Industrial Revolution* (Newton Abbot, 1971), pp. 145–72. Also, R. G. Wilson, 'Georgian Leeds', in Derek Fraser (ed.), *A History of Modern Leeds* (Manchester, 1980), pp. 24–43; and Rimmer, *Marshalls*. The following account benefits greatly both from these works and from the publications of the Thoresby Society.

[3] This study has used the *ESTC* to trace the surviving output of particular Yorkshire booksellers and publishers and their London and country partners and agents. Notable amongst published studies is Elizabeth A. Swaim, 'The Auction as a Means of Book Distribution in Eighteenth-Century Yorkshire', *Publishing History*, 1 (1977), 49–91.

[4] R. J. Morris, 'Middle-Class Culture, 1700–1914', in Fraser, *Modern Leeds*, pp. 200–22.

[5] Alf Mattison, 'A Renowned Leeds Artist', and other unpublished articles and memoranda, Leeds Central Reference Library, Mattison MSS; and John Rothstein, 'Famous Leeds Artists and Scientists', *Yorkshire Post*, 21 May 1938.

A sophisticated print culture was also in evidence. More than 150 book auctions took place in Yorkshire between 1691 and 1781 and of these a quarter were in Leeds.[6] J. Richardson, probably the first Leeds bookseller, had opened shop in 1700. Hirst's *Leeds Mercury* began publication in 1718 and in 1754 Griffith Wright and his son Thomas established the rival *Leeds Intelligencer*. From before mid-century the rival booksellers James Lister and George Wilson competed for custom, and in the mid-1760s John Binns opened his bookselling premises, issuing his first catalogue in 1767. The son of a highly successful bookseller of Halifax, Binns had studied his craft under Crowder of Paternoster Row and pursued a career which made him one of the most enterprising and certainly one of the most knowledgeable booksellers in the north of England.[7] He established several shops and stalls in Leeds, with retail outlets on market-days in neighbouring towns and a network of alliances with other booksellers in York and Halifax.[8] The catalogue issued by Binns in 1789, the year he accepted subscriptions for Mrs Gomersall's work, listed 7,486 titles for sale. Both Binns and Thomas Wright became highly respected members of the community. Binns took up a partnership in the Leeds Commercial Bank and Wright was elected Assistant to the Borough Corporation in February 1787.[9]

Within this framework an approach can be made to the works of Anna Gomersall. Their sale, promotion, and reception can all be examined. Only Mrs Gomersall's personal details remain sketchy.[10] We know little more than that she was born in 1750, married in 1781, and died in 1835. Her husband died in 1814.[11] In

---

[6] Swaim, 'Auction', p. 50.

[7] Nichols, *Literary Anecdotes*, vii. 468–9. John Binns died in 1796 and is buried beneath an impressive memorial in St Peter's, Leeds. Much material about Binns is collected in Leeds Reference Library, Mattison MSS.

[8] From the 1750s Nathaniel Binns of Halifax had a Tuesday shop in Huddersfield and, briefly, in Elland.

[9] Leeds City Archives LC/M, M9, Admissions Book of the Corporation, 2 Feb. 1787.

[10] In May 1790 the first Poor Rate Assessment Book for 16 years (with property evaluations) (LO/RB 34) was compiled just after the apparent Gomersall business failure. The correspondence in the Temple Newsam estate papers (the obvious source for alleged letters between the authoress and her patron) has a long gap, 1777–93. The Leeds Vestry Committee Minute and Order Book fails after 1770.

[11] These details are pieced together from the preface of Mrs Gomersall's *Creation* and from the county archives, the Isle of Wight. Anna Gomersell and her husband, William 'Grombersell' are buried in the now razed burial ground of Church Litten, Newport. Mrs Gomersall died 17 June 1835; her husband, aged 57, 14 Aug. 1814. One William, son of John

the mid-1790s the Gomersalls moved to south-west England, from where Mrs Gomersall's family seems to have originated. From the preface to her last, appalling poem, *Creation*, published by the generosity of friends in 1824, we also know that the authoress lived on the Isle of Wight for the last thirty years of her life.[12] It is likely that Mr Gomersall did not recover from his business failures. At least he did not provide for his widow, who died in near poverty.

Mrs Gomersall published three didactic works: *Eleonora* in 1789, *The Citizen* in 1790, and *The Disappointed Heir* in 1796.[13] All were a defence of the merchant and the values of commerce. In each book the author fought a rearguard action against what she saw as rising anti-business prejudice. She explained the necessity of encouraging commerce in the locality, but was also deeply troubled by the work of fellow authors and magazine contributors whom she regarded as responsible for unwarranted disparagement of trade. The nation was becoming infected with 'narrow prejudices... imbibed entirely from books, whose authors, merely for the pleasure of sacrificing to their splenetic dispositions, have delineated citizens and traders as the off-scouring of all things'.[14]

What is striking about Mrs Gomersall's work is not only that she devotes so many pages to considering the characters of local tradesmen, but that she explicitly differentiates between types of businessmen and their respective social and moral worth. While defending the merchant Mrs Gomersall savages the upstart merchant-manufacturer and petty trader. These, the villains and buffoons of her works, are presented in direct contrast to her portrayals of the Leeds merchant and his family. The merchant is depicted as the repository of social rectitude, of charity to the

Gumersal of Chirwell, Leeds, was baptized at Beeston, 6 Jan. 1757, *Thoresby Publications*, 23 (1915–16), 271. For other references I am grateful to Canon Buckett of Newport and the Hampshire county archivist, Mr C. D. Webster.

[12] Preface, *Creation, A Poem By A. Gomersall* (Newport, 1824), pp. iii–v. Also evidence from subscription lists.

[13] Mrs Gomersall, *Eleonora: A Novel, In a Series of Letters, Written by a Female Inhabitant of Leeds in Yorkshire*, 2 vols. (London, [1789]); Mrs Gomersall, *The Citizen: A Novel*, 2 vols. (London, 1790); A. Gomersall, *The Disappointed Heir: or, Memoirs of the Ormond Family: A Novel*, 2 vols. (Exeter, 1796). All three books are now extremely rare. Until recently the only known surviving copy of her final prose work *Disappointed Heir* was that held by the Houghton Library, Harvard. A further (cleaner) copy has now come to light at the library at Schloss Corvey, Germany. I am grateful to Prof. R. Schöwerling, Dr W. Huber, and Dr G. Tiggesbäumker.

[14] Gomersall, *The Citizen*, i. 134.

poor, of discrimination, of the highest moral standing. The manufacturer or petty trader is depicted as deceitful, uneducated, selfish, and socially destructive. Moreover, Mrs Gomersall's characterizations were accepted, especially in London, as accurate representations of northern merchants and manufacturers. The authoress received high praise from the critical reviewers for her realistic portrayals of characters associated with trade.[15] Of *The Citizen* the *Monthly Review* wrote that Mrs Gomersall 'represents the manners of middle life with great exactness, and has a happy facility in sketching familiar conversations. Her citizen, the hero of the piece, is an excellent character, and well supported'.[16] The *Monthly Review* was also delighted by the characters in *Eleonora*, particularly those 'taken from the middle or lower classes of society'.[17]

Significantly, in upbraiding Mrs Gomersall for portraying the manufacturing classes with 'too much of their coarse and ungrammatical dialect', the reviewers did not charge the author with any distortion of reality, but rather with the too accurate representation of it. The *Critical Review* further claimed that *The Citizen* was 'more interesting from the humourous scenes with which it is interspersed, than from any plot or dexterous development'.[18] This humour was largely derived at the expense of an upstart wool-stapling family, the Elwoods, and their inverted notions of propriety.

Mrs Gomersall also claimed to have based her leading characters upon specific individuals. In the *Disappointed Heir* she writes of her heroic merchant, Westby, 'as it is one at present really in existence (though under a borrowed name) I shall restrain my pen under the subject; from a consciousness, that is so superlatively excellent, I am incapable of doing justice to it'.[19] Tempting comparisons could be made with several Leeds merchanting firms of the 1780s. The eponymous hero of *The Citizen* is almost certainly the self-made merchant Matthew Rhodes, one of the

---

[15] The *Town and Country Magazine* carried independent and encouraging notices; the *Scots Magazine* repeated verbatim the verdicts of the *Monthly Review*; and the *Attic Miscellany* and *English Review* closely followed the *Critical Review*: AM 3: 40 (1792); CR, NS, 2: 355 (July 1791); ER 17: 312–3 (1791); MR, NS, 3: 223 (Oct. 1790); ScM 52: 493 (Oct. 1790); T&C 21: 416 (Sept. 1789); and 23: 356–7 (Aug. 1791).

[16] MR, NS, 3: 223 (Oct. 1790).   [17] MR 80: 552 (June 1789).

[18] CR, NS, 2: 355 (July 1791).

[19] Gomersall, *Disappointed Heir*, i. 236.

most prominent of Leeds merchants in the 1780s. The Citizen's daughter is also given the name 'Rhoda'. Further vaunting her local authority, Mrs Gomersall's title-pages advertised the author to be 'a Female Inhabitant of Leeds'. Few London periodical reviewers could claim detailed knowledge of that town. By itself, however, intimacy with the subject was not enough. Of much greater importance to the acceptance of the Gomersall portrayals was the extent to which they squared with existing assumptions about the northern merchant and manufacturer, their characters and their life-styles.

Leeds had been controlled since its incorporation in 1626 by an oligarchy of urban merchant gentry. In 1782 Thomas Hill's memorandum book lists seventy-three merchant houses in Leeds. These ranged from the Denisons, dealing with £50,000 worth of cloth per annum, to the Mirfields, with annual sales of little over £1,000.[20] Of these, six merchant families effectively controlled the corporation, its magistracy, and the political and social life of the town during the 1780s.[21] In all, a dozen merchant dynasties dominate the history of Leeds in the eighteenth century. There was never any question of confusing a wool merchant of Leeds with a West Riding clothier, wool-stapler, or, in the early years, the rising class of merchant-manufacturers. Many leading merchants retired from business to landed estates, and almost all acquired country seats, generally for social cachet but also for economic interest.[22] Between 1759 and 1770, one such family, the Denisons, invested in large tracts of Lincolnshire, Nottinghamshire, and the East Riding. Of John Denison's eleven sons, one became Speaker of the Commons, another Governor-General of Australia, and another the Bishop of Salisbury.[23] When William Denison died in 1782, he left over £700,000.[24]

In contrast to the clothiers, many of the merchants were also descended from landed families established in the West Riding

---

[20] *Publications of the Thoresby Society*, 34 (1919), 37.

[21] Blayds, Cookson, Denison, Dixon, Lee, and Oates.

[22] This is still the subject of some debate, but even if we accept W. D. Rubinstein's warnings against automatic mercantile landownership, and note G. E. Mingay's argument that alliances with local gentry and nobility were made as much through marriage as by land purchase, the Leeds area in the 18th cent. exhibits a dozen or more clearly indentifiable cases of mercantile land-purchasing on the grand scale—for whatever reason.

[23] Wilson, 'Denisons and Milneses', p. 167.   [24] *Leeds Mercury*, 30 Apr. 1782.

by the early seventeenth century.[25] Proud of their ancestry and marrying into a local gentry in which they were fully accepted, the merchants zealously guarded entry to their ranks. An apprenticeship in the 1780s could cost £400, a guarantee of extreme selectivity in recruitment. Even after apprenticeship, a partnership could not be bought for under £1,500. The merchants were no caste, however. Early in the century foreign entrants such as the Busks and Bischoffs settled into the merchant hierarchy within the first generation. A dozen or more apprenticed merchants, including Medhurst, Rawsthorne, and Markland also succeeded in establishing themselves. A few, like the Elams and Rhodes, even advanced from the status of clothier or cloth-dresser.

Given the social background of the Leeds merchant, his aloofness from manufacturing, but also the possibility for a qualified few to enter his calling, Mrs Gomersall's characterization of the merchant becomes more understandable. Her merchants are gentlemen defined by virtues and accomplishments which are the likely but by no means inevitable consequences of birth. Mr Oswald of *Eleonora* is 'a very opulent merchant,—a man of great piety and liberality of sentiment;—his understanding and ideas much enlarged by education and travel;—he was in short the finished gentleman'.[26] Kindly, but economic with words, Bertills, or the title-character of *The Citizen*, is a sincere, plainly dressed, and patriotic Yorkshireman. Following such maxims as 'defer not till tomorrow what should be done today', he exemplifies industry, economy, and honesty. The merchant's frequent acts of charity are performed without ostentation and he will not 'plead business to excuse himself from the exertion of benevolence'.[27] He founds an institution to educate poor female orphans and rescues a young merchant from imminent financial ruin. In this, the Citizen's benevolence to the poor is strikingly reminiscent of so many of the glowing *Leeds Intelligencer* and *Leeds Mercury* reports of the munificence of individual Yorkshire merchants. An obituary to Rhodes concluded that 'the most unwearied industry was united [with] the most boundless public spirit; in the midst of his mercantile pursuits his heart was ever open to relieve the distresses of

---

[25] A minority, including the Denisons, did acquire their capital from wealth derived from cloth manufacture in the Leeds district, Wilson, *Gentleman Merchants*, p. 15.

[26] Gomersall, *Eleonora*, ii. 2.   [27] Gomersall, *The Citizen*, i. 146; ii. 167.

the poor, and to promote every species of benevolence and public charity'.[28]

The Gomersall works further detail concerns central to every mercantile house of the period: questions of inheritance, of apprentice succession to a partnership, and of the economic and social significance of the marriage settlement. The hero of *The Citizen* is taken on as an apprentice, not only because of his poor prospects elsewhere but because of the firm's own crisis of inheritance. His eventual marriage to his heiress cousin is typical of the marriage settlements within the Leeds merchant community during the century. In nearly a third of all merchant marriages reported in Leeds newspapers between 1740 and 1830, both parties were the offspring of Leeds merchants.[29]

The commercial history of Leeds in the 1780s and 1790s is also reflected in the portrayal of new textile manufacturers and their families. Mrs Gomersall was writing at a time when the calm mercantile control of Halifax, Wakefield, and Leeds was shaken not only by financial difficulties—these had been faced before—but by the challenge of new products and manufacturing processes. The last quarter of the eighteenth century witnessed the greatest changes in the Leeds textile industry since the reign of Elizabeth. In the worsted and woollen trades the application of machinery from about 1770 widened commercial opportunity, while the cotton and linen industry advanced into the West Riding later in the next decade. After the contraction in trade between 1776 and 1783, the subsequent boom attracted new men into the industry. This class of merchant-manufacturers grew rapidly and ostentatiously. In 1781 there were three woollen-cloth merchant-manufacturers in Leeds: by 1830 there were forty-six. The wealth of virtually self-made entrepreneurs such as Marshall, Benyon, and Bowers was both quickly created and soon in excess of that of many traditional merchanting firms.[30]

These entrants to the woollen and linen trades do not fare well in contemporary literature. Mrs Gomersall identified three major objections: the vulgarity of their families and values; unacceptable haste in rising through the ranks; and the rude disturbance to existing civic and political order. Dozens of Mrs Gomersall's

---

[28] *Leeds Intelligencer*, 20 Sept. 1802.   [29] Wilson, *Gentlemen Merchants*, p. 212.

[30] Pat Hudson has recently confirmed the merchant-manufacturers' key role in financing and factory building, *Industrial Capitalism*, pp. 261–2.

characters, led by 'Old Ringworth' in *Eleonora,* display the follies
of those unqualified to receive riches overnight. Ringworth, his
wife, and son, quickly amass a fortune of £3,000 and 'fancied they
possessed vast perfections'. Although their capital is far short of
the wealth of the leading merchants, 'in company their conversation turned upon their abundant wealth'.[31] The Ringworth heir
is a tonnish vulgarian. He has sacrificed his health and prospects
by gaming and other delights of the town and yet is bereft of all
social accomplishments. In the same novel, the widow Grigson
demonstrates her unsuitability as the beneficiary of a fortune.
Fanny Elwood, the manufacturer's daughter of *The Citizen,*
who specializes in 'the artful machinations of a vile designing
creature', is 'a painted jade' who eventually marries 'a beau of
affected gentility'.[32] Guilty of the greatest of vices, dissimulation,
she is 'made up of art, inside and out'. Fanny becomes the mistress
of several London peers, and in the closing chapter 'suffered the
natural consequence of her abandoned conduct'. She is carried
into the Poultry Compter, 'her face flushed with liquor; her person emaciated with disease; and reduced almost to a skeleton—
Her dress tawdry, ragged and dirty. The offence with which she
was charged ... was such as would subject her to the severest
punishment of the law'. This she escapes, expiring 'in a state of
insensibility and intoxication too horrid to be described'.[33] Sixty
years later, in industrial Manchester, *Mary Barton*'s Aunt Esther
reappears in the denouement to die and reveal the consequences
of aspiring to gentility and fashion upon the receipt of even a little
new income. Fanny Elwood was an earlier equivalent, but one
drawn as the daughter of a new-rich wool-stapler with £1,000 in
assets.

What determine the worth of both established and new men of
commerce in Mrs Gomersall's fiction are questions of inheritance
and education. Her despised traders belong to the more recent
groups of entrants to merchant and now manufacturing ranks.
Such men contrasted sharply in background and substance with
former *arrivistes.* Even the *émigré* merchants of early in the
century were men of substantial means, while the apprenticed

[31] Gomersall, *Eleonora,* ii. 12. In an apparent printer's error, Ringworth is introduced in
the novel as 'Ringwood'.
[32] Gomersall, *The Citizen,* i. 78, 89, 117; 'Her mind has lain fallow from birth; and the soil
is now overrun with weeds', i. 69.
[33] Ibid. ii. 209–10.

merchants necessarily derived from wealthy families. All were men of accomplishment and commercial training. By contrast, Montgomery cannot

avoid perceiving in both [Mr and Mrs Elwood] many [defects] so glaring as totally unfit them for polite circles—Nor is it to be wondered at, if we consider their situation a few years back, when Mr. Elwood lived in a house not many degrees superior to a cottage, his occupation that of a working manufacturer [i.e. clothier or below]. By the exertions of his own and his wife's industry, he, at length, realized a sum sufficient to purchase a tolerable quantity of wool; part of which he used in his business, and the rest he sold amongst those who could only buy a small quantity at a time: this by degrees, increased his property, and the death of a relation in London, who bequeathed him five hundred and his daughter a thousand pounds, enabled him to remove, with his family, to Leeds—commence the business of wool-stapler—and rise into a style of more gentility—Yet, his want of education will forever preclude his claim to the title gentleman.[34]

Here Mrs Gomersall was faced by a contradiction. Elwood, a clothier from the hills around Leeds, has worked laudably hard, but in so doing has exceeded his station: 'Do these circumstances render him [Elwood] less estimable?', enquires Montgomery. 'Surely the man who raises himself by honest industry has a claim to general respect, and deserves to be esteemed as a valuable member of the community'. In answer, his father agrees, but with heavy qualification:

No one entertains a higher respect for the character of honest industry than myself: but give me leave to observe, at the same time, that tho' we respect the man for his useful qualities, and the propriety with which he conducts himself, in that sphere wherein it has pleased providence to place him, yet those who possess the superior advantages of birth, fortune and education united, cannot avoid considering the want of those advantages, particularly the latter, as an insurmountable barrier in the way of matrimonial alliances or social intercourses.[35]

The author measures social acceptability by the velocity of social climbing, starting-line assets, and the birth-test of knowing what to do with newly and suddenly acquired commercial fortunes.[36]

---

[34] Ibid. i. 65–6.   [35] Ibid. i. 67.

[36] This is often subtle: Gomersall differentiates, for example, between the elder Elwoods and their daughter. The mother and father are preposterous and vulgar, but at least 'appear what they are'. Fanny, however, 'wishes to appear what she is not, nor has any right to aspire to'.

Mrs Gomersall has great amusement with her vulgar characters. The widow Grigson is suddenly worth £40,000 and cavorts indecorously through *Eleonora*'s promenades and balls. These social gatherings, she announces, make her 'all over of a muck sweat'. When Mrs Grigson is tricked into marrying a sharper who sells all her stocks, Eleonora felt no sorrow but 'on the contrary, I considered she was only returning to that sphere of life, for which providence had originally designed her for; for which she was by nature and education best fitted'.[37]

Consistent with this argument, the virtue of Mrs Gomersall's characters associated with the East India Company was dependent upon the speed of acquisition and the nature of dispersal of wealth as well as the inherent qualities of the participants. Eleonora is ultimately given the hand of one Carlton, who is introduced with a new commission in the East India Company and whose search for a fortune in the sub-continent is a recurrent allusion throughout the novel. Carlton, like the returned nabob, Mr Delmore, knows how to handle wealth. By contrast, Mrs Gomersall presents Delmore's wife and daughter as the typical stereotyped spoilt dependants of the rich Company servant.[38] Mrs Gomersall also adopts the trick so beloved of Fanny Burney in *Evelina* of a comic reversal of the use of the term 'vulgar'. The wrong-headedness of Mrs Delmore's opinions are shown by her exclaiming against her daughter being sent to a local school—'a vulgar proposal'—because the girl would mix with the sons and daughters of traders.

But how accurate were these imaginative portrayals of the *arriviste* businessmen? In certain respects, the new captains of industry led by William Marshall and Benjamin Gott were not as dramatically different in outlook and upbringing from the merchants as the Gomersall novels would suggest. As a merchant apprentice Marshall had learned accounts, the principles of commerce, geography, languages, and the skills of correspondence. Gott had also been apprenticed to a leading Leeds firm. At the end of their lives they both lived as country gentleman in much the same fashion as the established merchants of the 1780s.

<hr />

[37] Gomersall, *Eleonora*, i. 129, 160.

[38] Their types can be found in the novels of Mrs Smith and Mrs Parsons and in other contemporary favourites such as Graves's *Plexippus: or, The Aspiring Plebeian*, 2 vols. (London, 1790), and Mrs Hervey's *Louisa*.

Why then the attack upon the new men? How had circumstances changed in the reception of successful merchants between the 1720s and the 1780s? One consideration has to be religious association: as every account notes, by the mid-nineteenth century, Leeds politics hinged on the opposition between Anglican Toryism and Dissenting and largely new-manufacturing Liberalism. Rimmer suggests that the merchant oligarchy shunned the Nonconformist Marshall as they had blocked the advancement of another dissenter, Armitage. However, Mrs Gomersall's works reflect no division between merchants and manufacturers according to religious affiliation. She seems to have considerable admiration for dissenters. Mrs Wright, tutor to Eleonora, and the wife of the dissenting minister, is regarded as an angel by the local community. More than that, she readily appreciates the full worth of trade.[39]

In the 1780s, however, the great changes taking place in textile manufacture in Leeds brought other fears and hostilities. Although in comparison with later manufacturers, new men such as Gott and Marshall had advanced by traditional and respectable means and were to end their days in traditional and respectable style, the initial successes of the merchant-manufacturers were derided by the established oligarchy. When the local booksellers were advertising *The Citizen*, the *Leeds Intelligencer* was publishing a number of charges against upstart manufacturers, and the corporation sought to check any disturbance to the political life of the community. In his early years, Marshall found all paths to local influence blocked. Socially he was tolerated and yet also regarded as an outcast. In the Leeds library catalogues the selective appellation 'Esq' in the subscribers' lists was not appended to the names of the merchant-manufacturers, even though many of them had been accepted as near-founder members.[40] Rimmer describes how in middle life Marshall grew 'increasingly aware of the social limitations of self-made wealth'.[41] Nevertheless, this was to change within a decade or so. Even in

---

[39] She is also incensed by the 'inhumanity' of Eleonora's 'despicable relations', the trade-loathing Bartons, *Eleonora*, i. 34.

[40] *A Compleat Catalogue of the Books in the Circulating Library at Leeds; a Copy of the Laws, As they are now in Force; and a List of the Subscribers* (Leeds, printed by Thomas Wright, 1785), Munby Collection, Cambridge University Library. Jeremiah Marshall and his family held subscription no. 80.

[41] Rimmer, *Marshalls*, pp. 20, 97-8.

the late 1780s the *Leeds Mercury* was able to announce marriages and charitable donations by 'very eminent wool-staplers' and the merchants were just as exercised by Methodism and the possibility of food riots as by the threat posed by the manufacturers.

At another level, however, Mrs Gomersall does portray a very real fear expressed by the mercantile class: the possibility of disastrous marriage. As can be seen from the wordy accounts in local newspapers of merchant marriages, and more especially, of the character of the bride, merchants and their heirs looked to more than just the financial settlement in the choice of a wife. In addition to the formal ranking of the merchant in the corporation, vestry, church-pews, even the library and theatre, the accomplishments of the merchant's wife set the social tone of the family and firm. Her social poise decided her husband's respectability. The vulgarity of a tuft-hunting manufacturer's daughter was more than a laughing matter. Even the London reviewers, delighted and also shocked by the vulgar caricatures in the Gomersall works, probably underestimated the importance of the subject in Leeds.

Even if such local writing and caricature can be related directly to the changes in the textile industry in the late 1780s, there remains one outstanding feature of Mrs Gomersall's characterization of the heroic merchant. The gentlemanliness of merchants is patiently explained to what is expected to be a sceptical audience. Following Lillo, Brooke, and other examples discussed in the previous chapter, Mrs Gomersall's central design in all her works is to articulate and then refute specific prejudices against men of commerce. Through Montgomery in *The Citizen*, Gomersall gives a hearing to the anticipated objections to the merchant. Denied the fortune which he had confidently expected to inherit, Montgomery does not know where to turn. 'Trade I am wholly a stranger to', he reflects, 'nor do I think I could bring my mind to submit to all the servile situations which the trader must necessarily be thrown into very frequently'.[42] Bertills welcomes his anti-trade nephew into his business and re-educates him in his attitudes towards commerce. As a result of the example and instruction of Bertills, Montgomery reverses his beliefs and realizes the merchant's worth: 'how noble, how generous, how exalted in his conduct!'[43] The young man has learnt his lesson well and is

[42] Gomersall, *The Citizen*, i. 126.   [43] Ibid. ii. 67.

rewarded with the hand of Bertill's beautiful and virtuous daughter.

In addition to aristocratic snobbery of the commercial, the objections to the merchant which Mrs Gomersall anticipates are those of avaricious profit-making and unmannerly social conduct. If the first is reminiscent of nineteenth-century disdain for manufacturers and 'shoppy people', the last two objections are close to her criticism of upstart manufacturers. Montgomery is reluctant to apply to his uncle Bertills who 'must of course have imbibed opinions and sentiments despicably narrow and contracted'. He was convinced that 'it would be romantic indeed to build a hope upon the generosity of a man, who, in the city phrase, knows the value of money'. Sir Edward Melworth upbraids Montgomery for this attitude, praising the benefits of commerce, denying that a mercantile or city life 'should make him less of a gentleman in his manners', and urging Montgomery to disregard the anti-trading prejudices of contemporary literature.[44]

Mrs Gomersall attacks anti-business prejudice where this entails disrespect for the merchant or the hard-working and honest tradesman. Aristocratic pride is intolerable when it unjustifiably denigrates the talented man of commerce. Eleonora's mother, 'of small fortune, tho' of high birth', precipitates the business failure of her husband, the merchant Sheldon, by her insistent spending to keep up appearances during trading slumps. When both die of shock from the resultant bankruptcy, the orphaned Eleonora is cared for by the splendid Mr Nelson, a man of liberal education with the manners of a gentleman but who has always been treated as a menial by Mrs Sheldon because he was her husband's confidential clerk. Eleonora and her sister are abandoned by their mother's sister, Lady Barton, because the Sheldons' alliance with trade is regarded only 'as a circumstance highly disgraceful'.[45]

Convinced of the need to overcome anti-trade prejudice, Mrs Gomersall refought literary battles to acknowledge the worth of the man of commerce. In doing so, the author's defence of the benign British merchant was presented in a very particular tradition. While scornful of the aspirations of lesser traders, Anna Gomersall devotedly illustrated the integrity and munificence of

---

[44] Ibid. i. 127, 128, 134.   [45] Gomersall, *Eleonora*, i. 21.

successful, hard-working Leeds and London merchants, defending them against general anti-trade charges in a style familiar since at least mid-century. Her respectful portraits of trustworthy and generous British merchants were largely restatements of the literary portrayals flourishing during the second quarter of the century. Melworth employs Lillo's sentiments in praise of Bertills, noting that 'the engagements of commerce keep both body and mind in action; it engrosses the faculties; and, imperceptibly, exhilarates the spirits'.[46] With the importance of the wool trade gaining increasing recognition, Yorkshire was singled out for special praise. Tucker and Arthur Young both specifically applauded the enterprise of the West Riding, and as Dyer wrote:

> Of busy Leeds, up-wafting to the clouds
> The incense of thanksgiving; all is joy;
> And trade and business guide the living scene
>
> .   .   .   .
>
> What bales, what wealth, what industry, what fleets!
> Lo, from the simple fleece how much proceeds.[47]

Reviewers recognized the antecedents. 'The character of the citizen, though too obviously borrowed from the *English Merchant* [by Lillo] is well drawn and supported', concluded the *Critical Review* of Mrs Gomersall's 1790 contribution.[48] Mrs Gomersall was clearly fearful that rising prejudice against the trader and manufacturer would undermine public regard for the merchant. In order to dissociate anti-trade criticism from the merchant, she deflected attacks towards a bastard form of commerce and so kept her work within the parameters of the traditional defence. In *The Citizen* Mrs Gomersall deliberately set up the vulgar family of petty traders and wool-staplers to contrast with the great merchant.

There remains, however, the question of where the anti-trade prejudice was believed to be coming from. As seen, Mrs Gomersall placed much of the blame for the negative attitudes upon her fellow writers. She regarded books as the main distributor of the 'narrow prejudices' against commerce and had little doubt about their effectiveness. Even so, she did not specify any particular

---

[46] Gomersall, *The Citizen*, i. 134.

[47] John Dyer (1699–1758), *The Fleece* (1757), Bk. iii. The extract was repeated in Phillips's *Tour Through England*, 3rd edn. (London, 1811), p. 148, to stand as the commentary on Leeds.

[48] *CR*, NS, 2: 355 (July 1791).

author by name, nor did she provide any explicit indication of which readerships—either geographically or professionally—were most affected by the anti-business line. What type of reader, therefore, had Mrs Gomersall in mind when she composed the speeches of Montgomery? Equally, how idealized was the portrayal of commerce in Leeds? To a local readership, would the images of the merchant and manufacturer be acceptable largely because of the mediating influence of a strong and accessible literary tradition?

It is, of course, impossible to know with complete certainty what the people of Leeds were reading in the last quarter of the eighteenth century, but it is possible to distinguish both bookselling policy and bookselling success from the local newspapers. In each week's issue the *Leeds Mercury* and the *Leeds Intelligencer* contained many advertisements for new publications, book auctions, library lots, or subscription proposals. The largest advertisements were those on behalf of the London wholesalers, with energetic notices by Cooke for his *British Poets*, Bell for his *British Theatre*, and Coote and Robinson for their *Lady's Magazine* and *Town and Country Magazine*. The latter magazines were given particular provincial puffs. William Lane, the novel publisher, appears to have concentrated upon a few weeks of bold coverage. In the Christmas season just prior to Mrs Gomersall's announcements, Lane filled several columns of the Leeds newspapers with notices for his latest and forthcoming publications, informed country booksellers of his readiness to supply them with ready-made circulating libraries, and requested manuscripts for publication.[49] In the *Leeds Mercury*, Bell announced the several reprintings of Lillo's *Merchant* in confident headings. The play had enjoyed four issues in 1776 alone. The newspapers also attest to Binns's fame for buying up large libraries to resell. From his surviving catalogues, his coverage does appear to have been extremely wide, with a large selection of both standard mercantile reference works and classical imaginative writings.[50] Both he and Wright advertised

---

[49] The series of notices in the *Leeds Intelligencer*, 11, 18, and 25 Nov. 1788, amongst other examples.

[50] *A Catalogue of Books, Containing Several Valuable Libraries, lately purchased, with a large and Good Collection of Modern New Books ... For Ready Money Only: By John Binns, Bookseller, Bookbinder, Stationer, Print-Seller and Music-Seller, Leeds*. In the 1789 edn., *Eleonora* was no. 6343.

their own publications, Wright having the *Leeds Intelligencer* at his disposal.[51]

The catalogues of the Leeds Library also provide direct insights into the reading of a select part of the community. The Leeds Library Society was founded in 1768, after an abortive attempt ten years previously by Wilson, the bookseller.[52] The society's membership rose steadily from a healthy 150 at foundation, to some 374 by 1786. Annual subscription was five shillings with the initial entrance fee or share raised from one guinea to three guineas in 1786.[53] By 1780 the library stocked 2,300 volumes. By 1790 it contained over 4,500 volumes, and had developed a formidable body of rules and reader services, including reservation lists and individual ordering facilities. The minutes of the society, as well as the columns of the local newspapers, record lively debates over the stocking policy of the library.[54]

The cultural development of Leeds went hand in hand with local mercantile self-esteem. The first library committee was dominated by merchants. Its first president was James Kenion, cloth merchant and recent mayor. Successful mercantile families such as the Denisons and Milneses, accumulated extensive personal libraries and were handsome contributors to the success of Binns and other booksellers in the area. Amongst the subscribers to the Leeds Library, proudly listed in each printed catalogue, were representatives of all the major merchant families. The Bischoffs, Rhodes, Elams, and later, Gotts, were all members. John Denison and his wife were early subscribers.[55] The merchants also used the local printing presses for more than announcing the sale of property, the sailing of ships, or reporting latest trade figures. The *Leeds Intelligencer*, in particular, was used as a platform for commercial self-congratulation. In the two years before the publication of *Eleonora*, the West Riding newspapers carried various grateful addresses from listed merchants to Pitt and other

---

[51] It is not known how large the sales were for the book Wright was advertising at the time of the launch of *The Citizen*, Isaac Swainson's *Letters to a Friend on the Properties and Effects of the Original Syrup of Mr Denos*.

[52] Frank Beckwith, *The Leeds Library, 1768–1968* (Dewsbury, 1968), p. 12.

[53] Frank Beckwith, 'The Beginnings of the Leeds Library', *Thoresby Miscellany*, II (1936–42), 145–65. Joseph Priestley was the first secretary, 1768–69, and the second president, 1768–73.

[54] Notably, the objections raised to the purchase of Boydell's *Prints of Shakespeare*, *Leeds Intelligencer*, 1 May 1787.

[55] Wright, *A Compleat Catalogue ... and a List of Subscribers* (Leeds), 1785 and 1793 edns.

ministers, with full publication of the elaborate replies received. These congratulated the merchants and people of Leeds on their support of commerce and their personification of all the ideal virtues associated with honest trade, from examples of local phil- anthropy to the protection of civil liberties and the defence and enrichment of the realm. The self-advertisement was symp- tomatic of the control exercized by the town's fathers over the cultural outlets of the community. They permitted the theatre to open, they enabled the operation of the newspapers, they imported artists and architects, they effectively ran the local library committee. They, as much as Trusler or Mrs Gomersall, feared the loss of control over the press. In 1795 when a rival library was established in the town, it was immediately labelled the 'Jacobin Library'. It failed within two years.

The stock of the local library and the publications advertised in the newspapers and in booksellers' catalogues were certainly carrying in plenty the traditional representations of commerce and the merchant. A wealth of eighteenth-century popular fic- tion can be found listed in the 1785 and 1793 Leeds Library cata- logues. These included not only such standard authors as Smol- lett, Richardson, Fielding, and Sterne, but also the latest works of Charlotte Smith, and volumes by Frances Brooke, S. J. Pratt, Robert Bage, Henry Mackenzie, and Charlotte Lennox. *The Fool of Quality* and Lillo's *The Merchant* were both prominent, as was a number of discursive contributions to the East Indian debate, *The Saddle Put on the Right Horse* (hot from the press), Samuel Foote's *Nabob*, *The Asiatic Miscellany*, Burke's *Charges against Hastings*, the anonymous novel *The Nabob*, and Major Scott's defences of Has- tings. Also listed by 1790 and of particular importance to the negative portrayal of commerce, were Mrs Smith's *Emmeline* and *Ethelinde*, Mrs Lennox's *Euphemia*, *The Devil Upon Two Sticks in England*, and Dr John Moore's *Zeluco*.[56] As will be explored in later chapters, all these works reinforced the imaginative divisions between the gentleman merchant and the unsavoury new-rich manufacturer, financier, nabob, or petty trader.

It is noticeable that the proportion of plays and romances stocked by the library increases with each surviving catalogue. The Leeds Library Society held 150 prose romances by 1785.

[56] *Compleat Catalogue of the Books in the Circulating Library at Leeds.* In 1793 *Eleonora* is at no. 847, *The Citizen* (two copies) at no. 875.

Imaginative literature represented some 35 per cent of the total stock, with 42 per cent devoted to biography, history, commerce, law, and politics, and 22 per cent to geography and the sciences. Between 1785 and 1790 three translations of the classics were added to the collection as against eighty-eight volumes of plays and verse and forty-nine 'Prose Epics'. The 1793 catalogue introduced the placing of asterisks after books which, though catalogued, could not be found on the shelves. There were far more stars in the fiction sections than in all the others, with de Vergy and some of the most melodramatic and allegedly socially realistic pieces included amongst the losses. Unless this was censorship by a back-door method, one must assume that the more sensational literature of social manners was highly prized material.

From Leeds publications themselves we can see the effect of the accumulated literary representations of modern trade. The few satires against commerce published in the town during the century were all attacks upon specific individuals.[57] Locally, the broadly based benefits of commerce had appeared incontestable. In the 1784 election, the aristocratic interest in the county suffered a crushing defeat and many local pamphlets were issued to explain the result. The earlier North administration was charged with commercial ineptitude and with failing to understand the needs of communities like Leeds. Steadying its nerve at the height of the commercial crisis of 1780, the *Leeds Intelligencer* reassured the townspeople of its confidence in the merchants—'Cool, cautious, frugal and industrious, they will always survive'.[58] Likewise, the newspaper reviewed the question of the recent succession of bankruptcies at the close of 1788. This, the crisis which felled the Gomersalls, was believed by the local newspapers to be the most serious yet—certainly in terms of numbers. The *Leeds Intelligencer* also warned that not all men of business were blameless. The extravagance of upstart merchant-manufacturers could initiate credit crises with catastrophic domino-effects for an otherwise decent, hard-working community:

One thing however, is certain, that while gaming and every species of luxury so much prevail among men of business, we are not to be surprised if bankruptcies continue more frequent than when men were

---

[57] Notably, the attack upon the merchant gentry by Berkenhaut's son in 1751.
[58] *Leeds Intelligencer*, 15 Aug. 1780.

contented with a more simple mode of living, and did not grasp at riches beyond their returns of trade.[59]

In addition to such orthodox explanations for trading blight, the citizens of Leeds were treated to an even more black-and-white comparison of the merchant with the manufacturer. In 1793 the *Leeds Intelligencer* determined that 'clothiers cannot more consult their true interest than by behaving with the strictest fidelity and most inviolable respect, remembering that by the ordination of heaven, merchants are superior links of that Chain which connects the various ranks of Society in the firm bonds of mutual necessities'.[60] The same newspaper was particularly critical of the activities of William Marshall and seemed to set itself up as the spokesman of popular belief regarding the actions of merchants and merchant-manufacturers.

The scenario was repeated on the local stage. Early in 1789 *The Lucky Escape* by the Wakefield writer, Richard Linnecar, was playing at the Leeds theatre, to be made available in print by the end of the year in his widely subscribed *Miscellaneous Works*. In the season after the appearance of Mrs Gomersall's Sheldons, Nelsons, and Oswalds (in *Eleonora*), and before that of Bertills (in *The Citizen*), *The Lucky Escape* presented Clarissa, only and angelic daughter of Worthy, a benevolent merchant, perilously close to entrapment by Cashlove, a wicked money-grasping trader. The playwright's message was that the merchant community must be rid of Cashlove-like delinquents who sullied the name of commerce. Linnecar introduced one Trueman, a dashing and younger version of Worthy who saves the day and takes the hand of the merchant's daughter. Cashlove is tricked into marrying a dowry-less maidservant—'if ever man had cause for hanging himself, I have'—but his most fitting punishment is said to be his ostracism from merchant ranks and 'the honest merchant's contempt of such a man'.[61]

The acceptance of such scenes depended upon the already idealized image of trade as presented by its defenders in fiction and drama. This apology for commerce never contained specific

---

[59] Ibid. 11 Nov. 1788.

[60] *Leeds Intelligencer*, cited in Wilson, 'Leeds Woollen Merchants, 1700–1830', Ph.D. thesis (Leeds, 1964).

[61] *The Lucky Escape*, *The Miscellaneous Works of Richard Linnecar of Wakefield* (Leeds, printed by Thomas Wright, 1789).

business details. Many contributing authors, as stocked by the Leeds Library and bookshops, lived in London and based their representations upon merchants of the City. Beyond vignettes of individual charity and integrity, there is sparse description of how the benefits of mercantile fortunes are actually transferred to the citizenry. It is not surprising that Yorkshire merchants and writers shared common concern that the existing representation of the gentleman merchant would be tainted by other London-based charges against ostentatious fortune-making and social climbing. Mrs Gomersall was clearly fearful that rising prejudices would undermine local regard for the merchants of Leeds. In order to dissociate anti-trade criticism from the merchant, she and writers like Linnecar deflected attacks towards the purportedly vulgar families of merchant-manufacturers, petty traders, and wool-staplers.

Such proselytizing style was certainly not aimed at Leeds alone. Here the patronage and readership of Mrs Gomersall and Linnecar can be examined further. Mrs Gomersall relied upon subscription as the means of launching her work. To announce the proposals for subscription, a single advertisement was placed in the front page of the *Leeds Mercury* and two others on inside pages of the *Leeds Intelligencer* and the *York Courant*.[62] It could hardly have been realistic for Mrs Gomersall to have expected, as she announced in the advertisement, to re-establish her husband's business from the proceeds of two subscription novels.[63] Perhaps she anticipated particular generosity from her patron, Frances, Viscountess Irwin of Temple Newsam, or from other wealthy friends and admirers. Perhaps she was influenced by the example of Charlotte Smith, who embarked upon a writing career after accompanying her merchant husband to the King's Bench gaol. After a flurry of publicity upon the publication of *Emmeline* in 1788, Mrs Smith was the current sensation of London and the wholesale booksellers. In addition, there were numerous local examples of successful subscriptions—notably that of Linnecar's *Works* printed by Wright. It had taken two seasons to advertise,

---

[62] *Leeds Mercury*, 20 Jan. 1789; *Leeds Intelligencer*, 3 Feb. 1789; *York Courant*, 24 Feb. 1789.
[63] She and her booksellers did insist, however, on payment at the time of a subscription—an insurance not without good cause according to F. J. G. Robinson and P. J. Wallis in their survey of the century's subscriptions, *Book Subscription Lists: A Revised Guide* (Newcastle, 1975).

but it gained an impressive 946 subscribers for 1,018 copies, or a virtual complete market-sized edition immediately.[64]

In eight months Mrs Gomersall received 219 subscriptions to *Eleonora* and 246 to *The Citizen*.[65] The first subscription edition was sent to John Trusler at his Literary Society. Mrs Gomersall assumed that all readers of the *Leeds Mercury* were familiar with Dr Trusler's work at his 'Logographic Press' and with his design to help poor authors.[66] Hers was one of the earliest publications of the Press. Although it is not clear how many copies of the works were sold on the open market, the likelihood is that after payment of Wright's expenses, net profits were not high. At six shillings a copy, total initial subscription to *Eleonora* amounted to £66, and to *The Citizen*, £73. 16s. Alone, these sums could not have covered the sort of edition publication costs calculated by Trusler.[67] Even an edition of 500 would have run up heavy publication expenses, with unit costs far higher than for an edition three times the size. It is probable, however, that Mrs Gomersall expected a buying and borrowing readership well beyond her initial backers. Certainly, the *Critical Review*, in a rare puff for an impoverished author, urged 'the success which she so well deserves'.[68] Most of the surviving copies of Gomersall works belonged to circulating libraries.

The subscriptions can also provide a more precise indication of the location of Mrs Gomersall's patrons. Fig. 4 shows the distribution of subscribers to both works.[69] In contrast to the predominantly Yorkshire subscriptions to Linnecar, both *The Citizen* and *Eleonora* were largely supported by subscribers from outside the West Riding and the north of England.[70] The majority of the Gomersalls' familial and business contacts lived in London, the Portsmouth and Newport district, and in various parts of the

[64] The earliest notice of the proposals I have found is in the *Leeds Intelligencer*, 27 June 1788, and the latest, in the same newspaper, 20 Jan. 1789.

[65] This includes the extra copies requested by a handful of the listed subscribers. Most subscribers supported both works; 30 individuals subscribed to *Eleonora* but not to *The Citizen*, 60 new subscribers enlisted for *The Citizen*.

[66] *Leeds Mercury*, 20 Jan. 1789.

[67] BL, Add. MSS, 28,121, fos. 1, 381, notes to MS copy of 'Luxury No Political Evil'.

[68] *CR*, NS, 2: 355 (July 1791).

[69] The two surviving copies of *The Disappointed Heir* (see n. 13) do not contain subscription lists.

[70] Most surprising is the support from the Warden, the chaplain, and some of the teaching fellows of Dulwich College. No copies of Gomersall works remain at the college.

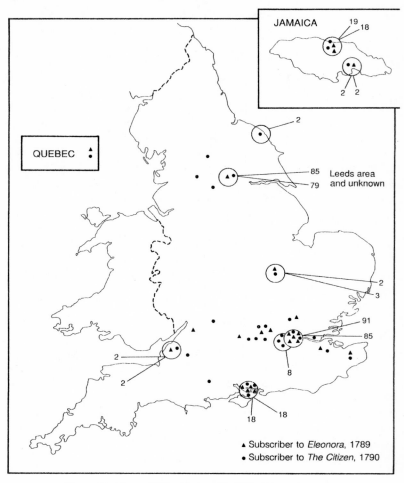

FIG. 4. Residence of Mrs Gomersall's Subscribers, 1789–1790

Home Counties. Subscribed readership was much wider than
known commercial centres, however. Many country addresses
close to London or in the Thames valley are included, as well as a
good sprinkling of aristocratic and clerical households. This does
help to explain the didacticism of her portrayals: Mrs Gomersall
seems to have had good grounds for expecting a large part of her
audience to be untutored in matters of Yorkshire trade.

Civilization in Leeds was an unexpected discovery for many visitors. As Boswell recorded when passing through the town in 1779, 'in Leeds where one would not expect it, there is a very good public library, where strangers are treated with great civility'. Mrs Gomersall's defence of Leeds was echoed in accounts throughout the next century (and not wholly absent today). In his 1821 address to the Leeds Philosophical and Literary Society, C. T. Thackray opened by agreeing that 'a notion has prevailed that Philosophy is not calculated for mercantile men',[71] and in 1927 Professor A. J. Grant, addressing the British Association meeting in the town, still had to insist that 'Leeds has no reason to be ashamed of the contribution she has made to the intellectual life of England'.[72] The point has to be that once again time was spent on proving what Leeds and its trading and industrial community were not, not what they were. While the people of Leeds had a more than sufficient diet of confident images of trade to accept Mrs Gomersall's work, they must also have been aware of growing prejudice against certain products of manufacturing towns.

In Leeds itself there was nothing new in the animosity shown towards an upstart group seeking power and position within the existing order. Between 1550 and 1800 successive waves of immigrants invaded the established merchant oligarchies: the original gentlemen who arrived in the West Riding in the years following the Dissolution, the wealthy foreign immigrants in the early eighteenth century, the continuing selective influx from apprenticeships and partnerships, the merchant-manufacturers rising from the apprenticeships or from clothier status, and finally the new manufacturing barons from the late 1790s, many of whom had no former contact with merchanting at all. The hostility towards the new men in the late 1780s, so bitter and long-lasting, was not only the result of critical change in the structure of the industry. New tensions were also created from the printed and unprecedentedly public defence of controlling interests. The works of Mrs Gomersall illustrate perfectly the arguments used to gain sympathy and respect for the traditional fathers of commerce. In terms of its publishing and book trades, Leeds was an exhilarating

---

[71] Cited in E. D. Steele, 'The Leeds Patriciate and the Cultivation of Learning, 1819–1905', *Proceedings of Leeds Philosophical and Literary Society*, 16/9 (1978), 183–202.

[72] A. J. Grant, 'The Development of Thought in Leeds', in C. B. Fawcett (ed.), *General Handbook of the British Association: Leeds Meeting 1927* (Leeds, 1927), p. 142.

town in which to live in the late 1780s. Mrs Gomersall's writing has all the gusto of a confident preacher. A store of long-accepted images was available to her; they influenced both her writing and its reception. To this were added convenient, local, and new-found candidates to explain away the attacks upon commercial and industrial activities now appearing with increasing regularity in newspapers and *belles-lettres*. The local press and Library Society were employed to reinforce the ideological mainstay of mercantile patrician control.

Mrs Gomersall's writing also suggests the particular contribution to the debate made by more widely available imaginative literature. The growth of a female readership, of circulating libraries, and a new market for fiction, was paralleled by the concentration of popular literature upon domestic manners and social etiquette. The novel as conduct book was used to illustrate the vulgarities set out in new and self-improving guidebooks as deviations from acceptable, polite behaviour. In fact, Mrs Gomersall and her fellow local writers did not discuss in any detail the economic benefits of the existing trading and industrial structure in the West Riding. So close to commercial and industrial society, Mrs Gomersall deliberately misrepresented the business world around her. Despite, or indeed, because of this, she won critical acclaim for her realistic writing, for her idealized portrayal of commerce, and for her detestation of *nouveaux riches* manufacturers and vulgar upstarts. The personal strengths of her merchants are so clearly drawn that even the most imperceptive of readers could not have failed to associate charity, sobriety, politeness, wisdom, and general good citizenship with the existing mercantile community. Bertills and his like were always the gentlemen: the belief Mrs Gomersall sought to overturn was that a trading life had robbed him of his gentility, not that he had been born completely outside polite society and might now aspire to it. The leading Gomersall merchant endorses and is endorsed by the same key values transgressed by undeserving brethren in this and other contemporary tales and novels. Trade and its professors are ultimately judged by values extraneous to commercial activity.

The 'commercial' ideals of civility and philanthropy were repeated widely in nineteenth-century histories of Leeds and of British merchants and approved traders. In 'Who is the Gentleman?', the first chapter to John Reid's *Illustration of Social Depravity* of 1834—largely a defence of trade and manufacturing in Glasgow—the wise father ridicules at length his son's desire to abandon trade and enlist, like Montgomery, in the army. Certain types of worthy trade can still be a gentlemanly occupation. Parsons's mid-nineteenth-century history of the West Riding abounds with similar sentiment.[73] Like the early nineteenth-century obituaries to merchants and early merchant-manufacturers, eminent Victorian historians of Leeds, seeking to chronicle the contribution of the merchants to the town's development in the last century, focused upon William Denison's donation of thirty loads of corn and four hundred corves of coal to the poor of the Kirkgate district in the winter of 1776.[74] Beyond Smilesian accounts of heroic engineers and of Arkwright and Watt, very few early manufacturers were given any attention by Victorian local historians. As for their former adversaries, when commerce could not be accommodated within its traditional idealized portrayal, or the anti-manufacturing line was sufficiently explanatory or too powerful to require any qualification, the contribution of the merchant to the *economic* development of the region was simply ignored.

[73] E. Parsons, *The Civil, Ecclesiastical, Literary, Commercial and Mercantile History of Leeds ... and the Manufacturing Districts of Yorkshire*, 2 vols. (Leeds, 1834).

[74] Retold by R. V. Taylor, *Biographia Leodiensis* (London, 1865), p. 181, and John Mayhall, *The Annals of York, Leeds, Sheffield* (Leeds, 1861), p. 155.

7

VULGARITY AND SOCIAL GRAMMAR

The hucksters with their wares, their cries and their vulgarities are excluded from this to another part of the city in
order that their turmoil may not intrude upon the orderly
life of the cultured.

Xenophon, *Cyropaedia* (trans. 1728).

DESCRIPTION of the language, learning, behaviour, and status
of the common people as 'the vulgar' had been in currency since
at least the fifteenth century and survived through the nineteenth
century. The use of 'vulgar' to mean 'ordinary' or 'commonplace'
was still in evidence in the eighteenth century. As a description of
the lower social orders, however, the idea of 'the vulgar' was in
the late eighteenth century increasingly linked to deviance from
standards of taste. In much imaginative literature of the period,
'vulgarity' became less a specification of class and status than a
measure of disparity between social actions and station. The new
definition complemented rather than replaced its original
meaning. Given that the rank assumed by the *nouveau riche* was
deemed bogus, the continuance of the older sense of the vulgar as
the lower and unlettered classes underpinned the new usage.
Earlier in the century, the use of 'vulgar' was less complicated.
Defoe's attempt to rescue tradesmen from charges of being
'mechanicks' was an attempt to remove the slur of being 'vulgar,
low, base'.[1] As late as 1770, 'Peter Pennyless', apostrophizing the
poor, was simply proud that his family was 'distinguished by the
names of vulgar, rabble, mob'. Ten years later, however, popular

[1] Michael Shinagel, *Daniel Defoe and Middle-Class Gentility* (Cambridge, Mass., 1968),
pp. 214–15.

writers such as Thomas Vaughan expected readers to appreciate the double meaning of 'the vulgar' in topical skits about society.[2]

The changing definition of vulgarity was reflected by the dictionaries, themselves competitive publications vaunting up-to-date coverage and attracting avid contemporary interest. The first edition of Bailey's dictionary in 1721 offered a double listing of 'vulgar' as 'trivial, low, mean', and as 'the common sort of People, the Rabble'.[3] The equivalent entry in Dyche and Pardon's dictionary of 1735 introduced the idea of coarse and ungenteel, a significant transition and close to later interpretations of 'vulgarity' as ungentlemanly taste or behaviour.[4] The *Oxford English Dictionary* gives the earliest recorded usage of 'vulgar' to define 'a person not reckoned as belonging to good society' as being in a letter from Gilly Williams to George Selwyn, dated 1763.[5] Pinpointing subtle changes in usage is a very problematic exercise, however. The example from the Williams letter is certainly not unequivocal in its meaning. Similarly, although the *OED* lists several seventeenth-century instances of the use of 'vulgar' to mean lacking in refinement or good taste, none bear the unambiguous sense of the attributes of a person outside polite society which becomes clear in popular literature by the late 1760s. At about the same time, 'taste' was the topic of parallel debate in popular magazines and essays. Swiftly changing representations of 'modishness', 'the ton', and 'fashion' were supplanting notions that 'good taste signify no more than ordinary accuracy in determining, in certain cases, that two distinct things are the same or of different kinds'.[6] The recognition of good taste, or rather the lack of it, was to be a key feature in new assessments of vulgarity.

Literary derision of traders was not in response to unprecedented coarseness on the part of the entrepreneur. Irregular manners and accents had been the pride of many self-made merchants and financiers of the past. For centuries men (and some women) had

---

[2] *Sentimental Lucubrations: By Peter Pennyless* (London, 1770), p. 51; [Thomas Vaughan], *Fashionable Follies: A Novel*, 2 vols. (London, 1781), particularly Folly xcviii.

[3] Nathan Bailey, *An Universal Etymological English Dictionary* (London, 1721).

[4] Thomas Dyche and William Pardon, *A New General English Dictionary; Peculiarly Calculated for the Use and Improvement of Such as are Unacquainted with the Learned Languages* (London, 1735).

[5] John Heneage Jesse, *George Selwyn and his Contemporaries; With Memoirs and Notes*, 4 vols. (London, 1843–4), i. 264.

[6] *A Dialogue on Taste*, 2nd edn. (London, 1757), p. 4.

made their own fortunes or set up local industries, without necessarily being condemned by their tongue or gait. In the same way, country gentlemen from all parts of the country boasted a diversity of accents as great as in any comparison between the self-made trader and the established landowner. There were, of course, the age-old gibes, of lesser or greater destructiveness, used as convenient reproofs against the pompous and the ambitious. Defoe claimed to 'open the door to the politer son ... despise him as you will, he will be gentleman in spite of all the distinccions we can make', but he also acknowledged that he was 'willing to giv up' on at least one founder of a commercial firm:

Purse-proud, insolent, without manners, and too often without sence, he discovers his mechanick quallificacions on all occasions; the dialect of the Alley hangs like a brogue upon his tongue, and if he is not clown clad in his behaviour, 'tis generally supplyed with the usuall air of a sharper and a bite, and he can no more leav the ravening after money, *Fas aut nefas*, than an old thief can leav off pilfering, or an old whore leav off procuring.[7]

What was so different in the late eighteenth century was the fresh definition of social awkwardness and the particular consciousness of inferiority that went with it. Most tracts condemning parvenu bad taste presupposed generally accepted notions of good taste and propriety. Most late eighteenth-century writers mocking manufacturers' dialect speech presupposed a uniformity of accepted polite English. The period saw the escalation of London-based pleas for standardized grammar and pronunciation. Literary contributions nurtured and reacted to the enlarged social sensitivities of a middle-class public. In defence of their new commercialism, booksellers and writers boasted of their production of books of social instruction, from teach-yourself manuals to exemplary moral fables. Dozens of publications educated readers in the definitions of the tasteful. Some of these books and magazines offered straightforward explanations; many more presented subtly instructive tales which took care implicitly to congratulate the readers on being able to understand the message without having it spelled out for them.

The difference in the tone and recurrence of the charge of vulgarity can also be seen in the contemporary response. It was an

[7] Defoe, *Compleat English Gentleman*, p. 258.

attack to which the victims were clearly sensitive and the association of vulgarity with first generation merchants, tradesmen, and industrialists is still an appealing aside for modern histories of the eighteenth and nineteenth centuries. It was this which Miss Meteyard strove to avoid in her Victorian biography of Wedgwood, and which Smiles anxiously hoped to counter in his Olympian *Lives.*[8] By the time of their contributions, social labelling had become recognizably modern, with the widespread adoption of terms such as 'working class', 'middle class', and 'industrial'. In the second half of the eighteenth century, the emergence of a new notion of vulgarity was one part of that complex evolution of a 'language of class'. 'Class' was to replace 'sort' and other such terms in the linguistic representation of social relationships and groupings, but 'language' itself was to be in new ways an indicator of 'class'. Together with other behavourial traits, language was exploited as a totem of taste, politeness, and vulgarity.

It is in the commercial literature of the late eighteenth century that these new associations can best be seen. The novel, in particular, popularized revised notions of vulgarity, at first by occasional, flamboyant examples, but later, from the mid-1780s, by a brigade of stock 'vulgar' caricatures. Again, we must be careful not to claim that everything was entirely unprecedented. Stereotypes of the wives and daughters of tradesmen had flourished before, notably in the free portrayals of Restoration drama. 'City-wives', such as those of Gripe and Moneytrap, were shown as both grasping and pretentious. In de Bellegarde's basic guide to polite behaviour, the 'new-vamp'd Trades-women' exposed themselves to ridicule through their social pretensions.[9] Detailed mockery of false taste, however, was not conveyed. Recognizable comic types appeared on the stage and in prints and broadsides, but no obvious series of replicated models of the 'vulgar' served to warn and instruct. These gained currency only in the 1770s, with popular women writers prominent in boosting the definition of vulgarity as the deviance from particular ideals of the polite. In 1778, the Duchess of Devonshire's *Sylph* (advertised with *Evelina*)

[8] Neil McKendrick, 'Josiah Wedgwood and the Commercialization of the Potteries', in McKendrick, Brewer and Plumb, *Consumer Society*, pp. 100–45 (pp. 108–9); Eliza Meteyard, *The Life of J. Wedgwood* (London, 1865); Samuel Smiles, *The Life of George Stephenson* (London, 1857), and *Lives of the Engineers*, 3 vols. (London, 1861).
[9] de Bellegarde, *Reflexions upon Ridicule*, pp. 211–12.

liberally and unambiguously used 'vulgar' to mean 'underbred'. Fanny Burney, Charlotte Smith, and their imitators devoted many pages to describing vulgar women cavorting in the 'Vortex of Fashion'. Such characters became essential props in English domestic tales of the second half of the century. Later novels and serialized stories duplicated almost exactly the opening descriptions of the female vulgar. By the 1780s, a full gallery of stereotypes was available. External appearance provided immediate recognition of worth, rank, and character. Very similar patterns were followed in hundreds of Row and Fleet Street publications. Contempt was directed not only at the foibles of fashion, but also at the deceit and worthlessness of the pretensions of low rank. Readers of the 1790 season of novels must quickly have recognized that pearls and simple coiffure signalled respectability; gold, silver, feathers, and ornate hairdressing, contrasting vulgarity.

Given below is just one, devastating example of this type, from Mrs Parsons's *Miss Meredith* of 1790:

To our mutual relief the Jankins's were soon announced; when in bounced the mother, stuck out in stiff brocade with roses on it as big as a fruit-plate, and this in the middle of August; flaring pink bows, green satin shoes bespread with tarnished gold flowers; and her head-dress, O Heavens! 'tis impossible any description can do it justice. Figure to yourself an immense load of black hair, for the most part false, decorated with such a profusion of pink riband, laced lappets, and diamonds, that the weight was too much for the feeble, scraggy neck to sustain; consequently this pile of elegance fell from side to side, like the pendulum of a clock. An enormous hoop compleated the lady's dress.[10]

Such creations were reproduced in more than a dozen of the 1790 novels alone. They formed a distinctive subgroup of the large number of minor trading characters in the novels of the period. Smith's Mrs Ludford was introduced with 'her ample person dressed in a gown of fine muslin, a fashionable hat surmounted with a plume of feathers and her whole appearance displaying more wealth than taste'.[11] Mrs Harley, the source of corruption in *The Fair Cambrians*, makes her entrance: 'Her dress was excessively full and showy; her hair in the very extreme of the mode, and loaded with powder. Indeed it was necessary that the foundation

---

[10] Parsons, *Miss Meredith*, i. 75–6. The Jankins were 'the greatest treats you ever saw', i. 75.

[11] Smith, *Ethelinde*, ii. 122.

should be substantial to support so mighty a fabric of feathers and flowers as were placed upon it'.[12] Lady Roseville, mother of the heroine of *Louisa* and later revealed as a prostitute to Russian nobility, looks absurd on a country visit, 'her high turbanned hat, shaded with an enormous plume of feathers, her hair waving in ringlets down her back; her pink lustring jacket and white petticoat, and ... the liberal use she had made of both *rouge* and white'.[13] Henrietta Willmore describes the horror of being dressed by her unseemly mother: 'My gown was white sattin, richly starred with silver and trimmed with an intermixture of sable and silver fringe, my hoop sufficiently large, but my head was preposterous beyond conception! a stupendous structure composed of feathers, flowers, jewels and powder'.[14] When 'dressed quite in taste' by her hairdresser, the Duchess of Devonshire's heroine, Julia Stanley, is horrified to find that

with curls, flowers, ribbands, feathers, lace, jewels, and ten thousand other things, my head was at least from one side to the other full half an ell wide, and from the lowest curll that lay on my shoulder, up to the top, I am sure I am within compass, if I say three quarters of a yard high; besides six enormous large feathers, black, white, and pink, that reminded me of plumes which nodded on the immense casque in the castle of Otranto.[15]

In a popular 1770 work, *The Placid Man*, the joking element remains; the subject of the jest, the size of feminine coiffure:

'Pray, Madam,' said Sir Charles, 'may I beg the favour of the name of your head?'
'This, Sir,' said she, 'is *un tete de mouton*'.
'Pardon me', replied he, 'the air it gives you has so little of the sheepish in it, that I should never have imagined it'.[16]

The crucial point, however, is that by the end of the period, the subjects of almost all such fictional stereotypes were trading families. It was the dependants of the suddenly opulent who were most savagely pilloried as the carriers of extravagance and the 'Rage of Fashion'. The family of the businessman became an imaginative creation capable of explaining and illustrating the

[12] *Fair Cambrians*, i. 128.   [13] Hervey, *Louisa*, ii. 15–16.
[14] Mary Pilkington, *Delia: A Pathetic and Interesting Tale*, 4 vols. (London, 1790), i. 15.
[15] Duchess of Devonshire, *The Sylph*, 5th edn. (Dublin, 1784), i. 41–2.
[16] Charles Jenner, *The Placid Man; or, Memoirs of Sir Charles Beville*, 2 vols. (London, 1770), ii. 78.

horrors of parvenuism and extravagance. In part, descriptions of family life served as indictments of the individual businessman. The good governance of the family was an ideal repeated in countless religious tracts and sermons, from Baxter's *Christian Directory* of 1673 to Allestree's *Whole Duty of Man*. In post-Restoration England, argued Schlatter, the last vestiges of belief in the superiority of celibacy were replaced by a religious consensus about the positive moral and spiritual benefits of marriage and family life. As an ideal with its origins in the laws of God and Nature, the proper, paternal management of the family supplied a microcosm for patriarchal society as a whole.[17] On the other hand, exposés of preposterous wives and children avoided further direct accusations against the man of trade himself, and hence the charge that the author might be indulging in disloyalty to the commerce upon which Britain was built. Thus, even Mr Jankins was 'plain and decent (like what he once was, a wealthy tradesman)'.[18]

Such associations between trading families and new vulgarities were advanced intermittently from the early 1760s to the late 1770s. Their use accelerated after the recovery and renewed social interest of the domestic novel in the 1780s. There was also a marked increase in the portrayal of businessmen's families, however incidental to the plot. Of the characterizations of daughters of merchants in the 1760 season very few were depicted as worthless coquettes, and vulgar *nouveaux riches* characters were not instantly recognizable.[19] In 1770 Mrs Woodfin chose not to caricature the wife of Gravelook the self-made apothecary, a man 'now in the higher Rank of People in Business'. Gravelook 'had Prudence enough to restrain her Extravagance'.[20] It was exactly the sort of opportunity not resisted in the next decade. In the 1770 season *Delicate Embarrassments* featured an early caricature of the fashionable modern lady who was eager for her daughter to marry a 'sober, industrious, money-getting citizen', and 'very wisely opining, that an handsome fortune, though acquired by "filthy trade" (her own common expressions), would enable Charlotte to make a more spirited appearance than she could

[17] Schlatter, *Social Ideas*, p. II.   [18] Parsons, *Miss Meredith*, i. 75.
[19] There are two major portrayals of heroic daughters of merchants in the 1760 season: Polly Witts in *The Rake of Taste*, and Letitia in *The Romance of a Day; or, An Adventure in Greenwich-Park last Easter* (London, 1760).
[20] Woodfin, *Sally Sable*, i. 157.

possibly keep up for her, with her scanty income'.[21] Five years later the season of novels brought many representations of the giddy, foolish vulgarian, notably that of Lucy Lightairs, daughter of the considerable tradesman in *The Adventures of a Corkscrew*. In the 1780 offerings, the tawdry Cokers were emphatically traders, and *The Relapse* indulged in a florid description of Mrs Palmerstone, with her 'scarlet face' and 'various carbuncles', as a shop-soiled dependant of commerce.[22]

Certain writers exercised a disproportionate influence. In particular, the early work of Fanny Burney popularized the vulgar trader. According to Burney at least, Dr Johnson marvelled at her vulgar characters, particularly enjoying Mr Smith of *Evelina*: 'such a fine varnish of low politeness!—such a struggle to appear a gentleman! ... there is no character better drawn anywhere—in any book or by any author'.[23] It was the portrayal of the coarse, trading Branghtons in *Evelina* which made the most impact. Mr Branghton was modelled on a silversmith from Snow Hill, a commercial district between Holborn Bridge and Newgate.[24] His family, as shown throughout and explicitly stated in one episode, are 'all *at home*' amongst the 'gaudy', 'pert', and 'low-bred'.[25] Their type was repeated in *Cecilia* of 1786, with the 'vulgarity and avarice' of the Briggs' household, and the characterization of Mrs Belfield, a trader's wife. The 'Burney-school' of novelists was particularly impressed by such low characters, and a rash of imitations followed.[26] 'Being a Branghton' was noted as a catch-phrase of journals and letters of the period, and later commentators were to accept unquestioningly the typicality of the Burney portraits. As Turbeville declared, 'In the Branghtons Fanny Burney introduces us to the typical vulgar aspirants to gentility. The Branghtons are characters in ... *Evelina*, than which there is perhaps no more faithful or attractive guide to the contemporary world'.[27] Burney

---

[21] *The Delicate Embarrassments*, 2 vols. (London, 1769), i. 2–3.

[22] *Fatal Obedience; or, The History of Mr. Freeland*, 2 vols. (London, 1780), i. 135; *The Relapse: A Novel*, 2 vols. (London, 1780), i. 220.

[23] Dobson, *Diary of Madame D'Arblay*, i. 72.

[24] Fanny Burney, *Evelina; or, A Young Lady's Entrance into the World*, 3 vols. (London, 1778). Mr Branghton introduced, i. letter xvii.

[25] Burney, *Evelina*, ii. letter xiv.

[26] As noticed in a review of *Henry and Isabella*, *CR* 65: 485 (June 1788); and in a comment on Burney's influence on Charlotte Smith, *AR* 1: 333 (July 1788).

[27] A. S. Turbeville, *English Men and Manners in the Eighteenth Century: An Illustrated Narrative*, 2nd edn. (New York, 1957), p. 72.

herself was most concerned with the authenticity and public reception of her uncouth Mincing Lane folk. The disadvantage to
her success, she feared, was that it would be thought that she had
'an innate vulgarity of ideas to assist me with such coarse
colouring for the objects of my imagination'.[28]

Impolite, shameless trading families were graphically portrayed in the 1790 season. The Jankins were in trade, and so was
the awful Miss Thomas (of *Plexippus*), the daughter of a retired
retailer from a provincial town. Her flawed learning leads to
disgrace and elopement to Scotland with her Methodist writing-
master. In *Arley*, the family of Frederick's trading uncle, Mr
Jonathan Arley, was carefully drawn. Country-bred Frederick's
reaction to his 'City relations' was fully detailed, being 'a great
trial of temper to bear the fulsome compliments, and overstrained
civility of people of low breeding'. Polly Arley was portrayed as
wholly contemptible. Her 'assurance and vulgarity' disgust
Frederick, she thinks only of money and material possessions, and
she debates with her father as to whether Frederick might be
worth £5,000 or £3,500 a year if she were to 'level the whole
artillery of her charms against our hero'.[29] The 'Lord!' or 'Lor!'
which preface all her remarks merely confirm her vulgarity.
Again, distinctions were drawn between merchants and the new
vulgar. Most heroines from the world of 'old commerce', like
Louisa Wharton, the daughter of 'a very successful merchant',
inherit their fathers' excellence only to find themselves rubbing
shoulders with parvenu petty traders, nabobs, or the sons and
daughters of common factory-owners.[30]

The concept of 'the vulgar' was self-reinforcing. In order to act
as a further moral deterrent, vulgarity was associated with what
was already deemed to be outcast from the public interest. Thus
gambling and attentiveness to cards distinguished the vulgar from
the polite. Similarly, poorly managed, reckless, or upstart trade,
could, like cards, instantly define the vulgar. Such associations
were explicit in Charlotte Smith's *Ethelinde*, first published in 1789
and reprinted three times by 1790. Mrs Smith, still writing to
support her family, was anxious to continue her honeymoon with

[28] Dobson, *Diary of Madame D'Arblay*, i. 37, 42, 49–50, 275–6.

[29] *Arley; or, The Faithless Wife*, 2 vols. (London, 1790), i. 17, 21.

[30] *Louisa Wharton: or, A Story Founded on Fact* (London, 1790), or from the beginning of this
period, the lively heroine of *Almira: Being the History of a Young Lady of Good Birth and Fortune,
but More Distinguish'd Merit*, 2 vols. (London, 1762).

the public after the success of *Emmeline* in 1788. In her second novel she included a range of characters designed to be accepted by her readership as amusing and instructional comments upon contemporary society. The novelist delicately crafted two impudent yet contrasting cameos of the domestic man of commerce and of the grand East India merchant and contractor. Both Mr Ludford, the Bristol merchant, and Mr Maltravers, the nabob, exhibit the vanities and self-assured vulgarities of the *nouveau riche*. The effect which self-made wealth has upon these characters was presented as the norm:

Mr Maltravers, like most men who accumulate sudden and opulent fortunes, was wrapped up in the contemplation of his own consequence, and in the project he was ever forming to aggrandize his family by procuring an higher title for Sir Edward Newenden's heirs.[31]

Newenden is Maltravers's blue-blooded son-in-law, and Mrs Smith lost few opportunities to express her repugnance at the grandiose ambitions of returned East India men to invade an ancient English aristocratic caste.[32] The Ludfords were similarly denounced for ridiculous and shocking pretension:

Their equipage was a coach and four; very shewy, and attended by four servants in liveries equally gaudy: for Mr. Ludford, though still in business, had no longer any occasion to adhere to the œconomics of mercantile life; but, having purchased an estate about three miles from Bristol, had commenced country gentleman.[33]

Respectability is further apportioned according to the degree to which the heads of the two families are engaged in money-making. Maltravers does retain an honesty denied to Ludford. Although Mrs Maltravers and her family are drawn as arrogant and irresponsible, the true lack of taste is displayed by the Ludfords. While Mr Maltravers 'was not interested in the commerce which wholly engrossed the ideas of his brother-in-law', Ludford House, boasting servants in 'unnecessary numbers', was 'built by its present possessor in a situation the very worst he could have

---

[31] Smith, *Ethelinde*, i. 20.

[32] Literary references to the nabob began in the 1760s. Foote's *The Nabob*, first performed in 1772, heralded the massive interest in the returned Anglo-Indian of the next two decades. The nabob became a stock character of the popular novels. Study of this question is central to the developing hostility towards parvenu wealth. It is separately discussed in Ch. II.

[33] Smith, *Ethelinde*, ii. 159–60.

chosen on the estate. The building was substantial and expensive; but heavy and inelegant'. Here, new wealth was at its worst. Ludford dinners, like the architecture, were ponderous and over-rich. Mrs Ludford treats her niece, the orphaned but high-born Ethelinde, with the 'affected pity and affected forgetfulness [which] was the mere insolence of purse-proud prosperity'. The true worth of the Bristol merchant's wife is affirmed by her con-formity to the stereotype of female indecorum. Clarinthia Lu-dford, daughter and novel-reader, is also dressed absurdly, look-ing like Marmontel's 'Shepherdess of the Alps'. Unusually, Mrs Ludford remains alive and unharmed at the close of *Ethelinde*, and is last seen 'in all the unwieldy splendor of recent wealth and self-created importance'. Miss Ludford, however, does bring the inevitable disgrace—an elopement to Scotland with a fashionable officer of the regiment.[34]

The periodical reviews stressed both the authenticity and the typicality of such caricatures, and applauded their moral design. Both the *Monthly Review* and the *Critical Review* delighted in *Plexip-pus the Aspiring Plebeian* with its high-spirited treatment of the appalling Miss Thomas, the tradesman's daughter: the author 'aim[s] at copying from nature, without distorting the features to render the pictures ridiculous, or the portraits caricatures'.[35] Similar critical attention was paid to the differences between the Ludfords and the Maltravers in Mrs Smith's *Ethelinde*. 'The sub-ordinate characters are well-preserved, and prove that Mrs Smith is, generally speaking, a nice and accurate observer', wrote the *Monthly Review*. 'Mr. Maltravers, whose consequence arises from money *somehow* acquired, and the family of the Ludfords, whose importance is likewise derived from their wealth, are very ably portrayed'.[36] Although the *Critical Review* found the idea of the Maltravers *passé* because 'they no longer have the attraction of novelty', it believed that 'they are properly, as well as characteris-tically, employed'. The reviewer also delighted in the more recent, and what was regarded as the even more authentic portrayal of the *nouveau riche* trading family. The type was said to be capable of effective and sundry reworking. In summary, the Ludfords were

---

[34] Smith, *Ethelinde*, ii. 122, 181–2, 186, 123; v. 316.   [35] *CR* 70: 97 (July 1790).
[36] *MR*, NS, 2: 164–5 (June 1790).

'masterly drawings, well discriminated, and supported with great judgment'.[37]

Acceptance of the caricatured trader, therefore, was urged as a credible and authentic representation of the living, and as an example to be avoided. In order to sustain the stereotyping of ill-bred business families, writers and reviewers reinforced the latest examples of deviance from social propriety and elegance. Moreover, in imaginative literature, implicit instruction in false taste enabled the reader to make a self-congratulatory recognition of the way in which social deviance was portrayed. It was a powerful means of reinforcing fashionable notions of refinement and unacceptable business types, inviting the reader to take pleasure in identifying the derided. It ensured the repetition and sophistication of stereotyped features and jokes. Particular play, for example, was made of inverted theories of vulgarity credited to *nouveaux riches* characters. In *Evelina*, Burney's shocking Miss Branghton has the idea that 'Miss will think us very vulgar … to live in London, and never have been to an Opera'. Miss Branghton 'hates the city, though without knowing why; for it is easy to discover she has lived no where else'.[38] In her diary, Burney delighted in describing how certain auditors at invited readings of *Evelina* failed to understand the cause of the general laughter over the Branghtons' speeches.[39] Many novelists incorporated an ironic use of 'vulgar' dependent upon the double meaning. In *Delicate Embarrassments*, the new wife of the former city businessman is soon lost to a world of frivolity and extravagance. She draws her City husband 'out of, what she called, the "sink of vulgarism" to the "centre of gentility"'.[40] In the 1780 season, Miss Minifie's vulgar creation, Emily, cries, 'A Coronet—A Countess—there are charms even to the vulgar in these sounds'.[41] Mrs Gomersall's awful parvenu figure, Mrs Delamore, and her horror at the 'vulgar proposal' to educate her daughter in the company of common traders was yet another of these comic reversals.[42] Such elaborations tantalized readers with the possibility of mistaking the socially unacceptable. It also heightened the pleasure in correctly identifying characters

[37] *CR*, NS, 3: 58 (Sept. 1791).   [38] Burney, *Evelina*, i. letter XVII.
[39] Dobson, *Diary of Madame D'Arblay*, i. 42.
[40] *Delicate Embarrassments*, i. 8.   [41] Minifie, *Count de Poland*, i. 104.
[42] Gomersall, *Eleonora*, i. 66. See above, p. 122.

transgressing the boundaries of the polite and destined for untimely ends.

All this was very closely bound to changing appraisals of refinement. During the final third of the eighteenth century the blush extended its domain. Delicacy demanded fewer oaths, greater personal hygiene, and the removal of new-found indecencies from public life. As modesty expanded, so the Wedgwood fig leaves grew more abundantly and capaciously, and the speeches of Shakespeare were shortened.[43] The eager reception and reproduction of the didactic vulgar caricatures was one further advance for the march of delicacy. The impact of literature can certainly be measured in terms of the development of 'taste'. The output of Paternoster Row and Leadenhall Street established and defended politeness and elegance, defined norms of social behaviour, and distinguished between the ranges of tastes available. Visible changes in social organization affected the standards and categories of refinement that were represented. Changing consumer preferences and the schizoid posturing of the literature industry on questions of fashion further sharpened consciousness of the polite. In this discussion, the 'taste' in popular imaginative literature was of a wholly social nature, not a philosophical abstraction. It was seen as proliferating, either as a derivative of increasing luxurious effeminacy which would ensure the decline of the empire, or as 'the superabundancy of taste' in architecture, furniture, literature, and the kaleidoscopic variety of consumer goods obsessing mid-century periodical publications and their imitators. Number 117 of the *World* (27 March 1755) considered 'the desire of NOVELTY'. Number 120 of the *Connoisseur* (13 May 1756) was on 'Taste' as 'the darling idol of the polite world'.

What is important to understand about such productions is their double-edged anxiety over the whirligig of fashion and the changing winds of 'public partiality'.[44] The modish public which Steele and Addison had discovered and cultivated for their own use was as anxious to copy new style as it was to discriminate between the compass of tastes presented by contemporary litera-

---

[43] McKendrick, 'Commercialization of the Potteries', p. 113; Porter, *English Society*, 321–6.

[44] A phrase of the opening number of the *General Magazine*, 1 (June 1787), 5–7.

ture.[45] A public anxious to read about itself was quick to appreciate cumulative judgements upon popular fads and fashions. The eager response of magazines merely fuelled desire for ever greater discrimination. Readers wanted to learn not only of fashion, but also of its excesses. Study of the outlandish and the grotesque would reaffirm the rules of polite behaviour and present object lessons in the observance of correct taste. Once again, social norms and ideas of deviant taste were established by detailing the bad as well as the good.

The most significant development, however, was that taste was being sold. Instruction in taste and discrimination was the basis for the popularity of the Row and Minerva novel, for the reprintings of children's guides to the great world, and for pocket books advising youth and young married women. During the second half of the eighteenth century, magazine contributions and tales conveying new ideas of propriety and elegant discrimination included highly successful and long-running publications. As a young man gaining his first interest in literature, Leigh Hunt adored the *Connoisseur* with its witty arbitration between models of taste.[46] Novels and collections by prolific publishers including Bew, Hookham, Stalker, and Cooke, carried earnest advertisements for the pocket-books and moral primers which formed the supportive encyclopaedia of *politesse*. Such works emphasized the necessity of both good manners and good breeding for the preservation of the polite. In 1783, Trusler, differentiating between 'good-manners' and 'good-breeding', noted that 'good-breeding is of much larger extent than good-manners; it includes all the fashionable accomplishments; whereas good-manners is confined to our conduct and address'.[47]

The key consideration in this was the producer–consumer relationship. Just as Wedgwood drapes were placed according to the anticipated class and sensibilities of the customer, popular literature was moulded according to an expected readership.

[45] Alexander Beljame, *Men of Letters and the English Public in the Eighteenth Century, 1660–1774; Dryden, Addison, Pope*, trans. E. O. Lorimer (London, 1948); Charles A. Knight, 'Bibliography and the Shape of the Literary Periodical in the Early Eighteenth Century', *Library*, 6th ser. 8/3 (Sept. 1986), 232–48.

[46] J. E. Morpurgo (ed.), *The Autobiography of Leigh Hunt* (London, 1949), p. 139.

[47] John Trusler, *Distinction Between Words esteemed Synonymous in the English Language Pointed Out, and the Proper Choice of them Determined: Useful to all who would either write or speak with Propriety and Elegance*, 2nd edn. (London, 1783), p. 3. The contrast was not included in the 1st, 1766, edn.

Issues were carefully selected in order to cultivate opinions and new subscribers. The literature so crucial to making rigid notions of proper behaviour and civilization during the second half of the century, employed other public concerns about social mobility and acceptability to pursue its sale of taste. Authoritative manuals poured from the presses expounding standard spelling, correct grammar, the rules of deportment and conversation, the right mode of education, and the correct subjects for study, contemplation, discussion, and emulation. Both compilers and booksellers were anxious to pursue public concerns as well as to inspire them.

The sheer volume of output is impressive. Conduct books, secretaries, even manuals of conversation, had enjoyed a long and distinguished history,[48] but now the pronunciation of words, the correct construction of a letter, and the minutiae of polite manners were addressed by a torrent of primers, pocket-books, and even serial magazine pieces and number books. Many accompanied the frequent reissue or 'improvement' of designated 'standard' works. The most notable contribution to spelling manuals was the reprinting of Dyche's classic of 1707, *A Guide to the English Tongue*, which went through sixty-four editions by 1800. His *Spelling Dictionary* of 1725 enjoyed a score of subsequent editions. George Fisher's *The Instructor* reached a sixty-eighth edition in 1800. There were many successes for schools, including John Shaw's *Methodical English Grammar: Containing Rules and Directions for speaking and writing the English Language with Propriety: Illustrated by a Variety of Examples and Exercises*, first published in 1778. Of the many guides to pronunciation, the most famous were William Perry's *Only Sure Guide to the English Tongue; or, New Pronouncing Spelling Book* of 1776, John Entick's *New Spelling Dictionary, Teaching How to Write and Pronounce the English Tongue*, which went through forty editions by 1800, and *Newbery's New Spelling Dictionary of the English Language*, issued in 1788.

A recent study of the printed language of the late eighteenth century has most persuasively argued that 'civilization' 'was largely a linguistic concept, establishing a terrain in which vocabulary and syntax distinguished the refined and the civilized from

---

[48] Since at least William Fulwood's letter-writer, *The Enimie of Idlenese* (1568) and Angel Day's *English Secretarie* (1586), considered in Wright, *Middle-Class Culture*, ch. 5, and Katherine Gee Hornbeak, *The Complete Letter Writer in English*, 1568–1800, (Smith College Studies in Modern Languages, 15/3–4; (Northampton, Mass., 1934).

the vulgar and the savage'.[49] As Olivia Smith shows, the new grammar books for English were offered for the middle classes and carried the obvious assumption that correct usage of English derived from the governing classes and automatically conveyed desired status, sensibilities, and standards of moral virtue. The battle for the middle-class bookshelf and classroom was a highly commercial one, however. It was fought at a furious tempo, and often, it seems, with little regard to any dignity for the subject. Many contributors were little more than hack compilers or writer-booksellers with a quick appreciation of market potential. *Trusler's Principles of Politeness* was sold as a work 'translated into every European language'. Between 1760 and 1769, at least twenty-two separate grammars were issued, between 1770 and 1779, at least twenty-eight, and between 1780 and 1789, at least thirty-one. Many of these titles were issued in dozens of editions.[50] Alston's bibliography readily shows the tonnage of grammatical guides, dictionaries, and instructors in writing, letter-writing, and pronunciation produced in this period. Robert Lowth's *Short Introduction to English Grammar* of 1762 went through at least thirty-three English and Irish editions before 1790. John Ash's *Grammatical Institutes* of 1760 went through at least twenty-one editions. Many, of course, were destined for the schoolroom, but many also were designed for the home library. The anonymous *Complete Letter-Writer* of 1755 had enjoyed eighteen London and Dublin editions by 1790.[51] Some primers and grammars were written by popular novelists and moralists. Alexander Bicknell achieved a notable success with a work which discussed and dismissed all his main rivals and provided extraordinarily detailed grammar rules.[52]

The keen competitiveness of booksellers is obvious in these publishing ventures. Advertisements, prefaces, and commentaries in the works themselves made haste to describe the social ostracism inevitably faced by those withholding their custom. This was especially true of the works aimed specifically at

[49] Olivia Smith, *The Politics of Language* (Oxford, 1984), p. vii.

[50] The most concise listing of these, with their editions, is found in R. C. Alston, *A Bibliography of the English Language from the Invention of Printing to the Year 1800* (Ilkley, 1974).

[51] *The Complete Letter-Writer; or, New and Polite English Secretary* (London, Crowder and Woodgate, 1755).

[52] Alexander Bicknell, *The Grammatical Wreath; or, A Complete System of English Grammar* (London, Baldwin and Debrett, 1790).

a young readership.[53] One of the earliest works of Dr Trusler, ever an exploiter of market possibilities, was his 1766 version of Girard, the *Difference Between Words*, whose title proclaimed its use 'to all, who would, either, write or speak, with Propriety, and, Elegance'.[54] Again, his work, like that of so many others, stressed the labour required to attain the necessary accomplishments: vulgarity in both learning and taste indicated a failure to endure the study of the essentials of social etiquette.[55] The emphasis of all such works was upon a uniformity of behaviour and uncompromising notions of what was and was not correct. The commercial opportunities for selling indispensable knowledge were not overlooked. For the publishing industry, its writers, and its entrepreneurs, the representation of vulgarity and the indelicate provided more than just entertainment and self-justifying instruction: it could also be the safest and most profitable type of publication undertaken.

Nevertheless, in defining the vulgar and condemning the purely fashionable, popular publishers faced an embarrassing dilemma. Within the magazines, anti-fashion and anti-town contributions nestled uneasily amidst 'têtes-à-têtes', other city-gossip features, and accounts of the latest dresses, nosegays, *coiffeur*, and cuisine. Literature itself was part of the fashion industry and supported by the leisured and the moneyed. Lowndes, the bookseller, recorded a customer begging a copy of *Evelina* in early 1778 and complaining that he was 'treated as unfashionable for not having read it'.[56] Other ironies of commercial double-speak were abundant. Minerva, goddess of both Arts and Trade, was the symbol and name of William Lane's prolific, and many said profligate, press. She was also portrayed in magazine frontispieces as the protectress of innocence against vice.[57] The first number of

[53] Amongst many, Cooke's offering of George Wilson's *Youth's Pocket Companion* [1756], 3rd edn. (London, 1777), and William Woolgar's *Youth's Faithful Monitor: Or, The Young Man's Companion* (London, 1761), and J. Rothwell, *A Comprehensive Grammar of the English Language for the Use of Youth*, reviewed *GM* I: 531 (1788); and *ER* II: 150 (1788).

[54] Based on Abbé Gabriel Girard, *Synonymes françois, leurs différentes significations, et le choix qu'il en faut faire pour parler avec justesse*, 10th edn. (Geneva, 1753).

[55] Trusler, *Distinction Between Words*, 2nd edn. (1783), preface.

[56] Lowndes to Burney, 2 July 1778, cited in Dobson, *Diary of Madame D'Arblay*, i. 39; and the original, confirming Burney's record, survives in NYPL, Albert Berg MSS, Burney Diary, pp. 673–4.

[57] As for example, *GM* 2, frontispiece, 'Minerva Protecting Innocence Against the Allurements of Vice' (1788).

Bellamy's *General Magazine*, carrying fashion advice and town gossip, could only assume haughty bluff to justify its publication as a reformist journal. Rival magazines were worthless:

Among the sons of literature some have proved rebellious to Virtue, and have endeavoured to lay waste her kingdom with the firebrands of licentiousness; while others have subverted her authority by satanical delusions.[58]

Hookham's *Hive* opened its account with similar blustering ferocity.[59] The expansion of the reading public in the provinces also increased the sophistry of editors and authors in their treatment of country–city issues. The dual appeal of 'Sylvanus Urban', fictional editor of the *Gentleman's Magazine*, was paralleled by that of the *Town and Country Magazine* two decades later.

Such attention to the dangers of fashion and the isolation of specific exemplars of the ton was a direct result of the vulnerability of magazine and lighter literature to charges of frivolity and immorality. Falconer, surveying popular beliefs, considered that 'the passion for novelty has, in the present age, pervaded not only our manners and behaviour, but also our studies and literary taste'.[60] Reviewers were castigating novel after novel as the immoral and faddish products of market-conscious writers and publishers. As the *English Review* commented of a 1790 offering,

All the business consists of assemblies, vanities, parties of pleasure, and the whole round of dissipation which absorbs the votaries of fashion, and which is nothing more than the reiterated collisions of vanity, pride, and insignificance.[61]

The result was an even greater, often desperate discrimination between the acceptable and unacceptable, the polite and impolite.

Once again, the general method adopted in popular imaginative literature was to satirize specific aspects of contemporary society as a means of mixing entertainment with instruction. As Cumberland put it in the introduction to his *Observer* of 1785, 'to

[58] *GM* 1: 6 (June 1787).
[59] *The Hive: A Hebdomadel Selection of Literary Tracts; Comprising Every Thing Moral, Literary, or Entertaining that has any claim on the Public Attention … To be continued Every Saturday* (London, 1789), 'To the Public'.
[60] William Falconer, *Remarks on the Influence of Climate, Situation, Nature of Country, Population, Nature of Food, and Way of Life on … Mankind* (London, 1781), p. 516.
[61] *ER* 16: 151 (Aug. 1790).

administer moral precepts through a pleasing vehicle seems now the general study of our Essayists, Dramatists and Novelists'.[62] Old attacks upon vice and folly were reworked, and the dependence upon Addison and Steele's early century models showed. Ridicule was to be aimed at identifiable men, and although many writers were now engaging in little more than generalized caricature, the obsession remained with isolating supposedly authentic fools and scoundrels. The alternative tradition of rumbustious, often facetiously crude burlesque, was clearly suppressed in all but the lower end of the market. Smollett was its last distinguished champion in *belles-lettres*. The aim of continuing satire was to reform the individual by exposing violations of good taste and illustrating the minutiae of social manners. Correct behaviour was outlined by depicting the folly and evil of its antithesis. The gentleman was contrasted with the nabob and businessman, just as the stately image of the prince-merchant was defined by gentlemanly values and continued in opposition to that of the petty, self-seeking trader. The association of vulgarity with the trading world also quelled doubts about the validity of other attacks upon the newly-wealthy. Similarly, deviance in taste was now highlighted in order to describe the respectable. The definition of propriety was a defence for writers and booksellers eager to prove their responsibilities towards the public. A detailed illustration of vulgarity eased consciences over the double standards adopted in the discussion of fashion and the continuing consumer boom, while at the same time actually promoting another 'fashion'—that of appreciating the current totems of respectability.

---

[62] Cumberland, *Observer*, i. 5.

8

REACTIONS TO FASHION
AND LUXURY

> Since luxury may be consider'd, either as innocent or
> blameable, one may be surpriz'd at those preposterous
> opinions, which have been entertain'd concerning it.
>
> David Hume, 'Of Luxury', *Political Discourses* (1752).

Iᴛ is only recently that detailed investigation has been made of
the consumer revolution of the late eighteenth century.[1] Much
work remains to be done on the nature of the demand for consumer products and the commercial manipulation of fashion and
social emulation.[2] One aspect of changing consumer behaviour
has been particularly neglected. Even a cursory survey of late
eighteenth-century literature reveals the extraordinary vigour of
published reaction to the take-off in home demand. Despite the
use by economic historians of colourful contemporary comments
to sketch the otherwise gaunt contours of increasing demand,
there has been little questioning of why these reactions occurred
and what their effects were. The literary reception of the commercial revolution—and the deliberate artifice of published outrage—was crucial to the formation of hostile images of the businessman and business activities.

Literary responses to consumer behaviour focused on the dual

---

[1] Jones, 'Fashion Manipulators'; McKendrick, Brewer, and Plumb, *Birth of a Consumer
Society*; Lorna Weatherill, *Consumer Behaviour and Material Culture in Britain*, 1660–1760 (London, 1988), and 'Consumer Behaviour and Social Status in England, 1660–1750', *Continuity
and Change*, 1/2 (Aug. 1986), 191–216.

[2] Early suggestions towards the history of fashion are offered in the collected articles in
Business History Review, 37/1–2 (1963); and H. Leibenstein, 'Bandwagon, Snob, and Veblen
Effects in the Theory of Consumers' Demand', *Quarterly Journal of Economics*, 44/2 (May
1950), 183–207.

condemnation of luxury and fashion. During the consumer revolution of the second half of the century literary charges of luxury gained new ferocity and social specification. Accusations were far more detailed and numerous than the traditional warnings of the dangers of over-consumption and a life of ease. Across a broad range of literature the evocation of 'Fashion' as a social evil prompted and was prompted by the association of 'Luxuries' with worthless consumer products.

Such reaction against fashion and luxury had various causes. On the one hand, concern was voiced over the economic uselessness of consumer goods and the apparent wastefulness of extravagant expenditure. It was an anxiety echoed by new manufacturers. Boulton wrote to Eckhart in 1796, pleased by the plan to abandon 'all his manufactory which depended on Fashion & taste & in lieu thereof is building Iron Fournices & Foundrys which he knows is more perminent & more profitable in proportion to being usefull to the publick'.[3] On the other hand, such responses often disguised more expedient reactions against fashion. A range of social resentments encouraged the isolation of supposed malefactors and condemned parvenu wealth and conspicuous consumption. In association with this, contemporary writers and booksellers promoted and reformulated moral questions according to changes in personal wealth-holding and patterns of expenditure. As A. W. Coats has complained, 'historians of literature seem much more aware of the significance of this point than historians of economics'.[4] In question is the relationship between the growth of domestic consumption, its social and economic consequences, and the discourse available to explain it. In order to try to understand this more fully, we need first to identify the popular literary reaction against consumer spending and fashion, and then trace its relationship to changing intellectual and popular concepts of luxury and the attacks against the flagrant misuse of riches by the newly-wealthy.

Although there remains considerable dispute over the precise economic effects of the growth in home demand for manufactured goods, there can be no doubt about the rapid rate of change

---

[3] Cited in Robert E. Schofield, *The Lunar Society of Birmingham: A Social History of Provincial Science and Industry in Eighteenth-Century England* (Oxford, 1963), p. 380.

[4] A. W. Coats, 'The Relief of Poverty: Attitudes to Labour and Economic Change in England, 1660–1782', *International Review of Social History*, 21/1 (1976), 98–115 (p. 103).

in fashions, begotten by growing consumer industries and an increasing ability and willingness to spend on leisure and consumer goods.[5] Despite this, the precise timing and regional variation in changes in consumption patterns remains unclear. So also does the exact growth in the output of consumer goods during the final third of the century.[6] Recent work on eighteenth-century domestic inventories suggests increasing expenditure throughout the period.[7] Lorna Weatherill's research in particular, while confirming that the market for consumer goods 'had considerable social depth, as well as geographical extension', supports the view that by far the most important and increasing market lay 'somewhere between the upper gentry and the labourers, that is to say in the middle ranks'.[8] This endorses contemporary impressions of an increase in material possessions at all levels of society and in the ability of the humbler ranks to gain material comforts over a working lifetime. But it also gives renewed emphasis to the belief that the key variable in the support of fashion industries was not so much change in average consumption levels as change in the distribution of income and the stimulation of demand among the middle orders. Only the general contours of consumption patterns can be guessed from the statistics available on the receipt of excised commodities. The changing distribution of incomes is similarly

[5] The effects of home demand upon 18th cent. economic growth is a controversy beyond the scope of this study. For the most sceptical view, Berrill, 'International Trade', and Mokyr, 'Demand vs. Supply'; and by contrast, Harold Perkin, *The Origins of Modern English Society, 1780–1880* (London, 1969), pp. 91–6. During the second quarter of the century low and stable wheat prices increased the margin between working-class income and expenditure, and also boosted spending upon consumer goods at upper income levels, Crafts, 'English Economic Growth'. A fall in the rate of increasing *per capita* domestic demand for non-agrarian products in the second half of the century (with obvious regional variation) has been suggested, and also that the *average* level of consumption did not rise appreciably above the level of the 1760s until the 1820s, W. A. Cole, 'Factors in Demand, 1700–80', and C. H. Feinstein, 'Capital Accumulation and the Industrial Revolution', in Floud and McCloskey, *Economic History of Britain*, i. chs. 3 and 7.

[6] P. Deane and W. A. Cole, *British Economic Growth, 1688–1959* (Cambridge, 1962), ch. 2, on the difficulty in calculating the volume of imports retained for consumption. Also, the pioneering work on the expansion of consumer-goods industries in Walther G. Hoffmann, *British Industry, 1700–1950*, trans. by W. O. Henderson and W. H. Chaloner (Oxford 1955), esp. part b. iii and table.

[7] J. S. Moore (ed.), *The Goods and Chattels of our Forefathers* (London, 1976); Weatherill, *Consumer Behaviour*; and for the earlier period, Paul Glennie, 'The Emergence of a Consumer Society in Early Modern England', unpublished conference paper, 1986.

[8] Weatherill, *Consumer Behaviour*, p. 193.

hazy.[9] Even so, the huge increases in the import of tea, sugar, tobacco, and the spiralling production of fabrics, soap, pottery, candles, and a vast range of other commodity goods of the final third of the century, are impressive general testimony to the strength of domestic demand for new 'decencies'.[10] Many colourful accounts record the Topsy-like growth of button, buckle, and cutlery towns.[11] The famous technical innovations in the cotton and textile industries of the 1770s enabled the well-documented expansion of the next ten years. These were also accompanied by experiments in promotional sales techniques and the manipulation of demand by Wedgwood, Boulton, and a host of lesser figures anxious to copy and compete.

The proliferation of consumer industries stimulated concern over the retail of inessential extravagancies, and provided increasingly recognizable commercial products to be associated with bad taste, vulgarity, and parvenu spending. A comparison between literary verdicts from the popular literature of 1760 and 1790 clearly shows the development of the attack upon fashion and of the association of luxuries with irresponsible parvenu wealth and the gaudy philistinism of overweening traders and nabobs. In 1760 the *Narrative Companion*, reprinting the *Connoisseur* of 1755, attacked the social pretensions of tradesmen precisely because merchant visitors to the suburbs were said to be dowdy and unfashionable.[12] That sort of attack was unthinkable thirty years later. By 1790 almost all popular literature identified a commodity fetish, assigned its origins to a new variety of contagious luxury, and identified its participants as the reckless newly-wealthy. It was argued that money wasted in vain gratification was as dangerous an omen for Britain as the hoarding of riches or the dissipation of fortunes in gambling.

The reaction against fashion, particularly against dress and

[9] For the statistical underpinning of most accounts: E. B. Schumpeter, *English Overseas Trade Statistics, 1697–1808* (Oxford, 1960); Deane and Cole, *British Economic Growth*, esp. p. 47; and B. R. Mitchell and P. Deane, *An Abstract of British Historical Statistics* (Cambridge 1962).

[10] Peter Mathias, *The Transformation of England* (London, 1979), pp. 162–3.

[11] Perhaps the most famous is William Hutton's *An History of Birmingham to the End of the Year 1780* (Birmingham 1781), with its record of the astonishing development of the town's industries after 1750.

[12] *Narrative Companion: or, The Entertaining Moralist*, 2 vols. (London, 1760), ii. 142–6, from [George Colman and Bonnell Thornton], 'Description of a London Tradesman in the Country', *Connoisseur*, no. 79.

display, was not a new English phenomenon, and discussion of the 'ton' had been a staple for many essayists since the early eighteenth century. Even the contrast between populist conservatism and the intellectual acceptance of fashion as an economic good was no complete novelty. Largely as a result of responses to East India Company imports during the last two decades of the seventeenth century, a new understanding was gained about the elasticity of home demand. Writers including Houghton, North, and Barbon rejected blanket condemnations of luxury as a threat to the balance of trade.[13] Barbon had even welcomed fashion, albeit somewhat eccentrically:

Fashion or the alteration of Dress, is a great Promoter of *Trade*, because it occasions the Expence of Cloaths, before the Old ones are worn out: It is the Spirit and Life of *Trade*; It makes a Circulation, and gives a Value by Turns, to all sorts of Commodities; keeps the great Body of *Trade* in Motion; it is an Invention to Dress a Man, as if he Lived in a perpetual Spring; he never sees the autumn of his Cloaths.[14]

During the second half of the eighteenth century, however, the increasing demand for consumer goods provoked an unprecedented reaction. The outcry was broadcast to a keener readership than ever before by the booksellers and their outlets. It was given new authority by the uniformity of so many representations within Row and Fleet Street publications. Protest contrasted more than ever with the now highly organized fashion industries, the pace of change, and the published advertisements, prints, and advice columns encouraging consumer spending.

The hostile reaction of popular magazines and novels towards fashion continued to diverge sharply from advancing intellectual appreciation of consumer practice. Among scholars and legislators there was growing belief that a rising standard of living for all members of society was an indication of national well-being, and that money might be a positive stimulus to economic activity rather than remaining as a 'passive store of value'.[15] Letters to

[13] William Letwin, *The Origins of Scientific Economics: English Economic Thought, 1660–1776* (London, 1963), ch. 2; Joyce Oldham Appleby, *Economic Thought and Ideology in Seventeenth-Century England* (Princeton, NJ, 1979), pp. 256–64; and Appleby, 'Ideology and Theory: The Tension Between Political and Economic Liberalism in Seventeenth-Century England', *American Historical Review*, 81/3 (June 1976), 499–515.

[14] N[icholas] B[arbon], *A Discourse of Trade* (London, 1690), p. 65.

[15] A. W. Coats, 'Economic Thought and Poor Law Policy in the Eighteenth Century', *Ec.H.R.* 2nd ser. 13/1 (1960), 39–51.

editors and the verdicts of novels and tales, however, were in direct contrast to those economic works welcoming progressive levels of spending as a stimulus to economic growth. By the 1770s this contrary reaction was loud and confident. In the 1760s, only a handful of novels and short tracts described the stupidity of fashionable excess as part of their avowed task to expose folly and vice. Comment was not socially specific and at least three of the reprinted works were more concerned with portraying the salacious than sermonizing upon the evils of fashion.[16] From the 1770s to the 1790s the reaction against rampant consumer spending grew increasingly strident in the novels and moral tales. It was considered that 'fashion' had always represented the modish taste of an élite, but that 'people of fashion' had limited their desires out of respect for others. In the new age, it was held, all restraint was abandoned. The notion of a beneficial consumption of manufactured goods, if intellectually unexceptionable, was regarded with splenetic hostility by the fiction and magazine industry. A stock of characters and story-lines was assembled to illustrate the evils of luxurious conspicuous consumption.

Almost without exception, writers depicted London as the crucible of fashion and the source of all vice. Again, this was nothing new. The horrors of the city had been vividly depicted since the beginning of the century in an attempt to discourage mobility to the metropolis. In the first half of the eighteenth century, moral tracts had been obsessed by the depopulation of the countryside, the size of London, its polyglot populace, and the crimes committed in its streets. Erasmus Jones's celebrated *Luxury, Pride and Vanity* had asked:

Is it not an ungrateful Spectacle to see so many noble and ancient Families Houses mouldring into Ruin, and dropping down for want of Inhabitants; and then to behold the prodigious Growth and Encrease of this unwieldy *City*, and to observe what a strange multitude of People there is jumbled together in it?[17]

In the 1770s, the *Town and Country Magazine* revived old-style warnings about the growth of the capital, advising proscriptive

---

[16] *The Adventures of a Black Coat* (London, 1760); *Did You Ever See Such Damned Stuff?* (London, 1760); and *Memoirs of B——Tracey* (London, 1760?).

[17] [Erasmus Jones], *Luxury, Pride and Vanity, The Bane of the British Nation*, 3rd edn. (London, 1737), p. 2.

legislation, for 'in such *tempora*, can we wonder at such *mores?'*[18]

After mid-century, however, it was London's emergence as the recognized centre of fashion which aroused greatest concern in the magazines and novels. A metropolitan population of 575,000 in 1700 had risen to 675,000 by 1750, and to 900,000 by 1800. In 1750, one Englishman in every ten lived in London. The gross turnover in London's population was far greater than the net increase.[19] Between 1760 and the end of the century London's expanding Season and fashion industries provided writers with new evidence of the follies and aspirations of new wealth and revived well-rehearsed fears of unrest amongst the lower orders. Once Plexippus, the 'Aspiring Plebeian' and fictional hero, has secured his fortune, baronetcy, and wife, he sets out to

reform the manners of his servants—as he was convinced, that the profligacy which prevailed in the metropolis proceeded, in great measure, from the habits of luxury and extravagance which the servants in great families contracted, and diffused amongst the lower ranks of people: to support which, they were under a *moral* necessity of having recourse to picking pockets, house-breaking, and robbing on the highway.[20]

John Trusler, producing his *London Adviser* to supply every need of the newcomer to London, warned that the choice of servants must be well attended: 'London is so much the sink of vice, that the lower class of people are very much corrupted'.[21] The metropolis provided both the social example and the financial enticements which led to economic ruin. The capital was credited with a destructive magnetism which attracted the young and ambitious away from an honest home to new and terrible temptation. Both learned and hack writers lectured upon the dangerous dominance of London and its apparently increasing dissipation. A self-perpetuating Season furnished evil example to the individual and to the rapidly growing provincial and northern cities. Trusler

[18] 'On London being over-built', *T&C* 9: 378–9 (p. 379) (July 1777).

[19] E. A. Wrigley, 'A Simple Model of London's Importance in Changing English Society and Economy, 1650–1750', *Past and Present*, 37 (July 1967), 44–70; George Rudé, *Hanoverian London, 1714–1808* (London, 1971); and P. J. Corfield, *The Impact of English Towns, 1700–1800* (Oxford, 1982), ch. 5.

[20] Graves, *Plexippus*, ii. 213–14.

[21] John Trusler, *The London Adviser and Guide: Containing Every Instruction and Information Useful and Necessary to Persons Living in London, and Coming to Reside There* (London, 1786), p. 47.

warned that 'the several cities and large towns of this island catch the manners of the metropolis, and are vicious and extravagant, in proportion to the wealth and number of their inhabitants'.[22] Alarmed essays and serialized magazine stories were appalled by London diseases spreading to the provinces. In the 1780 season, complaints in the *Lady's Magazine* ranged from country damsels dressing and behaving 'as town-bred belles', to Mrs Tasty shocking the north by her outrageous London garb.[23] Mackenzie's 'plain country gentleman', Mr Homespun, contrasted the fearsome debauchery of the city with the ideal purity of the country and enumerated the much-repeated consequences of extravagance: poverty, enforced departure from the ancestral home, emigration, illicit love, illness, criminality, and disgraceful and agonizing death.[24] In a parable from 1790, a genteel but doomed country lady arrives in town and, 'as it were, in a moment she was seized with the contagion of fashion; elated by the consciousness of dignity, and hurried into all the folly, affectation, and expense of modish life'. Soon she 'glories in the design she has formed of introducing folly, fashion and luxury, into the circle of her provincial acquaintance'.[25]

Such fashion became the great bogy of imaginative literature despite and because of the success of consumer industries in the contemporary world. London was the dominant centre of both production and consumption. To many visitors the spectacle of London was without compare.[26] The West End was the resort of the fashionable; the pleasure gardens and the Pantheon, the parade-ground of society.[27] Many changes in consumer

---

[22] John Trusler, *The Way to be Rich and Respectable, Addressed to Men of Small Fortune*, 4th edn. (London, 1784), pp. 8–9.

[23] 'The Fortunate Sequel; or, The Adventures of Ella Worthy: A Novel in a Series of Letters', *Lady's*, Jan. 1780–July 1782, 32 parts (*Lady's*, II: 6 (Jan. 1780); II: 171 (Apr. 1780).

[24] The Homespun family had been a great success for Mackenzie, first introduced in Essay XII of the *Mirror* (Mar. 1779), and continued in the *Lounger* (1785–7) and elsewhere throughout the decade. Extracts were reprinted in *The Companion: Being a Choice Collection of the most Admired Pieces from the Best Authors*, 3 vols. (Edinburgh, 1790–1), i. 259–60.

[25] Combe, *Devil Upon Two Sticks*, iii. 82, 84.

[26] Pierre Jean Grosley, *A Tour to London; or, New Observations on England and its Inhabitants*, trans. by Thomas Nugent, 2 vols. (London, 1772); Williams, *Sophie in London*, pp. 90–284; Balderston, *Thraliana*, ii. 682 (21 May 1787); d'Archenholz, *Picture of England*, pp. 76–9; Nettel, *A German in England*, pp. 27–48.

[27] Sir John Summerson, *Georgian London*, rev. edn. (London, 1970); Warwick Wroth, *The London Pleasure Gardens of the Eighteenth Century* (London, 1896); 'Ranelagh Gardens', a scrapbook of contemporary advertisements, newspaper-cuttings, and prints, BL (840. m. 28).

behaviour—and certainly their discussion—originated in the capital of fashion. Pastor Wendeborn was assured that over a quarter of all English manufactories were in London.[28] The 'demonstration effect' as a key to the development of high consumption,[29] produced reaction as well as emulation, and the most frequently reprinted new novels, including works by Parsons, Pratt, Burney, and Smith, ferociously condemned the city and the fashionable. The very success of emulative spending and the outpouring of home-produced commodities in the 1780s was a major stimulus to the fulminations against fashion. In a decade when the Exchequer pointedly considered the first shop tax, and retailers were adopting revolutionary marketing techniques, foreign and British travellers noted not only the tremendous activity of the home market, but also its recent, explosive advance.[30] Worse, the new luxuries both followed and directed weathercock fashions. The Duchess of Devonshire affected to be appalled by the fickleness of modern taste. Her heroine in her highly successful *The Sylph*, is astonished by the ton:

I always looked on taste as genuine and inherent to ourselves; but here, taste is to be acquired; and what is infinitely more astonishing still, it is variable.[31]

The change appeared to quicken with each season, the consumer society to be out of control. A tract for sale in the same season as the *Sylph* warned that 'the World is unhappily governed by Fashion; Scarce two, in a thousand, think for themselves. People indolently go with the stream, rather than be at the Trouble of turning their Face against the Torrent'.[32]

New consumer industries were also central to the link between this growing attack upon fashion and a notable transformation in the ancient idea of luxury. From the late 1760s condemnation of 'Luxury' was accompanied by attacks upon 'Luxuries', the

---

[28] Wendeborn, *View of England*, i. 162.

[29] David S. Landes, *The Unbound Prometheus* (Cambridge, 1969), p. 243.

[30] Williams, *Sophie in London*, pp. 83–7, 141–4, 165–6; Wendeborn, *View of England*, i. 136–41, 154–79 ('the rage of tea-drinking among all ranks of people in England, is beyond conception', p. 155); d'Archenholz, *Picture of England*, pp. 61–2; [E. D. Clarke], *A Tour Through the South of England, Wales, and Part of Ireland* (London, 1793), pp. 373–7; and B[arthélemy] Faujas [de] Saint-Fond, *Travels in England, Scotland, and the Hebrides*, 2 vols. (London, 1799), ii. 339–48.

[31] *The Sylph*, 5th edn. (Dublin, 1784), i. 22.

[32] *Thoughts on the Times, but Chiefly on the Profligacy of our Women* (London, 1779), p. 19.

manufactured products of the new age. As might be expected, the most expansive accounts of the transformation in the idea of luxury were contained in the increasing number of serious contemporary social commentaries. Changes here filtered into representations of luxury in other types of literature.

A staple notion of two centuries of economic and social thought, the idea of luxury was refashioned to defend increasing levels of conspicuous consumption. As a defence against the charge of luxurious living, those supporting many of the new domestic industries were assured not only that certain luxury was acceptable, but that a very particular luxury was responsible for the outcries within contemporary literature. In a succession of tracts and pamphlets of the second half of the century an evil intemperate luxury was isolated and depicted as the responsibility of men and families of trade and fortune. Free-spending by the wealthy was re-examined in order to explain the apparent paradox of unprecedentedly large fortunes accrued from trade, manufacturing, and service under the East India Company, and the ever-predicted fall in the rate of British economic expansion. Redundant wealth and its promotion of worthless and rapidly changing fashion was associated unquestioningly with excessive luxury. Essayists and learned writers reformulated the familiar bogies of dangers from monopoly and the intrigues of an individual against state and community in terms of a growing disparity between rich and poor. Current 'luxury' was testified by extravagance, speculation, gambling, and a lust for money. Personal dishonesty was paralleled by financial irresponsibility and the corrupting influence of wealth. Pervasive classical influences reaffirmed the destructive power of luxuries, whatever their material form. Many publications held the contagion of luxury to be unprecedentedly sinister, a belief fuelled by fears of financial, moral, and political catastrophe. In turn, these were sustained by a continuing but extremely anxious pride in the mercantile and constitutional achievements of the last hundred years.[33]

Both imprecision in the meaning of luxury, and reaction to the work of Mandeville had ensured heated and prolonged debate.

---

[33] The importance of developmental, stage-led, and classical decline-and-fall notions of history to the crisis-thinking concerning trade and industry, is surveyed in Ronald L. Meek, *Social Science and the Ignoble Savage* (Cambridge, 1976), and Raven, 'English Popular Literature', appendix II.

'Luxury is a word of the most vague and indeterminate signification, and admits of almost infinite degrees', complained Nathaniel
Forster in 1767.[34] A very large number of contemporary publications attested to Forster's view.[35] The *Monthly* remarked that
'there is scarce any subject that has been more frequently treated
by political writers than that of luxury, and yet few have been
treated in a more vague and superficial manner'.[36] Since at least
Davenant's acceptance of the 'necessary evil', outright hostility
had to be squared with belief in luxury as a potential social
benefit. Mandeville's heretical claim that private vice was public
virtue had nourished writers and publishers for more than half a
century.[37] In the fall-out from the *Fable of the Bees*, disgusted
scholars, moralists, and hacks raced to condemn what was
regarded as a reversal of truths—that frugality or 'necessity' was
an abomination, that luxury was a prerequisite for national
greatness and prosperity, and that self-interest might become a
public benefit.[38] Mandeville's uncompromising thrust against the
self-deception involved in the luxury debate was passed over with
little compunction. Illustrations of the necessity of luxury were
popularized by the debate over Mandeville. Detailed discussion

[34] [Nathaniel Forster], *An Enquiry into the Causes of the Present High Price of Provisions*
(London, 1767), p. 36.

[35] Including David Hume, *Political Discourses* (Edinburgh, 1752): 'Luxury is a word of a
very uncertain signification, and may be taken in a good as well as a bad sense', opening to
Discourse II, 'Of Luxury', p. 23.

[36] *MR* 47: 508 (Appendix for 1772), review of *Théorie du Luxe—A Treatise upon Luxury*, 2
vols. (London, 1771).

[37] F. B. Kaye (ed.), *Fable of the Bees*, 2 vols. (Oxford, 1924), vol. i. xciv–xcviii, cxxxvi–cxlvi;
André Morize, *L'Apologie du luxe au XVIIIe siècle et 'Le Mondain' de Voltaire* (Paris, 1909; repr.
Geneva, 1970), pp. 72–8; Gordon Vichert, 'The Theory of Conspicuous Consumption in
the Eighteenth Century', in Peter Hughes and David Williams (eds.), *The Varied Pattern:
Studies in the Eighteenth Century* (Toronto, 1971), pp. 253–67; Hector Monro, *The Ambivalence of
Bernard Mandeville* (Oxford, 1975); and M. M. Goldsmith, 'Mandeville and the Spirit of
Capitalism', *Journal of British Studies*, 17/1 (Fall 1977), 63–81.

[38] Bernard Mandeville (?1670-1733), *The Fable of the Bees, or Private Vices, Public Benefits*
(London, 1714), an enlargement of his *Grumbling Hive* (1705), and after the revised edition of
1723, reaching a 9th edition in 1755. Mandeville was answered by John Dennis, *Vice and
Luxury, Publick Mischiefs: or, Remarks on a Book Intituled, the Fable of the Bees* (London, 1724);
Richard Fiddes, *General Treatise of Morality* (London, 1724); William Law, *Remarks upon ... the
Fable of the Bees* (London, 1723); Thomas Bluett, *An Enquiry whether a General Practice of Virtue
tends to the Wealth or Poverty, Benefit or Disadvantage of a People?* (London, 1725), and his *The True
Meaning of the Fable of the Bees* (London, 1726); Sir John Thorold, *A Short Examination of the
Notions advanc'd in a book intituled The Fable of the Bees* (London, 1726); and by Archibald
Campbell in Ἀρετη-λογία (Westminster, 1728) (authorship given as Alexander Innes on
title-page). John Brown first attacked Mandeville in his 1751 *Essay upon Shaftesbury's Characteristicks*.

did not appear until after mid-century, and was the result of two distinct developments: first, the expansion of the community of economic writers and moral philosophers re-examining the recent history of the British state, and secondly, the greater commercial sponsorship by booksellers and bookselling associations of tracts, histories, and guidebooks for the popular market.

The contrast between the two responses can be illustrated by comparing the very different contributions of Hume and Trusler. Hume attempted to refute many long-standing objections to luxury, although not without careful distinction between innocent, beneficial luxury and the pernicious luxury of excess. Interpretations of luxury, argued Hume, were dependent upon specific circumstance, and the concept was both as vague and as relativist as many other moral concepts. What he did stress, however, was that the consequences of luxury were to be evaluated in terms of the *advancement* of society.[39] The point is fundamental to the erosion of cyclical theories of history and that civic humanist insistence upon the essential pravity of 'luxurious' economic and social behaviour.

The plurality of Trusler's luxury definitions were much more commercial in origin. Trusler believed the luxury of a town to be 'an incontestible proof of the opulence of its inhabitants', and held it to be absurd that 'Luxury is charged with corrupting the manners, degrading the soul, stifling of virtue, introducing a thousand vices, and by such effects, working the ruin of States'.[40] Dr Trusler, however, more interested in sales than theory, was perfectly capable of arguing against this, as he proved in his opening statement to *The Way to be Rich and Respectable* of 1775: 'The great degree of luxury to which this country has arrived, within a few years, is not only astonishing but almost dreadful to think of'.

A significant shift within this debate was the increasing consideration of luxury in relation to vices practised not by the lower orders, but by the middling and upper classes, not by the illiterate but by the literate. Moreover, to provide added justification to the economic arguments, popular literature was to stress the social as much as the economic threat of such luxury, and, in illustration,

[39] 'Luxuries must be manufactured and hence provide employment'; 'Indulgences are only vices, when they are pursu'd at the expence of some virtue, as liberality or charity', *Political Discourses*, pp. 5, 23.

[40] John Trusler, *Luxury No Political Evil, But Demonstratively Proved to be Necessary to the Preservation and Propserity of States* (London, 1780), pp. 44, 60.

accuse parvenu families of self-indulgent and anti-social behaviour. In imaginative literature and in the contributions to the
magazines, criticism became more pungent as frivolous spending
was associated more and more with social and political pretension. The 'acceptance of modernity' in consumer affairs was not
only contradicted in some quarters by a hankering after tradition,[41] it was qualified by the degree of social change perceived
as acceptable to a specific reading public.[42] The new charges of
luxury attacked fashionable luxuries and the misuse of wealth
rather than the mere possession of wealth and comforts. Even by
1770, the luxury under intellectual and public discussion was far
removed from that condemned fifty years earlier.

A conception of luxury which identified as the true enemies of
society the indolent or wasteful rich (soon to be narrowed to
upstart men of commerce), derived in part from a growing sympathy for the poor. Essayists, historians, and economists from
Davenant to Bolingbroke, had envisaged a luxury as the harb-
inger of indolence, effeminacy, insubordination, and social and
political debility.[43] Such luxury was applicable to all social classes,
but especially to the lower orders.[44] From Mun to Henry Fielding,
economists and pamphleteers stressed the dangers of luxuries to
the poor as preventives to the labour necessary for the support
both of the labouring classes and of the existing structure of
society. Fielding blamed 'a vast torrent of luxury' for the unrest of
the poor in his 1751 *Enquiry into the Cause of the late Increase of Robbers*.
Typically, the amateur economist the third Viscount Townshend
outlined 'the idle and licentious behaviour which in general pre-
vails among this rank of people', as well as his plans for the
regulation of the poor in general.[45] Frequent essays on luxury in
mid-century journals such as the *London Magazine* concentrated
upon the dangers of the vice to the lower orders. Nevertheless,
however emphatic Defoe's and Mandeville's warnings against
alms-giving to beggars, humanitarian consideration of the poor

[41] J. H. Plumb in McKendrick, Brewer, and Plumb, *Birth of a Consumer Society*, p. 316.
[42] This is explored in greater detail in Ch. II.
[43] James William Johnson, *The Formation of English Neo-Classical Thought* (Princeton, NJ, 1967), pp. 48–50, 60–8.
[44] Assumptions of theories of leisure-preference are discussed in Mathias, *Transformation of England*, pp. 148–67.
[45] 3rd Viscount Townshend, *National Thoughts, Recommended to the Serious Attention of the Public* (London, 1751), pp. 1, 20–5.

was apparent from mid-century. Isaac Barrow, John Tillotson, and Francis Hutcheson (reworking Shaftesbury), made significant contributions to the development of the idea of 'benevolence' particularly as applied to the poor.

In writings on the economy, belief in the efficacy of providing a more positive work stimulus for the poor gradually displaced necessarian doctrines of the social utility of poverty. In 1734, Jacob Vanderlint argued that domestic real wages ought to be higher than abroad, as did other pre-1750 'high-wage economists', including Cary, North, and Defoe.[46] Berkeley in the *Querist* (1734), Postlethwayt in numerous reworkings of contemporaries, and Forster in his 1767 tract on prices, viewed improved living standards as an end in itself. Such attitudes were encouraged by distinctions made between high wages and high labour costs and an acknowledgement of the growing importance of industrial mechanization. Opposition was continued by resolute conservatives, notably William Temple, Arthur Young, and those condemning high wages from fear of declining exports.[47] By at least 1770, however, many economic writers held that the raising of living standards of even the poorest members of the community improved the prosperity of the whole of society.[48] Moreover, from the time of Malachy Postlethwayt and Josiah Tucker, new invective was trained upon the effects of upper- and middle-class extravagance, idleness, and non-productive conspicuous consumption. In 1772, the economist and historian Thomas Mortimer argued that there were too many idle aristocratic consumers and too few working people. He insisted that the manufacturing population was not 'the most idle, debauched and luxurious of any in Europe' as Arthur Young had suggested, but rather that the economy was undermined by the idle rich. Like so many others at this period, Mortimer singled out for attack 'all supernumerary servants' as 'the useless pageants of pride and luxury',

---

[46] *Money Answers All Things; or, An Essay to Make Money Sufficiently Plentiful* (London, 1734).

[47] William Temple of Trowbridge, *A Vindication of Commerce and the Arts* (London, 1758) and *An Essay on Trade and Commerce* (London, 1770) (sometimes attributed to J. Cunningham). The key texts are discussed in A. W. Coats, 'Changing Attitudes to Labour in the Mid-Eighteenth Century', *Ec.H.R.* 2nd ser. 11/1 (1958), 35–51.

[48] Of many statements, Thomas Mortimer (1730–1810), *The Elements of Commerce, Politics and Finances* (London, 1772); Francis Moore, *Considerations on the Exorbitant Price of Provisions* (London, 1773), and Smith's proposition that no society could prosper and be happy if a majority of its members were impoverished, *Wealth of Nations*, Everyman edn., 2 vols. (London, 1975), i. 70.

and the over-abundance of horses in England as the symbols of ostentation and pedigree insolence.[49] The explicit contrast between the benevolence and the luxury of the rich was some decades in reaching the popular magazines, however. 'Benevolence', particularly in terms of the evaluation of 'prudent luxury', is not commonly discussed by the magazines until the 1770s.[50]

From the mid-1750s, popular essayists and magazine writers had taken a revived interest in the ambiguous luxury debate. 'Civis', in one early contribution, inveighed against the 'Prevalence and Bad Effects of Luxury', while admitting it to be 'the daughter of commerce and promoter of trade'.[51] Essayists and magazine contributors continued to represent a neo-classicist vision of luxury undermining the fabric of the state. Warnings based on alleged classical precedent for the fall of empires, were also increasingly related to specific aspects of commercial and manufacturing prosperity. 'Luxuria——victum ulciscitur Orbem', supposedly written from 'Birminghamensis' in December 1755, was agitated by the growing number of these 'common-place declamations against the degeneracy of the present times', but nevertheless proceeded to add to their number.[52] No real *debate* was in evidence in the popular magazines, however——certainly not reflecting the propositions of intellectual economic and historical writing. In the popular essay contributions there were also few detailed discussions of the economic theory of luxury. While many sober essays related luxury to the material progress of society,[53] more populist tracts pursued all-out attacks on newfangled and manufactured extravagancies and fashions.

By the 1780s, however, a more genuine debate was opened up. Trusler was one of the first contributors to accept the real challenge of Mandeville: 'There is one striking observation that occurs upon this subject [Luxury]; though in theory the common opinion is against it; in practice, the world is for it: though moralists inveigh against it, wise statesmen have encouraged

---

[49] Mortimer, *Elements*, pp. 94, 105.
[50] Elizabeth J. Duthie 'Benevolence in English Poetry from the Seasons to the 1790s', unpublished Ph.D. thesis (Cambridge, 1976), p. 50.
[51] *LM* 23: 409 (Aug. 1754).   [52] *LM* 25: 15–17 (p. 15) (Jan. 1756).
[53] Notably, Adam Ferguson, elaborating Hume's argument that general luxury was a question of changing tastes developed in accordance with the new conveniences of the age, *An Essay on the History of Civil Society* (Edinburgh, 1767).

it'.[54] A rival publishing cleric condemned Trusler for praising the economic benefits of luxury 'in an Age, when both Art and Nature seem almost exhausted by the varied, ingenious Invention of new Luxuries; and are tortured, ransacked, and plundered on every side, in order to create new Appetites and Desires'.[55] The shriller tone in the discussion of luxury was in many cases forced by the tensions of war and financial crisis. Further aspects of this will be considered in later chapters, but contrasting contributions during the Seven Years War and the war with the American colonies, offer particular insights into changing responses, from moral, historical, and nationalistic generalities, to specific critiques of business development and its financial and social consequences.

The Seven Years War brought the hysterical last gasp of old-style, moral outrage, most famously embodied in the Revd John Brown's *Estimate of the Manners and Principles of the Times.*[56] Published in 1757, the tract was reprinted at least a dozen times by the end of 1758. The *London Magazine* also carried such articles as 'The Profligacy of the Present Times', its author, 'Britannicus', pointing out that 'the time of War ... seems the fittest to suppress Luxury', and complaining that 'every village must now have a publick assembly; every handycraftsman must have his horse and country-house, and every tradesman's wife, her routs'.[57] The Noble brothers issued *The Tryal of Lady Allurea Luxury*, in which Lady Allurea, a foreigner, is tried by a jury led by Sir Oliver Roastbeef, Bart. The charge is 'that the Prisoner, for near a Century past, hath most wickedly and maliciously plotted and conspired the Destruction of this Land by corrupting the Morals of our People'. Henry True-Briton testifies that she arrived in Britain with the Restoration, Charles II taking her to his bed. Lord Good-Mind recalls that after letting Luxury into his house, 'my old English hospitable Table was covered with nothing but Frenchified disguised Dishes'. She corrupted tradesmen and merchants, told sailors to stay at home, and 'used every Stratagem to corrupt, and render effeminate and cowardly, the B———h

---

[54] Trusler, *Luxury No Political Evil*, p. 2.

[55] Revd J. Fawel, *Observations on a Pamphlet entituled 'Luxury No Political Evil'* (Wigan, 1785), p. 40.

[56] John Brown, *An Estimate of the Manners and Principles of the Times* (London, 1757).

[57] *LM* 27: 223–4 (p. 223) (May 1758).

Soldiery'.[58] John Type, 'Printer and Bookseller', also gives evidence:

> She is the Author of all the Books that have been published these last fifty Years in Favour of Self-Murder, Gaming, Atheism, and every Kind of Vice, public as well as private—She wrote the Fable of the Bees, and published it under the Name of Mandeville—She likewise wrote the Book on Self-Murder, which goes under Count Passeran's Name—All the Books under the Names of Toland and Tindal, were likewise wrote by her. Nay, I am morally certain that Meursius was one of her Productions—Not to mention the Nun in her Smock—the new Atalantis, and the Poems said to be wrote by Lord Rochester... Nay, I have Cause to think that all those curious Treatises that go under Mr Hoyle's Name, were wrote by her.[59]

A defence is mounted, but the witnesses—including Jews, Frenchmen, and ladies of fashion—are discredited. The arguments which they put forward and which are rubbished by the prosecution, are nevertheless, those which gain respectability during the next two decades—that Luxury encourages 'a perpetual Circulation of Business', and that 'we had neither Trade or Wealth, till she came amongst us'. This is no debate, however. All defence 'witnesses' are cross-examined and exposed, but the evidence against Luxury is left to stand uncontested. As Mr Manly sums up for the prosecution, 'Punish that wicked Woman—and be forever renowned, for what your Ancestors with so much Reason gloried in. In a word—Be Britons'. Lady Allurea Luxury is found guilty of every charge, but before sentence, 'was rescued by a Mob of Nobility and Gentry, who now entertain and caress her in Defiance of all Law and Justice'.[60] The charges, the defence, the verdict, and especially the irresponsible supporters, had all changed by the time of the next war-induced revival of the luxury debate.

The American war encouraged a debate based on fears of economic crisis and of post-war and East India *arrivistes*, but also on the acceptance, by now, that certain luxury could bring benefits. While consumer industries disgorged a torrent of new decencies, the consensus of the discussions in the magazines during the 1780s allowed the necessity for luxury, while demanding a variety of measures to prevent its excess. Essays and letters in the

---

[58] *The Tryal of the Lady Allurea Luxury* (London, 1757), pp. 6, 8, 13, 17.   [59] *Ibid.*, p. 29.
[60] *Ibid.*, pp. 40, 52, 66, 91, 92.

Town and Country Magazine, for example, accepted as axiomatic the currency and appropriateness of the luxury controversy. In 1778 the magazine carried an article by 'Poplicola' ('Friend of the People') which pilloried 'locusts of the state', projectors, and false traders as promoting luxury and subverting true commerce. Even the tourist-traveller and antiquarian was attacked as a wanton:

> If our travellers studied the particular advantages of situations respecting commerce, rather than what time a castle was built or demolished, or by what route men traversed a province some twenty centuries ago, their excursions would be a benefit to their country, and an honour to themselves.[61]

The popular neo-classical Jeremiahs refused to be completely silenced. One article insisted that 'it is a mistake to say, that *luxury* is only criminal when it produces an expence disproportionate to a man's fortune'.[62] A letter 'to the Printer' in the next season warned of the viciousness of luxury, blaming 'the monstrous size of our capital'.[63] Thereafter, the response was more balanced. In June 1781, a *Town and Country Magazine* piece on 'National Luxury' decided that 'luxury produces vice, and vice misery; but luxury is, notwithstanding, essentially necessary to national greatness ... It is indeed true, that nations have been undone by luxury; but it is also true, that no nation can subsist without it'.[64]

Fresh essays and letters disturbed by excessive luxury carried warnings quite distinct from the forthright if unsophisticated anti-luxury sentiment sustained by the magazines in earlier decades. 'An Admirer of Ease and Convenience' of October 1781 debated the advantages and disadvantages of luxury, settling for a balanced compromise and the caution to 'let misers and cynics rail at imaginary luxury'. The author believed luxury to be necessary in order to promote industry and support labour—'the coffers of departed misers are opened, and their contents circulated'—but agreed with those who suggested that luxury encouraged wantonness, subverted manners, and 'in its ample field ... eventually must ruin the community'.[65] In 1782, a letter signed 'Voltaire' championed luxury, claiming primarily that it

---

[61] 'Essay on the State of the Nation', *T&C* 10: 24–6 (Jan. 1778). The author added, 'blind is the man who maintains that private vices are public benefits', p. 24.
[62] *T&C* 12: 63–5 (Feb. 1780).   [63] *T&C* 13: 67–8 (Feb. 1781).
[64] *T&C* 13: 318 (June 1781).
[65] To the editor 'On Luxury', *T&C* 13: 537 (Oct. 1781).

clothed the poor.[66] This was echoed in 1787 by a long, thoughtful article 'On the bad Consequences of National Avarice', arguing that because 'private vice as public benefit' was thought injurious to the cause of virtue, avarice might now be mistakenly advocated as socially advantageous 'as it prevents the indulgence of luxurious appetites'. Of 'superfluities', it claimed, 'individuals would, perhaps in time, be happier without them; but the body politic, as it now is constituted, would soon shew symptoms of a hasty consumption'. The author pleaded with the rich 'to be prudently luxurious'.[67] The most common argument was that the availability of new comforts was necessary to promote industry, but that sumptuary laws had to be revived as safeguards against luxury's over-development. The search was for standards of legitimate personal consumption; for justification for the purchase of decencies which went far beyond traditional concepts of the necessary. Such writing necessitated new discrimination in types of luxury and more refined levels of intolerance.

Here, all writers guided the attack away from increasing general consumption and towards specified extravagant groups and individuals. It was claimed that luxuries were the materialist fads of irresponsible and over-rich individuals, not of the general public. While magazines and occasional essays of the 1770s moved away from neo-classical outbursts against the 'Profligacy of the Times', the domestic novel contained increasing numbers of episodes devoted to exposing unacceptable aspects of 'luxury' in down-to-earth, contemporary parables and illustrations. The real assault was directed against the excessively fashionable. The fates which novelists allotted to adherents of the 'ton' became ever more alarming. Like most Paternoster Row fiction, the Duchess of Devonshire's work attacked fashionable individuals even more than fashion itself. This is perhaps unsurprising. The Duchess had no qualms about allowing Wedgwood to use her name in the advertisement and sale of à la mode pottery.

There were also other ways in which a literary demonstration of the dangers of fashion and luxury focused upon the extravagant individual. It was argued that large profits had been garnered from the consumer revolution, and that much extravagance derived from families made rich from their irresponsible promotion of fashion products. In a populist attack against a

[66] *T&C* 14: 31 (Jan. 1782).   [67] *T&C* 19: 394–6 (Sept. 1787).

marketing of luxuries which enjoyed increasing intellectual acceptance and undeniable popular participation, obvious targets were those who fuelled consumer excesses, not by buying, but by producing the goods. Business families were charged with growing fat from commercial profits without assuming the responsibilities of their wealth.

Certainly, the survey of the new imaginative literature of the period reveals the increasing obsession with the luxuries of individuals and with those supporting the ton. The jests of the 1770 works were mild rebukes compared to the later creation of major characters exemplifying the follies and consequences of fashionable living. Characterizations displaying specifically the horrors of the new fashions only became clear by the end of the decade.[68] Odes and comic verse of the 1770s vigorously and wittily denounced fashion—still a novelty in its mass-produced and commercialized form. *The Woman of Fashion*, issued during the financial crisis of 1778, inveighed against what were seen as the fads of irresponsible females. Such behaviour, the writer warned, tempted moral, financial, and mental catastrophe.[69] In the following season, the popular *Sylph* employed a heroine who herself fell victim to deep play, to comment upon the pains and absurdities she had to endure to remain '*au dernier goût*'.[70] *Fashionable Follies*, a heavily advertised and reprinted Dodsley publication of 1781, was little more than a catalogue of fashionable dissipation, from hair-architecture to phaeton-driving.[71] By the mid-1780s a range of malevolent and pathetic creatures were displayed as pandering to the worthless, ever-changing, often dangerous, values of whimsical fashion. Their fates became more dramatic and horrifying, the moral lessons all the more telling. The horrors of fashion were exposed in almost every 'History of a Young Lady' of the decade. They appeared not only in novels with domestic settings, but also in works set in Turkey, medieval France, Siberia,

---

[68] Two exceptions within the 1770 cohort remain the characterization of Mr Modish in *Female Friendship; or The Innocent Sufferer*, 2 vols. (London, 1770), and the even slighter portrayal of Sir John Modish of Modish Hall in Treyssac de Vergy, *The Mistakes of the Heart*, 3 vols. (London, 1769–70).

[69] *The Woman of Fashion: A Poem: In a Letter from Lady Maria Modish to Lady Belinda Artless* (London, Bew, 1778).

[70] Julia Stanley in *The Sylph*, 5th edn., i. 37–46, 80–90 (p. 39).

[71] Thomas Vaughan, *Fashionable Follies: A Novel: Containing the History of a Parisien Family*, 2 vols. (London, 1781).

and the moon.[72] The *Devil Upon Two Sticks in England,* which went through at least four three- to six-volume editions in two years, was a compendium of case-histories of the extravagant fashionable and their deserts. In Ryves's equally popular *Hermit of Snowden,* the star of the piece has many troglodyte years in which to lament his dalliance with the beau monde.[73] In such works the entertainment value of relief comic characters was combined with powerful preaching. The popular, reprinted novels of the 1780s not only parodied tonnish imbecility in numerous digressions, but directed the main structure of the plot to unveiling the horrific consequences of craving the fashionable world. Such works as Mrs Bennett's 1785 *Anna,* a Lane work and reprinted three times in the next decade, described the uselessness of 'feathered ladies and painted beaus', the physical decline of a follower of fashion, and the shocking demise of a dissipated man of pleasure.[74]

Reviewers continued to support the public utility of such writing. The *English Review,* for example, praised *Fashionable Infidelity; or, the Triumph of Patience* for knowing 'the vices and foibles of fashionable life, and copies them with correctness ... the story is so well told that few novels will, upon the whole, better repay the reader's perusal'.[75] Ryves's *Hermit,* which appeared to want realism, probability, fine language, and other merits usually essential for critical approval, was enthusiastically received by a *Critical Review* writer. Notwithstanding the trite subject matter, the novel taught a most salutary lesson: 'Read it, ye sons of fashion or of fortune, and change your conduct: be happy, if your hearts, depraved by vanity and dissipation, will permit!'[76]

The development in popular literature of the new luxury

---

[72] The most notable surviving novels and collections of tales from *c.*1781 to *c.*1787 with strident attacks on fashion include, Elizabeth Griffith, *Essays Addressed to Young Married Women,* 1782 and 1783; anon., *The Lascivious Hypocrite,* 1783; anon., *The Woman of Letters ... or Miss Fanny Bolton,* 1783; Thomas Holcroft, *The Family Picture,* 1783; anon., *The Denouement ... History of Lady Louisa Wingrove,* 1784; Mrs Parry, *Eden Vale,* 1784; John Potter, *Virtuous Villagers,* 1784; Agnes Maria Bennett, *Juvenile Indiscretions,* 1786; Anna Maria Mackenzie, *The Gamesters* (3 edns. in 1786); anon., *Juliana,* 1786; anon., *May Day or Anecdotes of Lydia Lively,* 1787; Miss Tomlins, *Victim of Fancy,* 1787. Attacks upon fashion in the novels of Bage are considered in Gary Kelly, *The English Jacobin Novel, 1780–1805* (Oxford, 1976), pp. 35–40.

[73] Elizabeth Ryves, *The Hermit of Snowden; or, Memoirs of Albert and Lavinia,* 2nd edn. (Dublin, 1790), esp. the hermit's remorse, pp. 26–8 (3 edns., 1789–90).

[74] Agnes Maria Bennett, *Anna; or, The Memoirs of a Welch Heiress,* 4 vols. (London, 1785), ii. 93–4; iii. 107, 143–9.

[75] *ER* 15: 306 (Apr. 1789).   [76] *CR* 68: 163 (Aug. 1789).

charges was linked to the attack on fashion. Direct condemnation
of luxury was subdued in the imaginative literature of 1760. In 1770
many works enthusiastically attacked the beau monde,[77] although
the most numerous and daring satirical attacks were confined to
scurrilous biographies of prominent men and women.[78] Although
compared to the 1790 season of novels, the tone of the 1780 works
was mild, the thrust of the assault on luxury was unmistakable.
The lure and timing of the Season were given comparatively
restrained attention but 'Pleasure' was clearly identified as a disease, derived from free-spending, ruining youth, and threatening
the whole nation: 'This passion for pleasure ... rages like a contagious distemper, among both sexes; but it is by no means confined to the younger part of the human species; all ages are infected with it.'[79] The heroine of Miss Pilkington's *Delia*
announced to a not unprepared readership, 'I cannot help
fancying that the present race of men is strangely dagenerated
[*sic*]. What swarms of animals infest each public place, the
effeminacy of whose persons corresponds with the enervation of
their minds.'[80] By the late 1780s, commercial imaginative literature constantly associated luxury with the folly of fashion, and
with the wasteful and harmful expenditure deemed unavoidable
in maintaining an assumed social rank. Older charges of luxury
were reworked to apply specifically to the life-style of the beau
monde and the *nouveaux riches*.

The new emphasis upon fashion generated in the popular press
from the 1770s was therefore concerned with a specific application
of luxury. It indicted the extravagant wealthy, not those affected
only by a marginal increase in their income. By the end of this
period, sympathy for the condition (if not the aspirations) of the
poor was extended in the great majority of novels, children's
books, and serializations.[81] Novel after novel emphasized ideals of

---

[77] Of many examples, *Female Friendship*, 2 edns. (London, 1770); Edward Bancroft, *The History of Charles Wentworth Esq.*, 3 vols. (London, 1770); and notably, Jenner's thrice reprinted *Placid Man*.

[78] As in *The Life, Adventures ... of the Celebrated Jemmy Twitcher* (London, 1770); *The Life and Adventures and Amours of Sir R[ichard] P[errot]*, (London, 1770); and *The Genuine Memoirs of Miss Faulkner* (London, 1770).

[79] *How She Lost Him; or, The History of Miss Wyndham*, 2 vols. (Dublin, 1780), i. 26.

[80] Pilkington, *Delia*, i. 26.

[81] Notable examples include the *Louisa* of 1790 (and esp. its 'Caroline Green' episode);
Maria Geertruida Van de Werken de Cambon, *Young Grandison* (London, *c*.1788, with 2 further edns., 1790), esp. 1790 London edn., 2 vols., i. 255; and the even more popular *History*

charity, benevolence, economy, and the proper responsibilities of wealth. These removed the application of the charge of luxury largely, if not completely, from the poor, focusing attention on the luxurious rich. In his broad examination of Smollett's fiction and voluminous non-fiction, John Sekora argues that much of Smollett's thought derived from the 'ancient concept of Luxury' of which the novelist and historian was the last champion. It is shown that Smollett conceived of luxury as a vice breeding extravagance, idleness, corruption, and dissoluteness in all classes.[82]

Many writers now advanced notions of the new luxury in order to prescribe the antidote: a gentlemanly morality of economy and benevolence, and a proper understanding of the responsibilities of wealth. The attack on luxury and fashion further reaffirmed charitable and economical ideals of gentlemanly behaviour in contrast to those of upstart and irresponsible men of wealth. Trusler urged that as the butt for all novelists and dramatists, the buffoon-like squire should be replaced by the malevolent man of fashion. Lampoons of backwoods dullards had always handicapped the promotion of country values, and a redirection of the assault upon the absurdities of fashion bolstered the calls for a reformation of manners:

For many years a *country 'squire* has been an object of ridicule: but, why? No other reason can be given, but that want of polish that too often characterizes the fops of the age. If we divest ourselves of prejudice, he will not appear in so contemptible a light: it is true, he may want taste and politeness, but he may possess qualities infinitely superior. Honest unadorned freedom is preferable to studied and fashionable deceit ...

In short, an effeminate life emasculates the fine gentleman, and renders him unfit for every thing but sipping of tea, and dealing the cards; whilst the robust and manly exercises of the 'squire keep him healthy and hardy, and, inured to hunger, danger, and fatigue, enable him, when called upon in the public cause, to be of *real* service to his country. But it is to be lamented, that the true country gentleman is seldom to be found. The luxuries and effeminacies of the age have

---

of Sandford and Merton by Thomas Day. In Day's work, Mr Barlow is shown to respect the poor: 'instead of widening the distance which fortune has placed between one part of mankind and another, he was continually intent upon bringing the two classes nearer together', *Sandford and Merton*, ii. 212.

[82] He cites *Humphrey Clinker* (1771) as 'the last major English literary work to be informed by the older sense of luxury', Sekora, *Luxury*, p. x.

softened down the hardy roughness of former times; and the country, like the capital, is one scene of dissipation.[83]

The stewardship of riches was re-emphasized, often in biblical terms. As an ideal of the gentleman it was carefully moulded and perpetuated in both imaginative and serious social literature. As the contribution entitled 'The Abuse of Riches' in a 1775 *Town and Country Magazine* explained:

The man who squanders his money with a wanton profusion, and the man who hoards it with a sordid parsimony, are equally strangers to the true use of riches ... Avarice and extravagance are undoubtedly the two rocks which men of fortune should, with the greatest caution, avoid; but it is a very nice point to draw the line of moderation between them.[84]

As seen, however, the greatest venom was reserved for profligate waste, not selfish hoarding. As the range of consumer products widened, most imaginative literature certainly insisted that expenditure could be as useless as and even more dangerous than selfish accumulation. The novel, *Rencontre*, by Albinia Gwynn (1785) neatly expressed current orthodoxy amongst the writers for Paternoster Row and Leadenhall Street over the stewardship of riches and the definition of the religious, honest, gentleman:

In prosperity, he is affable, humble, and benevolent; he regards his riches as intrusted to him for the benefit of his poor brethren, and distributes, with judgment and prudence, among them, what the thoughtless devote to their luxuries, or their lusts.[85]

The charity of the gentleman would prevent non-use of riches, his economy and natural good sense, its misuse.

From the interwoven arguments of the literary response discussed in this chapter, it should be clear that there were two underlying concerns, supportive but distinct. The implicit definition of the gentleman was concerned with problems of both financial and social legitimacy. In the first of these, imaginative literature reinforced notions of the importance of active, circulat-

---

[83] Trusler, *Way to be Rich and Respectable*, pp. 10, 11.

[84] *T&C* 7: 361–5 (p. 361) (July 1775).

[85] Albinia Gwynn, *The Rencontre; or, Transition of a Moment*, 2nd edn., 2 vols. (Dublin, 1785), i. 16.

ing, and redeployable wealth in society, and attempted a layman's analysis of unacceptable behaviour and its consequences. This clear middle-class morality of warnings against living beyond one's means, also used and was supported by an obsession with respectability and appearances. Misuse of wealth also plainly involved concepts of taste and propriety, and was entangled, like the ideas surrounding the accumulation of wealth, with judgements upon the acceptability of social mobility. Although condemnation of misused inherited wealth continued unabated, greatest hostility was directed to those misdirecting fortunes amassed in a single working career. Indeed, the misuse of wealth and its sudden accumulation were interchangeable as cause and effect. The prosecution of *nouveaux riches* also outlined the iniquities of an uneven distribution of wealth when this included large unused or misused fortunes.[86] It served as a proof that vast inequalities in wealth-holding provided no stimulus to work and justified the sympathy for the poor expressed in the recent novels and miscellanies. It was in the interests of popular writers to maintain mutually supportive arguments: fulminations against luxury and extravagance criticized the wealthy upstart by way of illustration, while attacks against the upstart depended upon concern over free-spending. It was a course eagerly pursued in the literature surveyed. Clearly, by the 1780s, the literary concentration upon extravagance and luxury became as much a consequence of the attack upon *nouveaux riches* and businessmen as its cause. Mackenzie, to take one of the most popular examples, was as anxious to identify culprits as he was to examine the crime:

In the country, it [the disease of Extravagance] will be productive of melancholy effects indeed; if suffered to spread there, it will not only embitter our lives, and spoil our domestic happiness, as at present it does mine, but, in its most violent stages, will bring our estates to market, our daughters to ruin, and our sons to the gallows... let all *little men* like myself, and every member of their families, be cautious of holding intercourse with the persons or families of *Dukes, Earls, Lords, Nabobs,* or *Contractors,* till they have good reason to believe that such persons and their households are in a sane and healthy state, and in no danger of communicating this dreadful disorder.[87]

The underlying threats posed by new men of trade were not only concerned with social and political order, but with specific worries about the proper deployment of wealth.

[87] The *Mirror*, no. 12 (6 Mar. 1779), 48; repr. (amongst other places) in the *Companion*, i. 259–60.

9

FEARS OF RUINATION

Of all the follies and absurdities which this great metropolis
labours under, there is not one, I believe, at present, appears
in a more glaring and ridiculous light than the pride and
luxury of the middling class of people ... You shall see a
grocer or a tallow-chandler sneak from behind the counter,
clap on a laced coat and a bag, fly to the E. O. table, throw
away fifty pieces with some sharping man of quality.

Oliver Goldsmith, 'Of the Pride and Luxury of the
Middling Class of People', *The Bee* (1759).

A MEMORABLE cast of characters was used by popular writers
during this period to spell out the economic threat of extravagance. Over-expenditure in attempts to maintain or extend
appearances, or as the consequence of sheer folly, was said to
devastate families and threaten the prosperity of the nation.
Economy was presented as the universal ideal. New exemplars
were found to demonstrate the dangers of free-spending and to
stress the vigilance required to avoid both personal and national
indebtedness. Novels and moral essays repeated charges that particular business and consumer activity could promote economic
instability, that credit crises affecting the whole community could
originate from action by an individual, and that there was a
determinable relationship between a right to a fortune and its
usage.

These themes were illustrated by the alleged activities of self-
made petty traders, entrepreneurs, nabobs, and later, manufacturers and their families. The expedient selection of targets was
plain. There is, for example, striking neglect of the speculator and
stockjobber in the fictional parables warning against gambling
and high-risk investment. The projector and financier had been
under almost constant attack since the end of the seventeenth

century, and especially after Davenant's 1702 portrait of Tom Double, shoeless before 1688, but worth £50,000 after twenty-four years as a stockjobber.[1] For Steele, the stockjobber had been 'that ravenous Worm in the Entrails of the State'.[2] In the fiction of the 1780s, however, only the loose collection of episodes in *The Devil Upon Two Sticks* included old-fashioned caricatures of men of finance similar to those of the first decades of the century. To some extent, familiarity with the national debt and share investments had eased anxieties, but it is also noticeable that concern was diverted to the use or misuse of wealth rather than to the manner of its accumulation. In imaginative literature, passages and caricatures depicting the traditional bogies of usury and financial swindling were brief and minor compared to the attention lavished on the way in which particular individuals employed new wealth. The individual or institutional means whereby investments were made or loans for new expenditure raised, was hardly discussed at all.

In identifying wastefulness, the businessman and parvenu was made a convenient butt to portray the consequences of intemperance. Such characters provided identifiable scapegoats for often inexplicable economic ills. The prosperous trader was placed centre-stage in tales illustrating economic threats to society. The alleged self-indulgence of the businessman and *nouveau riche* was shown not only to result in misuse (and sometimes under-use) of wealth, but also to encourage the neglect of business. Concern over the misuse of wealth was focused upon free-spending. Work-avoidance and negligence was said to be induced by luxury. Both elements were featured in the common narrative progression from the history of personal ruin to its effects upon the wider community.

The illustration of personal extravagance has left an indelible mark in the history of the period. The conventional historical wisdom has been, in the words of Mingay, that by the second half of the eighteenth century, 'the most likely cause of a family's downfall was now not a change of government, penal confiscation or burdensome taxation, but extravagance'.[3] Professor

---

[1] Davenant, *The Picture of a Modern Whig* (London, 1702).

[2] 'The Englishman', no. 4 (13 Oct. 1713), in [Sir Richard Steele and Joseph Addison], *The Englishman: Being a Sequel to the Guardian* (London, 1713–15), p. 26.

[3] Mingay, *English Landed Society*, pp. 47–8.

Habakkuk suggests that as claims on income and capital, gambling and foreign travel were much more important in the eighteenth century than earlier obligations to hospitality and 'port'. The principal causes of debt were not mounting losses on current account, but payments for items of capital expenditure. It is also argued that the increased rent-charge provision for younger sons and endowments for daughters forced up the debt burden and made the estate more vulnerable to profligacy.[4] Recently, however, the Stones have presented their rebuttal to an 'open élite' which, along the way, debunks the idea that the wealthiest families collapsed because of extravagance.[5] Although we learn little about lesser estate-owners and the 'parish gentry', no clear example can be found amongst the county grandees of any bankruptcy from building, gambling, or lavish living. If this is the case—and we may be in for a squall over the county gentry—then it makes the contemporary image all the more important. For here, surely, in popular, fashionable literature is the basis for the persistent legends of conspicuous consumption and familial decline which have partnered accounts of the upward mobility of businessmen in the traditional view of a socially fluid, money-into-land England.

In fiction, the most alarming illustrations of misused wealth concerned the extravagance of the individual. Magazine essays extended the imaginative parables by providing practical advice for readers. Mrs Grey's 'Matron', the long-running column in the *Lady's Magazine*, advised husbands upon treating their wives:

He would not, as a prudent man, indulge her in a course of unwarrantable extravagance, which might prove highly detrimental to himself and his family; urging him, at the same time, to avail himself of the authority of a husband when he found it necessary to exert it, fix proper limits to her expences, and set reasonable bounds to her pleasures, that is, confine them to a circle rather below than above his fortune; a point to which all prudent people ought to bring their desires.[6]

Even a glance at the output of popular booksellers of the period will find the dangers of personal ruination repeated in dozens of advisers to men of small fortune. Once again, Trusler led the field

---

[4] Sir John Habakkuk, 'The Rise and Fall of English Landed Families, 1600–1800', Part I, *TRHS* 5th ser. 29 (1979), 187–207 (pp. 198–9).

[5] Stone and Stone, *An Open Elite*, esp. ch. 5.

[6] 'The Matron', no. 83, *Lady's*, II: 263 (May 1780).

with his *Way to be Rich and Respectable*. In such pocket-books, demands for economy went hand in hand with fears of the consequences of living beyond one's means. Handbooks warned of the
economic ruin facing those who were tempted by the fashionable
life of the city. Several of these echoed more sophisticated publications by clerics, historians, and those attempting to analyse the
moral and economic state of the nation. Many learned authorities
regarded non-residence in the country as a threat to personal
solvency and to the balance of local society. Davenant's *Works*
were reprinted in 1771 and advised that all 'must be then very
moderate in all their appetites. Ancient frugality must be restored;
rents must be paid in kind, and the gentry must live at their own
seats'.[7] Thomas Mortimer believed that the benevolent duties of
the rich were threatened when the great landowner was 'far
removed from his country-mansion [and] he lives luxuriously in
the capital'. He also sternly advised the apprentice merchant to
learn languages, geography, and history, and to embark on the
Grand Tour to outshine 'those who are educated in this dissipated
metropolis, and comment on the laws of commerce at coffee-
houses or taverns, at Mrs. Cornelys', at the New Ranelagh, or in
the environs of Covent Garden; exhaust the funds of their fathers,
ruin themselves and their partners, and sink down into the tomb
of contempt, or oblivion'.[8]

During the second half of the century, novels and moral tracts
insisted at increasing length and with an increasing number of
examples that the extravagance of unthinking individuals could
bring about not only their own ruin but that of the whole nation.
The starting-point for an explanation of national crisis or decline
was a consideration of the state not of the national debt, as had
been common in earlier popular moralities, but of the health of
private—and identifiable—finances. Concern over the national
debt was represented in popular literature as the unsophisticated
and general need for economy. It was another proof offered
against extravagance—and one which may have contributed to
the later blurring of the distinctions between public and private
credit. Much of the language—though not the examples—was
derived from traditionalist tracts deploring the state of the

---

[7] Sir Charles Whitworth (ed.), *The Political and Commercial Works Of that celebrated Writer Charles D'Avenant*, 5 vols. (London, 1771), i. 348.

[8] Mortimer, *Elements*, pp. 44, 200–15 (p. 215).

national debt.[9] Attacks continued against the non-dispersal of fortunes and excessive thirst for riches, but by the end of the 1780s a much greater number of popular publications attacked the extravagant dissolution of wealth. Many works opened by describing the results of recent extravagance. Typically, the father of Miss Williams's heroine has to redeem a parental estate which has been 'dissipated by the imprudence and extravagance of his parents'.[10] From the first page of Pilkington's novel, Delia's confidante, Henrietta Willmore, continued to 'suffer under the effects of her mother's extravagance'.[11] Mrs Smith's Sir Edward Newenden had been forced to marry the appalling heiress of the equally appalling Mr Maltravers in order to pay off inherited debts. The wealth in question was almost always newly made. In attacking conspicuous wastage and warning of economic ruin, popular writers isolated culprits who were said to have no right to their fortunes. With deliberate emphasis upon the alleged rate at which wealth was gained, upstart and extravagant tradesmen were singled out as unjustified holders and irresponsible dispersers of new wealth. The size of such fortunes was equated with the supposed excesses of free-spending. What could not be disguised was the obsessive concern with the possession and use of new riches.

Certainly, the reasons for anxiety about economic matters are not difficult to understand, although the cause of individual ruination was never critically assessed. Fear of economic disaster could often be based on specific, but strictly non-economic concerns when, as John Brewer says, crises 'seemed just as arbitrary and cruel as a death, flood or plague'.[12] The gathering speed of domestic demand and of industrial output did not preclude short-term or individual failure. Indeed, in business, the instability of increasingly competitive enterprise, often forced to carry larger overheads and credit burdens, is marked during the 1770s and 1780s. In 1778 Boulton himself barely survived.[13] The number of

---

[9] This typically pointed out that a Debt which did not exist in 1688 'has intirely been since incurred', *An Address to the Landed, Trading and Funded Interests of England on the Present State of Public Affairs* (London, Stockdale, 1786), p. 8.

[10] Helen Maria Williams, *Julia: A Novel*, 2 vols. (London, 1790), i. 1.

[11] Pilkington, *Delia*, i. 4.

[12] John Brewer, 'Commercialization and Politics', in McKendrick, Brewer, and Plumb, *Consumer Society*, pp. 197–262 (p. 212).

[13] L. S. Pressnell, *Country Banking in the Industrial Revolution* (Oxford 1956), pp. 330–1; Schofield, *Lunar Society*, p. 27.

bankruptcy proceedings could increase dramatically in the very midst of rampant demand.[14] Himalayan peaks and troughs mark the bankruptcy records of the period. Of the bankruptcies recorded in monthly returns in the *Gentleman's Magazine* between 1731 and 1800, 40 per cent fell in the years after 1782.[15] A more recent and telling estimate suggests that about one out of every 605 businesses went bankrupt in any one year between 1756 and 1765, compared to about one out of every 263 between 1791 and 1800.[16] A new introduction to the 1774 edition of Postlethwayt's *Dictionary*, noted a hiatus in progress: 'really the face of things is so changed to what it was, that general industry and ingenuity seems to be at a stand among our mechanics and manufacturers; which must be owing to the general bankruptcies that prevail amongst the trading part of the kingdom'.[17] Many provincial newspapers carried extracts from the columns of the *Gazette* and major magazines contained listings or occasional summary articles of the most recent bankrupts together with births, marriages, deaths, and promotions. There were many other victims of financial failure, but by no means all or even the majority of them were bankrupts.[18]

The outpouring of charges and recriminations in the magazines also moved with the larger fortunes of the economy. War proved an important influence. The chronology of popular attacks upon *nouveau riche* spending can be linked closely to anxieties attendant on war and economic depression. In time of crisis, novelists and social commentators alike focused upon money-lust as a stimulus to extravagance and ruination. At such times, many writers complained of rampant materialism. The keynote was set by John Brown at the beginning of the Seven Years War. As he put it in a typical comment: 'the laurel Wreath, once aspired after as the highest Object of Ambition, would now

---

[14] Ashton, *Economic Fluctuations*, esp. pp. 125–30. A striking contemporary account of the 1772 crisis, which felled and then was fuelled by the collapse of Neale, James, Fordyce, and Down, is given in Jacob M. Price, (ed) *Joshua Johnson's Letterbook*, 1771–1774 (London, 1979), pp. xvi–xvii, 40–2, 57, 75–6.

[15] T. S. Ashton, *An Economic History of England: The Eighteenth Century* (London, 1955), p. 125. Ashton noted that a high level of bankruptcies over a period of years was the mark of an expanding economy.

[16] Hoppit, *Risk and Failure*, p. 51.

[17] Malachy Postlethwayt, *The Universal Dictionary of Trade and Commerce*, 4th edn., 2 vols. (London, 1774), p. x.

[18] Hoppit, *Risk and Failure*, pp. 29–41.

be rated at the Market-price of its Materials, and derided as a *threepenny Crown*.[19] In 1782, near the close of the American war, the reissued *Pleasant Art of Money-Catching* provided the inveterate comparison between the bygone days and the immoral behaviour of the present:

> I confess, if we look backward into the better and wiser ages of the world, Virtue, tho' clothed in rags, was more esteemed than the trappings of the golden Ass: 'tis in these last and worst of days, that Vice has got such an ascendant in the world; as to make men think all that are poor, are miserable: for in the primitive times, Poverty was the badge of Religion and Piety.[20]

Concern over the personal misuse of riches had further increased after the 1778 financial crisis, and attacks on misspent wealth and *nouveau riche* extravagance were strengthened by renewed anxieties over gaming and wagering. The 1780 season included broad parables encouraging thrift and detailing the lures of pleasure, novelty, and free-spending, as well as the false attraction of titles and wealth. By 1790 each of these themes was greatly elaborated and the forms of ruinous expenditure separately distinguished. Portrayal of gambling ranged over cards, dice, wagering, and the allied diversions of the state lottery and the Exchange.

Although protest against gambling enjoyed a long pedigree, a new urgency was introduced from the mid-eighteenth century. Erasmus Jones represented gaming as derived from the twin evils of covetousness and cheating.[21] Revised editions of the *Pleasant Art of Money-Catching* did not fail to survey the 'quicksands' of play and gambling. The 'fifth' edition of 1750 was the first to insist that once gamblers had succumbed, they shall so sink 'that hardly you shall ever see their heads appear any more'.[22] Dr Johnson's *Dictionary* of 1755 defined 'gaming'—which remained an innocent pastime in Bailey's lexicon—as 'to play extravagantly for money'. In 1757 Brown called gambling 'the last wretched Effort of bungling and despairing Luxury'.[23] In the following two decades public attention was held by a succession of gambling *causes célèbres*. Accounts were published about the excesses of notorious adventurers, wagers over the most unlikely disputes, and sensational suicides as

---

[19] Brown, *Estimate*, p. 59.
[20] *The Pleasant Art of Money-Catching* (London, 1782), p. 15.
[21] Jones, *Luxury, Pride and Vanity*, p. 24. [22] *Pleasant Art of Money-Catching*, p. 28.
[23] Brown, *Estimate*, p. 39.

the result of gambling debts. The private career of Fox was a centre-piece of town gossip, and Damer's suicide in 1776 was discussed avidly in newspapers and magazines throughout the nation.[24] The betting-book of White's Club records the heavy and eccentric wagering of mid-century and beyond.[25] William Guthrie, when assessing national characteristics, made the sardonic observation that 'the English are remarkably cool, both in losing and winning at play; but the former is sometimes attended with acts of suicide'.[26] Gaming now became the shibboleth for unthinking, addictive waste, for illegitimate and profligate risk. The term 'deep play', with its connotations of intractable sinking, became a common substitute for 'high gaming' during the 1780s.[27] In the reprinted fiction of that decade the horror of 'deep' play was forcefully conveyed. Gunning's Lady Lucy Blank suffers humiliation and ruin. Her one desire had been

to play the *deepest* of our dear delightful town circle ... Deep play, the dearest of all dear things, I must encore it—*deep play*—yes *deep play* it bears all down before it.[28]

Warnings of moral catastrophe were coupled with predictions of bodily ruin for the addicted gambler. 'Hollow eyes, haggard looks, and pale complexions, are the natural indications of a female gamester', declared a common type of instructional manual, and it remained a standard truth for novelists of these years.[29] The 1780, 1785, and 1790 seasons carried stark warnings against gambling.[30] In the 1780–1 season, a complete novel was devoted to chronicling the ill health resulting from deep play.[31]

It was the horror of financial destitution, however, that was paraded as the final deterrent to play. Novels and moral tracts

---

[24] The event is recorded in Lewis Melville (ed.), *The Berry Papers: Being the Correspondence Hitherto Unpublished of Mary and Agnes Berry* (1763–1852) (London, 1913), pp. 20–1; and d'Archenholz, *Picture of England*, p. 112.

[25] Algernon Bourke (ed.), *The History of White's with the Betting Book from* 1743 to 1878, 2 vols. (London, 1892), ii. pt. 1.

[26] William Guthrie, *A New Geographical, Historical, and Commercial Grammar*, 14th edn. (London, 1794), p. 213.

[27] The 17th- and 18th-cent. association of 'deep' with 'expensive' was applied to gaming at least by the reign of Anne.

[28] Mrs Gunning, *Coombe Wood: A Novel*, 2nd edn. (Dublin, 1783), pp. 24, 255.

[29] J. Hamilton Moore, *Young Gentlemen and Ladies Monitor* (London, 178–), p. 100.

[30] Notably, *The Relapse*, i. 173; *How She Lost Him*, ii. 172; Alexander Bicknell, *Doncaster Races; or, The History of Miss Maitland*, 2 vols. (London, 1790), ii. 203, 216, 249.

[31] *Fashionable Life; or, The History of Miss Louisa Fermor* (Dublin, 1781).

envisaged a contagion of ruin, resulting from the indebtedness and time-wasting of an army of gamblers. The paramount concern was economic wastage, rather than the specific vices which ensured it. The racecourse was depicted as a particularly evil temptation.[32] Speculation in stocks was credited with the deaths of good men impetuously trying to revive their fortunes. The Stock Exchange was described as 'the scene of a more deep and artful species of gambling, than has ever been practised at any time or period, in any part of the world'.[33] The state lottery was also a recurrent target. In *Amelia* in 1751, Fielding had painted a sorry picture of the consequences of entering the lottery, and his play *The Lottery* (1732) was revived and reprinted in 1788.[34] The *Monthly Review* devoted a remarkable eight pages to reviewing a novel of 1780 about a lottery ticket. The novel was said to be 'mean', but nevertheless held to contain warnings for all.[35] Cards and dice, however, remained the most frequent illustration of gambling. *The History of Miss Harriot Fairfax* was one of many 1780 novels in which the heroine's father was ruined by gaming, and, 'his affairs being desperate, he took a desperate resolution, which was to shoot himself through the head'. His wife dies of grief before she can appear in widow's weeds, but the moral was clearly spelled out for even the most imperceptive of readers:

O, ye frequenters of gaming tables! call Reason to your aid; stop your hand one moment, and reflect on what may be the consequence of setting the last you have in the world on chance! ruin, perhaps, hangs over your head; destruction is under your feet; fly from them in time.[36]

The vice of gambling was deemed so insidious that in the 1790 popular novels it could tempt even characters who ultimately vindicated approved values. Bicknell's hero, Charles Clayton, despite his impeccable background (his mother lives at 'Woodland Cot'), succumbs to play in the metropolis. Albert, the Hermit of Snowden and adolescent gambler, accumulated a debt of

[32] *Doncaster Races* aimed to expose this centre of vice. Mrs Gomersall also featured an unflattering episode concerning Doncaster races, *The Citizen*, i. 101–3. Plexippus warns his friends against the races at Newmarket as 'the greatest danger a young man of fortune is exposed to', Graves, *Plexippus*, i. 103.

[33] Combe, *Devil Upon Two Sticks*, i. 191.

[34] Henry Fielding, *Amelia*, 4 vols. (London, 1752 [1751]), bk. xii, ch. 2.

[35] *MR* 63: 121–9 (Jan. 1781), on *Edal Village; or, the Fortunate Lottery Ticket*, 2 vols. (London, Lowndes, 1780). The novel has not survived.

[36] *The History of Miss Harriot Fairfax* (London, 1780), p. 4.

£30,000 and lived out the remainder of his life in a Welsh cave.[37] 'The itch for gaming seized him', mourns Charles Hamilton of his father in *The Perfidious Guardian* —he 'lost his senses and died in three months, leaving me but two years old'.[38] The weak, but well-meaning Sir Arthur Williams, who marries Parsons's Miss Meredith, loses over £20,000, sells the family jewels, and mortgages the family estates, all as a result of gambling.[39] Mrs Smith's *Ethelinde* is dominated by the temptations of play. It is the 'only blemish' of the heroine's father, and the colonel's son, Harry Chesterville, is driven to the Fleet Prison and twice to the point of suicide by gaming debts. The highly charged horror scenes in the debtors' gaol make the many 1780 card rout episodes and even the much later and famed scenes of *Little Dorrit*, seem limp by comparison.

By the same token, sympathy was still expressed for the genuine misfortune befalling those engaged in trade, good and wicked businessmen being the respective victims and promoters of excessive risk. The verdict of almost all the popular literature considered supports suggestions that self-presentation as 'sober, reliable, candid, and constant was not merely a question of genteel manners, but a matter of economic survival'.[40] This fear of ruination from the irresponsible extravagance of a few newly-rich, was picked up by mid-century magazines and featured in dozens of articles and letters:

when the tables of the shopkeeper, the mechanick and artificer, are replenished with cates and dainties unbecoming their rank; their rooms furnished in a sumptuous manner, and themselves and their families appear cloathed in costly garments, much exceeding their stations in life, then it is that luxury and extravagance not only prejudices them, but detriments others of the same degree, by the frequent bankrupting, insolvencies, and shutting up of shop doors it occasions.[41]

In the sharpened images after the 1778 crisis, personal ruin was causally linked with the decline of the local or national economy. If a father found that his son had misused his allowance, asked

---

[37] Ryves, *Hermit of Snowden*.
[38] *The Perfidious Guardian; or, Vicissitudes of Fortune, Exemplified in the History of Lucretia Lawson*, 2 vols. (London, 1790), i. 104–5.
[39] Parsons, *Miss Meredith*, ii. 98.
[40] Brewer, 'Commercialization and Politics', p. 214.
[41] 'Civis', *LM* 23 (1754), 410.

'On National Frugality' of 1780, 'would such a father be justified in giving him any other treatment than that due to a prodigal, and striking him out of his will? Nations as well as families are undone by profuseness'.[42] Albinia Gwynn's 1785 *Rencontre* recounted the misery of the dependants of those who overextended their resources:

Tradesmen complain of this rage [the desire to appear rich] in their great customers, which enlarging their appearance beyond their income, leaves long accounts in their books, which can never be expunged; drawing down unexpensive and thrifty families to ruin by their unlimited extravagance.[43]

Honest tradesmen were ruined by those 'forgetting that their own country-houses, their double set of servants, their neglect of business whilst they are amusing themselves at them, the dress of their wives and daughters, with their diversions, greatly accelerate their downfall'.[44] In 1790 the *Town and Country Magazine* warned:

So that let a man be ever so well able to afford either magnificence or profusion in his way of living, the duty he owes the public obliges him to live within his fortune, that he may not give encouragement to general waste, and become a means of introducing universal poverty and misery.[45]

Ultimately, it was claimed, free-spending blighted the reputation, prosperity, and internal stability of the nation itself. New periodicals such as the *Town and Country Magazine* had denounced gaming as a spur to general and ruinous luxury.[46] Their conclusions were echoed by an array of weighty essays. Cumberland believed that gaming had been integral to the fall of Rome. In his world survey, Falconer was anxious to comment upon the propensity to gaming within each of his outlined climate types. The 1787 Royal Proclamation attempted to prohibit cards, dice, and gaming on the sabbath. In 1783, the university of Cambridge, offering the first prize since 1756 for a dissertation of practical

---

[42] *T&C* 12: 532–4 (p. 533) (Oct. 1780).   [43] Gwynn, *Rencontre*, ii. 229–30.
[44] Ibid. *Rencontre*, ii. 230.
[45] *T&C*, 23: 64 (Feb. 1790).
[46] Of various examples, 'Essay on Gaming', *T&C* 2: 685–6 (Supplement for 1770); 'Strictures on Modern Luxury', *T&C* 8: 377 (July 1776); 'On the Present Rage for Gaming', *T&C* 13: 305 (June 1781); 'Essay on Gaming', *T&C* 14: 124–5 (Mar. 1782).

service, set the essay subject as gaming.[47] The winning Cambridge dissertation by Richard Hey stated succinctly the orthodox arguments. Gaming was shown to have no natural boundary, and to injure both the individual and his community. A gambler's health would disintegrate through worry and long hours, gambling was socially unbalancing by 'confounding ranks', and 'nothing perhaps could more effectually ruin the Commerce of a nation, than an universal prevalence of Gaming'.[48] The *Monthly Review* commented: 'should the author's sentiments be read and adopted as generally as they deserve, he would be entitled to a rank among the greatest benefactors of his country'.[49]

Many magazine essays of the 1780s were close to Hey's analysis. The *Lady's Magazine* of 1780 devoted a long essay to the national effects of a legion of lady-gamblers:

Woman was intended by the Great Creator as the most amiable of terrestrial beings: with beauty little inferior to that of angels, with sensation equal to the brightest son of reason; and invested with the rose of modesty to give an additional lustre to all her actions.

Gaming led women to sacrifice their virginity, their beauty, or their husbands' estates: 'and what a race of warriors, patriots, and Britons is *poor Britain* to expect will be brought into the world from the wombs of such dissolute mothers?'[50] Where fears were expressed over a luxury of the poor, it was not necessarily because of the increased income to the lower orders, but more because of their emulation of the bad example of the rich. Such example might encourage the middling ranks as well as the poor to make ill-judged risks or to live beyond their means. 'It is on the poor that the vices of the rich fall heavy', wrote Miss Willmore in the opening to *Delia*, echoing scores of other heroes and heroines of novels of these years.[51]

Despite the overwhelming attention to the deployment of wealth, it would be incorrect to suggest that there was no interest

---

[47] Cumberland, 'On Gaming', *Observer*, i. 286–95 (pp. 290–1); Falconer, *Remarks*; Cambridge University Archives, Char. I. 1.

[48] Richard Hey, *A Dissertation on the Pernicious Effects of Gaming* (Cambridge, 1783), pp. 3, 21, 77, 80.

[49] *MR* 56: 479 (Dec. 1783).

[50] 'On the Practice of Gaming among Ladies of Quality', *Lady's*, ii: 65–6 (p. 66) (Feb. 1780).

[51] Pilkington, *Delia*, i. 4.

at all in the means by which fortunes were gained. Literary interest in personal financial concerns was often ambiguous and contradictory. Card gaming, wagering, and the lottery, for example,
were condemned because of continuing public fascination with
wealth and risk. Popular interest in the lotteries had redoubled in
the 1760s and 1770s, exactly when the state lotteries abandoned
safe investment tickets for larger prizes and all-or-nothing
chances. In 1777 the *Annual Register* was attacking lottery-office
schemes and a lottery craze of lottery tea-merchants, lottery
barbers, and lottery oyster-stalls.[52] Fashionable periodicals such
as the *Lady's Magazine* and *New Lady's Magazine* offered readers
both the service of full listings of the prize-winning ticket numbers, and also essays and letters explaining why no respectable
reader would be caught gambling. Such tension was paralleled in
political debate. Fox, the most notorious gambler of his day, led
the parliamentary opposition to the Chancellor of the Exchequer's permissive lottery bill in 1787—an event well publicized
by the magazines.[53]

Opportunities for new credit arrangements and greater financial risk-taking in business and estate management explains much
about why such anxiety over economic instability developed so
rapidly in the late eighteenth century. Debate focused upon what
was and was not a legitimate risk. As Professor Mathias has
pointed out, in the final third of the century there was increasing
diversification in the means of negotiating the short-term personal credit arrangements which were the life blood of both estate
and business.[54] Expansion in the manufacturing sector was certainly dependent upon short-term circulating capital. Trades-

---

[52] *Annual Register ... for the Year* 1777 (London, Dodsley, 1778), pp. 206–7. The state
lottery, inaugurated in 1694, was virtually an annual event by 1760. Its history is surveyed
by John Ashton, *A History of English Lotteries: Now for the First Time Written* (London, 1893); R.
D. Richards, 'The Lottery in the History of English Government Finance', *Economic
History*, 3 (1934–7), 57–76; C. L'Estrange Ewen, *Lotteries and Sweepstakes* (London, 1932); and
James Raven, 'The Abolition of the English State Lotteries', *Historical Journal*, 34/2 (June
1991), 371–89.
[53] The *Town and Country Magazine* earnestly reported that it was Fox's 'opinion, that by
enhancing the price of lottery tickets, it would operate as an encouragement to gambling',
T&C 19: 56 (Feb. 1787).
[54] Peter Mathias, 'Capital, Credit and Enterprise in the Industrial Revolution', *Transformation of England*, pp. 88–115. Also, Julian Hoppit, 'The Use and Abuse of Credit in
Eighteenth-Century England', in Neil McKendrick and R. B. Outhwaite (eds.), *Business
Life and Public Policy* (Cambridge, 1986), 64–78, and 'Attitudes to Credit in Britain,
1660–1790', *Historical Journal*, 33/2 (June 1990), 305–22.

men's tokens and paper-chases of negotiable transaction-bills proliferated during the second half of the century. Although actual cash requirements were lessened by new credit facilities, these could also be worryingly meagre if the gentleman determined to follow the advice books and live within real cash limits. Given the recurrence of local and national liquidity crises, the increasing availability of credit served to swell the number of defaulters, and perceptions of risk-taking altered according to local conditions and the nature of personal credit arrangements.[55]

Increasing sophistication in the raising and transfer of credit and in borrowing on bond and by mortgage, was also based far more upon local and face-to-face transactions than upon central or institutionalized development.[56] Credit founded upon personal worthiness placed a premium on confidence and heightened anxieties over any tremor in economic fortunes which might devalue trust and assurance.[57] Moreover, the raising of credit by personal, rather than anonymous or institutional means, was a routine and a necessity to more than the large business. It was a part of the life of the smallest estate- and property-owner. Again, default was not anonymous; it was known to a wide community and its consequences for creditors and upon future transactions could be traced without difficulty. Honesty, therefore, was more than a moral nicety: it was the mainspring of a system seen to rely on individualized trust and goodwill.

Recurrent default and the form of new credit opportunities had a number of important effects upon the literary image. Default stimulated a search for the reasons for failure, which, facing a mechanism largely mysterious beyond personal transactions, focused upon personal expenditure and conspicuous consumption. This, with new opportunities for greater risk-taking or survival on credit, emphasized personal failure as likely to bring the whole edifice of credit and confidence crashing down. Interest

[55] B. L. Anderson, 'Provincial Aspects of the Financial Revolution of the Eighteenth Century', *Business History*, 11/1 (Jan. 1969), 11–22.
[56] B. A. Holderness, 'Credit in a Rural Community, 1660–1800: Some Neglected Aspects of Probate Inventories', *Midland History*, 3/2 (Autumn 1975), 94–115.
[57] Of the face-to-face society of personal and kinship links, Mathias suggested that 'in no set of business relationships were the implications of this more important than in the search for credit', *Transformation of England*, p. 101.

centred therefore upon the moral virtues, integrity, honesty, economy, even charity, as essentials to a structural stability mortgaged upon the discouragement of failures in others. Censure was focused on the alleged financial irresponsibility of a neighbour. The temperature of the debate was further raised by assessing the legitimacy of risk by measure of conspicuous expenditure rather than of the largely unknowable investment interests of established businesses or property-owners.

This led directly to the depiction of exemplary miscreants. The servants of the East India Company and petty traders and retailers were often pilloried by satirists and novelists in the 1780s exactly because of allegations about how they made their money. This is particularly clear in the storm of protest over the returning nabobs, culminating in the attacks upon Rumbold, Impey, and Hastings. The means of gaining riches was still not pursued in detail, however. What was highlighted was the suddenness and the blatant manner in which excessive new fortunes were created. Many argued that not only did low-born recipients of new wealth not know how to employ riches properly, but that their fortunes were made without talent or honest skills. Petty traders were singled out as filling their coffers by deception. The nabob was accused of rape and pillage, a charge for which the stories and the proofs were innumerable and exotic.

One cause of the charges against shopkeepers and petty traders was the introduction of fixed-price retailing and the abandonment of expected credit or abatement purchase. Here, for once, the honesty of money-making was scrutinized more carefully than the consequences of money-spending. The shock over the changes in retail practice was great. When Lackington, the creator of the greatest book emporium yet seen, declared in 1780 that he would in future require strict payment and would offer no abatement, he noted that such a practice seemed as easy to establish as to rebuild the tower of Babel. Certainly, traditional bargaining and credit allowances were not yet to be overhauled by the new practices, but fixed prices and no abatement policies did become more common during the 1780s. The reaction was immediate and grudging. Earlier, when retailers' credit had been regarded as a customer's right, great sympathy had been extended to the small shopkeepers and businessmen who had collapsed upon the default of a major creditor.[58] Now, as Wendeborn observed in 1790, the case was very different. Shopkeepers were demanding immediate payment to a fixed price, a practice which 'does not always, I believe, proceed from such commendable motives of honesty and integrity'. Hence, 'the splendid manner in which many shopkeepers live, and the short time in which some of them acquire fortunes, are proofs that such a supposition in many instances, is not ill-founded'.[59] Fixed-price retailing allowed commentators to compare prices at different establishments and to estimate profits. The tightening or even the abolition of credit terms boosted the image of the money-handling, money-grabbing trader.

Tolerance of credit was therefore ambiguous. The allowance of too much credit was associated with immoderate risk or extravagance which could set dangerous examples or lead directly to ruin. Too little credit, however, could be associated with over-caution and deceitfulness. Here, criticism was linked to attacks upon the under-use of wealth. Although less dramatic than the exposés of extravagance, charges of misappropriating wealth by not employing it profitably, accompanied calls for economy. Tracts and novels isolated those whose fortunes were said to have been gained from the same materialistic desire which promoted conspicuous wastage. Selfish hoarding was regarded as much an abuse of riches as profligate extravagance. Hoarding was attacked in *belles-lettres* as the wasted, non-productive, accumulation of riches. It was the main target of Topham's brief, but edifying biography of John Elwes, published in 1790. In the words of the author, 'the delineation of characters such as these, I consider as very moral instruction to mankind, and a lesson more demonstrative of the perfect vanity of *unused wealth*, than has hitherto been presented to the public'.[60] This was very much the idea behind numerous attacks levelled at 'some wealthy monster, who is now revelling in the superfluity of luxurious dainties'.[61]

In addition, it was claimed that such misdirection of riches

[58] The cause was still espoused in the 1780s by the reprinting of *The Swindler Detected: or Cautions to the Public: Containing a Minute Account of the honest and Industrious Tradesmen of this Metropolis* (London, Kearsley, 1781).
[59] Wendeborn, *View of England*, i. 138, 139.
[60] Edward Topham, *The Life of the Late John Elwes, Esquire; Member in Three Successive Parliaments for Berkshire* (London, 1790), preface, pp. v–vi.
[61] The phrase of *Adventures of a Corkscrew* (London, 1775), pp. 1–2.

could divert its owners from necessary industry. Popular writers expressed alarm that the pretension of traders would lead them to desert their businesses and leave London to ruin. This certainly inspired much of the satire about retirement to country estates and against the sons of traders who embarked upon gentrification and learned to despise trade.[62] In Mrs Smith's *Ethelinde*, for example, Ludford retires to his new estate, 'and his son, though his name was in the firm of the house, never sullied his dignity with any attention to that, which, though it had procured him all the consequence he boasted, he considered as much beneath the attention of a man of spirit, a man of fashion, and a *bel esprit*'.[63] Not only was the retired merchant's desire for a country seat suitably scorned, but Mrs Smith introduced a second level of sarcasm. Robert Ludford, heir to the mercantile fortune, disowns his trading background. While this allows the author to attack the dissipated London life of fashion he is to lead and further caricature the *arriviste* family from which he springs, Mrs Smith's implicit concern over lost industry also forces the admission that trade itself is not necessarily a disgraceful occupation—merely that certain present practitioners are immodest and irresponsible. Significantly, the novelists' wish to stress that swollen profits and luxury led to a neglect of business, served to exaggerate the image of businessmen retiring to opulent country estates.

Works devoted specifically to social enquiry made even clearer a double concern with hoarding and gambling, with excessive risk evasion and excessive risk acceptance. Many writers also voiced fear over the apparent polarization of wealth between a few very rich and a large number of very poor. The trader, financier, or speculator deemed to be too rich and against the public interest, became as much a traitor to the friends of commerce as a target for the abuse of the agrarian, anti-commercial, or philanthropic lobby. Defenders of commerce were anxious to isolate and condemn self-interest and the accumulation of huge, unused fortunes, dissociating this from the actions of the mercantile community. Commentators upon trade and industry expressed dismay at the apparent dissolution of a former parity in wealth-holding, proportionate—it went without saying—to respective ranks. Naismith, for example, criticized 'overgrown individuals'

---

[62] To be discussed in more detail in Ch. 10.   [63] Smith, *Ethelinde*, ii. 160.

and 'the cumberous wealth of the opulent few' in his attack upon the cotton industry in 1790:

> The wealth which is acquired, being distributed among the members of the society, like the children of one great family, will be useful and active, constantly employed in the support of its own industry, and always within reach to supply the exigencies of the state; not like great wealth in a few hands, which may be sometimes dead and unprofitable, sometimes hurtful and dangerous.[64]

If the benefits of peace and prosperity were to be available to all Englishmen, a harmony of interests between citizens had to be maintained by moderation in personal accumulation and the execution of the responsibilities of wealth. Certainly not an egalitarian concern, it was the potential unbalancing of order which fired the debate over forces accused of destabilizing or reversing commercially based national prosperity. Many were concerned with the ease with which the poor might become uneasy and contribute, in Brown's words, to 'Murmurs, Sedition, and Tumults'.[65] The 'equalizing' powers of Commerce continued to be stressed: 'commerce requires a fluctuation of property as a spur to industry, and as the means of preserving a due equality among the members of the state. Enormous fortunes, also, continued in families, would beget pride, idleness, and luxury, render personal distinction despised and bring trade into contempt'.[66] In the simplified and dramatic depiction of these targets in popular literature, fears of universal ruination and wastefulness could condemn the newly-moneyed even before consideration of their social or political intrusion.

---

[64] John Naismith, *Thoughts on Various Objects of Industry pursued in Scotland* (Edinburgh, 1790), pp. 20, 24, 25.
[65] Brown, *Estimate*, p. 196.   [66] Falconer, *Remarks*, p. 432.

10

PRETENSIONS TO LAND

The wealthy Cit, grown old in trade,
Now wishes for the rural shade.

.   .   .   .

While Madam doats upon the trees,
And longs for ev'ry house she sees.

Connoisseur, 135 (1756).

ON E of the most striking, popular, and stereotyped fictional settings developed during the second half of the eighteenth century
was that of the retired businessman in his 'bran-new' country
seat. Description of the tradesman's purchase or improvement of
a country estate became a common feature of works claiming
instructive and realistic attention to contemporary society. Their
depiction of commercial retirement and estate purchase illustrates vividly the set assumptions about the taste and ambitions of
men of trade. The portrayals have also been extremely influential. They are frequently repeated in historical accounts of mercantile and industrial breaches of the landed élite.[1]

London merchants retiring to their suburban villas were a
stock jest at mid-century. The *Connoisseur*—in the voice of 'Mr
Town'—was full of such satires. Novels of the 1760s and 1770s
rapidly followed Mr Town's lead. Of the 1770 works, *The Younger
Brother* devoted a detailed digression to 'contemplating the
surprizing taste of our citizens in the contrivance of their villas':

I have known some few Gentlemen ... who have been so stupidly
countrified as to study prospects, to bound their gardens by a Chinese
paling, an ha-ha, or a fish-pond plentifully supplied from the draining of

---

[1] It has been a sensitive issue. R. G. Wilson, for example, defended the results of
merchant Denison's commissions to Nollekens as 'ostentatious but not vulgar', 'Denisons
and Milneses', p. 162.

stables, and the ditches of the adjacent lanes and fields ... To these delightful places do our citizens repair in the summer-evenings, to strew the briary road of business with flowers, and, for the sake of their health, to sleep in the *country air*. In the morning they return, laden with green branches and bough-pots, and renew their daily toil with redoubled vigour. Every tradesman, almost, is ambitious of one of these retreats; for it sounds well in his own ears, when he invites a friend or two to take a Sunday's dinner with him *at his country-house*.[2]

Other publications strengthened the association between subur-ban villas and trading fortunes. In 1785 a handbook for the con-struction of country villas addressed its expected clientele:

Men of business there are, who all their lives have sidled along a passage thirty inches wide, or squeezed up a staircase two feet wide, while gaining their fortunes in London, and such will find themselves at ease, and be largely and comfortably accommodated with passages three feet, and stairs thirty inches wide, while enjoying the fruits of their labour in the country.[3]

The novels of the 1780s redirected attention from the summer villa to the permanent, newly-bought country seat. By 1790 descriptions of villas were rare, but where given, sarcastic and hostile. In the same chapter in which the 1790 'Devil Upon Two Sticks' describes the upstanding British merchant, he also draws attention to a Scotsman of 'mean appearance':

a character not uncommon among his countrymen, who by an active and persevering industry, have risen from the lowest situation of menial service, to the highest rank of mercantile profession ... [He] is become a very eminent American merchant, and lives in luxury and splendour. His country-house was purchased of a nobleman, who had lately built it, and whose title it still retains;—he has his park and his hot-houses,—he sees, in spring, the fruitage of summer on his walls, and is rolled in a coach and six from his accompting-house to his villa. While his son figures as a fine gentleman about town, and his daughters rival, in manners and accomplishments, the best education of the great world.[4]

These caricatures were largely in response to the well-publicized search for country estates by prominent business-men, nabobs, and manufacturers. They also provided convenient

---

[2] *The Younger Brother, A Tale*, 2 vols. (London, 1770–2), ii. 174, 176–7.
[3] José Mac Packe [James Peacock], Οἰκίδια, or Nutshells: Being Ichnographic Dis-tributions for Small Villas; Chiefly Upon Œconomical Principles (London, 1785), p. 4.
[4] Combe, *Devil Upon Two Sticks*, 2nd edn., 6 vols. (London, 1790), i. 181–2, 188–9.

illustration of the excesses of the upstart, his bad taste, and his idle pretension. Mrs Smith depicted the Ludfords squandering enormous sums on a country estate to which by nature they were not entitled. At the same time, she scathingly denounced young Ludford's contempt for his father's trade. Others repeated Beawes's mid-century claim that businessmen retired in order 'to look down on their quondam Business, as derogatory and now beneath them'.[5] 'I should be sorry', intoned the *Connoisseur*, 'that this abundance of wealth should induce our good citizens to turn their thoughts too much upon the country ... I am afraid therefore, that if the Villas of our future tradesmen should become so very elegant, that the shopkeepers will scarce ever be visible behind their counters above once in a month'.[6] Once again, the countrified businessman was attacked both for tempting economic ruination by neglecting business in the city and for squandering money in profligate and vain expenditure. This last charge was reinforced by further claims that his spending raised the price of basic provisions. The gentrified tradesman could not win. He was attacked for not making money as well as for making too much. His retirement encouraged the first charge and was the consequence of the second. The retired City financier was especially ridiculed where the non-productivity of his 'Change Alley dealings could be contrasted with respectable trades.

Startling digressions from the main plots of novels were devoted to satirical accounts of the bought-up estate. One of the best received of these was the relief passage in Dr Moore's sensationalist story of *Zeluco*. Here, in a 'work of genius and utility',[7] the reader is suddenly transported from the violent wilds of Sicily, where the book is set, to the peace of the English countryside. An extended episode considers the rural ease of one Nathaniel Transfer who has made a vast fortune in the City. The long account of the retired man of business remains an isolated and distinctive insertion in the plot:

Transfer, like thousands of others, had begun to accumulate money as the means of enjoying pleasure at some future time; and continued the practice so long, that the means became the end—the mere habit of

---

[5] Wyndham Beawes, *Lex Mercatoria Rediviva* (London, 1752), p. 32.
[6] *Narrative Companion*, ii. 90.
[7] *GM* 3: 263 (June 1789).

accumulating, and the routine of business, secured him from tedium, and became the greatest enjoyment of which he was susceptible.[8]

Moore pities rather than despises this condition and sympathizes when Transfer is eventually persuaded to retire to the country.

Two seasons before *Zeluco* was written, George Wright, author of *The Rural Christian*, had published his *Retired Pleasures*. The work was a sincere but pompous guide for the gentleman retiring to the country, training him in an appreciation of nature and teaching him how to develop a contemplative mood in which to pass his declining years.[9] Moore must have had such advice books in mind when he wrote the Transfer episode. Transfer 'quickly found rest the most laborious thing he had experienced ... while he yawned along his serpentine walks and fringed parterres, he thought the day would never have an end'. 'O Lombard-street! Lombard-street!' cries Transfer, 'in evil hour did I forsake thee for verdant walks and flowry landscapes, and that there tiresome piece of made water'.[10]

Moore provided a lengthy jest at the expense of his novice country gentleman. A passing Earl stops at the Transfer estate which is now the talk of the county, and its bored proprietor shows his lordship the grounds:

'Pray, Mr. Transfer,' said he [the Earl], pointing to one of the statues which stood at the end of the walk, 'what figure is that?'

'That, my lord,' answered Transfer, 'that there statue I take to be—let me recollect—yes, I take that to be either Venus or Vulcan, but upon my word, I cannot exactly tell which.—Here you, James,'—calling to the gardener; 'is this Venus or Vulcan?'

'That is Wenus,' answered the man; 'Wulcan is lame of a leg, and stands upon one foot in the next alley.' ...

'Perhaps it is not an easy matter to distinguish them,' said the Earl.

'Why, they are both made of the same metal, my lord,' said Transfer.
...

'You have so many of these gods, Mr. Transfer,' said the Earl, 'that it is difficult to be master of all their private histories.'

'It is so, my lord,' said Transfer; 'I was a good while of learning their names,—but I know them all pretty well now—That there man, in the

---

[8] John Moore, *Zeluco: Various Views of Human Nature, taken from Life and Manners, Foreign and Domestic*, 2nd edn., 2 vols. (Dublin, 1789), ii. 43.

[9] George Wright, *Retired Pleasures, or the Charms of Rural Life in Prose and Verse, with Occasional Notes and Illustrations* (London, 1787).

[10] Moore, *Zeluco*, ii. 43–4.

highland garb, is Mars. And the name of the old fellow with the pitch-fork is Neptune.'[11]

The episode won immediate fame. In her novel of the next season, Miss Williams made several allusions which presupposed her readers' familiarity with Mr Transfer, 'a personage whose acquaintance every reader of taste is, no doubt, proud to acknowledge'.[12] Moore's otherwise anomalous insertion made a similar impression upon the reviewers. 'The sketch of the life of Transfer', remarked the *European Magazine*, 'extends to a considerable length, and with little variation might bear a close resemblance to two-thirds of the wealthy citizens of London; it shews that the author is well acquainted with the genius, disposition, and manners, of the class of people he so accurately describes'.[13] The review also included an extensive quotation illustrating the Transfer character. The *Monthly Review* was similarly enthusiastic and even extended the censure of the retired trader. Like the *European Magazine*, the *Monthly Review* critic was also at great pains to authenticate the caricature:

The picture of Transfer, a wealthy citizen of London, will apply to many an original; and the common folly of men who have dedicated the whole vigour of their lives to one pursuit, that of accumulating money, and who yet expect in the wane of life to derive enjoyment from other occupations and other amusements, is placed in the most striking point of view.[14]

Criticism of the businessman's improved estate quickly became a set satire, and was still powerful in the writings of Peacock, eighty years after the *Connoisseur*. The target was the taste of the parvenu proprietor. Ridicule of the new villa and new estate-owners was offered in the belief that aspirants to gentility could be identified by obvious flourishes of bad taste. The country-house tradition, amplified by seventeenth-century contributions,[15] was paralleled by attacks upon the misguided ostentation of the modern villa. In the 1730s Pope's *Epistles* to

---

[11] Ibid. ii. 46–7.   [12] Williams, *Julia*, i. 214.
[13] *EM* 16: 347 (Nov. 1789).
[14] *MR* 80: 515 (June 1789).
[15] G. R. Hibbard, 'The Country House Poem of the Seventeenth Century', *Journal of the Warburg and Courtauld Institutes*, 19/1–2 (1956), 159–74; Howard Erskine-Hill, *The Social Milieu of Alexander Pope: Lives, Example and the Poetic Response* (New Haven, Conn., and London, 1975), esp. ch. 9.

Bathurst and to Burlington, with the latter's description of Timon's villa, became famed critiques of tasteless, ostentatious wealth. Richardson's *Sir Charles Grandison*, some twenty years later, presented Grandison Hall as a carefully constructed antithesis to the falsities of Timon's villa.[16] Specific contemporary allusions made by Pope and Mr Town were extended by later writers to the mockery of a full range of gentrifying accoutrements—zigzag avenues (instead of the fine gladed and straight avenues of true gentility), parterres, absurdly placed lakes, and most infamously, an extravagant love of classical statues, especially Cupids and Venuses. This last was to reach a glorious climax in Peacock's chapter on the Venus-mania of Crotchet, but ridicule of the parvenu's love of classical architectural allusion was strident throughout the 1780s.[17] Of many examples, there is a notable episode scorning the parvenu pretensions of a carriage covered by classical goddesses in the best-selling *Fashionable Follies* of 1781.[18]

The ingredients for such attacks on the parvenu were available from most London booksellers and librarians. Following the early success of books by Batty Langley in the 1740s, many booksellers issued guides and pattern books illustrating the plans and elevations for follies and garden buildings and ornamentation. The designs of William and John Halfpenny achieved enormous popularity during the 1750s. Their drawings were issued in finely produced pocket-guides to the latest Gothic and Chinese. Where the Langley books concentrated on highly detailed and elaborate designs for umbrellos, pavilions, and temples, and for porticoes, columns, windows, and other impressive additions, the Halfpenny pattern books included bridges, temples, triumphal arches, terraces, garden seats, palings, obelisks, termini, and a multitude of follies. The later Halfpenny collections included particularly grandiose suggestions, notably the Chinese floating pleasure islands (with temples) and Chinese snake boats to reach them.[19]

[16] F. W. Bateson (ed.), Alexander Pope, *Epistles to Several Persons*, 2nd edn. (London and New Haven, Conn., 1961), epistles III and IV, esp. pp. 146–51; David C. Streatfield and Alistair M. Duckworth (eds.) *Landscape in the Gardens and the Literature of Eighteenth-Century England* (Los Angeles, 1981), pp. 96–99.

[17] Thomas Love Peacock, *Crotchet Castle* (London, 1831), ch. 7, 'The Sleeping Venus'.

[18] Vaughan, *Fashionable Follies*, Folly CXIV.

[19] William and John Halfpenny, *Rural Architecture in the Gothick Taste: Being Twenty New Designs for Temples, Garden-Seats, Summer-Houses, Lodges, Terminies, Piers, &c ... With Instructions to Workmen, and Hints where with most Advantage to be erected* (London, 1752); *The Country Gentleman's Pocket Companion, and Builder's Assistant, For Rural Decorative Architecture, Containing*

It is unlikely that many Halfpenny drawings could ever have been reproduced in wood and stone with much exactness. No measurements or dimensional sense was given and no guidance was provided about materials or methods of construction. Inspiration could be all that the Halfpenny books offered to estate improvers and those commissioned to execute the designs. Many of the pattern books, however, such as the Langley editions and those issued by Thomas Overton and Thomas Wright, did include measurements and dimensional notes in their sketches of temples, arbours, and grottoes. By 1790, such publications as William Wrighte's *Grotesque Architecture* provided detailed indications of the wood, bark, and reeds to be used in construction.[20] A great number of the proposed hermitages, pavilions, bridges, and other follies were indeed attempted. Many are carefully recorded in a Dutch visitor's garden tour of 1791.[21] Langley and Wright both appear to have been very active executors of their own designs, with many surviving park and garden buildings ascribed to Wright at Badminton, Hampton Court House, Sudbury in Staffordshire, Horton Hall in Northamptonshire, Nuthall in Nottinghamshire, Shugborough in Staffordshire, Codger's Fort in Northumberland, and Belvedere House, Westmeath.[22]

Magazine essays and episodes in plays and novels took up references to specific designers and fashionable architects employed by 'Candidates for Sylvan Retirement'.[23] Although, as the survivals show, many of the new follies and garden buildings were commissioned by the rich and fashionable nobility, essayists and novelists associated many of the building plans with parvenu

Thirty-two New Designs Plans, and Elevations of Alcoves, Floats, Temples, Summer-Houses, Lodges, Huts, Grottos, &c., In Augustine, Gothic and Chinese Taste (London, 1753); and *Rural Architecture in the Chinese Taste: Being Designs Entirely New for the Decoration of Gardens, Parks, Forests, Insides of Houses, &c* (London, c.1754; 3rd edn., 1755, and repr. 1768 and 1774). William Halfpenny, alias Michael Hoare, (*fl.* 1752), resided in Surrey. His first book of designs was published as early as 1722.

[20] Thomas Overton, *The Temple Builder's Most Useful Companion* (London, 1774); Michael McCarthy, 'Thomas Wright's "Designs for Temples" and Related Drawings for Garden Buildings', and 'Thomas Wright's Designs for Gothic Garden Buildings', *Journal of Garden History*, 1 (1981), 55–66, 239–52; William Wrighte, *Grotesque Architecture, or Rural Amusement; Consisting of Plans, Elevations, and Sections* (London, 1790).

[21] Heimerick Tromp, 'A Dutchman's Visits to Some English Gardens in 1791', *Journal of Garden History*, 2 (1982), 41–58.

[22] Barbara Jones, *Follies and Grottoes*, 2nd edn. (London, 1974), pp. 140, 179, 180, 222; Gwyn Headley and Wim Meulenkamp, *Follies: A National Trust Guide* (London, 1986), pp. 32, 246, 284, 299, 304, 309, 310, 312, 418.

[23] The phrase of Wright, *Retired Pleasures*, p. 4.

bad taste—particularly the absurdities of the Composite which incorporated Japanese, Chinese, Indian, and High Gothic within one garden house or temple. There was some truth in this association. Many merchants and landowners with mercantile connections indulged in fashionable garden building. Thomas Goldney, a banker with overseas trading interests and a partner in the Coalbrookdale Iron Company, began a grotto at Clifton in the late 1730s and continued his temple, grotto, and cascade building for twenty-seven years. George Durant, a West Indian merchant from Worcestershire, built a new 'gothick' house in 1764 boasting a spectacular mixture of minarets, pinnacles, and Moorish domes. William Reeve, a self-made copper-smelter, built a castellated house at Brislington near Bristol in the late 1740s. During the next two decades, he added stables, called 'Arnos Castle', a bath-house, and a triumphal gate, all in eccentric gothic style. A grotto built by Samuel Scott, a Quaker linen-draper of Ware, was finished in 1773 at an estimated cost of £10,000.[24] This was no more than the aristocracy was doing. Indeed, merchant temple-builders and garden-improvers were relatively restrained contributors to grotto and folly building. The rage was taken up, amongst many other great landowners and luminaries, by Lord Hardwicke, Horace Walpole, Lord North, the Duchess of Richmond, and Alexander Pope himself. A few splendid examples of the commissions by rich tradesmen, however, were sufficient to associate them with tasteless pretension. As the *Connoisseur* complained:

If the taste for building encreases with our opulence for the next century, we shall be able to boast of finer country-seats belonging to our shopkeepers, artificers, and other plebeians, than the most pompous descriptions of Italy or Greece have ever recorded ... who has ever read of a Chinese-bridge belonging to an Attic tallow-chandler or a Roman pastry-cook? or could any of their shoemakers or taylors boast a Villa with it's tin cascades, paper statues and Gothic root-houses? Upon the above principles we may expect, that posterity will perhaps see a cheesemonger's Apiarium at Brentford, a poulterer's Theriotrophium at Chiswick, and an Ornithon in a fishmonger's garden at Putney[25]

Of the pattern books published, the Halfpenny volumes were especially littered with illustrations of classical statuary. Figures were arranged on terraces, in avenues, or surmounting Chinese

---

[24] Jones, *Follies and Grottoes*, pp. 63–5, 125, 152; Headley and Meulenkamp, *Follies*, p. 231.
[25] *Narrative Companion*, ii. 89–90.

and Indian temples. The *Connoisseur* made direct references to the Halfpenny taste of gilded classical architecture and Chinese temples:

> With many a bell and tawdry rag on
> And crested with a sprawling dragon
> A wooden arch is bent astride
> A ditch of water four foot wide;
> With angles, curves, and zigzag lines,
> From Halfpenny's exact designs
>
> .   .   .   .   .
>
> The Villa thus completely grac'd,
> All own, that Thrifty has a Taste:
> And Madam's female friends and cousins,
> With Common-Council-Men by dozens,
> Flock ev'ry Sunday to the Seat,
> To stare about them, and to eat.[26]

These caricatures of the architectural efforts of the newly rich focused on the rejection of simplicity and its replacement by ornate bad taste. The change was said to demonstrate wider failings. Counter-ideals were presented as 'antient hospitality', neighbourliness, and the proper stewardship of land and wealth. Towards the close of the century, dozens of novels and magazine contributions isolated Halfpenny-like proposals as indications of new vulgarity and new riches. There were many examples from the 1790 season, including the plans of Mr Changeall, the architect and landscape gardener employed at Boxley Grove in *The Maid of Kent*. Changeall has sweeping new schemes, culminating in the insistence that 'the straight walk from the house to the grove was to *convolute* to a considerable distance'.[27] When the owner of the Grove tries to pay off the architect, legal action is threatened. As the novel shows, the tonnish purveyors of piers, pilasters, and palisades are as pernicious as their fashionable clientele. All were undermining national values. Frivolous and foreign influences were at work. Straight avenues of English oaks were being replaced by Changeall's convolutions and Halfpenny zigzaggery.

---

[26] 'Humorous Account of the Villa's of London Tradesmen', *Connoisseur*, no. 135, repr. in *Narrative Companion*, ii. 91–4 (p. 94).

[27] *The Maid of Kent*, 3 vols. (London, 1790), i. 8–18 (p. 11).

The popularity of the fictional parvenu estate scene can partly be explained by these metaphorical possibilities. The relationship between landscaping and literary representation was a reciprocal one, with many contemporary garden designers drawing upon a literary inheritance for inspiration and direction. Capability Brown famously explained the merits of a garden design to Hannah More in terms of punctuation, phraseology, and composition. Many new gardens included busts of past and present literary figures and ornamental allusions to works of literature. Designers drew on a rich classical literature, from Virgil to Martial and Horace, to buttress their theories of recreating an Arcadia and of representing in landscape notions of liberty and control.[28]

Conversely, the garden was written about in relation to the broadest themes of civilization and nationhood. Horace Walpole described William Mason's 1772 poem, *The English Garden*, as 'a beautifull Set of Cuts to a Commentary on our once-blessed Constitution. When he gives laws to every man of property for the decoration of his grounds, he insinuates the blessing of laws that ascertain Property'.[29] The legal framework of landownership is mirrored by proscriptive laws on tasteful improvement and preservation. The ordering of the landscape further reflects the stability and orientation of the state. Two recent studies have suggested in new and illuminating ways how gardens and woodlands were read politically, offering specific allusions to national values, patriotism, political responsibilities, and social structure.[30] A pioneering history of attitudes to nature in England notes that in the eighteenth century 'trees were increasingly cherished, not just for their use, not even just for their beauty, but because of their human meaning, what they symbolized to the community in terms of continuity and association'.[31] Trees were crucial elements in the modern aesthetic

[28] William Roberts, *Memoirs of the Life and Correspondence of Mrs Hannah More*, 2nd edn., 4 vols. (London, 1844), i. 267, letter by Hannah More, Dec. 1782; Tromp, 'Dutchman's Visits', 46–58; Streatfield and Duckworth, *Landscape in the Gardens*, pp. 97–8.

[29] Paget Toynbee (ed.), *Satirical Poems Published anonymously By William Mason with Notes by Horace Walpole* (Oxford, 1926), p. 45.

[30] Stephen Daniels, 'The Political Iconography of Woodland in Later Georgian England', in Denis Cosgrove and Stephen Daniels (eds.), *The Iconography of Landscape: Essays on the Symbolic Representation, Design and Use of Past Environments* (Cambridge, 1988), 43–82; and Stephen Bending, 'Politics, Morality, and History: The Literature of the Later Eighteenth-Century English Landscape Garden', unpublished Ph.D. thesis (Cambridge, 1991).

[31] Keith Thomas, *Man and the Natural World: Changing Attitudes in England, 1500–1800* (London, 1983), p. 214.

of simplicity and 'naturalness', much of which was avowedly stylized and artificial. The placement of trees and natural features was carefully undertaken. It offered a powerful political and social iconography. Straightforwardness, simplicity, and a little, appropriate, craft were the basis for constitutional theories of gardening. In the 1780s Sir Uvedale Price was concerned about landscape improvement in terms of the reflection of known social boundaries. In 1794 Sir Humphrey Repton wrote that

the neatness, simplicity, and elegance of English gardening, have acquired the approbation of the present century, as the happy medium betwixt the wildness of nature and the stiffness of art; in the same manner as the English constitution is the happy medium betwixt the liberty of savages, and the restraint of despotic government.[32]

While Price worried about the fashion for planting conifers in representational terms as 'the upstart growth of deformity', Repton began to compare parvenu clients with the conifers they wished him to plant.[33] His gibes also had legal and economic implications. With a few additions peculiar to certain counties, timber was legally recognized as oak, ash, or elm of at least twenty years' growth. The cutting of timber by tenants was subject to legal constraint, and comparisons between conifers and trees of timber often involved statements about the relative productivity of plantation and the improvement of the freehold.

In the novels and magazines, most of the attacks on ostentation questioned the legitimacy of *nouveau riche* ownership of land and pointed malevolently to counterfeit pedigrees and the false values of new landowners. In 1785 Cumberland's enormously popular *Observer*, although generally sympathetic to business, told of Sir Theodore Thimble's improvements to his newly-purchased estate in Essex. After young Thimble inherits the estate, the heir of the previous owners returns to survey the alterations:

My favourite avenue no longer existed; the venerable tenants of the soil were rooted up, and a parcel of dotted clumps, composed of trumpery shrubs, substituted in their places; I was the more disgusted, when I perceived that by the nonsensical zigzaggery of the road, through

---

[32] Sir Uvedale Price, *A Letter to H. Repton, Esq ... to which is Prefixed, Mr Repton's Letter to Mr Price*, 2nd edn. (Hereford, 1798), p. 10.

[33] Daniels, 'Political Iconography of Woodland', pp. 61, 69.

which we meandered, I was to keep company with these new-fashioned
upstarts through as many parallels, as would serve for the regular
approaches to a citadel.[34]

The grounds of the *nouveau riche* exactly reflected the owner—his
ostentation, his newness, and his sudden transformation. He and
they were vulgar and superfluous to society as well as positively
destructive of the old and good. Such estates grew 'trumpery
shrubs' and their pretentious zigzag avenues created the allusion
of larger, more secluded estates. 'Noble' and 'gentle' oaks were cut
down and fast-growing conifers were planted in their stead. The
zealous collection of classical statuary was said to betray not only a
sham imitation of proper elegance, but also a pathetic craving for
a legitimizing tradition. Hardly incidental to the Transfer scene
was Moore's attention to the businessman's accent. Transfer was
shown to have risen from the lower orders, and his taste and
bewilderment in county society proved it. This and other attacks
against the purchase and improvement of estates by the parvenu
supported the belief that the newly-moneyed had no rights to
extensive landowning. The only possible response by *nouveaux
riches* owners—the imitation of the ideal virtues which led to the
assumption of new titles and pedigrees—merely opened up further opportunities for satire.

In fact, the evidence of major business entryism in the land
market is slim. Ever since Lang's work on Jacobean merchants, it
has been shown for ever more recent periods that the landowning
aspirations of men of trade were more restrained than formerly
believed.[35] It has already been long established that for investment alone, many were attracted by safe and profitable ventures
outside land.[36] The fall in the rate of interest in the seventeenth
century was largely a result of reducing the hazards of available
instruments of debt and improving their investment potential.[37]
Many affluent merchants did not, it seems, indulge in major land
purchases merely for social cachet. They therefore avoided the

---

[34] *Observer*, i. 32.

[35] R. G. Lang, 'Social Origins and Social Aspirations of Jacobean London Merchants',
Ec.HR 2nd ser. 27/1 (1974), 28–47 (pp. 40–7).

[36] H. J. Habakkuk, 'English Landownership, 1680–1740', *Ec.HR* 1st ser. 9/1 (1940), 2–17
(pp. 11–12); K. S. Davies, 'Joint Stock Investment in the Later Seventeenth Century', *Ec.HR*
2nd ser. 4/3 (1952), 283–301.

[37] H. J. Habakkuk, 'The Long-Term Rate of Interest and the Price of Land in the
Seventeenth Century', *Ec.HR* 2nd ser. 5/1 (1952), 26–45 (p. 41).

sort of rivalry between established and new gentry suggested by the literary attacks upon the parvenu estate of the 1770s and 1780s. Mercantile marriage alliance with the aristocracy did not necessitate extensive land purchase. There were long and fruitful associations between merchant oligarchies and rural proprietors, but as recent studies have shown, most merchants remained attracted to suburban living and the smaller estate.[38]

The obvious corollary of this is to ask whether competition in land increased in the second half of the century, fuelling the new bitterness towards the retired businessman. The broad consensus of present studies is that competition for great estates did not increase, but this is qualified by evidence suggesting greater activity in the market for smaller parcels of land. It was sales of these that were of greatest concern to the gentry. Modest land acquisition still attracted. As Henry Horwitz has argued, 'to perpetuate one's family name and to achieve social recognition, it was not enough to live in the expanding West End or to mingle with the "quality" during the months of the London season'.[39] Another qualification, however, is that despite much new research on questions relating to land and country houses, we still do not know whether the number of businessmen retiring to estates (irrespective of size) increased significantly during this period. Whether this is the case or not, it is quite clear that the contemporary debate was charged not so much by the aggregate number, as by the individual fame of the new owners, their use of the land, and the attention given to particular estates. The increase in criticism of the pretensions of businessmen and nabobs in the 1770s and 1780s also partly reflects contemporary awareness of trends in the land market. This could be used further to condemn *nouveaux riches* ambitions. There was certainly greater stress on changing landownership, a concern reflecting both increasing strains upon the retention of land and the influence of more general hostility towards new landowners.

The land market at this period and the accumulation of land by the great landowners has been under renewed investigation

[38] Rogers, 'Money, Land and Lineage'; Henry Horwitz, '"The Mess of the Middle Class" Revisited: The Case of the "Big Bourgeoisie" of Augustan London', *Continuity and Change*, 2/2 (Aug. 1987), 263–96.
[39] Ibid. p. 286.

for some time.[40] The original Habakkuk thesis of an increasingly limited land market in the second half of the eighteenth century, serving to protect the dominance of the great landholders, has been modified by evidence of a considerable turnover in small estates and by marked—if hardly surprising—regional variation.[41] In addition to long-term land exchange patterns, particular attention has been given to the question of the contraction of the land market during the second half of the century and the exclusion of certain types of new owner. For the smaller investor, the attractiveness of land was undiminished.[42] In numerical terms, however, newcomers to land were probably fewer than at any time during the previous two centuries.[43] Although the Habakkuk thesis has been revised in many parts, the consensus still suggests a drift in property in favour of the larger, existing landowner, both in the number of such proprietors and also in the proportion of the total acreage under their ownership. Moreover, on the question of business entryism into the greater landed élite, recent research impressively supports the early scepticism of W. D. Rubinstein. Concluding that there was no continuous 'process of rapid and substantial upward mobility of men of business into the landed classes', the count of the manors in three contrasting counties by Lawrence and J. C. F. Stone sets out to demolish the idea that businessmen bought big in land in the late eighteenth century.[44]

---

[40] Christopher Clay, 'Marriage, Inheritance, and the Rise of Large Estates in England, 1660–1815', *Ec.HR* 2nd ser. 21/3 (1968), 503–18; B. A. Holderness, 'The English Land Market in the Eighteenth Century: The Case of Lincolnshire', *Ec.HR* 2nd ser. 27/4 (1974), 557–76; J. V. Beckett, 'English Landownership in the Later Seventeenth and Eighteenth Centuries: The Debate and the Problems', *Ec.HR* 2nd ser. 30/4 (1977), 567–81; Lloyd Bonfield, 'Marriage Settlements and the 'Rise of Great Estates: The Demographic Aspect', *Ec.HR* 2nd ser. 32/4 (1979), 483–93. An overview is given in Habakkuk, 'English Landed Families', Part I; with Part II, *TRHS* 30 (1980), 199–221; and Part III, *TRHS* 31 (1981), 195–217.

[41] Attention has focused upon the representativeness of the original Bedfordshire and Northamptonshire study—Holderness, 'English Land Market', and Beckett, 'English Landownership'—and upon the demographic assumptions within the older model— Clay, 'Marriage, Inheritance', and Lloyd Bonfield, *Marriage Settlements, 1601–1710: The Adoption of the Strict Settlement* (Cambridge 1983).

[42] Beckett, 'English Landownership'; Holderness, 'Credit in a Rural Community', pp. 111–12.

[43] Most firmly stated in H. J. Habakkuk, 'The English Land Market in the Eighteenth Century', in J. S. Bromley and E. H. Kossmann (eds.), *Britain and the Netherlands* (London, 1960), pp. 154–73, (pp. 155–6).

[44] Rubinstein, 'New Men of Wealth'; Stone and Stone, *An Open Elite*, ch. 7. They base their conclusions on intensive study of Hertfordshire, Northamptonshire, and Northumberland. Included are all country houses of over 5,000 square feet.

The heightened concern about land transactions would therefore seem puzzling. It is clear that the literature of the final third of the century with its mounting anxiety over increased consumer spending gave prominence to very particular images of the purchase and improvement of land. Novelists provided much detail in fictional estate descriptions. Frequently, the size of new and old estates was noted precisely, together with rentals, expected returns from timber, and the nature of other holdings. Writers denounced the rapid turnover in land and the purchase of estates by those not born gentlemen. Only working possessors of land should be allowed to modify those antique buildings and furnishings too ponderous for modern taste. The 1790 *Fair Cambrians* is one of many imaginative publications of the season in which gentlemen improvers are favourably presented.

One obvious explanation for the response is that the image of widespread entryism in a *particular* section of the market was not unfounded, even if threats of social intrusion were exaggerated. Large estate buyers might indeed be few, but small entrants were there in plenty. As Professor Habakkuk emphasized, 'the *nouveaux riches* of the eighteenth century established themselves on a more modest scale than had their counterparts before 1640. In this sense more of the newcomers established gentry-sized estates in the eighteenth century than before 1640'.[45] Competition in the market for small estates clearly increased. While J. V. Beckett's research supported Professor Habakkuk's contention that it was the lesser gentry who were in decline, this was because the Cumbrian merchant and newly-wealthy buyers were able to find and buy the smaller-sized estates they were looking for. Greatest land transaction and market competition occurred at the level of the medium-sized properties of the gentry and smaller occupiers.[46] From this it seems that the prestige of land increased at a time when the smaller landowners were increasingly hard-pressed. The fight to retain estates was often hard and protracted. Moreover, even if the Stones' new work leaves the advocate of *nouveau riche* land-lust with only the pastures of the lesser gentry, these remain extremely extensive.[47] It is also exactly

[45] Habakkuk, 'English Landed Families: Part III', p. 217.

[46] Beckett, 'English Landownership', pp. 579–80; Clay, 'Marriage, Inheritance', pp. 515–16.

[47] In addition, of course, it is not yet established that the Stones' conclusions do hold for the English counties (38) outside their study.

here where competition would have impinged most directly upon the lesser gentry and the middle classes featured in the novels and to whom most novels appealed. Land prices were primarily determined by demand, itself reflecting, amongst other factors, the attractiveness of government securities. Their low price during the American conflict brought down land prices and values, making land purchase easier for would-be small estate-owners in the 1780s.

One other important consideration in the making of the contemporary image has been given added weight by the Stones' study. There was a significant increase in the sale of great estates near to London in the final third of the century. The Stones point out that the trend was not sustained, that purchasers were transient entrants to the landed élite, selling again in their own lifetime or with sales after death, and that the movement was not repeated elsewhere in the country. Nevertheless, the centre of the literature industry was London and literary distribution was clearly skewed towards the Home Counties. Even if the trend in the sale of great estates was not continued, the disruption in this part of the country was marked. In Hertfordshire, at least, there was 'a substantial influx of monied men, sufficient after 1760 seriously to affect the composition of the county élite'.[48]

In parts of the country where land sales did not accelerate, it is tempting to suggest that calls for economy and retrenchment were indeed sufficiently heeded—despite isolated but publicized bouts of exuberant spending—to enable the retention of estates and the contraction of particular selling-markets. More certainly, however, the estate was preserved by an increasing ability to support indebtedness, with the mortgage as a common instrument of long-term debt. It also, of course, heightened concern over the actual retention of property and redoubled the calls against extravagance. Sophie von la Roche sarcastically denied the popularity of Trusler's *Way to be Rich and Respectable* :

But this useful English book cannot be very well known, even in its own country, as in the latest papers I saw a number of estates up for sale; it seems to me as long as paint *à la* Ninon Enclos, soap-bubbles of Venus, hair-oil of Athens, and exaggerated fashions are sought by the 'ladies', as this paper reports, and as long as there are men who dodge the ban upon

[48] Stone and Stone, *Open Elite*, pp. 221–5 (p. 222), and cf. chronological and comparative trends in fig. 6. 1.

the coming fashion of tying shoes with laces, which threatens to ruin buckle-makers ... so long there will be family estates on the market, and this booklet will need to go through more than five editions ... for the nation cannot always count on a William Pitt to succeed with virtuous precepts in counteracting this irresponsible squandering.[49]

Moreover, in the second half of the century it is probable that a majority of the smaller landowners faced rising burdens of accumulated debts whose effects upon the condition of the estate are hidden by desperate yet successful attempts to prevent sale. Land tax was a sore complaint, and the diversion of capital into taxation precluded many estate improvements. Landowners faced taxes on houses, servants, carriages, horses, dogs, and windows. During the American war the land tax was restored to four shillings. More merchant than gentlemen landowners appear to have been able to release disposable capital for their estate improvements. There are a significantly high number of references to commercial wealth in a recent study of the development of landscape parks and gardens in Sussex during its major period of park development between about 1750 and 1780.[50] Adam Smith noted that the mere country gentleman, 'if he improves at all, it is commonly not with a capital, but with what he can save out of his annual income'. By contrast, the merchant who buys up land 'is not afraid to lay out at once a large capital upon the improvement of his land'.[51] Grudges surfaced in literary comment and popular jest. Some were real; many were thought likely to find an appreciative audience.

Discussion of landownership was often the issue within the luxury debate most associated with a 'country' voice. Civic virtue and public action were shown to be founded on the ownership of land, which ensured independence and responsibility. The interests of the whole country could best be directed by those not in the pocket of the city financier or one whose commercial operations were based upon credit and speculation. As much as the loss of the financial investment in a property, landowners fought against any devaluation of land as a symbol and purveyor of

[49] Williams, *Sophie in London*, pp. 296–7.

[50] Sue Farrant, 'The Development of Landscape Parks and Gardens in Eastern Sussex, c.1700 to 1820—a Guide and Gazetteer', *Garden History*, 17 (1989), 166–80.

[51] Adam Smith, *Wealth of Nations*, cited in H. J. Habakkuk, 'Economic Functions of English Landowners in the Seventeenth and Eighteenth Centuries', in W. E. Minchinton (ed.), *Essays in Agrarian History*, 2 vols. (Newton Abbot, 1968) i. 189–201 (p. 194).

social and political status, as the repository of traditional, permanent values, and as the conspicuous emblem of leisure. The estate provided a sense of identity between generations—a true 'vehicle of family purpose'.[52] Sales of land by gentry and smaller owner-occupiers were often traumatic crises in a long family history, and resistance to sale was famously demonstrated by the institution of trusteeships. The corner-stone of the eighteenth-century strict settlement was the appointment of trustees in an attempt to preserve contingent remainders and ensure successive resettlement.[53]

At the same time, certain social fluidity was proudly defended by popular authors, commercial writers, politicians, and contemporary biographers alike. Trade was held to contribute to the 'equalizing tendency' of society. This, however, merely confirmed the residual importance of the anciently held family estate. A preserve of privilege and real local influence and a node in the country-house federation, the landed estate gained in prestige as its inviolability was threatened by market activity and *nouveau riche* ownership. The family estate could be represented as the very antithesis of that form of dreaded self-interest and private accumulation popularized by the writings of Addison, Swift, and their successors. Property was held in trust for future generations as the family inheritance. It was not to be squandered on personal pleasure, nor was it said to be derived from suddenly accumulated riches. Insistence on the pedigree of estates, did, of course, disguise the fact that the great majority of estates were established or enlarged by grant on marriage or purchase after a mercantile career. In Northamptonshire most of the landowning squires were second or third generation merchants who had bought estates in the sixteenth or early seventeenth centuries.[54] The concern with longer-term holding was clearly conceptualized in the very agreement of so many 'years' purchase' as the declared price of sale.

For many of those holding lands, or, more pointedly, for those in recent or proposed acquisition, there was therefore something

---

[52] H. J. Habakkuk, 'England', in A. Goodwin (ed.), *The European Nobility in the Eighteenth Century: Studies of the Nobilities of the Major European States in the Pre-Reform Era* (London, 1953), pp. 1–21 (p. 2).

[53] Bonfield, 'Marriage Settlements'. The form of marriage settlement with strict entail had developed from the early 17th cent.

[54] Habakkuk, 'English Landownership'.

inherently contradictory in the very idea of an estate market, even before the rights and suitability of ownership were considered. Yet the more that land was viewed as a special preserve of status, the more attractive it became to those ready to call themselves gentlemen. Whatever contraction in the market, and whatever alternative investments to land were offered, land did not lose its own special investment attractions. As J. V. Beckett notes, 'the social and political prestige it conveyed far outweighed its diminishing economic return'. Land itself, as Sir Lewis Namier observed, embodied the ultimate entitlement to citizenship.[55]

Despite certain limitations to both the land market and business entryism in the second half of the century, fears of parvenu intrusion were heightened by increasing difficulties in maintaining landed property and keeping up appearances. New and threatening forces fuelled further disquiet. As a result, protest focused upon the social and political pretensions of nabobs, merchants, and manufacturers, and upon a consumer world of new tastes and upstart riches. In identifying new threats to the traditional estate, it was unexpectedly large purchases of land or sudden, spectacular improvements which won attention. The sharpest reaction was reserved for the newest identifiable group—the manufacturing and nabob land purchasers. The retired financier and petty businessman could—though not always—escape with scornful rebuke. Modest mercantile estate-buying had become commonplace, while many merchant families were well established in county politics by the second half of the century, with a corresponding interest by many landed gentlemen in the finer points of overseas trade.

By contrast, returned Anglo-Indians and new industrialist buyers made outstanding targets. Although more prominent than numerous, they were presented as a teeming force. As *The Topographer* believed, 'every year produces an inundation of *new men*, that over-run almost every county in the kingdom, expell the ancient families, destroy the venerable mansions of antiquity, and place in their stead what seemeth good in their own eyes of glaring brick or ponderous stone'.[56] Dominating the lists were

---

[55] Beckett, 'English Landownership', p. 578; Sir Lewis Namier, *England in the Age of the American Revolution*, 2nd edn. (London and New York, 1961), pp. 18–26.

[56] *The Topographer, For the Year* 1789 (London, 1789), p. iii.

Arkwright's Willersley Castle, Wedgwood's Etruria Hall and Barleston Hall, the Strutts' Milford House and Derby and Nottingham estates, the Peels' Drayton Manor and Tamworth estates, and the Whitbreads' grandiose collection of estates in Bedfordshire and Northamptonshire.[57] Of those returning from India, Sulivan bought Ponsborne Manor in Hertfordshire, and Clive bought homes in Berkeley Square and Shropshire, as well as Chatham's house at Bath and Newcastle's at Claremont. The unseemly haste of the rise was all too apparent, particularly if retirement was in mid-life or if the estate was an obvious showpiece. Potential buyers of more modest means who required a real return on their property might remain unsatisfied in the land market for several years, perhaps for a generation. The Ryder family failed to establish an estate until 1777, two decades after the death of the founder of the family fortunes.[58] All this was in sharp contrast to the alleged army of mushroom manufacturers and Anglo-Indian estate buyers.

At heart, therefore, the satire on the *nouveau riche* estate illustrates a fundamental cause of the renewed attack upon the vulgarity and false taste of the parvenu. The financial success of certain men of business posed a social threat to those jealously defining particular routes to repute and esteem. The threat was keenest to those attempting to preserve, or to adopt as their own, a traditional life-style in the face of the increasing burden of supporting a small estate. The ambiguous literary representation of fashion was paralleled by the denigration of those whose material accumulation, achieved by the otherwise acceptable avenues of industry and perseverance, lifted them beyond respectable social limits. The limits partly erected by polite literature were strengthened by the exemplary illustration of the outcast. This is clearly seen in the emphasis upon the origins of the successful businessman—now castigated as a parvenu whatever his social derivation.

---

[57] Harold Perkin, *The Origins of Modern English Society, 1780–1880* (London, 1969), pp. 88–9; Dean Rapp, 'Social Mobility in the Eighteenth Century: The Whitbreads of Bedfordshire, 1720–1815', *Ec.HR* 2nd ser. 27/3 (1974), 380–94; Beckett, 'English Landownership', p. 579. All give further examples.

[58] Habakkuk, 'English Land Market', p. 157.

II

ASSUMPTIVE GENTRY AND
THE THREAT TO STABILITY

If any of our readers will take the trouble to search in the
dusty recesses of circulating libraries for some novel published sixty years ago, the chance is that the villain or sub-
villain of the story will prove to be a savage old Nabob, with
an immense fortune, a tawny complexion, a bad liver, and a
worse heart.

Thomas Babington Macaulay,
Critical and Historical Essays (1843).

N E w ambitions provoked new hostilities. During the final third of
the eighteenth century popular literature reflected increasing
resentment against the social and political aspirations of three
arriviste types: planters, manufacturers, and nabobs. Both the
speed and the extent of social advancement was emphasized by
novelists and magazine contributors. Sudden social climbing was
portrayed as deceitful and dangerous, and writers touched upon
many of the concerns discussed so far—the social and financial
fears of luxury and fashion, the establishment of standards of
taste, and the preservation of traditional features of status. Underpinning such contributions was the need to create a saleable cause
to explain ills and to broadcast a simple, positive message. Many
arguments were interwoven: their impact depended upon their
interconnectedness and their confusion.

By far the greatest attention was given to self-made men
returning after service with the East India Company. West Indian
fortunes were familiar to English society by the mid-eighteenth
century, and the commercial worth of the plantations was the
subject of continued congratulation. Industrial fortunes were not

deemed sufficiently large or destabilizing until the late 1780s. The great shock to the observers of society from about 1760 was the influx of flagrantly wealthy nabobs, rather gradually in the early years and then sensationally during the 1780s. In this decade in particular, unprecedented hostility was fuelled by the well-publicized estate-buying of a few Anglo-Indians and other 'assumptive gentry'.[1] Laurence Sulivan and most of the early returned East Indians took up London residences and activities, but many nabobs of the next generation 'returned to live like a county magnate'.[2]

Published accounts of the ventures of the East India Company increased after the victories on the subcontinent in 1756–63. This early period of territorial conquest and alliances revived accusations about the bullion allegedly flowing to India in return for a damaging flood of imported eastern luxuries. Scholarly dissent from this traditional critique, notably that by Mildmay,[3] contrasted with the populist response which repeated the standard charges. There were, however, an increasing number of portrayals of the behaviour of individual adventurers on their return to England. In March 1761, in what seems to be one of the very first transferences of the term 'nabob', Horace Walpole complained that 'West Indians, conquerors, nabobs and admirals, attack every borough'. A month later, he was horrified by English nabobs appearing at St James's.[4] In 1763 the *Schemer* suggested that 'C———e' was a 'dirty ————'. 'C———e has conquered for us it is true, but C———e is a dirty ———— I will not say what. See how rich he is. Do you think all that m———y was honestly come by?'[5] Infamous by-elections, parliamentary investigations, and unseatings were popular targets for ballads, prints, and satirical verse. In 1758 and 1764, the *Annual Register* still had to explain the term 'nabob' (as a native ruler) for the wider public.[6] By the early

---

[1] The phrase used by Margaret Rudd, *The Belle Widows: With Characteristic Sketches of Real Personages and Living Characters*, 2 vols. (London, 1789), ii. 6.

[2] Lucy S. Sutherland, *The East India Company in Eighteenth-Century Politics* (Oxford, 1952), p. 62.

[3] William Mildmay, *The Laws and Policy of England, Relating to Trade* (London, 1765), pp. 82–3.

[4] W. S. Lewis (ed.), *The Yale Edition of Horace Walpole's Correspondence*, 48 vols. (New Haven, Conn., 1937–83), xxi. 484, Walpole to Mann, 3 Mar. 1761; xxi. 518, Walpole to Mann, 23 July 1761.

[5] *The Schemer; or, Universal Satirist* (London, 1763), p. 202 (no. 26, dated 13 July 1762).

[6] *Annual Register*, 1 (1758), p. 13, and 7 (1764), pp. 189–92.

1770s, however, print-shops responded eagerly to the activities of Rumbold and the 'Christian Club' at New Shoreham and such disreputable nabob by-elections as that at Worcester in 1773.

Both at the time, and in later assessments, animosity towards the nabob was seen as encouraging disaffection with commerce at large.[7] The return of Clive in 1767 was followed by the parliamentary inquiries of 1772–3, established after the Company almost collapsed in the economic slump of the previous year. Horace Walpole had 'no public news, but new horrors coming out every day against our East India Company and their servants'. Soon afterwards he declared himself 'impatient for the result of the inquiry, and to hear that the legislature has made all the amends in their power by condemning those harpies to regorge the gold and diamonds they have so infamously extorted'.[8] The parliamentary inquiry of 1772–3, although more penetrating than that of 1766-7 and culminating in the first Regulating Act, did not condemn Walpole's smiling villains. Walpole was outraged when Clive—'as white as snow'—received the Commons' praise rather than its censure: 'Cortez and his captains were not more spotless heroes'.[9] When charged with financial misdealings, the directors of the East India Company blamed the activities of individual nabobs. Moreover, just when the Company was forced to ask parliament for financial assistance, Indian groups in the Commons were gaining in numbers and notoriety. Four returned nabobs held parliamentary seats in December 1765, thirteen in November 1774, and eighteen in November 1783. By the end of that year, the East Indian interest boasted thirty-one members of parliament, with a further twenty-seven members claiming a Company or city and shipping attachment. After the Spring general election of 1784, at least fifty Company men were returned, seventeen of whom sat in the Commons for the first time. The *Public Advertiser* reported that Pitt had been carried into office on the strength of seventy-four MPs from the 'Bengal Club'.[10] At

---

[7] McVeagh, *Tradefull Merchants*, pp. 92–7.

[8] Lewis, *Walpole's Correspondence*, xxiii. 451, Walpole to Mann, 22 Dec. 1772; xxiii. 457, Walpole to Mann, 30 Jan. 1773.

[9] Ibid. xxiii. 484–5, Walpole to Mann, 29 May 1773.

[10] P. J. Marshall, *The Impeachment of Warren Hastings* (Oxford, 1965), pp. 23–5; C. H. Philips, *The East India Company, 1784–1834*, 2nd edn. (Manchester, 1961), pp. 24–30; James M. Holzman, *The Nabobs in England: A Study of the Returned Anglo-Indian, 1760–1785* (New York, 1926), pp. 103–30; Robert Palk to William Goodlad, 2 Feb. 1772, Historical Manuscripts Commission, Report no. 74 (London, 1922), Report on the Palk Manuscripts, p. 170.

the time, Walpole observed that it was not only fears of the political machinations of the 'nest of monsters . . . and their spawn of nabobs', 'but it was the gold of the Company that really conjured up the storm, and has diffused it all over England'.[11]

Nabob wealth was seen to be buying political power. Despotism at home and abroad was rooted in the money-lust. The trial of Sir Thomas Rumbold in April 1783 inspired numerous angry critiques. Tracts and ballads alleged that Pitt's 1784 election victory and his subsequent taxation proposals were bought by nabob money.[12] Prints had acquired a virtual immunity from prosecution and the Wilkes crusade and the Indian questions transformed them into powerful political weapons. The Carlo Khan prints, following Fox's India Bills, were hugely popular and influential. Numerous contemporary commentators remarked on their impact. Magazines reproduced the most popular squibs and cartoons.[13]

The most inflamed attacks upon the nabob, however, date from after the return to England of Warren Hastings. Hastings's arrival in 1785 marked the beginning of five years of uproar, even though his £80,000 gains were paltry compared to Clive's earlier million and the million pounds of Rumbold, both gathered over a much shorter period. The *Rolliad* and other squibs attacked Hastings and his wife for offering presents to the Crown, ridiculing their extravagant life-style.[14] Typical of the attacks on Mrs Hastings was Tickell's ode, first printed in the *Morning Herald* and *Daily Advertiser*:

[11] Lewis, *Walpole's Correspondence*, xxv. 484, Walpole to Mann, 30 Mar. 1784.

[12] Goldsmiths' Library Broadsides, v, *Poor Old England: Billy Boy and the East India Nabobs; or Taxation for Ever* (c.1785), and *Billy's Nabobs for England* (c.1784).

[13] M. Dorothy George, *English Political Caricature to 1792: A Study of Opinion and Propaganda* (Oxford, 1959), pp. 169–70, with examples; Frederic George Stephens, Mary Dorothy George, *et al.* (eds.), *Catalogue of Prints and Drawings in the British Museum*, 11 vols. (London, 1870–1954), v and vi, nos. 6276, 6285, 6462, 6558, 6886 (from Carlo Khan series); 5341, 5351 (nabob by-elections); 6966, 6978 (from more than four dozen on Hastings); and from the Inquiry period, *T&C* 4: 705 (Supplement 1772), 'The India Directors in the Suds'; and *Oxford Magazine*, 10: 144 (Apr. 1773), 'The Present Times or the Nabobs Cl–ve and C–l–ke brought to Account'.

[14] Philip Lawson and Jim Philips, '"Our Execrable Banditti": Perceptions of Nabobs in Mid-Eighteenth Century Britain', *Albion*, 16/3 (Fall 1984), 225–41 (p. 227); *An Asylum for Fugitive Pieces, in Prose and Verse* (London, 1785) includes the 'Extract from the Rolliad' and 'Criticisms on the Rolliad', pp. 169–248.

Gods! how her diamonds flock
On each unpowder'd lock!
On every membrane see a topaz clings!
Behold! her joints are fewer than her rings![15]

Hastings and his wife were regarded as the perfect exemplars to illustrate the crimes of the newly-moneyed, of their luxury, extravagance, and upstart pretension. The climax came with the parliamentary charges against Hastings of 1786–7 and the final impeachment a year later. In the words of one historian of the trial, the Commons' move to impeach Hastings 'seems to have been a genuine expression of the idealism and prejudices of ordinary members and not the result of any Machiavellian plot by ministers'.[16] Hastings's arraignment before the Lords in Westminster Hall was the focus of the 1788 fashionable season. Fanny Burney's remarkably vivid eyewitness reports confirm the hysteria of the opening days, the scramble for admission tickets, and the social necessity of making an appearance at Westminster Hall. The trial opened in February 1788 and, after many long interruptions, did not complete its proceedings until 1795.[17]

Dozens of defences and charge-sheets were commissioned by the partisans. Language became increasingly extravagant. Burke's opening speech at the trial spanned four daily sessions, and prompted new invective against the accused: 'for years he lay down upon that sty of disgrace, fattening in it, lying feeding upon that offal of disgrace and excrement, and everything that could be opprobrious to the human mind'.[18] Hastings had 'a heart blackened to the very blackest—a heart dyed deep in blackness— a heart corrupted, vitiated and gangrened, to the very core'.[19] Fanny Burney, caught up in the imaginative feast of the trial, but trying to maintain her belief in Hastings's innocence, noted in astonishment the extent of opinion against the prisoner.[20] The trial was grand drama. Gilbert Elliott, one of the managers, could not remember 'so heartily and copiously crying on any public

[15] [Richard Tickell *et al.*], *Probationary Odes for the Laureatship by Sir John Hawkins Knt.* (London, 1785), p. 52.

[16] Marshall, *Impeachment of Warren Hastings*, p. 62.

[17] Dobson, *Diary of Madame D'Arblay*, iii. 408–80. The trial is detailed in Marshall, *Impeachment of Warren Hastings*, and Michael Edwardes, *Warren Hastings: King of the Nabobs* (London, 1976).

[18] E. A. Bond (ed.), *Speeches of the Managers and Counsel in the Trial of Warren Hastings*, 4 vols. (London, 1859–61), ii. 69–70, 25 Apr. 1789.

[19] Ibid. i. 57.   [20] Dobson, *Diary of Madame D'Arblay*, iii. 424–37.

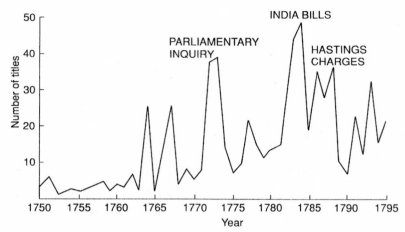

FIG. 5. The Publication of Tracts and Pamphlets (by title) concerning the East India
Company and Indian Affairs, 1750–1795
Sources: L. W. Hanson, *Contemporary Printed Sources for British and Irish Economic History,
1701–1750* (Cambridge, 1963); Henry Higgs, *Bibliography of Economics, 1751–1775* (Cambridge,
1935); *ESTC* (BL base only); and *PHIBB* (title check only).

occasion'. Gibbon recorded that Sheridan, at the close of his
speech, 'sunk into Burke's arms, but I called this morning, he is
perfectly well. A good actor.'[21] For all her defence of Hastings,
Burney also joined in the castigation of the extravagances of his
wife. 'I have always been very sorry that Mrs Hastings ... should
have an indiscretion so peculiarly unsuited to her situation, as to
aim always at being the most conspicuous figure wherever she
appears. Her Dress now was like that of an Indian Princess ...
every body else looked under dressed in her presence'.[22] Even the
rural diary of the Revd Edmund Nelson, father of Horatio, testifies
to the currency of such scorn for nabob wealth.[23]
    A fuller literary response to Indian affairs between 1750 and

---

[21] Cited in Edwardes, *Warren Hastings*, p. 169. There are memorable asides, noting the
collapse of speakers and of members of the audience, in Bond, *Speeches of the Managers*.
    [22] Joyce Hemlow (ed.), *The Journals and Letters of Fanny Burney (Madame D'Arblay)*, 12 vols.
(Oxford, 1972–84), i. 166.
    [23] M. Eyre Matcham (ed.), *The Nelsons of Burnham Thorpe: A Record of a Norfolk Family
Compiled from Unpublished Letters and Notebooks*, 1787–1842 (London, 1911), pp. 53, 54, 57.

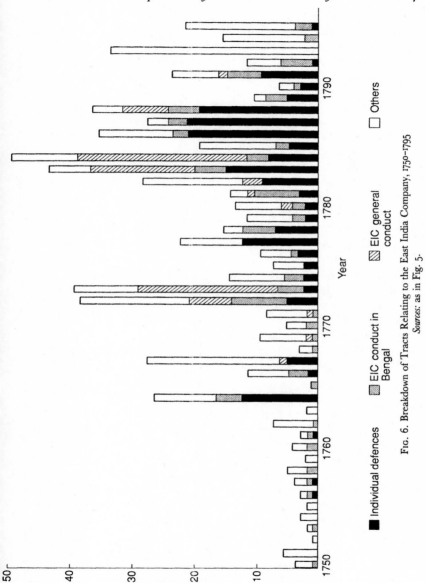

Fig. 6. Breakdown of Tracts Relating to the East India Company, 1750–1795
Sources: as in Fig. 5.

1800 is indicated in figs. 5 and 6. Especially striking is the number of tracts concerning the India Bill, the sustained interest in the Hastings trial, and the dramatic rise in the number of published individual defences in the 1780s. In imaginative writing, reactions to the influx and activity of nabobs was swift. It would be wrong, however, to believe that popular literature did not include debate about the issues raised by the home-coming of rich Anglo-Indians. The much-used Walpole letters convey typical accusations against the nabobs, but no sense of the counter-arguments. By contrast, the fictional treatment of the returned nabob remained ambivalent for twenty years after the first return of Clive. Even during the 1770s and 1780s, a nabob or West Indian planter could be presented as beneficial to contemporary society. *The Clandestine Lovers* boasts a finale featuring a legacy from a rich uncle in India. The self-made and avuncular Sir Robert Raymond, Bt. returns from India in Pratt's *Emma Corbett*, worth £50,000 and dispensing good cheer and counsel.[24] Admiral Harrison appears in Charlotte Palmer's *Female Stability* as a bluff immigrant nabob. Many novels provided the sort of romantic interest in the Indian states attempted by *The Indian Adventurer or the History of Mr. Vanneck* in 1780. Here, the hero does not return to Europe, but concludes his memoirs when still in Bengal. The text makes allusions to those who 'will return home with fortunes, equal to those of the Nabobs, whose riches have lately made such a figure in the commercial world'.[25] The ultimately reformed hero of *The Perfidious Guardian* amasses a vast fortune in Bengal before doubling his money in Indostan.[26] In 1790, Mr Clifford in Williams's *Julia* returns from the East Indies replete with the fortune to rescue the ancestral estate and its oppressed community from the clutches of parvenus.

Frequently an enabler of benevolence, Indian wealth was sanctioned or condemned according to the manner in which it was accrued and according to the social origin of its recipient. Once again, the guiding principle was the disposal of the fortune and the pursuit of the proper responsibilities of wealth. The exact origin of a foreign-made fortune was ignored when its holder

[24] *ER* 15: 466 (June 1790); Samuel Jackson Pratt, *Emma Corbett; or, The Miseries of Civil War* (Dublin, 1780), pp. 69, 81–2.

[25] *The Indian Adventurer; or, History of Mr. Vanneck* (London, 1780), pp. 54–5.

[26] *Perfidious Guardian*, ii. 105–6.

enjoyed an acceptable social status and used his windfall for the benefit of the community. When such wealth was deemed to belong to the presumptuous upstart, its derivation was given in ruthlessly simple terms. As Richard Clarke's much-reprinted poem *The Nabob: Or, Asiatic Plunderers* insisted, the immorality of such gain was confirmed by the means of its acquisition. In 1770, William Guthrie's *Grammar* illustrated the point:

The vast fortunes made during the late and the preceding wars, the immense acquisitions of territory by peace, and above all the amazing encrease of territorial as well as commercial property in the East Indies, have introduced a species of people among the English, who have become rich without industry, and by diminishing the value of gold and silver have created a new system of finances in the nation. Time alone can shew the event: Hitherto the consequences seem to have been unfavourable, as it has introduced among the commercial ranks a spirit of luxury and gaming that is attended with the most fatal effects, and an emulation among merchants and traders of all kinds, to equal, or surpass the nobility and the courtiers. The plain frugal manners of men of business which prevailed so lately as the accession of the present family to the crown, are now disregarded for tasteless extravagance in the dress and equipage.[27]

An important watershed in popular responses, however, came with Samuel Foote's play *The Nabob*, first performed at the Haymarket in July 1772. As the *Town and Country Magazine* commented, 'the character of a Nabob has, for some time, been a subject of so much animadversion, as well within, as without doors, that Mr. Foote judiciously thought he would be a proper personage for dramatic satire'.[28] Revived throughout the 1770s, the play's last London appearance was in June 1786.[29] In the prologue to *The Bankrupt* of 1773, Foote attacked the Clive acquittal in a parody of his defence speech before the Commons.[30] Richard Tickell also exploited the Foote success with a further stage caricature, that of Sir Peter Pagoda in *The Carnival of Venice*. First performed in 1781, the play offered a merciless assault on Rumbold.

Such caricatures, as well as the continued reportage of nabob

---

[27] William Guthrie, *A New Geographical, Historical, and Commercial Grammar* (London, 1770), p. 119.

[28] *T&C* 4: 373 (July 1772).

[29] Samuel Foote, *The Nabob; A Comedy: In Three Acts* (London, 1778); Grzegorz Sinko, 'Samuel Foote: The Satirist of Rising Capitalism', *Prace Wrocławskiego Towarzystwa Naukowego*, ser. A, 47 (1950), 5–72; Ben Ross Schneider, Jr. (comp.), *Index to the London Stage, 1660–1800* (Carbondale and Edwardsville, Ill., 1979), p. 319.

[30] Simon Trefman, *Sam. Foote, Comedian, 1720–1777* (New York, 1971), p. 215.

politics, influenced representations in the domestic novel. The fictional Anglo-Indian became increasingly loathsome. A sketch of an 'English Nabob' in Mrs Bonhote's *The Rambles of Mr. Frankly*, notes that 'sickness and fatigue had made large furrows in his forehead. He leaned upon his companion, as if unable to support himself—"And is this the price of accumulated wealth?"'[31] By 1790 most portrayals of the nabob were without any saving characteristics. In *Ellen Woodley*, a later work by Mrs Bonhote, Sir Henry Alford has gained 'more wealth than he could well know how to spend':

Having amassed in a few years, by rapine, cruelty, and injustice, an immense fortune, he returned, determined to spend the remainder of his days with luxury and splendour in old England ... he remained no longer in London, than just to pay his devoirs at Court, and settle his affairs, before he hurried into the country, to enjoy himself at his favourite villa. This sudden retreat was much against the inclination of Lady Alford, who was impatient to exhibit some of her Asiatic splendour before she left town.[32]

As Mrs Bonhote further explained,

The arrival of these great folks, their numerous retinue of servants, the splendour of their equipage, the extravagance and voluptuousness of their manner of living, which were told with additions and exaggerations, furnished the whole village with sufficient subjects for conversation. One heard, that the bed in which Lady Alford slept, was decorated with a crescent of diamonds, and the curtains ornamented with festoons of pearls;—another, that the tables were solid gold, and the stoves silver, and that master Edwin was not suffered to walk a yard, but had a dozen black men to carry him to bed.[33]

In the same season, Mrs Smith's nabobess,[34] Mrs Maltravers, recalls the 'luxurious magnificence to which she was accustomed in the East', and Mrs Lennox's heroine experiences rural life under immigrant 'sons and daughters of sudden opulence', the extravagant, uncharitable, price-rising 'Indian plunderers'.[35]

[31] Mrs Bonhote, *The Rambles of Mr. Frankly*, 2 vols. (London, 1772), i. 36–7.

[32] Mrs Bonhote, *Ellen Woodley*, 2 vols. (London, 1790), i. 15–16.

[33] Ibid. i. 20–1.

[34] The term first used in fiction in *Hartly House, Calcutta*, 3 vols. (London, 1789), i. 117–18, ii. 88.

[35] Smith, *Ethelinde*, ii. 198; Lennox, *Euphemia*, i. 123–7. Fuller quotation is also given, above, pp. 80–1. It is likely that Mrs Smith adapted the name Maltravers from 'Mountravers' the St Nevis estates of the Pinney family of Bristol, and discussed in Richard Pares, *A West-India Fortune* (London, 1950).

Ghastly cruelties towards native East and West Indians were suggested by both serious writers and magazine contributors. In 1768, Colonel Alexander Dow's extremely influential *History of Hindostan* adopted a very hostile view of British activity in India.[36] Humanitarian concerns about Indian natives were given special prominence. 'Their grievances were unparalleled in history', argued Burke, amid extravagant condemnations of nabob action in the subcontinent.[37] Of all the charges against Hastings, most attention was given to allegations about his involvement in the Benares revolt and his treatment of the Begums of Oudh with their lurid claims of assault and humiliation. A typical newspaper letter denounced the conduct of a Mrs F——g——d whose behaviour 'could only come from the *dregs of the people*, a *lunatic*, or one of those whose Asiatic cruelties have filled their purses; but left their heads as empty as their hearts, of sensibility or delicacy'.[38]

The perceived motive for cruelty was greed. It was the sheer wealth of many of the returned nabobs and planters that attracted most comment.[39] In a society obsessed by monetary value and yet unwilling to admit that this could ensure status, huge hostility was generated by the creation of sudden overseas fortunes. Exotic descriptions appeared of the actions of men risen from the lowliest of dunghills to the heights of affluence. The size of personal wealth was not the only concern. Many returned planters claimed enormous fortunes, some gathered over a single generation. As important as its extent was the manner of wealth-holding. The West Indian usually maintained an interest in West Indian estates, but the out-of-service nabob severed his connections with India, was resting upon his fortune, and had no special interest to protect but himself. Unlike the planter, he was not tied to landed interests before his arrival in England.[40]

In addition to this, India was a land of speculation in more than the monetary sense. Fascination with India and the nabobs came

---

[36] Wylie Sypher, 'The Anti-Slavery Movement to 1800 in English Literature', unpublished Ph.D. thesis (Harvard, 1937); Holzman, *Nabobs*, p. 93.

[37] *Parl. Hist.* xxiv. 1255, 30 July 1784.

[38] *Morning Herald, and Daily Advertiser*, 28 June 1784.

[39] Of many examples, the popular 'India Game', repr. in John Freeth, *Political Songster: or, A Touch on the Times*, 6th edn. (Birmingham, 1790), p. 93.

[40] The returned West Indian is examined in Wylie Sypher, 'The West-Indian as a "Character" in the Eighteenth Century', *Studies in Philology*, 36/3 (July 1939), 503–20. Also, L. J. Ragatz, 'Absentee Landlordism in the British Caribbean, 1750–1833', *Agricultural History*, 5/1 (Jan. 1931), 7–24; and Pares, *West-India Fortune*, ch. 8.

in great measure from their mystery and immense imaginative possibilities. India, source of pillage and ill-gained riches, was that 'mine of exhaustless wealth' or 'that region of gaiety and pleasure'.[41] In at least half the novels featuring India, the hero (or heroine) sets off to the East to recover his fortune.[42] Even Mackenzie's John Homespun admitted to the allure of nabob wealth:

There are such accounts of nabobs, rajahs, and rajah-pouts, elephants, palanquins, and processions; so stuck full of gold, diamonds, pearls, and precious stones; with episodes of dancing girls and otter of roses!—I have heard nothing like it since I was a boy, and used to be delighted with reading the Arabian Nights Entertainments.[43]

From the unknown came the tales of horror with which to confront the *nouveau riche*. Ignorance fathered hostility. Unprecedentedly large spoils were spent on status-building, without any clear idea of how the moneys were derived. For Walpole, the conflicting images of India were 'an endless labyrinth'. His respondent concluded that 'the immense riches that those barbarians brought home, alone pronounce their condemnation'.[44] No knowledge of India was required save that it was the fount of riches, the land of rapine, and the school for upstarts.

In this respect, India was frequently included in novels to add simple up-to-the-minute appeal. Dozens of novels published during the 1780s feature dramatic Indian episodes. A fashion for India contributed much to the intense, bubble-like interest in fiction of the five years, 1785–90. In *Juliana* of 1786, the hero rescues an Indian princess from the clutches of a low-born Company official. The 1787 *History of Captain and Miss Rivers* encouraged readers to immerse themselves in Indian affairs. The final volume of *Hartly House* of 1789, even opens with the startling revelation by the heroine that 'I am become a convert to the Gentoo faith, and have my Bramin to instruct me *per diem*'.[45] All responses, however, remained largely dependent upon the currency of nabob estate-buying, political activity, and trials of the returned Company grandees. Popular literary interest in the nabob fails almost

---

[41] *Hartly House*, i. 1; *Disinterested Nabob: A Novel*, 3 vols. (London, 1787), i. 1.

[42] Notably, in *Adeline; or, The Orphan*, 3 vols. (London, 1790), and *The Disinterested Nabob*.

[43] Henry Mackenzie, *Works*, 8 vols. (Edinburgh, 1808), v. 165–75, 'The Lounger', no. 17, 28 May 1785 (pp. 172–3).

[44] Lewis, *Walpole's Correspondence*, xxiii. 392, Walpole to Mann, 27 Mar. 1772; xxiii. 397, Mann to Walpole, 28 Mar. 1772.

[45] *Hartly House*, iii. 1.

completely after the end of the Hastings trial. After 1800 the nabob makes no more villainous appearances and very few complimentary or derisory ones.[46]

It should be added, by way of comparison, that many 1780s' attacks against northern manufacturing upstarts were also fuelled by the mystery of industrial operations. Several southern-bound writers admitted that much of the north was as unknown as India. For those that did travel, plans to visit industrial sites were often frustrated. The assumption that country houses and commercial establishments would be open for viewing by the itinerant gentleman, made the refusal of access all the more annoying and noteworthy. Gentlemen travellers were exasperated when factory visits were curtailed by limited access, complex touring procedures, or complete refusal of entry. Closure, however, stimulated the imagination. Byng, Viscount Torrington, was barred from Arkwright's mills.[47] Faujas de Saint-Fond was infuriated to find that he was not allowed to enter the great chemical works at Prestonpans and could not expect, as Fiennes and Defoe had done, to stride into any factory in his path. As he noted of 'the greatest manufactory of the oil of vitriol in Britain':

> The whole of the place is surrounded with a very high wall, which does not permit the eye to discover even the chimney tops of the works ... every thing is so carefully enveloped in mystery, that the harbour itself is surrounded with walls of a great height ... The only thing known is, that the oil of vitriol which it produces, forms an article of very extensive commerce.[48]

Many factory-masters and mill-owners—notably Arkwright— were reluctant to grant visiting rights because of the genuine difficulties and dangers of access. Manufacturers also limited viewing in order to protect trade secrets. Such precautions were not taken without good reason, as revealed by the records of the Baron Stein espionage of 1779.[49] The frustration of would-be visitors increased during the 1780s when manufacturers became

[46] *The Nabob's Wife*, 3 vols. (London, 1837), and Mrs Monkland, *The Nabob at Home; or, The Return to England*, 3 vols. (London, 1842). Returned Company men occasionally appear as figures of ridicule, notably Thackeray's Joseph Sedley in *Vanity Fair* (1847–48).

[47] Andrews and Beresford, *Torrington Diaries*, ii. 190–91 (cf. his successful visits, i. 49, 120, 188; ii. 62).

[48] Saint-Fond, *Travels*, i. 177.

[49] Jennifer Tann (ed.), *The Selected Papers of Boulton and Watt* (London and Cambridge, Mass., 1981), pp. 156–65.

even more protective of their businesses and closed premises which had formerly been open to gentlemen tourists. Fanny Burney made her one and abortive factory visit to the pin factory at Gloucester, toured by Byng the year before, and recorded that 'they discouraged us by an account of its dirt'.[50] 'They will not now shew their Manufactures', complained Mrs Thrale of her 1787 stop-over at Birmingham, contrasting this with the memorable excursion of 1774 to Clay's papier mâché works and Boulton's button factory.[51] Wendeborn, writing 'On Manufacturies' in his 1791 *View of England* recorded that 'among the English themselves, I have heard complaints, that nothing satisfactory, and which could be depended upon, has been written upon this subject, which requires infinite pains to become acquainted with, even to a moderate degree'.[52] In addition, writers accused the City and the Bank of clandestine financial and business activities. According to Wendeborn, the latter was 'wrapped up in mysterious darkness; and I have been told, that even not all the directors themselves are admitted behind the curtain, or shewn the caves of Plutus, where the treasures of the Company are deposited'.[53]

In the representation of the nabob, however, mystery was an enabling but not sufficient ingredient. The most common depiction of the Anglo-Indian was as the exemplar of social presumption. The trading or Company upstart became the literary model for the man of humble origins whose sudden social elevation posed a far more serious threat to society than did the fashionable man of ton. The fates assigned to those who overreached themselves were increasingly tremendous. Throughout the 1780s, the stereotype of the nabob illustrated the dangers and follies of the upstart. One heroine, writing from the subcontinent, reported that 'at this very time have I a most noble Nabob, whose father for ought I know, may be a cobler, if one may judge by the elegance of the son sighing at my feet'.[54] The wife of Rudd's General Nabob Sumpter was handicapped by vulgar accent and manners.[55] The heiress of the cake and sugar-plum seller who marries the East Indian in *The Twin Sisters* is self-opinionated, extremely coarse,

[50] Dobson, *Diary of Madame D'Arblay*, iv. 27, 19 July 1788.

[51] Balderston, *Thraliana*, ii. 688 (Sept. 1787), and cf. G. B. Hill, ed., L. F. Powell, rev., *Boswell's Life of Johnson*, 6 vols. (Oxford, 1934–50), v. 458, 20 Sept. 1774.

[52] Wendeborn, *View of England*, i. 159.   [53] Ibid. i. 143.

[54] *Disinterested Nabob*, i. 82.

[55] Rudd, *Belle Widows*, ii. 2–6.

and '*kivered* all over with diamonds'.[56] Foote's *Nabob* had presented Sir Matthew Mite as an extravagant gamester, pompous, raised from the lowest of social orders, and providing a notorious example of sham gentility and reckless extravagance. Lady Oldham observes, 'with the wealth of the East, we have too imported the worst of its vices. What a horrid crew!' Mite first appears 'in his macaroni dress for the hazard-table', while he practises his technique so that 'in a couple of months, I shall be able to tap, flirt, stamp, dribble, and whirl, with any man in the club'.[57] During the next few scenes Mite shuns his old working-class friend, Putty, and by means of ludicrous presents, becomes a member of a supposedly élite antiquarian society. Sykes and Rumbold—'one of our Indian mushrooms'—were both featured as former tavern waiters in innumerable satires and lampoons.[58] Of her low-born Nabob Sumpter, Mrs Rudd concluded that he was

the quintessence of Eastern pomposity. He mistook ostentation for dignity; glare for splendour; superficial smattering for literature; and ferrago observation, gleaned from his former motley situations, for correct and extensive knowledge of life. Yet he had some good sense, and some good qualities, and was one of the least exceptionable of our 'Asiatic quality'.[59]

The 'mushroom' rise and 'dunghill' origins became stock metaphors. Bailey's *Dictionary* of 1721 was the first to acknowledge that 'in a Figurative Sense', 'mushroom' is 'used for an upstart'. Bailey's twenty-fifth edition, in 1789, recognized the dunghill as a 'vile abode' and as 'a mean pedigree'. It was explained by Barclay's *Dictionary* of 1779 as 'a situation of meanness ... a man descended from mean parentage ... sprung from the dunghill ... figuratively mean, base, or worthless'. Barclay defined mushroom as 'an upstart; a person that rises to grandeur from a mean and poor birth'.[60] Notably, it was grandeur rather than power that was

---

[56] *The Twin Sisters; or, The Effects of Education*, 4 vols. (London, 1788–9), iv. 24.

[57] Foote, *Nabob*, pp. 13, 26, 28.

[58] Walpole embroidered upon the charge with relish, Lewis, *Walpole's Correspondence*, xxv. 274, 400, xxix. 35, Walpole to Mann, 5 May 1782, 30 Apr. 1783, and Walpole to Mason, 19 May 1780; xxix. 122, Walpole to Mason, 30 Mar. 1781; xxv. 274, Walpole to Mann, 5 May 1782.

[59] *Belle Widows*, ii. 2.

[60] Bailey, *Universal Etymological English Dictionary*; Revd James Barclay, *A Complete and Universal English Dictionary on a New Plan* (London, 1779). Both Dyche and Bentinck listed only a 'botanical' meaning.

stressed. The popular moralist in the *Sentimental Lucubrations* of 1770 reviewed mankind 'from the king upon the throne to the beggar on the dunghill'.[61] 'To mushroom' even became a verb.[62] New industrial towns were also overnight growths—'Sheffield is an old oak: Birmingham, but a mushroom'.[63]

Until at least the 1770 season, however, warnings continued to be given about applying the mushroom image to worthy trading families. *Sally Sable* of 1770 cautioned against calling merchants 'upstarts'. The fatal consequences of an argument between the fictional Traffick and Vere families over this issue were condemned as 'a Sacrifice to the vainest of all Vanities, family Pride'. The hero of *Eliza Musgrove* described himself as a 'mushroom' in order to suggest how truly sorry he was that his own birth denied his nephew the family title and estate.[64]

During the 1780s such discrimination was dulled by new fears aroused by parvenu activities. The author of the 1780 *Fatal Obedience* provided a tongue-in-cheek verdict on the trading characters, the Cokers:

What low-bred, aukward devils! ... Mrs Coker has forgot that she once lived up three pair of stairs in chambers ... Her carriage is quite of a piece with her origin—What, my dear Harry, do you apprehend her to be of the mushroom breed?—Positively, the very refuse of a dunghill, by Gad.[65]

Prints of parvenu representatives carried such titles as the 'Mushroom Frogstool', with its slogan, 'Here today gone tomorrow', and 'From a Dunghill'.[66] Political overtones were also frequent.[67] A satirical squib, *The Boletarium* of 1786, referred to the 'mushroom

---

[61] *Sentimental Lucubrations*, p. 21. Dunghill as applied to the overweening man of humble origin was of ancient origin—as, for example, the dunghill grooms in *Henry VI Part I*, Act I, Scene iii.

[62] 'None but the prosperous upstart, MUSHROOM'D into rank ... was arrogantly proud of it [good sense and honour]', Samuel Richardson, *Clarissa: or, The History of a Young Lady*, 7 vols. (London, 1748), i. 268.

[63] Jeremy Bentham, *Defence of Usury* (London, 1787), p. 179, in response to Birmingham being called a 'projecting town'.

[64] Woodfin, *Sally Sable*, i. 24–55 (p. 55); *The History of Eliza Musgrove*, 2 vols. (London, 1770), i. 8.

[65] *Fatal Obedience*, i. 196, 197, 198.   [66] George, *Catalogue*, no. 5793 (1780).

[67] Its usage was at least two centuries old: Christopher Marlowe had scorned the 'night growne mushrump', *Edward II* (1598, Act I, Scene iv, l. 284); and Ben Jonson had attacked 'mushrompe gentlemen, that shoot up in a night', *Every Man Out of his Humour* (1599), Act I, Scene ii.

contest' at Carlisle in that year. New freemen admitted to the corporation for political purposes were designated 'mushrooms'.[68] Wendeborn, writing in 1790, reflected an attitude shared by dozens of diarists, letter-writers, and other witnesses:

Many of them [English East-India nabobs] arrive very hungry, and in an emaciated condition in India; they suck as eagerly as leeches, to fill themselves the quicker, that they may return the sooner to their own country, and move in a higher and more brilliant sphere on their own island; for most of those, who are styled in England nabobs, are of low extraction, and starting up, like mushrooms out of their obscure condition, are naturally the more infected with national pride and prejudice... They think, that to be created an English baronet, to procure, by bribery and corruption, a seat in parliament, and to live, upon the frequently ill-gotten Indian wealth, in a splendid manner, in the English mode, is far more honourable and consistent with the happiness of life, than to slumber in Asiatic luxury, like a mogul, or be adored as an Indian nabob.[69]

In his *Memoirs*, the self-made Lackington ironically boasted of his achievement by citing a text attributed to Shakespeare and which scorned the dunghill from which 'minions do advance'.[70] The text can now be traced to a spurious Shakespeare play issued by Tonson in 1734. What is particularly striking about the work, in its attempt to imitate the bard and benefit from the massive commercial success of Shakespeare plays and memorabilia, is its recurrent stress upon upstart social climbing and the striking images describing it.[71] When Lackington first borrowed the reference, however, he printed it as 'millions do advance'.[72] The army of mushroom-men must have seemed large indeed.

The upstart's ill-gotten wealth was also shown to have disastrous and socially damaging effects upon his dependants and his neighbourhood. The portrayals were forerunners for the later depiction of the manufacturer's family and others unable to act responsibly with suddenly acquired riches. Of many examples,

---

[68] I am indebted to Dr Penelope Corfield for this reference. Peter Borsay gives a similar usage in the Warwick borough election of 1734, in 'All the Town's a Stage', in Peter Clark (ed.), *The Transformation of English Provincial Towns, 1600–1800* (London, 1984), pp. 228–58 (p. 234).

[69] Wendeborn, *View of England*, i. 126.   [70] Lackington, *Memoirs*, 1795 edn., p. 24.

[71] *The Life and Death of Thomas, Lord Cromwell: By Mr. William Shakespear* (London, 1734), pp. 3–4. I am indebted to Emma Crichton-Miller for identifying the quotation.

[72] Lackington, *Memoirs*, 1791 edn., p. 6.

Lady and Miss Silvertop, wife and daughter to Thomson's honest
Sir George, were represented in a quite different way from the
nabob himself. Lady Silvertop is 'assuming without dignity, gar-
rulous without communication, contradictious even to vulgarity'.[73] Her daughter, who has a fortune of fifty to sixty
thousand pounds, shocks respectable circles by her ignorance of
Paradise Lost and her inability to converse on any topic save
fashion and Court dress. In Mrs Smith's *Ethelinde*, Mrs Maltravers's daughter, Lady Newenden, is spoilt, arrogant, and
idle.[74] In Mrs Rudd's *Belle Widows* of the same season, 'that renowned conqueror of rupees', Nabob General Sumpter, boasts
the typical wife and son. The son's 'character of ton [was] completed by the accomplishments of deep play, Bacchanalian *éclat*,
expensive courtesans, and fashionable oaths'.[75] Mackenzie's
Lounger described the 'Influence in the Neighbourhood of a rich
Asiatic, in a letter from John Homespun'.[76] Here, the young Mr
and Madame Mushroom are first seen at church, 'where their
pew was all carpeted and cushioned over for their reception, so
bedizened—there were flowered muslins and gold muslins, white
shawls and red shawls, white feathers and red feathers; and every
now and then the young Mushroom girls pulled out little bottles,
that sent such a perfume around them'.[77] Madame Mushroom is
shown to bear no contradiction. The influence of the Mushrooms
in the local community rekindles the folly of the female
Homespuns, who attempt to adopt the fashions and morals of the
new arrivals.

   Where there was conflict between approved values, most
writers now emphasized the permanency of rank in preference to
the merits of industry and thrift. Representation of the nabob
caused few difficulties, but charges of mushroom growth were
problematic in many later considerations of the domestic businessman or industrialist. Industry and economy were abstract
ideals for all writers. They were practised by, and in turn defined,
the ideal gentleman. They were clearly also to be promoted
amongst businessmen, traders, and all of the lower ranks. In *Young
Grandison*, the translated moral primer for children of 1788–9,
sympathy for the poor was combined with a lesson on the dignity

---

[73] Thomson, *Denial*, i. 24.   [74] Smith, *Ethelinde*, i. 16–18.
[75] Rudd, *Belle Widows*, ii. 2.
[76] Title from *Lounger*, no. 17.   [77] Mackenzie, *Works*, v. 170.

of labour.[78] Praise for industry could be sustained where the poor remained content with a humble station, but many writers were caught between the need to encourage industry by depicting a splendid carrot, and the need to prevent the donkey from moving forward too far and too quickly. To this extent, conservative attitudes towards labour in the popular literature had not changed. It was acknowledged that greater productivity derived more from incentive than necessity, but there remained the residual anxiety that encouragement to self-advancement might result in a contagion of irresponsible *arrivistes*.

In his *Observer*, Cumberland attempted a critical survey of this problem of portraying rapid social advancement. Self-made men had more than ordinary merit, he suggested, and yet they remained friendless:

All the world must be sensible of the danger attending sudden elevation, and how very apt a man's head is to turn, who climbs an eminence, to which his habits have not familiarized him. A mountaineer can tread firm upon a precipice and walk erect without tottering along the path, that winds itself about the craggy cliff, on which he has his dwelling; whilst the inhabitant of the valley travels with affright and danger over the giddy pass, and oftentimes is precipitated from the heighth to perish in the gulph beneath his feet. Such is the fate of many, who by the revolutions of fortune are raised to lofty situations: It is generally the lot of such people to make few friends; in their danger there are none to give them warning, in their fall there are few to afford them pity.[79]

The eighteenth-century concept of the gentleman, it has been argued, was not proscriptive and allowed for surprising tolerance of low origins and the purchase of rank.[80] There was, however, a very pointed and important difference between practice and representation. Most novelists and moralists of the 1770s and 1780s tried to insist upon the impossibility of a full conversion to gentility. They did so in the face of widespread contemporary social emulation. It seems to have been anticipated that readers who assumed the mantle of gentility were anxious to insist upon its exclusiveness. Once again, social advancement was defended by highlighting the extremes of current practice and by creating outcasts to illustrate model conduct and the bounds of acceptability. 'Emulation' and false appearance were the key charges. They were said to be

[78] De Cambon, *Young Grandison*, i. 254–65.   [79] Cumberland, *Observer*, i. 184–5.
[80] Shinagel, *Defoe*, ch. 6; Shirley Robin Letwin, *The Gentleman in Trollope: Individuality and Moral Conduct* (London, 1982), pp. 14–21; Stone and Stone, *Open Elite*, pp. 19–21.

caused by too much credit being available or by the sudden arrival of vast wealth. All who had sufficient money might buy the appurtenances and symbols of status and privilege: equipage, property, houses, land, dress, seats in parliament. The fashion boom continued to reduce outward divisions between *nouveaux riches* and established gentry or nobility. Fashion consciously promoted emulation. As a 1780 novel commented, 'dress in the present age but little distinguishes the peer from the plebeian'.[81] The stress on vulgarity was based upon an attempt to continue particular distinctions of rank in the face of the sudden ability of those successful in industry and overseas commercial service to support the traditional badges of high station.

Conspicuous, emulative consumption was cited in evidence of the unbridled social ambition of the *nouveau riche*. As London-led excess invaded all parts of the land, provincial misses aped their betters, 'For Fashion now alike Pervades | The gorgeous Roof, and sylvan Shades'.[82] Tales highlighted this by carefully illustrating the divergence between appearance and reality. In the modish and fashionable world, manners that reflected true breeding were all the more important when appearances—especially dress— had become so deceptive. Values of the ton were worthless and even destructive. Externals were strictly subordinate to inner worth. Simplicity and frankness were applauded. Affectation of manners was roundly condemned. 'Good understanding had taught him to connect the polish of fashion, with plainness and simplicity', wrote Helen Maria Williams of her 1790 hero. The flawed hero of *The History of Miss Meredith* is fundamentally honourable, his manners, frank and unaffected. Charlotte Smith continually stressed frankness as the dominant characteristic of her heroines. Mrs D—— in her instructions to William at the beginning of *Young Grandison* insisted: 'regulate your thoughts, and let your expressions appear easy and not studied'.[83]

In so defining gentility, dissimulation was the arch-vice. In 1780 Miss Minifie was especially concerned to stress the deceptiveness of wealth and fashion in the much-reprinted *Count de Poland*. With her friends and fortune 'frittered away', the virtuous but misled Maria

[81] *Letters Between Clara and Antonia*, ii. 14.
[82] [Christopher Anstey], *Speculation; or, A Defence of Mankind: A Poem* (London, 1780) p. 19. Reprinted many times, 1780–82 and beyond.
[83] Williams, *Julia*, i. 87; Parsons, *Miss Meredith*, i. 45; de Cambon, *Young Grandison*, i. 6. Mrs de Cambon appeared not to have noticed the irony of the demand to act with frankness.

'now for the first time saw what is called the *great world* in its true colours; it was no longer varnished over with the *smile* of *treachery*'. The heroine, Emily, is similarly saved from a dissipated life: 'I have been, said the charming Countess, since my earliest remembrance, blinded by custom, misled by appearances, and the dupe of fashion'.[84] Also in 1780, the satirical *Parsonage-House* introduced Mrs Davers as having made an unfortunate marriage, merely one demonstration of 'how fallacious a criterion is the outward appearance of things'.[85] In the equally popular *Rencontre*, the authoress observed that 'such indeed is the present rage for dress, in all ranks of people, that the desire of *being* rich is lost in the wish to *appear* so; and the happiness of families, and the peace of society, are sacrificed to show'.[86] According to another writer, it was 'an age that abounds with falsehood and dissimulation'.[87] By 1790 the lessons are increasingly colourful and severe. The sparkle of superficial attractions trick many of the 1790 fictional husbands into marrying ignorant, spendthrift, and unworthy wives. Of many examples, Colonel Dorville, father of the Fair Cambrians, had been 'deceived' into accepting a foolish woman of low rank and understanding.[88] The reader was able to distinguish such women as much by their dress as by their thoughts and opinions. As Mackenzie's Mr Homespun observes: 'there is, it seems, a fashion in morality, as well as in dress; and the present mode is not quite so strait-laced as the stays are'.[89] Villainous women may hide behind the façade of beauty, as does Maria de Vellorno, the stepmother and bigamist of *A Sicilian Romance*, 'a woman of infinite art, devoted to pleasure, and of an unconquerable spirit'. The hero of *The Baron of Manstow* declared, 'I prefer reality to external appearance, temperance to luxury, the convenient to the superfluous, and simple nature to ostentation'.[90]

False appearances were further used to attack the attractiveness of titles for their own sake. Honest, middle-class characters were contrasted with worthless arrays of privileged aristocrats. The

[84] Minifie, *Count de Poland*, Dublin edn., 1780, 4 vols. in 2, ii. 163; iii. 144.

[85] Elizabeth Blower, *The Parsonage-House: A Novel*, 3 vols. in 1 (Dublin, 1781), p. 80.

[86] Gwynn, *Rencontre*, Dublin edn., 2 vols. in 1, 1785, p. 229.

[87] *Letters Between Clara and Antonia*, ii. 34.   [88] *Fair Cambrians*, i. 6–7.

[89] *The Companion: Being a Choice Collection of the most Admired Pieces from the Best Authors*, 3 vols. (Edinburgh, 1790–1), i. 267.

[90] Mrs [Ann Ward] Radcliffe, *A Sicilian Romance*, 2 vols. (London, 1790), i. 6; *The Baron of Manstow: A Novel*, 2 vols. (London, 1790), i. 108.

[91] Minifie, *Count de Poland*, i. 7, and later.

unthinking pursuit of titles was portrayed as injurious and wide-spread, another example of deceptive social illusions. In 1780 title-lust becomes the ruin of Miss Minifie's Emily.[91] Ten years later, Arabella Burrell, self-confessed 'mistress of the art of ogling', also aspires to nobility.[92] Fiction of the 1790 season was crowded with similar examples. 'An Earl!', exclaims Mrs Parsons's ill-fated Emma Montague, 'a coronet is a pretty ornament to one's coach'. 'Coronets and titles had taken strange possession of her brain', wrote Mrs Smith as she described the flirting of the spoilt Miss Ludford with the unwholesome Lord Danesforte. Miss Ormsby, having spent most of *The Fair Hibernian* searching for ermine or sable, finally marries Sir Peter Ball, 'a poor city knight': 'You see she is determined to be a lady at any rate; and that, as Sir Peter is considerably the wrong side of fifty, must I presume be her principal inducement to wed him'. Windham, the unprincipled friend of Clayton in Bicknell's *Doncaster Races* and a 'professed libertine', marries the forty-year-old sister to the Earl of ———.[93] In their reviews, critics concentrated on praising novelists' scorn for the worthlessness of appearances over true worth. There was congratulation for 'smart retorts' over title-mania.[94]

Economic fears both inspired and contributed to criticism of emulation. As the *Town and Country Magazine* of February 1790 announced, the man imitating his superiors became

a means of introducing universal poverty and misery ... it is obvious to every man's knowledge that the meaner sort of people are perpetually treading on the heels of those immediately above them, and aping the manner of life in fashion among such as are called persons of distinction, which every man is to some others of those who are below him.[95]

Similar notions had been expressed throughout the century as a concern with the social consequences of old-style luxury among the lower and middling orders. Erasmus Jones had complained that 'Scarce *one* Family in *ten,* keeps strictly within the Compass of its Income ... The *Contagion,* as I have said, hath spread itself over the whole Kingdom; the grand Controversy among all Ranks and Degrees, being only who shall *Out-Dress, Drink* or *Eat*

---

[92] Bicknell, *Doncaster Races,* i. 30.
[93] Parsons, *Miss Meredith,* i. 27; Smith, *Ethelinde,* ii. 182–3; *The Fair Hibernian,* 2 vols. (London, 1789), ii. 171; Bicknell, *Doncaster Races,* ii. 256–7.
[94] *MR,* NS, 2: 225 (June 1791).
[95] *T&C* 22: 64 (Feb. 1790), 'The Observer', no. 94.

his Neighbour'.[96] Such criticisms were now transferred to the pretensions of the leisured businessman. As well as preventing industry, emulation led to the default of the extravagant, the undermining of credit confidence, and local financial collapse. Trusler was insistent that

Luxury, disproportioned to a man's fortune in life, is certainly blameable; nay, though proportioned to his fortune, it is still reprehensible, when the expences it leads him into, and the indulgences he gives way to, carry him beyond the proper bounds of decency and moderation.[97]

The social conservatism of the popular press became more strident in response to both the volatility of economic life and the visible wealth of notable manufacturers and nabobs. Manuals and imaginative literature depicted consumer spending and new wealth as a threat to the social order. Many of the attacks upon gambling derived from fear of 'the confusion of ranks' by successful players. Those whose wealth alone allowed them to climb above their social station, would soon find their reason overbalanced.[98] The popularity of the mid-century best-seller, *Pamela*— the archetypal tale of the humble maiden who does become the lady—declined in the final third of the century. Reprintings of Richardson's contrasting *Sir Charles Grandison* increased. Imitations of the *Pamela* theme almost disappeared. One of the last successful attempts was the 1770 *Maid of the Mill*.

With gathering assurance, the novel and serial magazine warned of the social dislocation threatening the peace and stability of the nation. Mackenzie's successful Mr Homespun serial was entitled 'On the Affectation of High Life'. The Homespun theme—the need to keep within one's means—was also interpreted as the need to keep within one's station. Men of commerce and their families, from the petty trader to the haughty Indian adventurer, were isolated as the propagators of fashion and dangerous emulation:

Here lies the whole grievance: parents are, now, in a state of the worst depravity: the lowest tradesman, nay, even the mechanic, will strain beyond what his circumstances in life will oftentimes afford—to do what?—to spoil the natural disposition of his child with ideas of false

---

[96] Jones, *Luxury, Pride and Vanity*, p. 1.
[97] Trusler, *Luxury No Political Evil*, p. 33.   [98] Hey, *Pernicious Effects of Gaming*, p. 77.

grandeur and splendid appearance. The violent rage for Imitation is inexpressible.[99]

John Trusler, in his *Difference Between Words*, believed social emulation to be the direct link between the foolish fashionable and the upstart trader. In defining 'Of Fashion, Of Quality', he noted that, 'as synonymous, as these expressions may be ... they, still, imply particular characters ... The last of these expressions, rises upon the first, and signifies the nobility; whereas, by the other, is, only understood the gentry. The pride and folly of the world is grown to so great a pitch, that persons in trade are continually apeing people *of-fashion*; and those, *of fashion*, people *of-quality*'.[100] Mrs Thrale's brewer husband was featured in affected, pretentious finery in caricatures sold at the print shops in the Strand and St Paul's Churchyard.[101] Novelists such as Mrs Smith further condemned the unnaturalness and the hypocrisy of commercial upstarts who outshone the gentry:

Mrs Ludford, while she affected to despise every thing but the substantial comforts of riches, was yet very solicitous to be noticed by 'people of quality'; and was never so well pleased as when she compared that affluence acquired by trade, to the more brilliant but frequently ill supported splendor of such of the nobility as believed themselves obliged to make an appearance more equal to their rank than to their fortune.[102]

Undoubtedly, age-old suspicions of the self-made man of commerce had been submerged rather than destroyed by the sympathetic reaction to commerce at mid-century. Even at the height of commercial enthusiasm, revelations of 'real-life' mercantile indiscretions were avidly read and reprinted. *The Amorous Merchant* of 1752–3, was published to 'let the world judge of the Principles of this Man'—a merchant portrayed as an adulterous hypocrite, respectable in appearances, but remaining 'the Wolf in Sheep's Cloathing'.[103] Thirty years later, many novels demon-

---

[99] Dr Typo [pseud.], *The Affecting History of Two Young Gentlewomen* (London, 1780), pp. v–vi.

[100] John Trusler, *The Difference Between Words, Esteemed Synonymous in the English Language* (London, 1766), pp. 125–6.

[101] 'The Southwark Macaroni', published 24 Apr. 1772 by M. Darly, the Strand, George, *Catalogue*, no. 4691.

[102] Smith, *Ethelinde*, iii. 1–2.

[103] *The Amorous Merchant: or, Intriguing Husband: Being a Curious and Uncommon Process of Love and Law ... Written by Mrs Graham, now Barry, in the Manner of Constantia Phillips* (London, [1753]), p. 62. The BL copy has a title-page MS addition, 'A true story. This pamphlet was never published, the merchant ... having bought up the whole Impression'; Mrs Barry rewrote the tale as published in two editions in 1753.

strated far more elaborately the evils of practising charity—that shibboleth of the gentleman—merely for appearances. The character of Lady Beverly in *Harcourt* (1780) was designed to expose the counterfeits of the newly-moneyed. Miss Williams's harridan, Mrs Melbourne, was presented as the daughter of an eminent but lately bankrupted city merchant. 'Morose and ill-humoured', Mrs Melbourne commits the unforgiveable sins of shouting at her servants and of making benevolent gestures just for show.[104]

Many writers accused the dependants of self-made men of practising a more basic deceitfulness. The author of the 1790 *Fair Hibernian* featured the responses of two true gentlemen to the attractions of parvenu wealth. Marchmont writes to Methuen of his infatuation with the daughter of a merchant, Ormsby, with a market value of £40,000. Marchmont acknowledges the now commonplace cautions against a *nouveau riche* mercantile match, but the attractions of the heiress prove superior.[105] Methuen rehearses familiar arguments to dissuade Marchmont, which, by the shabby fate allotted to the merchant's daughter, are endorsed by the author:

'I do not approve your precipitate choice' ... ''tis a prudent one with regard to fortune; but as to birth, I could wish you had been a little more nice. Her father, I find, has the character of a worthy, honest, rich man, but he may have dropt from "heavens above" or—more applicable, indeed—ascended from the earth beneath, for anything I know to the contrary; for inspite of my strictest researches, I cannot possibly learn he had a single forefather.'[106]

It required an usually long read—and purchase of the second volume—before the reader had these early suspicions confirmed, that indeed, 'Miss Ormsby is a mean, artful and wicked woman who basely betrays your confidence and love and meditates the deepest wound upon your honour'.[107] Coarse and rakish friends of the merchant's daughter are soon produced and the full horror is revealed. Miss Ormsby, trade, and humble origins, should never have been trusted.

For other authors, exceptions only proved the rule. Readers were meant to be surprised by portrayals of benevolent returned West Indian planters and East Indian nabobs. An early example of the singular West Indian was given in Mrs Scott's *The Man of*

[104] Williams, *Julia*, i. 10.   [105] *Fair Hibernian*, i. 52.
[106] Ibid. i. 58.   [107] Ibid. ii. 23.

Real Sensibility or the History of Sir George Ellison, reprinted in 1760, 1770, and 1797. Mrs Smith's Harcourt in *Ethelinde* is a benevolent returned planter, but the work is balanced by her portrayal of the pompous Maltravers, a returned nabob who, 'like most men who accumulate sudden and opulent fortunes, was wrapped up in the contemplation of his own consequence'.[108] The key explanation offered was that the benevolent returned adventurers were gentlemen before they went out to the Caribbean or the Indies (and were often driven to do so by the wickedness of defaulting creditors or of land-hungry *arrivistes*). A splendid example is the hero of the 1786 *Innocent Rivals,* where the benevolent Norton is not only a gentleman from the outset, but the only civilized male character in the whole book.

Mrs Brooke's Charles Mandeville was not, it seems to all, born a gentleman, but returns 'laden with immense treasures'. Despite his lack of formal education, however, Mandeville displays benevolence and good breeding in equal measure: 'no classical knowledge—has not been taught the Graces; and yet, one can discover no deficiency either in his conversation, or his manner'. He even boasts 'the air of a monarch'.[109] Indian opulence is only a credit to such a man. This deftly removed any difficulties over the acceptability of gentlemen adventurers, while their behaviour after their success merely confirmed their pedigree. Hence Miss Williams described Mr Clifford as 'a man of a plain understanding and an excellent heart. Just in his principles, and generous in his disposition, he acquired wealth slowly, but honourably'.[110] More than once, the author qualified such fortune-making, insisting upon the decent reluctance to make money. Clifford, apparently, was in no unseemly hurry and the riches arrived more as a result of his innate disposition than of his material ambitions. India is also used as a convenient journey's end for the exile. In this novel, the author's improbable solution to the problem of Seymour's lust for Mrs Meynell is to dispatch Mr Meynell to Bengal to amass new wealth.[111] The unfortunate, but virtuous Mrs Raby in *Louisa,* places her last hope in the success of her young and industrious husband who has embarked for India.[112] Other acceptable nabobs are dissociated from martial excess and large-scale commercial operations. An administrator rather than a trader,

---

[108] Smith, *Ethelinde,* i. 20.   [109] Brooke, *Charles Mandeville,* i. 44, 77.
[110] Williams, *Julia,* i. 4.   [111] Ibid. ii. 242.   [112] Hervey, *Louisa,* i. 163.

Thomson's Sir George Silvertop, is 'an open, worthy, intelligent man'.[113]

The few benevolent portrayals of self-made men were not reworked and extended in their own day, however; nor were they remembered after it. Holzman's pioneering study of the nabob considers few of the more sympathetic verdicts upon the Anglo-Indian during the first decade of the great returns.[114] It is the caricatures of the wicked and presumptuous which are repeated in set form. Most famously, perhaps, Macaulay's essays on Clive and Hastings recorded that nabobs 'raised the price of every thing in their neighbourhood, from fresh eggs to rotten boroughs'.[115] The image of the upstart nabob reinforced protests against business pretension and the social and economic damage it would cause. Works which set out to defend groups of traders and Anglo-Indians by identifying the deviant, faced a difficult, if not impossible, task. Price's *Saddle Put on the Right Horse* illustrated at length the themes of many works discussing the return of the nabob and the 'sprouting of the mushroom'.[116] In the belief that he was vindicating the overall reputation of East Indian gentlemen, Price isolated the corrupt black sheep, but thereby confirmed and extended their ill-repute. In his examination of 'spurious' and 'mushroom' nabobs, Price highlighted many of the common suspicions about those with self-made fortunes—in particular, their lavish spending and the depths from which they began their ascent. In discussing 'spurious nabobs', for example, Price defined a man whom he preferred not to call a nabob, but of whose existence he had no doubt:

When men, whose origin is so obscure, that no parish register can be found, which bears their name, obtain wealth so suddenly, that nobody can account for the means, and at the enormous mass of which, they themselves seem surprised, conjectures injurious to their moral rectitude, will and must have place. If it be true that such upstart beings, intoxicated with pride, drive furiously on in the public way, covering with dust and filth, people of all ranks, general contempt is what they deserve. If there be such, who, purchasing manors on which their fathers kept sheep, or building palaces on the spot, where heretofore, in a blue apron, they themselves drew ale, and where they now exceed in

---

[113] Thomson, *Denial*, i. 23.   [114] Holzman, *Nabobs*, ch. 5.

[115] Macaulay, *Critical and Historical Essays*, iii. 109–206, 327–466 (p. 190).

[116] Joseph Price, *The Saddle Put on the Right Horse; Or, An Enquiry into the Reasons why certain Persons have been denominated Nabobs* (London, 1783).

luxurious expence, pomp of equipage, and every ostentatious, frivolous, and useless act of costly extravagance, the first nobles of the land, they deserve, and richly too, the infamous appellation of *spurious Nabobs*.[117]

In 'shewing how and when, these prejudices first took their rise, how they have since been propagated and supported', Price attested that 'falsehoods often repeated, and never contradicted, in time come to be considered as real facts, and at last are adopted by creditable historians, and go down to posterity as parts of true history'.[118] As Mite confronts Lady Oldham:

Mite: What, you, I find, adopt the popular prejudice, and conclude that every man that is rich is a villain?

Lady Oldham: I only echo the voice of the public ... we every day see what has been treacherously and rapaciously gained, as profusely and full as rapidly squandered.[119]

Or as Walpole wrote during the theatricals in Westminster Hall: 'I have followed up Hastings's trial as far as the newspapers have given it, and from the first day formed my judgment of its conclusion, though I don't pretend to have more penetration than the vulgar ... I have not yet looked into the charge, which fills a thick octavo. My opinion is formed more summarily: innocence does not pave its way with diamonds, nor has a quarry of them on its estate'.[120]

---

[117] Price, *The Saddle Put on the Right Horse*, p. 30.   [118] Ibid. p. 4.

[119] Foote, *Nabob*, p. 65.

[120] Lewis, *Walpole's Correspondence*, xxv. 639, 651, Walpole to Mann, 30 Apr., 3 June 1786.

HISTORICAL PERSPECTIVES

> For a long time I have felt that the contribution by busi-
> nessmen to society is widely misunderstood and constantly
> maligned by those who should know better.
>
> Margaret Thatcher, *Let Our Children Grow Tall* (1977).

ONE of the most influential contributions to recent overviews of
the modern British economy has been the insistence that cultural
conditions created anti-industrial attitudes, that the heirs of
entrepreneurs were hijacked by the attractions of aristocratic
leisure, and that business recruitment suffered because British
commercial achievement was viewed with growing disdain and
hostility. Anti-business sentiment, it has been argued, was
generated during the nineteenth century at the very height of
British industrial success and has been reinforced ever since. As
identified, the anti-business lobby included attacks against the
conditions of industrial employment, the effects of bankruptcy,
speculation and industrial pollution, and a pervasive suspicion of
commercialism, profit-making, mass-advertising, and material
and technological progress. For the past two centuries, it is said,
the combined assault has been carried by acclaimed imaginative
literature, by a selective literary tradition (in turn suppressing and
distorting alternative, sympathetic verdicts), by educational
syllabuses, and by a multifarious range of political, religious, and
moral crusades. In these, the entrepreneur was treated as a political Aunt Sally—a convenient and identifiable target attacked by
both the Left and Right of Victorian and Edwardian Britain. The
top-hatted capitalist of Radical polemic was the same vulgar
arriviste despised and feared by aristocratic and landed society.[1]

These views were not just fodder for after-dinner conversation.

[1] Martin J. Wiener, *English Culture and the Decline of the Industrial Spirit*, 1850–1980 (Cam-
bridge, 1981); reviewed, with examples of the influence of such ideas, in James Raven,
'British History and the Enterprise Culture', *Past and Present*, 123 (May 1989), 178–204; Neil
McKendrick, ' "Gentlemen and Players" Revisited: The Gentlemanly Ideal, the Business

The charges were sharp, damning, and widely promoted. During the past decade, many of the arguments of those identifying a 'luddite' cultural tradition have been popularized in magazine and newspaper articles, personal political manifestos, and television documentaries. Contributors insisted that gentlemanly values had inhibited economic development, that firms had collapsed because of the country-seat aspirations of those inheriting the business, and that modern Britain had lost out on the technological revolution.[2]

By contrast, most historical investigations of the industrial spirit were more cautious. Many of the more fashionable claims were incompatible with studies dismissive of entrepreneurial causes of British economic decline.[3] The reaction as identified was also a selective one. It focused more upon industrialism than upon general commerce, and in the absence of studies for the eighteenth century, many contributors were forced to accept origins for various aspects of modern business hostility in the mid-nineteenth-century response to industrialism and in the philanthropic and intellectual movements of later Victorian Britain. It was never established when anti-industrial and anti-commercial attitudes first emerged or even what they fully entailed. With so much attention given to a new luddism, few investigated the survival and influence of more traditional assaults upon the profit-making of the businessman and of older animosities towards the social climbing and political pretension of the suddenly moneyed.[4] The problem of timing is made most

Ideal and the Professional Ideal in English Literary Culture', in McKendrick and Outhwaite (ed.), *Business Life and Public Policy*, pp. 98–136; D. C. Coleman and Christine Macleod, 'Attitudes to New Techniques: British Businessmen, 1800–1950', *Ec.HR* 2nd ser. 39/4 (1986), 588–611; Paul Warwick, 'Did Britain Change? An Inquiry into the Causes of National Decline', *Journal of Contemporary History*, 20/1 (Jan. 1985), 99–133 (pp. 103–5).

[2] Wiener's work 'has become almost a cult book in management circles in Britain', according to Samuel Brittan, 'A Very English Status System', *Financial Times*, 7 Mar. 1983, p. 15. Further examples are given in Raven, 'British History'.

[3] Vigorous criticism of the hypothesis of entrepreneurial failure is offered by Donald N. McCloskey, 'Did Victorian Britain Fail?', *Ec.HR* 2nd ser. 23/3 (1970), 446–59, reprinted with earlier contributions to the debate in McCloskey, *Enterprise and Trade in Victorian Britain: Essays in Historical Economics* (London, 1981); and L. G. Sandberg, 'The Entrepreneur and Technological Change', in Floud and McCloskey, *Economic History of Britain*, ii. 99–120. There are many issues in dispute here beyond the scope of this book.

[4] The literary and historical treatment of businessmen was surveyed in Neil McKendrick, 'The Enemies of Technology and the Self-Made Man', in Roy Church, *Herbert Austin: The British Motor Car Industry to 1941* (London, 1979), pp. ix–lii, and general introduction to R. J. Overy, *William Morris, Viscount Nuffield* (London, 1976), pp. vii–xliv.

apparent by the split between those identifying a discomfort with industry derived from a pre-industrial commercial–landed ethos and those locating the origins of anti-business attitudes in actual change during the Victorian period.[5] All this re-emphasizes the importance of the late eighteenth century as a period requiring more detailed examination. The larger question remains of whether alienation from the business world was dependent upon the development of industrialism or whether it was inherent in or a consequence of the reception given to earlier success in overseas trade.

Earlier chapters have offered a contribution to the wider debate. During the second half of the eighteenth century, new manufacturers guided industrial expansion, extending the depth and diversity of the domestic market. At the same time, short-term credit crises provoked urgent discussion both of the causes and results of economic instability and of the definition of legitimate risk-taking. The home-comings of laden East Indiamen and wealthy nabobs brought debate to a head. Visible commercial expansion and its apparent fitfulness was accompanied by the creation and disposal of well-publicized personal fortunes. In another commercial sector, the fundamental question posed by writers of didactic, imaginative literature was whether value in society was to be measured by wealth, station, or behaviour. In reality, late eighteenth-century society was dominated by monetary considerations. Even if 'the actual volume of social mobility has turned out to be far less than might have been expected',[6] status and privilege could certainly be bought. The emulation writers and readers themselves pursued was justified by setting limits to what was acceptable. Social pretension was attacked in order to defend the illusion that exclusivism was dependent upon far more than material fortune. New potential for upward mobility in a relatively caste-free society promoted even greater attention to the gradations of rank and to marks of success and achievement. Judgements upon the businessman were clearly part of a concern over the preserves of social status in the face of a continuing increase in the proportion of the population

[5] Cf., e.g., the emphasis on a continuity of anti-industrialism from a hegemonic old-bourgeois form of commercial capitalism, as set out in Anderson, 'Origins of the Present Crisis', and Tom Nairn, 'The Future of Britain's Crisis', in Isaac Kramnick (ed.), *Is Britain Dying?* (Ithaca, NY, 1979), pp. 233-68.

[6] Stone and Stone, *Open Elite*, p. 402.

able and willing to buy from fashion and élite commodity industries, and able and anxious to acquire land and the traditional
badges of rank. Renewed literary attention to luxury focused
almost exclusively upon the newly-rich, not upon the traditional
subject of concern, the mechanics and the artisans.

It is clear, of course, that in the study of popular literary images,
very difficult (and sometimes impossible) gaps have to be negoti-
ated. The authorship of much of the commercial literature of the
second half of the eighteenth century is unknown. It is still impossible to record the personal circumstances of most of the contributors to the popular magazine, novel, and miscellany. With
the steady accumulation of foundation bibliographical work and
guides to the regional book trade, local studies of authorship
can supplement an otherwise London-based national picture.
Although others are in preparation, only one regional study has
been attempted here. Readership is even more intangible. Estimates of size vary. Ultimately, no one can be completely certain
about the effects of particular works on particular readers or even
particular groups of readers. Inevitably, we have to accept that
ignorance will remain about many aspects of the historical sociology of popular literature. One aim of this research has been to
indicate certain new routes which may be passable with future
work.

The survey of literature has been built upon the reconstruction
of bibliographical production and distribution and the close study
of recovered texts. Foremost has been the attempt to consult
reprinted imaginative prose literature of the second half of the
eighteenth century and all surviving works from calendar years
taken at five-yearly intervals. The leading assumption is that in
the absence of other representative sources, assessments of the
total output of publications, of the most popular of works, and of
the images conveyed, provide the best available insight into the
change in literary verdicts as it would have appeared to contemporary readers. A number of features support this approach. In
instructional aims, even in specific typologies or techniques of
characterization, uniformity is evident across the majority of
works of each season. If most new literature, and especially most
reprinted new literature, was saying much the same thing, failure
to identify all texts and all authors can be attenuated. Audience
interest can be measured from the sale of literature itself—and

without the usual reliance upon occasional and subjective direct references within the texts. Technological and commercial constraints, limiting variations in edition sizes, suggest that reprinting rates (according to the number of editions) offer an acceptable measure of literary popularity. The significance of new portrayals can be suggested by reprinting, direct feedback from the audience, and other indicators arising from the commercial basis of the book trade. At the same time, the reissue of older works provided both points of comparison with new literature and also images and arguments for incorporation or modification by new writers and compilers.

This approach highlights the importance of the change in the structure of the book trade. Analysis of the commercialization of literature reveals the prominence of the bookseller as a manipulator of public taste. There are, of course, dangers in relying too heavily upon the printed notices and advertisements of booksellers, particularly in an age of puffing and exaggeration, but evidential problems are eased by the surviving witness of newspaper columns, critical reviews, and trade and circulating library catalogues. Under new market conditions, commercial considerations also narrowed the gap between writer and reader. By accepting manuscripts for outright sale without the insurance of prior subscription or private patronage, truly commercial bookselling had to take stock of market interests as well as promoting them.

Omissions noted at the beginning of this study should not be forgotten. Poetry and drama have not been entirely neglected, and were broadly considered both as comparative examples and in the local case-study. The focus, however, has been upon popular imaginative prose in all its various forms. The choice was both deliberate and necessary: the novel and magazine grew disproportionately quickly over the period and the instructional merits of novels, magazines, and associated miscellanies were seized upon by both booksellers and readers. Not only were they self-consciously responsive to social change, but in terms of assessing the contemporary popularity and appeal of literary images they are also the most accessible works for the historian, even given the labours required to recover so many of them. Playbooks and poetry await study, but the publication of verse (much in magazines and periodicals) offers such bibliographical problems that the methodological approach would have to be revised.

Against a continuing fictional milieu of country gentlemen and provincial nobility, the literary representation of men of trade gained new specificity during the two decades after 1760. By 1780 many imaginative writers maintained a clear distinction between types of business profession, from the overseas merchant to the minor shopkeeper. Caricatures of vulgar trading families and the malevolent newly-wealthy and upstart were established as familiar types. New representations of the dress, behaviour, language, houses, and expenditure of the *arriviste* businessman were well developed by 1780 and became more elaborate in successive seasons.

In the broadening of the attack upon luxury and fashion, three main consequences can be distinguished. Firstly, the threat of luxury came to be associated less with the lower orders than with the rich and the parvenu. Secondly, economic threats posed by fashion and extravagance were isolated as warnings against financial speculation, over-expenditure, and the wastefulness of riches applicable to all who could afford to be reading modern literature. Finally, economic ruination was associated with the over-extension of resources caused by social emulation. Underlying concern with the social threat of upstart ambitions encouraged more detailed definition of the vulgarity and absurdities promoted by luxury. Such analyses were pragmatic and homespun, certainly far removed by the end of the century from the strictures of neo-classical rhetoric. Popular, self-evidently bourgeois literature instructed and entertained in a modern, determinedly accessible idiom. It did this not only by diluting the vocabulary of what has come to be labelled 'civic humanism', but by mixing contemporary parables with the traditional language and imagery of plain English courtesy books and manuals of popular piety.

Much of the actual language of debate also gained a modern appearance. Standardization was an important result of the commercial maturing of the book business. Particular values which were fixed upon words and images during this period had lasting effects. During the 1770s, as the crusade against extravagance advanced, luxury charges were directed at the pretensions of the rich rather than at those of the poor. In the same decade, vulgarity was first generally defined as a deviation from taste. Raymond Williams's seminal discussion of the emergence of a modern structure of meanings identified new definitions and usages for such key words as 'culture', 'class', and 'industry'. Detailed study of the historical formation of much of this, however, is still wanting. A few more avenues have been explored here. 'Luxury' disappeared as a portmanteau term in economic and social debate during the nineteenth century, and the use of 'vulgarity' was to become more sharply focused and less dependent on the play with its other definitions. For more than a hundred years, however, both terms were important verbal hooks upon which to display an often limited, prejudiced, and self-justifying understanding of economic change and the practice of businessmen.

The imaginative literature studied at five-yearly intervals reveals an escalating criticism of new wealth, with distinctions increasingly made between a number of typologies and portrayals. The origins of certain stereotyping can be dated specifically—particularly the attack upon the nabobs from 1768. In the literature of the 1755 and 1760 seasons, satirical depiction of the trader and 'cit' vied with that of men of the ton and the backwoods squire. By 1770, the characterization of businessmen was both more prominent and uniform, with commonly shared caricature and innuendo. Humorous satirical sketches of the petty trader and vulgar *nouveau riche* were developed in contrast to the long-established and continuing stately image of the 'merchant prince'. The 1780 season brought eager discussion of self-made wealth. Vilification of the parvenu was balanced by arch playfulness. The author of *Fatal Obedience* advertised the developing target: 'the moment people quit the humble sphere in which providence has placed them, having not the least pretensions to a higher, they become absurd, and are liable to the severest ridicule'.[7] Such ridicule included a revamped image of sprouting, 'mushroom' wealth, and from this a more comprehensive and rigorous denunciation of the newly-moneyed. Fictional works from 1785 and 1790 probed the origins of self-made or trading families and the morals and activities of their dependants. The light-hearted obsession with 'vulgarity' obvious by the early 1780s, was replaced by much fiercer condemnation of upstart pretensions. Heroines are depicted struggling against arranged marriages with men of recently acquired fortunes. Parvenu vulgarians

[7] *Fatal Obedience*, i. 159.

are courted by indebted intending father-in-laws. Heirs of impoverished estates are forced to make disastrous alliances with the unschooled daughters of the City and of the East India Company. Invariably, both spouse and in-laws are found to be small-minded, foolish, extravagant, and proud. Much of the upstart imagery was not new, but although vulgar *mushrumpes* had sprouted in the sixteenth century and before, modern charges were more specific and extensive. They were both responses and stimulants to increasingly rigid and widely shared codes of social conduct.

Throughout the period, unblemished portrayals of the English overseas merchant continued, even though virtually every other trading profession was subject to attack. Approval for the overseas merchant, however, was measured in new terms. He was increasingly depicted not as the representative of the sort of commercial values spelled out in early eighteenth-century tracts, but as the worthy citizen and neighbour who used his wealth to the benefit of the local community. In many deliberately contrasting cameos, he outgentlemanned the gentleman. Those merchants who did not conform to the behavioural code were excluded from the saintly cast, whatever they were doing to boost the British economy or to enlarge the nation's overseas interests. In the same way, familiar vindications of middle-class values were reinforced. Imaginative literature continued to attack the worthlessness and social deviance of redundant aristocracy as a means of illustrating idealized values of economy, charity, and a proper stewardship of wealth and position. Assaults upon misused wealth, however, led to still more devastating attacks upon the vulgarity of parvenus and the ambitions of traders and industrialists. In order to instruct as well as to entertain, many writers attempted a contemporary social commentary which was more than just a reaffirmation of the responsibilities of wealth and biblical or classical warnings against conspicuous consumption. Popular literature conveyed fears of the social, economic, and political dislocation threatened by upstart traders. Particular commercial and Indian *causes célèbres* of the 1780s were sensationalized by writers and booksellers satisfying the demand for satire and moralities. The twelves and octavos were self-appointed spokesmen for an increasingly self-conscious and self-confident section of society. Condemnation of unacceptable materialism justified 'moderate' participation in a consumer jamboree.

Much of the readership of the new literature was vulnerable to the very charges of money-lust, fashion-craving, and social pretension levelled by best-selling works. Literary demonstrations of the dangers of fashion and materialism were therefore crafted to specify and condemn excess and to do so by judgements upon correct taste, good breeding, and the legitimate and illegitimate aspirations of rank. The need for scapegoats was urgent given that the criticisms of fads and pretensions within popular literature could be applied not only to certain readers, but also to the fiction industry itself. The consequence was a bitter denunciation of the upstart wealth of particular trading families in a powerful literary crusade easily pre-dating Victorian scorn for industrial *arrivistes* and petty traders.

Self-imposed conservatism was similarly justifying social advancement. Hostile stereotypes of the self-made man became a means to advocate restraint upon ambition but not its proscription. Rapid and lofty social elevation was shown to be simple, not only to imply that the status of the social climber was of little worth in its own right, but also that others could gain riches— and use them more responsibly. Stress upon the use rather than the gain of a fortune did not deny the rights of certain individuals to better their own position in the new society. The presentation of parvenu pretensions as dangerous and deceitful re-emphasized the importance of social accomplishments.

By the turn of the nineteenth century, under-breeding was depicted as violating a precisely formulated code of conduct. New wealth—in the form of a middle-class readership—sought legitimacy from avowedly traditional models of social structure and behaviour. The aim was dissociation from extravagant display and the alleged frivolity and materialism introduced by rapidly accumulated wealth. In a continuing preoccupation with financial resources and social station, novels and moral tracts reaffirmed that duties, sanctioned by tradition, were expected of wealth and position. Charity, benevolence, and the responsible values of a sadly missed antique age, legitimized the retention of riches. Polite behaviour was demure, deferential, simple, and unobtrusive—the antithesis of that supposedly displayed by the provocatively rich. Amassing of wealth for wealth's sake was intolerable. Authentic, natural worth, which transcended the occasional disasters of material fortune, could be perceived only by those who both understood and practised its values. Nevertheless, the myth of the born gentleman was fragile and difficult to sustain: 'natural' breeding was distinguishable from and yet also through education and accomplishment. Increasingly, writers sought to prove the value of their ideals by the depiction of those denying them.

In turn, these ideals of good conduct and of the limits of social advancement were illustrated by literary distinctions between men of business. It was in terms of the proper use of riches, central to the definition of the gentleman, that the charity and thrift of the merchant came to be contrasted with the life-style and activities of the nabob, petty trader, and parvenu manufacturer. Many writers continued to produce enthusiastic portrayals of the overseas merchant. No longer, however, were they primarily illustrations of mercantile contributions to British prosperity and success; rather, their role was to define the values by which other men of business were condemned. By 1790 the parvenu was allowed few escape-routes from attack. The low origins of the trader were emphasized to reaffirm both that only vulgar people (the lower orders) sullied the name of trade, and that such tradesmen exhibited vulgar, ungenteel taste. He was charged with the hypocrisy of despising the aristocracy whom he aped. The parvenu's generosity after gaining wealth, even though this conformed to the ideal, was often scornfully dismissed as the insincerity of ostentation and as evidence of an anxiety to respond to the strictures of literature itself.

Economic instability in the midst of expanding demand and novelly derived commercial fortunes recharged the argument. In the search for explanations, attention was directed to the misuse of wealth and the necessity of husbanding resources. The alleged extravagance of the newly-wealthy was prime supportive evidence for theories of both classical and developmental decline and fall. In portrayals of the iniquities of trading and *nouveau riche* behaviour, intellectual purviews of contagious luxury and fashion were themselves used to reinforce belief in the potential destructiveness of the businessman's actions and social ambition. It was similarly argued that the excessive success of individual men threatened economic ruination either because of their over-extravagance or because of their retirement from trade. At the same time, activities which damaged the economy were presented as detrimental to social order. The leisure of the newly-rich was as much dangerous pretension as it was unproductive. The self-made man suffered from both the social and the economic attack, the one supporting the other.

All this has important consequences for the understanding of long-term responses to trade and industry. The most lasting effects of late eighteenth-century portrayals derived from representations designed for very particular middle-class market interests. The key values by which the tradesman and the *nouveau riche* were judged in the 1780s remained central to the literary portrayal of business for the next century or more. Even by 1790, many commentators were worried that attacks on businessmen were contributing to disdain for trade and industry. It is also clear that the sort of charges carried by this literature were attended to not only by writers, civic debating groups, and the heirs of established gentry, but also by second generation industrialists. The vilification of new wealth was emphatic, but the characteristics of the accepted and the valued were further elaborated. Interest was greatly heightened in the traditional accompaniments of station. Even if it was only at the parish level that most businessmen did or could buy landed property, the set image of the gentlemanly ideal encouraged ambitions for the country seat. The number of merchants sending their sons to mercantile academies or to the Scottish universities decreased in favour of gentrification at Oxford and Cambridge. New gentry of the early nineteenth century were quick to take up badges of Society—new houses, new names, new pedigrees, and new coats of arms. The sons of commercial booksellers and woollen manufacturers alike burned their fathers' business records. The idealization of charity as a mark of status brought its due crop of charitable institutions. In all this, of course, Victorian entrepreneurs continued as prisoners of the catch-all satires against vulgarity, newness, and sudden climbs in social station. Attention to dress and education and to the symbols of status were exactly the traits continued in contemporary parody, and always it seemed, as Dickens summarized in his creation of the Veneerings, that 'the surface smelt a little too much of the workshop and was a trifle stickey'.[8]

The late eighteenth-century obsession with proper behaviour

---

[8] Charles Dickens, *Our Mutual Friend* (London, 1864–5), ch. 2.

in a consumer society and the posturing necessary to make accumulation acceptable to one's peers remained unquelled in Victorian society. Modern versions of the vulgarian upstart were vigorously repeated. The parvenu estate entered the novels and the textbooks. Mushroom follies and outrages were popularized in a new generation of nineteenth-century periodicals, in children's books, and on the stage. Such characterizations coloured beliefs about how to write a business biography—and autobiography. The depiction of the rough manners and ostentatious behaviour of captains of industry was reproduced in dozens of Victorian school histories. The Bounderby figure had also clearly emerged by the end of the eighteenth century, with extended mockery of the self-made man whose absurd pride in his own achievement and low origins was shown to be in blustering response to gentlemanly prejudice against trade. Similarly, Victorian biographers of the pioneers of commercial and manufacturing enterprise were to stress the gentlemanly values and the conquest of both ambition and the profit-motive. They were to place their subjects in a carefully framed social context with no attention to their business skills. Even modern studies of late eighteenth-century manufacturers have been anxious to respond to the challenge first laid down in the period of their subjects' own industrial activity.

Such preoccupations also help to explain an apparent paradox between contemporary image and historical reality. Against increasing evidence for the dominance of a landed–commercial élite which thwarted manufacturing ambitions, most commentators, and as Professor Stone acknowledges, most historians, were apparently misled by the myth of an 'open gentry'. The failure of the new industrialist to buy land appears to confirm the theory of a continued landed–commercial hegemony. It might still be possible to argue that for the British entrepreneur 'the ultimate proof of success in business was the ability to leave it',[9] but if the businessman made so few attempts to buy into the preserves of the upper élite, how could he or his sons be said to enjoy its privileges or accept them as a means to escape a commercial or industrial career? One explanation for the persuasive myth of manufacturer entryism is found in the potency of the particularized attacks on the *nouveau riche*. Created to support specific

[9] David Cannadine, cited in Porter, *English Society*, p. 87.

interests, literary characterizations extended and perpetuated the myth of rampant entryism. By the same token, idealized mercantile heroes had in the long term limited staying power and attraction as instruments of moral instruction. Few benevolent merchant portrayals were remembered after this period. Their use declines towards the end of the century and by the 1820s their appearance in popular literature is rare indeed. By contrast, representations of the vulgar *nouveau riche* businessman were widely adopted. They appear in the evangelical crusade against the millocrats in the 1840s, they surface in Peacock, Dickens, and Trollope. They feature prominently in Fabian interpretations of an Industrial Revolution. They are alive and well in Belloc, Buchan, and Waugh, and much more besides.

The first question which this study set out to resolve was how and why the literary image of business changed so dramatically between the beginning and the end of the eighteenth century. Several conclusions have been given about the nature of the images carried during the final decades of the century. Readers were offered simple messages which handed out blame and praise, distinguished between right and wrong, and defined social acceptability. A strong case can be made for the forcing role of popular commercial literature in late eighteenth-century attacks upon upstart pretensions and the definition of legitimacy in social and economic affairs. Literature of the period broadcast to a wide audience and with the enthusiasm of both teacher and defending counsel. It stressed the importance of the values of the gentleman, tradition, charity, economy, the ownership of land, good birth, and the proper accomplishments of station. All these were pivotal to the nineteenth-century assault upon overreaching new wealth.

Such responses also suggest several ways in which literary images have been misinterpreted or isolated from their wider historical context. In the depiction of the businessman, precise business activities were little to the purpose of the popular portrayals. Representations of the outcast and parvenu man of trade were taken up to define by negative example the financially and socially respectable in an increasingly acquisitive and competitive society. Business caricatures became devices to instruct upon the use of wealth in relation to conduct and status in a consumer society. Financial gain was implicitly condoned by literature containing both the vaguest notions of the means by which individual fortunes were made and explicit and new-style attacks upon excessive wealth, extravagance, and luxury.

This counterpoint has been in evidence throughout the study. One of the key reasons for the changing presentation of men of new wealth also alters fundamentally the historical significance of the type of anti-business prejudice generated. Not the least ambiguity of the reaction identified is that although hostility to businessmen certainly increased, criticism was directed more to the particular agents of business than to basic business ethics. Anti-business portrayals were intended to explain disorder and sanction particularized profit-making and social mobility in a period of marked social and economic upheaval.

One way of seeing this is to compare again the popular literary verdicts with those of similar works of a century later. Imaginative works of the late eighteenth century carried neither the specificity nor the wide range of Victorian anti-industrial crusades. No attention was paid to the location of industrial activity, employment practices, or industrial pollution. Anxieties over the deteriorating quality of urban life were restricted to fears of social unrest. In literature, London was still the shock city, and the readership, however rapidly advancing in the provinces, still attended to London news and affairs. Early humanitarian concern had not yet broadened into lobbies for the reform of factory conditions and there was no horrific depiction of child labour and the sadistic factory-owner of the type appearing in novels by the close of the 1830s. In the 1780s the only interest in the suffering resulting from commercial enterprise arose either from accounts of those ruined upon the default or local greed of the extravagant trader or from charges against the nabob. Domestic exploitation of labour was not discussed within the literature. Sympathy for the poor was strictly limited—often the tool rather than the cause of attacks upon *nouveaux riches*. It is a salutary caution for accounts of the growth in humanitarian attitudes to the poor in this period.

Another way of highlighting the counterpoint is to note that if this interpretation of the popular literature is correct, then the courting of 'improving' readerships contributed as much to a favourable climate for advancing industrialism as it contributed to any disdain for business. Economic threats highlighted by the literature were based on fears not of too much business activity, but rather of the misuse or under-use of wealth derived from it.

Alarms over money-into-land entryism and the heightened importance of land conveyed by the literature, must not be used too simplistically in the anti-business interpretation of nineteenth-century social history. Acceptance of the worth of trade was carried by almost all works, if automatically and without great panache. The envisaged social threats were more complex, most reflecting real fears of dangers to familial, local, or national prosperity, and many serving to legitimize notions of advancement. Here, images can easily be misread. The literary verdict clearly reflects a balance between attitudes conducive to economic achievement and an array of images and arguments which could condemn business activity. Later historians would not be alone in questioning the continued support of trade. Its lack-lustre presentation and the images denouncing certain businessmen clearly worried many contemporaries. Writers rallied to the defence of the merchant and the values of commerce at the end of the century, attacking what they saw as a growing mistrust of trade. A paradox is suggested—that middle-class literature offering, for largely commercial reasons, instruction and reassurance about changes in a developing capitalistic society, created anti-business prejudices which were to have an extensive effect even by the next generation. Underlying the increased emphasis on status in England in the late eighteenth century were fears of the possible deprivation of new 'decencies' amidst growing numbers seeking to legitimize financial and social improvement. Print developed and fixed shared attitudes by and for an emergent and increasingly affluent sector of society. Popular writers sought to rank different social groups and establish referential norms. What we are looking at are not only the reactions of consumers to new consumption patterns and of credit-holders and credit-seekers to new financial relationships, but the role of print in creating, packaging, and reinforcing class attitudes and antagonisms. Attitudes to business are not only important because they can be shown to have specifically economic effects.

BIBLIOGRAPHY

To assist those seeking further reading, the secondary material is divided into three thematic groups. The longer eighteenth-century titles have been shortened.

The arrangement is as follows:

SELECT MANUSCRIPT SOURCES

Beinecke Rare Books and Manuscript Library, Yale University
   Osborn papers [letters to Lowndes].
Birmingham Reference Library
   Garbett–Shelburne papers.

Bodleian Library, Oxford
Douce papers.
Papers from the John Johnson collection.

Bristol Public Library
Bristol Library Society loan registers.

British Library, Department of Manuscripts
Additional MSS
4,272, fos. 35 ff., letters from Trusler to Birch.
4,319, fo. 200, letter from Trusler to Birch.
5,852, Cole papers, Hubbard's Journal, 1741–69.
28,121, fos. 1–305, 'A Series of Interesting and Animated Essays on the Affairs of Life', MSS for press, by Trusler.
28,121, fos. 306–81, 'The Theory of Luxury', MSS for press, by Trusler.
28,121, fos. 381 ff., Trusler accounts.
28,275, fos. 200–17, 382–498. Tonson papers.
32,555, fo. 4 ff., Defoe's MSS of 'The Compleat English Gentleman'.
32,717, 32,732, 32,735, 32,869, 32,873, Newcastle papers.
36,499, fo. 372, letter from Trusler to Cumberland.
36,504, fos. 316 ff., letters from Trusler to Cumberland.
38,728, William Upcott papers.
38,729, Upcott papers, letters, accounts, and copyright receipts.
38,730, Upcott papers, Rivington and Fletcher bankruptcy papers, copyright sales receipts, and transaction papers.
39,306, fos. 25–75. Berkeley's MSS 'Sermon on Charity'.
Egerton MSS
3,695 ff., Barrett papers.
'Ranelagh Gardens', a scrapbook of contemporary advertisements, newspaper-cuttings, and prints (BL 840. m. 28).

Cambridge University Library
University Archives, Grace Book I.
University Archives, Grace Book K.
University Archives, CUR 24, Addresses of the Senate, 1715–.
University Archives, CUR 38 To-Yo, Prizes and Scholarships.
Char. I. 1. Registrum Praemorium.
Char. I. 18. Prize Subjects.

Gloucester Public Library
Adams papers.

Goldsmiths' Library, University of London
Goldsmiths' Library broadsides, volumes i–v.

Leeds Central Reference Library
Alf Mattison papers.

Leeds City Archives
LC/M 3, Leeds Corporation Court Book, 1773–1835, iii, Minutes and Orders.
LC/M 9, Admissions Book of Leeds Corporation.
O/K 1–6, 18–33, Oates papers, 1894–7.
LO/RB 34, Leeds Poor-Rate Assessment Books, Nov. 1774 and May 1790.
Leeds Vestry Committee Minute and Order Book.
Oates papers.
Temple Newsam papers, 1761–1801.
Lewis Walpole Library, Farmington, Connecticut
Contract with Dodsley and receipt for payment by Trusler, May 1766.
'Memoirs of the Life of the Rev. Dr. Trusler', Part II, MSS for press.
New York Public Library
Berg papers.
New York Society Library
Catalogue of the Hammond circulating library.
Suffolk County Record Office, Ipswich branch
Ethel Mann papers.

PRINTED PRIMARY SOURCES

I. NOVELS, PLAYS, POETRY, AND MISCELLANEOUS IMAGINATIVE LITERATURE

Novels consulted during research for this book are asterisked in the check-list of my *British Fiction, 1750–70* and subsequent volumes in preparation (a preliminary presentation of the later decades is given in the one volume appendix to Raven, 'English Popular Literature', unpublished Cambridge Ph.D., 1985). The following section is therefore a select listing.

Anonymous works:
Adeline; or, The Orphan, 3 vols., London, 1790.
The Adventures of a Black Coat, London, 1760.
The Adventures of a Corkscrew, London, 1775.
The Adventures of Oxymel Classic Esq; Once an Oxford Scholar, 2 vols., London, 1768.
Almira: Being the History of a Young Lady of Good Birth and Fortune, but More Distinguish'd Merit, 2 vols., London, 1762.
Anna: A Sentimental Novel: In a Series of Letters, 2 vols., Dublin, 1782.
Arley; or, The Faithless Wife, 2 vols., London, 1790.
An Asylum for Fugitive Pieces, in Prose and Verse, London, 1785.
The Baron of Manstow: A Novel, 2 vols., London, 1790.

The Birmingham Counterfeit; or, The Invisible Spectator, 2 vols., London, 1772.

The Companion: Being a Choice Collection of the most Admired Pieces from the Best Authors, 3 vols., Edinburgh, 1790–1.

The Convent; or, The History of Julia, 2 vols., London, 1767.

Count D'Aubigny: An Historical Tale, Dublin, 1783.

The Country Cousins; or, A Journey to London, 2 vols., London, 1767.

Crazy Tales; and Fables for Grown Gentlemen, London, 1780.

Criticisms on the Rolliad, 8th edn., London, 1788.

The Delicate Embarrassments: A Novel, 2 vols., London, 1769.

The Delicate Jester; or, Wit and Humour divested of Ribaldry, London, 1780.

The Denouement ... The History of Lady Louisa Wingrove, London, 1784.

A Dialogue on Taste, 2nd edn., London, 1757.

Did You Ever See Such Damned Stuff?, London, 1760.

The Disinterested Nabob: A Novel: Interspersed with Genuine Descriptions of India, its Manners and Customs, 3 vols., London, 1787.

The Distrest Wife; or, The History of Eliza Wyndham, 2 vols., London, 1768.

Fables for Grown Gentlemen, London, 1770.

The Fair Cambrians: A Novel, 3 vols., London, 1790.

The Fair Hibernian, 2 vols., London, 1789.

Fashionable Life; or, The History of Miss Louisa Fermor: A Novel: By a Lady, Dublin, 1781.

Fatal Obedience; or, The History of Mr. Freeland, 2 vols., London, 1780.

Female Friendship; or, The Innocent Sufferer, 2 vols., London, 1770.

The Female Jester; or, Wit for the Ladies ... Containing Every Comical Jest, Smart Repartee, Brilliant Bon-Mot &c, London, 1780.

The Fortunate Lottery Ticket, London, 1797.

Francis, the Philanthropist: An Unfashionable Tale, Dublin, 1786.

The Fugitive; or, Happy Recess: A Dramatic Pastoral: In Two Acts, London, 1790.

Gabrielle de Vergy; An Historic Tale, London, 1790.

The Gentleman: An Heroic Poem, Dublin, 1747.

*The Genuine Memoirs of Miss Faulkner; otherwise, Mrs D***l**n, or Countess of H*****x*, London, 1770.

Gilham Farm; or, The History of Melvin and Lucy: In a Series of Letters, 2 vols., London, 1781.

Harcourt; A Sentimental Novel: In a Series of Letters by the Authoress of Evelina, 2 vols., Dublin, 1780. Not by Fanny Burney.

Hartly House, Calcutta, 3 vols., London, 1789.

The History of Captain and Miss Rivers, 3 vols., London, 1787.

The History of Eliza Musgrove, 2 vols., London, 1770.

The History of Frederick the Forsaken, 2 vols., Dublin, 1761.

A History of the Matrimonial Adventure of a Banker's Clerk, London, 1762.

The History of Miss Harriot Fairfax, London, 1780.

The History of Miss Katty N———, London, 1757.
How She Lost Him; or, The History of Miss Wyndham, 2 vols., Dublin, 1780.
The Indian Adventurer; or, History of Mr. Vanneck, London, 1780.
The Innocent Rivals: A Novel, Taken from the French, 3 vols., London, 1786.
Juliana: A Novel, 3 vols., London, 1786.
The Lascivious Hypocrite, London, 1783.
Letters Between Clara and Antonia, 2 vols., London, 1780.
Letters to Honoria and Marianne on Various Subjects, 3 vols., London, 1774.
The Life and Adventures and Amours of Sir R[ichard] P[errot], London, 1770.
The Life, Adventures . . . of the Celebrated Jemmy Twitcher, London, 1770.
The Life and Death of Thomas, Lord Cromwell: By Mr. Shakespear, London,
    1734.
The Lottery; or, Midsummer Recess, 2nd edn., Uttoxeter, 1797.
Louisa; or, The Reward of an Affectionate Daughter, 2 vols., London, 1790.
Louisa; or, Virtue in Distress, London, 1760.
Louisa Wharton; or, A Story Founded on Fact, London, 1790.
The Maid of Kent, 3 vols., London, 1790.
The Man of Taste, London, 1733.
May Day or Anecdotes of Lydia Lively, London, 1787.
Memoirs of B– Tracey, London, c.1760.
The Memoirs of Jonathan Splittfig, London, 1773.
*Memoirs of an Unfortunate Young Lady, which appeared in No's IV, V, and VI of
    the 'Citizen' just published in 'The Bristol Mercury'*, Bristol, 1790.
*The Merry Jester, or Convivial Companion; A Collection of Wit and Mirth, suited
    to all Companies, and adapted to every Capacity*, London, [178–].
The Modern Fine Gentleman: A Novel, 2 vols., London, 1774.
*The Nabob; Or, Asiatic Plunderers: A Satyrical Poem: In a Dialogue Between a
    Friend and the Author*, London, 1772.
The Nabob's Wife, 3 vols., London, 1837.
Narrative Companion; or, The Entertaining Moralist, 2 vols., London, 1760.
Original Love-Letters Between a Lady of Quality and a Person of Inferior Station,
    2nd edn., Dublin, 1811.
*The Perfidious Guardian; or, Vicissitudes of Fortune, Exemplified in the History of
    Lucretia Lawson*, 2 vols., London, 1790.
The Rake of Taste; or, The Elegant Debauchee: A True Story, London, 1760.
Ranelagh House: A Satire in Prose, London, 1747.
The Relapse: A Novel, 2 vols., London, 1780.
The Romance of a Day; or, An Adventure in Greenwich-Park last Easter, London,
    1760.
The Schemer; or, Universal Satirist: By the Great Philosopher Helter von Scelter,
    London, 1763.
Sentimental Lucubrations: By Peter Pennyless, London, 1770.
A Sketch of the Times: A Satire, London, 1780.

The Slave of Passion, London, 1790.

Sophia, or, The Embarrassed Wife: Containing the History of Mira, the New Foundling, 2nd edn., 2 vols., London, 1788.

Thoughts on the Times, But Chiefly on the Profligacy of our Women, London, 1779.

The Trial; or, The History of Charles Horton, Esq., London, 1781.

Trials for Adultery or the History of Divorces: Being Select Trials at Doctors Commons ... from 1760 to the Present Time, 7 vols., London, 1779–80.

The Tricks of the Town Laid Open, London, 1699.

The Trip to Weymouth, 2 vols., London, 1790.

The Twin Sisters; or, The Effects of Education, 4 vols., London, 1788–9.

The Undutiful Daughter; or, The History of Miss Goodwin: In a Series of Letters, 3 vols., London, 1771.

The Universal Director, London, 1763.

The Upstart, London, [before 1710].

The Whimsical Jester, London, 1788.

Witty and Humourous Jester, London, 1789.

The Woman of Fashion: A Poem: In a Letter from Lady Maria Modish to Lady Belinda Artless, London, 1778.

The Woman of Letters ... or, Miss Fanny Bolton, London, 1783.

The Younger Brother, A Tale, 2 vols., London, 1770–2.

AMHURST, NICHOLAS, *Terrae-Filius: or, The Secret History of the University of Oxford*, 2 vols., London, 1726.

ANSTEY, CHRISTOPHER, *Speculation; or, A Defence of Mankind: A Poem*, London, 1780.

BAGE, ROBERT, *Hermsprong, or, Man as He is Not*, 2 vols., London, 1796; and 2nd edn., 3 vols., London, 1799.

BALLIN, ROSETTA, *The Statue Room: An Historical Tale*, 2 vols., London, 1790.

BANCROFT, EDWARD, *The History of Charles Wentworth Esq.*, 3 vols., London, 1770.

BARRY, MRS, *The Amorous Merchant; or, Intriguing Husband: Being a Curious and Uncommon Process of Love and Law*, London, 1753.

BELOE, WILLIAM, *Incidents of a Youthful Life; or, The True History of William Langley*, London, 1790.

BENNETT, AGNES, *Anna; or, The Memoirs of a Welch Heiress*, 4 vols., London, 1785.

—— *Juvenile Indiscretions*, 5 vols., London, 1786.

BICKNELL, ALEXANDER, *Doncaster Races; or, The History of Miss Maitland*, 2 vols., London, 1790.

BLOWERS, ELIZABETH, *The Parsonage-House: A Novel*, 3 vols. in 1, Dublin, 1781.

BOLAS, THOMAS, *The English Merchant; or, The Fatal Effects of Speculation in the Funds*, 2 vols., London, 1795.

BONHOTE, MRS, *Ellen Woodley: A Novel*, 2 vols., London, 1790.

—— *Olivia; or, The Deserted Bride*, 3 vols., London, 1787.

—— *The Parental Monitor*, 2 vols., London, 1788.

—— *The Rambles of Mr. Frankly: Published by his Sister*, 2 vols., London, 1772.

BOWLES, W. L., *Verses to John Howard*, London, 1789.

BROOKE, FRANCES, *The History of Charles Mandeville*, 2 vols., London, 1790.

BROOKE, HENRY, *The Fool of Quality; or, The History of Henry, Earl of Moreland*, 2nd edn., 5 vols., London, 1767.

BURNEY, FANNY. *Cecilia; or, Memoirs of an Heiress*, 5 vols., London, 1782.

—— *Evelina; or, A Young Lady's Entrance into the World*, 3 vols., London, 1778.

DE CAMBON, MARIA GEERTRUIDA VAN DE WERKEN, *Young Grandison*, London, *c.*1788.

CARTER, JOHN, *The Scotch Parents; or, The Remarkable Case of John Ramble, Written by Himself*, London, 1773.

CENTLIVRE, MRS, *The Gamester: A Comedy*, London, 1705.

CHATER, JOHN, *The History of Tom Rigby*, 2 vols., Dublin, 1773.

COLLYER, MARY, *The Death of Cain: In Five Books*, London, 1789.

COLMAN, GEORGE, THE ELDER, *Prose on Several Occasions; Accompanied with some Pieces in Verse*, London, 1787.

[COLMAN, GEORGE, THE ELDER, and THORNTON, BONNELL], *The Connoisseur: By Mr. Town, Critic and Censor-General*, 2 vols., London, 1755.

COMBE, WILLIAM, *The Devil Upon Two Sticks in England*, 4 vols., London, 1790; 2nd edn., 6 vols., London, 1790.

COOKE, JOHN, *Cooke's Pocket Edition of English Poets Superbly Embellished*, London, [1788–].

—— *Cooke's Pocket Edition of Sacred Classics, or Moralists Instructive Companion*, London, [1787–].

—— *Cooke's Pocket Edition of Select Novels, or, Novelists' Entertaining Library, containing a Complete Collection of Universally Approved Adventures, Tales &c by the most Esteemed Authors*, London, [1788–].

COVENTRY, FRANCIS, *The History of Pompey the Little; or, The Life and Adventures of a Lap-Dog*, London, 1751.

CROFT, SIR HERBERT, *The Abbey of Kilkhampton; or, Monumental Records for the Year 1780*, London, 1780.

CUMBERLAND, RICHARD, *The Observer; Being a Collection of Moral, Literary, and Familiar Essays*, 4th edn., 5 vols., London, 1791.

—— *The West Indian*, London, 1771.

—— *The Wheel of Fortune, A Comedy*, London, 1795.

DARWIN, ERASMUS, *The Essential Writings of Erasmus Darwin*, ed. Desmond King-Hale, London, 1968.

DAWE, ANNE, *The Younger Sister; or, The History of Miss Somerset*, 2 vols., Dublin, 1772.

DAY, THOMAS, *The History of Sandford and Merton*, 3 vols., London, 1783–9.

DELL, HENRY, *The Booksellers: A Poem*, London, 1766 (Cambridge University Library copy with manuscript annotations).

DEVONSHIRE, GEORGIANA, DUCHESS OF, *The Sylph: A Novel*, 2 vols., London, 1779; 5th edn., Dublin, 1784.

DYER, JOHN, *The Fleece: A Poem: In Four Books*, London, 1757.

FIELDING, HENRY, *The Complete Works of Henry Fielding*, Wesleyan edn., ed. W. B. Coley *et al.*, 9 vols., Oxford, 1969–.

—— *The Works of Henry Fielding*, ed. G. H. Maynadier, 12 vols., London, 1903.

—— *Amelia*, 4 vols., London, 1752 [1751].

—— *The History of Tom Jones, A Foundling*, 6 vols., London, 1749.

—— *The Lottery*, London, 1732; 2nd edn., London, 1788.

FILMER, EDWARD, *A Defence of Plays*, London, 1707.

FOOTE, SAMUEL, *The Minor: A Comedy*. London, 1760.

—— *The Nabob, A Comedy: In Three Acts*, London, 1778.

FREETH, JOHN, *Political Songster; or, A Touch on the Times*, 6th edn., Birmingham, 1790.

GOLDSMITH, OLIVER, *The Collected Works of Oliver Goldsmith*, ed. Arthur Friedman, 5 vols., Oxford, 1966.

GOMERSALL, ANNA, *The Citizen: A Novel*, 2 vols., London, 1790.

—— *Creation: A Poem*, Newport, 1824.

—— *The Disappointed Heir; or, Memoirs of the Ormond Family: A Novel*, 2 vols., Exeter, 1796.

—— *Eleonora: A Novel, In a Series of Letters, Written by a Female Inhabitant of Leeds in Yorkshire*, 2 vols., London, 1789

GRAVES, RICHARD, *Columella; or, The Distressed Anchoret: A Colloquial Tale*, 2 vols., London, 1779.

—— *Eugenius; or, Anecdotes of the Golden Vale: An Embellished Narrative of Real Facts*, 2nd edn., 2 vols., London, 1786.

—— *Plexippus: or, The Aspiring Plebeian*, 2 vols., London, 1790.

—— *The Spiritual Quixote; or, The Summer's Ramble of Mr. Geoffry Wildgoose*, 3 vols., London, 1773.

GRIFFITH, ELIZABETH, *Essays Addressed to Young Married Women*, London, 1782.

—— *A Series of Genuine Letters between Henry and Frances*, 3rd edn., 6 vols., London, 1767–72.

GUNNING, SUSANNAH, *Barford Abbey: A Novel in a Series of Letters*, 2 vols., London, 1768.

—— *Coombe Wood: A Novel*, 2nd edn., Dublin, 1783.

GWYNN, ALBINIA, *The Rencontre; or, Transition of a Moment*, 2 vols., Dublin, 1785.

HAYWOOD, ELIZA, *The Invisible Spy; By Exploralibus*, 4 vols., London, 1755.

HERVEY, ELIZABETH, *Louisa: A Novel*, 3 vols., London, 1790.

HOLCROFT, THOMAS, *Alwyn; or, The Gentleman Comedian*, 2 vols., London, 1780.

—— *The Family Picture*, London, 1783.

JENNER, CHARLES, *The Placid Man; or, Memoirs of Sir Charles Beville*, 2 vols., London, 1770.

JENYNS, SOAMES, *A Modern Fine Gentleman*, London, 1746.

JOHNSTON, CHARLES, *Chrysal; or, The Adventures of a Guinea*, 4 vols., London, 1760–5.

JONSON, BEN, *Ben Jonson: Poems*, ed. Ian Donaldson, Oxford, 1975.

KILNER, DOROTHY, *The Rotchfords*, London, 1786.

LENNOX, CHARLOTTE, *Euphemia*, 4 vols., London, 1790.

LILLO, GEORGE, *The London Merchant or the History of George Barnwell*, London, 1731.

LINNECAR, RICHARD, *The Miscellaneous Works of Richard Linnecar of Wakefield*, Leeds, 1789.

MACKENZIE, ANNA MARIA [later MRS JOHNSON], *The Gamesters: A Novel*, 3 vols., London, 1786.

MACKENZIE, HENRY, *Julia de Roubigné, A Tale: In a Series of Letters*, 2 vols., London and Edinburgh, 1777.

—— *The Works of Henry Mackenzie*, 8 vols., Edinburgh, 1808.

[MARSHALL, JEAN], *The History of Alicia Montague*, 2 vols., London, 1767.

MASON, WILLIAM, *Satirical Poems Published anonymously By William Mason with Notes by Horace Walpole*, ed. Paget Toynbee, Oxford, 1926.

MASSINGER, PHILIP, *The City Madam: A Comedie*, London, 1658.

—— *A New Way to Pay Old Debts*, London, 1633.

MINIFIE, MARGARET, *The Count de Poland*, 4 vols., London, 1780.

MONKLAND, MRS, *The Nabob at Home; or, The Return to England*, 3 vols., London, 1842.

MOORE, JOHN, *Zeluco: Various Views of Human Nature, taken from Life and Manners, Foreign and Domestic*, 2nd edn., 2 vols., Dublin, 1789.

NASH, THOMAS, *Quaternio, or a Fourefold Way to a Happie Life*, London, 1633.

NEWBERY, JOHN, *The Circle of the Sciences*, 7 vols., London, 1745–6.

PARRY, CATHERINE, *Eden Vale: A Novel*, 2 vols., London, 1784.

PARSONS, ELIZA, *The History of Miss Meredith*, 2 vols., London, 1790.

PATERSON, SAMUEL, *Joineriana; Or the Book of Scraps*, 2 vols., London, 1772.

PEACOCK, THOMAS LOVE, *Crotchet Castle*, London, 1831.

PILKINGTON, MARY, *Delia: A Pathetic and Interesting Tale*, 4 vols., London, 1790.

Pope, Alexander, *Epistles and Satires of Alexander Pope*, ed. Anthony Trott and Martin Axford, London, 1961.

Potter, John, *Virtuous Villagers*, London, 1784.

Pottinger, Israel, *The Methodist: A Comedy*, London, 1761.

Pratt, Samuel Jackson, *Emma Corbett; or, The Miseries of Civil War*, Dublin, 1780.

—— *The Pupil of Pleasure*, 2nd edn., 2 vols., London, 1783.

—— *The Triumph of Benevolence; or, The History of Francis Wells*, 2 vols., London, 1772.

Purbeck, Jane and Elizabeth, *Raynsford Park: A Novel*, 4 vols., London, 1790.

Radcliffe, Ann Ward, *A Sicilian Romance*, 2 vols., London, 1790.

Reeve, Clara, *Edwy and Edilda: A Gothic Tale: In Five Parts*, Dublin, 1783.

—— *The Progress of Romance, Through Times, Countries, and Manners*, 2 vols., Colchester, 1785.

—— *The Two Mentors: A Modern Story*, 2 vols., London, 1783.

Richardson, Samuel, *Clarissa: or, The History of a Young Lady*, 7 vols., London, 1748.

—— *The History of Sir Charles Grandison: In a Series of Letters*, 7 vols. London, 1753.

—— *Pamela; or, Virtue Rewarded*, 7th edn., 4 vols., London, 1754.

Ripley, James, *Select Original Letters on Various Subjects*, London, 1781.

Rudd, Margaret, *The Belle Widows*, 2 vols., London, 1789.

Ryves, Elizabeth, *The Hermit of Snowden; or, Memoirs of Albert and Lavinia*, 2nd edn., Dublin, 1790.

Seally, John, *The Lady's Encyclopaedia; or, A Concise Analysis of the Belles Lettres, the Fine Arts and the Three Sciences*, 3 vols., London and Edinburgh, 1788.

—— *Moral Tales, After the Eastern Manner*, London, 1780.

Smith, Charlotte, *Ethelinde; or, The Recluse of the Lake*, 2nd edn., 5 vols., London, 1790.

Steele, Sir Richard, *The Conscious Lovers: A Comedy*, London, 1723.

[Steele, Sir Richard, and Addison, Joseph], *The Englishman: Being a Sequel to the Guardian*, London, 1713–15.

[Steele, Sir Richard, Addison, Joseph, et al.], *The Guardian*, 2nd edn., 2 vols., London, 1714.

Swift, Jonathan, *The Works of Jonathan Swift*, ed. Herbert Davis et al., 2nd edn., 16 vols., Oxford, 1966.

Thomson, James, *The Castle of Indolence*, London, 1748.

Thomson, Revd James, *The Denial; or, The Happy Retreat*, 3 vols., London, 1790.

[Tickell, Richard, et al.], *Probationary Odes for the Laureateship by Sir John Hawkins Knt*, London, 1785.

TOMLINS, MISS, *Victim of Fancy*, London, 1787.

TREYSSAC DE VERGY, *The Mistakes of the Heart*, 3 vols., London, 1769–70.

TYPO, DR [pseud.], *The Affecting History of Two Young Gentlewomen*, London, 1780.

[VAUGHAN, THOMAS], *Fashionable Follies: A Novel: Containing the History of a Parisien Family*, 2 vols., London, 1781.

WILLIAMS, HELEN MARIA, *A Farewell for Two Years to England*, London, 1791.

—— *Julia: A Novel*, 2 vols., London, 1790.

WOODFIN, MRS. A., *The History of Sally Sable*, 2 vols., London, 1770.

WRIGHT, GEORGE, *Retired Pleasures, or the Charms of Rural Life in Prose and Verse, with Occasional Notes and Illustrations*, London, 1787.

YOUNG, EDWARD, *Imperium Pelagi: A Naval Lyric*, London, 1730.

II. DIARIES, LETTERS, AND AUTOBIOGRAPHIES

ANDREWS, C. BRUYN, and BERESFORD, JOHN, eds., *The Torrington Diaries: Containing the Tours through England and Wales of the Hon. John Byng (later Fifth Viscount Torrington) Between the Years 1781 and 1794*, 4 vols., London and New York, 1970.

D'ARCHENHOLZ, M., *A Picture of England: Containing a Description of the Laws, Customs and Manners of England*, Dublin, 1790.

BAIN, IAIN, ed., *A Memoir of Thomas Bewick Written by Himself*, London, 1975.

BALDERSTON, KATHERINE C., ed., *Thraliana: The Diary of Mrs Hester Lynch Thrale (later Mrs Piozzi), 1776–1809*, 2 vols., Oxford, 1942.

BETTANY, LEWIS, ed., *Diaries of William Johnston Temple, 1780–1796*, Oxford, 1929.

LE BLANC, MONS. L'ABBÉ, *Letters on the English and French Nations*, 2 vols., London, 1747.

BLENCOWE, R. W., ed., 'Extracts from the Journal of Walter Gale, Schoolmaster at Mayfield, 1750', *Sussex Archaeological Collections*, 9 (1857), 182–207.

BRAY, WILLIAM, *Sketch of a Tour into Derbyshire and Yorkshire*, London, 1777.

CAINE, CAESAR, ed., *Strother's Journal: Written by a Tradesman of York and Hull, 1784–1785*, London, 1912.

CARTWRIGHT, JAMES JOEL, ed., *The Travels Through England of Dr. Richard Pococke, Successively Bishop of Meath and of Ossory, during 1750, 1751, and later years*, London, 1888.

CHRISTIE, O. F., ed., *The Diary of the Revd. William Jones, 1777–1821, Curate and Vicar of Broxbourne and the Hamlet of Hoddesdon, 1781–1821*, London, 1929.

[CLARKE, E. D.], *A Tour Through the South of England, Wales, and Part of Ireland Made During the Summer of* 1791, London, 1793.

DOBSON, AUSTIN, ed., *Diary and Letters of Madame D'Arblay (*1778–1840*): As edited by her Niece, Charlotte Barrett*, 6 vols., London, 1904–5.

ELLIS, ANNIE RAINE, ed., *Early Diary of Frances Burney*, 1768–1778, 2 vols., London, 1889.

GRAY, MRS EDWIN, ed., *Papers and Diaries of a York Family*, 1764–1839, London, 1927.

GRIFFEN, JOHN, ed., *Memoirs of the Rev. Thomas English, late of Wooburn, Bucks*, Portsmouth, 1812.

GROSLEY, PIERRE JEAN, *A Tour to London; or, New Observations on England and its Inhabitants*, trans. Thomas Nugent, 2 vols., London, 1772.

HEMLOW, JOYCE, ed., *The Journals and Letters of Fanny Burney (Madame D'Arblay)*, 12 vols., Oxford, 1972–84.

HILL, GEORGE BIRKBECK, ed., *Johnsonian Miscellanies*, 2 vols., Oxford, 1897.

—— ed., and revised L. F. Powell, *Boswell's Life of Johnson*, 6 vols., Oxford, 1934–50.

HOOPER, MR, trans., *Letters of Baron Bielfield, Secretary of Legation to the King of Prussia*, 4 vols., London, 1770.

HUTCHINSON, WILLIAM, *An Excursion to the Lakes: In Westmoreland and Cumberland: August* 1773, London, 1774.

KIELMANSEGG, COUNTESS, *Diary of a Journey to England in the Years* 1761–62: *By Count Frederick Kielmansegge*, London, 1902.

LACKINGTON, JAMES, *Memoirs of the Forty-Five First Years of the Life of James Lackington, the Present Bookseller in Chiswell-Street*, London, 1791, and 1793 and 1795 London edns.

—— *The Confessions of J. Lackington, late Bookseller at the Temple of the Muses: In a Series of Letters to a Friend*, London, 1804.

LANSDOWNE, MARQUIS OF, ed., *The Queeney Papers: Being Letters Addressed to Hester Maria Thrale*, London, 1934.

LEWIS, LADY THERESA, ed., *Extracts from the Journals and Correspondence of Miss Berry from the Year* 1783 to 1852, 3 vols., London, 1865.

LEWIS, W. S., ed., *The Yale Edition of Horace Walpole's Correspondence*, 48 vols., New Haven, Conn., 1937–83.

LOVEDAY, JOHN OF CAVERSHAM, *Diary of a Tour in* 1732 *Through Parts of England, Wales, Ireland and Scotland*, Edinburgh, 1890.

LUCAS, JOSEPH, trans., *Kalm's Account of his Visit to England, On his way to America in* 1748, London, 1892.

LUCE, A. A., and JESSOP, T. E., eds., *The Works of George Berkeley, Bishop of Cloyne*, 9 vols., London, 1948–57.

MACKY, JOHN, *A Journey Through England in Familiar Letters from a Gentleman Here, to his Friend Abroad*, 2nd edn., 2 vols., London, 1772.

MARCHAND, JEAN, ed., *A Frenchman in England, 1784: Being the 'Melanges sur l'Angleterre' of François de la Rochefoucauld*, Cambridge, 1933.

MATCHAM, M. EYRE, ed., *The Nelsons of Burnham Thorpe: A Record of a Norfolk Family Compiled from Unpublished Letters and Notebooks, 1787–1842*, London, 1911.

MELVILLE, LEWIS, ed., *The Berry Papers: Being the Correspondence Hitherto Unpublished of Mary and Agnes Berry (1763–1852)*, Edinburgh, 1913.

MORPURGO, J. E., ed., *The Autobiography of Leigh Hunt*, London, 1949.

MORRIS, CHRISTOPHER, ed., *The Illustrated Journeys of Celia Fiennes*, London and Sydney, 1982.

VAN MUYDEN, MADAME, ed., *A Foreign View of England in the Reigns of George I & George II: The Letters of Monsieur Cesar de Saussure to his Family*, London, 1902.

NETTEL, REGINALD, ed., *Journeys of a German* [Carl Philip Moritz] *in England in 1782*, London, 1965.

NICHOLS, JOHN, *Bibliotheca Topographica Britannica*, 8 vols., London, 1780–90.

OZELL, MR, trans., *M. Misson's Memoirs and Observations in his Travels over England*, London, 1719.

POWELL, G. H., ed., *Reminiscences and Table-Talk of Samuel Rogers*, London, 1903.

REESE, M. M. ed., *Gibbon's Autobiography*, London, 1970.

ROBINSON, ERIC, and McKIE, DOUGLAS, eds., *Partners in Science: Letters of James Watt and Joseph Black*, London, 1970.

SAINT-FOND, B. FAUJAS DE, *Travels in England, Scotland, and the Hebrides; Undertaken for the Purpose of Examining the State of the Arts, the Sciences, Natural History and Manners in Great Britain*, 2 vols., London, 1799.

SPENCER, ALFRED, ed., *Memoirs of William Hickey*, 3 vols., London, 1918.

TOPHAM, EDWARD, *The Life of the Late John Elwes, Esquire: Member in Three Successive Parliaments for Berkshire*, London, 1790.

TRUSLER, JOHN, *Memoirs of the Life of the Rev. Dr. Trusler, with his Opinions on a Variety of Interesting Subjects, and his Remarks, through a Long Life, On Men and Manners, Written by Himself*, Bath, 1806.

WEBB, EDWARD DORAN, *Notes on the Parishes of Fyfield, Kimpton, Penton, Mewsey, Weyhill and Wherwell in the County of Hampshire by the Rev. Robert Hawley Clutterbuck*, Salisbury, 1898.

WENDEBORN, FRED. AUG., *A View of England Towards the Close of the Eighteenth Century*, 2 vols., Dublin, 1791.

WILLIAMS, CLARE, ed., *Sophie in London, 1786: Being the Diary of Sophie von la Roche*, London, 1933.

WILLIAMS, JOHN, ed., *Memoirs of the Late Reverend Thomas Belsham*, London, 1833.

III. MAGAZINES AND NEWSPAPERS

Analytical Review; or, History of Literature, Domestic and Foreign, London, 1 (Jan. 1788)–ns 1 (Dec. 1799).

Annual Register; or, A View of the History, Politics and Literature, London, 1 (1758)–42 (1800).

Aris's Birmingham Gazette, 1740, 1761, 1772, 1785, 1791, 1798.

Attic Miscellany, or, Characteristic Mirror of Men and Things: Including the Correspondent's Museum, London, 1 (Jan. 1789)–3 (Dec. 1791).

Biographical and Imperial Magazine: Containing History, Philosophy, Politics, Arts, Manners, and Amusements, London, 1 (Jan. 1789)–5 (June 1791).

Critical Review; or, Annals of Literature, London, 7 (Jan. 1759)–ns 30 (Dec. 1800).

Diary, or, Woodfall's Register, London, Sept. 1789 and Jan. 1790–Oct. 1791.

Dublin Mercury, Dublin, Dec. 1769–Dec. 1770.

English Review; or, An Abstract of English and Foreign Literature, London, 1 (Jan. 1783)–28 (Dec. 1796).

European Magazine, and London Review: Containing the Literature, History, Politics, Arts, Manners and Amusements of the Age: By the Philological Society of London, London, 1 (Jan. 1782)–38 (Dec. 1800).

General Advertiser, London, Jan.–Dec. 1780.

General Evening Post, London, Dec. 1791.

General Magazine and Impartial Review, Including a History of the Present Times and an Account of New Publications, London, 1 (June 1787)–6 (Dec. 1792).

Gentleman's Magazine, London, 4 (Jan. 1734)–72 (Dec. 1802).

Hive: A Hebdomadel Selection of Literary Tracts; Comprising Every Thing Moral, Literary, or Entertaining that has any claim on the Public Attention, London, 1789.

Lady's Magazine; or, Entertaining Companion for the Fair Sex, Appropriated Solely for their Use and Amusement, London, 1 (Jan. 1769)–31 (Dec. 1800).

Leeds Intelligencer, Leeds, 1780–91, 1802.

Leeds Mercury, Leeds, 1782–91.

London Magazine; or, Gentleman's Monthly Intelligencer, London, 19 (1750), 23 (1754), 25 (1756), 27 (1758).

Lloyds Evening Post, London, 1769–71, 1779–81.

Merchants and Manufacturers Magazine of Trade and Commerce, London, 1785.

Monthly Magazine; or, British Register, London, 51 (1821).

Monthly Review; or, Literary Journal, London, 13 (1755), 14 (1756), 20 (Jan. 1760)–ns 33 (Dec. 1800).

Morning Advertiser, London, Feb. 1794.

Morning Herald; and Daily Advertiser, London, 1784.

New Lady's Magazine; or, Polite, Entertaining, Fashionable and Complete Companion for the Fair Sex: entirely devoted to their use and amusement, London, 1 (Feb. 1786)–6 (June 1791).

New Wonderful Museum and Entertaining Magazine, 6 vols., London, 1802–8.

The Economist, London, 1798.

Oracle: Bell's New World, London, Mar. 1793.

Oxford Magazine, London, 1768–76.

Public Advertiser, London, 1769–76, 1779–81, 1784–91.

Scots Magazine: Containing a General View of the Religion, Politicks, Entertainments, &c, in Great Britain, Edinburgh, 12 (1750)–62 (1800).

Town and Country Magazine; or, Universal Repository of Knowledge, Instruction, and Entertainment, London, 1 (Jan. 1769)–24 (Dec. 1792).

Universal Museum and Complete Magazine of Knowledge and Pleasure Containing the Greatest Variety of Original Pieces on the Most Curious and Useful Subjects in every Branch of Polite Literature Trade and Commerce, and Various Parts of Science and Philosophy, London, 1–2 (1765–6).

York Courant, York, 1788–91.

IV. LIBRARY AND BOOKSELLERS' CATALOGUES AND THE BOOK TRADE

A Catalogue of the Books of the London Library Instituted in 1785, London, 1786.

Further Remarks and Papers on the Booksellers Bill, London, 1774.

The Use of Circulating Libraries Considered, London, 1797.

BELL, JOHN, *New Catalogue of Bell's Circulating Library Consisting of Above 50,000 Volumes (English, French and Italian: In history, antiquities, voyages, travels, lives, memoirs, philosophy, geography, novels, divinity, physic, surgery, anatomy, arts, sciences, plays, poetry, husbandry, trade, commerce, gardening, coins, minerals*, London, 1778.

BINNS, JOHN, *A Catalogue of Books, Containing Several Valuable Libraries, lately purchased, with a large and Good Collection of Modern New Books . . . For Ready Money Only*, Leeds, 1789.

CADELL, THOMAS, *An Account of the Duties Payable on the like Species of Goods, Being the Growth Produce or Manufacture of Great Britain and Ireland*, London, 1785.

HARRISON, JOHN, *A Pleasing Publication* London, 1787 (handbill for the *Novelists Magazine)*.

HOOKHAM, THOMAS, *A New Catalogue of Hookham's Circulating Library; or a New and More Extensive Plan than any yet extant*, London, 1794 (Bodleian annotated copy).

LANE, WILLIAM, *Catalogue of Lane's General and Encreasing Circulating Library*, London, 1791.

RICHARDSON, SAMUEL, *Selected Letters of Samual Richardson*, ed. John Carroll, Oxford, 1964.

TRUSLER, JOHN, *A List of Books, Published by the Rev. Dr. Trusler*, London, 1790 (and similar lists appended to most other Trusler publications).

―――― *An Essay on Literary Property; Containing a Commentary on the Statute of Queen Anne*, London, 1798.

TUPMAN, S., *A Catalogue of a Valuable Collection of Books, Comprehending a Pleasing Variety of Approved Modern Publications*, Nottingham, 1790.

WRIGHT, THOMAS, *A Compleat Catalogue of the Books in the Circulating-Library at Leeds; a Copy of the Laws, As they are now in Force; and a List of the Subscribers*, Leeds, 1785 and 1793 edns.

V. ECONOMIC AND SOCIAL WORKS

An Address to the Landed, Trading and Funded Interests of England on the Present State of Public Affairs, London, 1786.

The Answer of Warren Hastings Esquire, to the Articles exhibited by the Knights, Citizens and Burgesses in Parliament Assembled, London, 1788.

Billy's Nabobs for England, London, *c.*1784.

The British Merchant: A Collection of Papers Relating to the Trade and Commerce of Great Britain and Ireland, 2nd edn., 3 vols., London, 1743.

The Defence of Warren Hastings Esq. (late Gov. General of Bengal) at the Bar of the House of Commons, London, 1786.

Of Gentylnes and Nobylyte: A Dyaloge Betwen the Marchant the Knyght and the Plowman Dysputyng who is a Verey Gentylman, London, *c.*1525.

The Genuine Speech of Mr. Sheridan, Delivered in the House of Commons on a Charge of High Crimes and Misdemeanours against Warren Hastings Esq. late Governor General of Bengal, 2nd edn., London, 1787.

The Historical Mirror, or Biographical Miscellany, London, 1775.

A Letter of Advice Addressed to All Merchants, Manufacturers and Traders, of Every Denomination in Great Britain by Oliver Quid, Tobacconist, London, 1783.

Live and Let Live: A Treatise on the Hostile Rivalships between the Manufacturer and the Land-worker, London, 1787.

Money Answers All Things; or, An Essay to Make Money Sufficiently Plentiful, London, 1734.

Observations on the Importance of National Manufactures; And particularly the Linen Manufacture, Edinburgh, 1780.

Œconomical Principles, London, 1785.

The Pleasant Art of Money Catching, 5th edn., Glasgow, 1750; rev. edn., London, 1782.

Poor Old England: Billy Boy and the East India Nabobs; or Taxation for Ever, London, *c.*1785.

A Review of the Principal Charges Against Warren Hastings Esq, London, 1788.

A Second Letter of Advice, Addressed to all Merchants, Manufacturers, and Traders, of Every Denomination in Great Britain, Concerning the Odious and Alarming Tax on Receipts: By Oliver Quid, Tobacconist, London, 1783.

The Swindler Detected: or Cautions to the Public: Containing a Minute Account of the honest and Industrious Tradesmen of this Metropolis, London, 1781.

Théorie du Luxe—A Treatise upon Luxury, 2 vols., London, 1771.

The Tryal of the Lady Allurea Luxury, London, 1757.

Vox Clamantis: Or an Essay for the Honour, Happiness and Prosperity of the English Society ... By P. A. Gent, London, 1684.

ALISON, REV. ARCHIBALD, *Essays on the Nature and Principles of Taste*, Edinburgh and London, 1790.

ANDERSON, ADAM, *An Historical and Chronological Deduction of the Origin of Commerce, From the Earliest Accounts to the Present Time*, 2 vols., London, 1764.

BAILEY, WILLIAM, *Bailey's Northern Directory*, London, 1781 and 1793.

BARBON, NICHOLAS, *A Discourse of Trade*, London, 1690.

BEAWES, WYNDHAM, *Lex Mercatoria Rediviva; or the Merchant's Directory*, 2nd edn., London, 1752.

BELLEGARDE, JEAN BAPTISTE MORVAN DE, *Reflexions upon Ridicule*, London, 1706.

BENTHAM, JEREMY, *Defence of Usury*, London, 1787.

BENTLEY, T., *Letters on the Utility and Policy of Employing Machines to Shorten Labour*, London and Dublin, 1782.

BLACKWELL, THOMAS, *Memoirs of the Court of Augustus*, 3 vols., Edinburgh, 1753–63.

BLUETT, THOMAS, *An Enquiry whether a General Practice of Virtue tends to the Wealth or Poverty, Benefit or Disadvantage of a People? In which the pleas offered by the Author of the Fable of the Bees for the usefulness of vice and roguery are considered*, London, 1725.

—— *The True Meaning of the Fable of the Bees*, London, 1726.

BOLINGBROKE, HENRY ST. JOHN, VISCOUNT, *Dissertation upon Parties*, 3rd edn., London, 1755.

BROOKE, HUMPHREY, *The Durable Legacy*, London, 1681.

BROWN, JOHN, *Essay upon Shaftesbury's Characteristicks*, London, 1751.

—— *An Estimate of the Manners and the Principles of the Times: By the Author of Characteristics etc*, London, 1757.

—— *An Explanatory Defence of the Estimate of the Manners and Principles of the Times*, London, 1758.

BURKE, EDMUND, *An Appeal from the New to the Old Whigs in Consequence of some late Discussions in Parliament, relative to the Reflections on the French Revolution*, London, 1791.

—— *Articles of Charge of High Crimes and Misdemeanours, Against Warren Hastings, Esquire, late Governor General of Bengal*, London, 1786.

BURTON, ROBERT, *Anatomy of Melancholy*, London, 1621.

C.-J., *The Coin-Act: By Way of Dialogue: Designed for the Use of Everyone that has Any Thing at all to do with Money*, London, 1775.

CAMPBELL, ARCHIBALD, Ἀρετη-λογία, London, 1728.

CHALMERS, GEORGE, *An Estimate of the Comparative Strength of Britain during the Present and Four Preceding Reigns, and of the Losses of her Trade from every War since the Revolution*, London, 1782.

—— *The Life of Daniel De Foe*, London, 1790.

COLE, THOMAS, *Discourses on Luxury, Infidelity, and Enthusiasm*, London, 1761.

COMBE, WILLIAM, *A Word in Season to the Traders and Manufacturers of Great Britain*, 6th edn., London, 1792.

COTSFORD, EDWARD, *Letters to the Honourable the Court of Directors of the East India Company*, London, 1784.

COTTON, CHARLES, *The Compleat Gambler: or, Instructions How to Play at Billiards, Tricks, Bowls and Chess*, London, 1674.

CRAUFORD, GEORGE, *An Essay on the Actual Resources for Reestablishing the Finances of Great Britain*, London, 1785.

CROSSINGE, RICHARD, *A Practical Discourse Concerning the Great Duty of Charity*, London, 1722.

DAVENANT, CHARLES, *The Picture of a Modern Whig*, London, 1702.

DEFOE, DANIEL, *The Compleat English Gentleman*, ed. Karl D. Bülbring, London, 1890.

—— *The Complete English Tradesman: In Familiar Letters*, 2 vols., London, 1726–7.

DENNIS, JOHN, *Vice and Luxury, Publick Mischiefs; or, Remarks on a Book Intituled, the Fable of the Bees*, London, 1724.

DOW, COLONEL ALEXANDER, *History of Hindostan*, 2 vols., London, 1768.

DUNBAR, JAMES, *Essays on the History of Mankind in Rude and Cultivated Ages*, 2nd edn., London, 1781.

EDWARDS, GEORGE, *The Aggrandisement and National Perfection of Great Britain; An Humble Proposal Comprehending ... the Means of Paying Off the Public Debt of Great Britain within the Space of Thirty Years*, 2 vols., London, 1787.

—— *The Great and Important Discovery of the Eighteenth Century, and the Means of Setting Right the National Affairs, by a Great Addition of Numerous and Inestimable Useful Designs and Public Improvements, by which the Nation is still capable of being Infinitely Benefited*, London, 1791.

ELYOT, SIR THOMAS, *The Boke Named the Gouernour*, London, 1534.

FALCONER, WILLIAM, *Remarks on the Influence of Climate, Situation, Nature of Country, Population, Nature of Food and Way of Life on ... Mankind*, London, 1781.

FAWEL, REVD J., *Observations on a Pamphlet entituled 'Luxury No Political Evil'*, Wigan, 1785.

FERGUSON, ADAM, *An Essay on the History of Civil Society*, Edinburgh, 1767.

FIDDES, RICHARD, *General Treatise of Morality*, London, 1724.

FIELDING, HENRY, *Enquiry into the Cause of the late Increase of Robbers*, London, 1751.

[FORSTER, NATHANIEL], *An Enquiry into the Causes of the Present High Price of Provisions*, London, 1767.

FULLER, THOMAS, *The Holy State*, Cambridge, 1642.

GUTHRIE, WILLIAM, *A New Geographical, Historical, and Commercial Grammar*, London, 1770; 14th edn., London, 1794.

HALFPENNY, WILLIAM and JOHN, *The Country Gentleman's Pocket Companion, and Builder's Assistant, For Rural Decorative Architecture, Containing Thirty-two New Designs Plans, and Elevations of Alcoves, Floats, Temples, Summer-Houses, Lodges, Huts, Grottos, &c. In Augustine, Gothic and Chinese Taste*, London, 1753.

—— *Rural Architecture in the Chinese Taste: Being Designs Entirely New for the Decoration of Gardens, Parks, Forests, Insides of Houses, &c*, London, c. 1754; 3rd edn., London, 1755; rev. edns., London, 1768 and 1774.

—— *Rural Architecture in the Gothick Taste: Being Twenty New Designs for Temples, Garden-Seats, Summer-Houses, Lodges, Terminies, Piers, &c ... With Instructions to Workmen, and Hints where with most Advantage to be erected*, London, 1752.

—— *Useful Architecture in Twenty-One New Designs*, London, 1752.

HARPER, WALTER, *The State of the Nation with respect to Religion and Manners*, London, 1789.

HARRISON, WILLIAM, 'An Historicall Description of the Islande of Britayne', *Chronicles of England, Scotlande and Irelande*, 2 vols., London, 1577.

HASTINGS, WARREN, *A Letter from the Honourable Warren Hastings Esq. Governor General of Bengal to the Honourable Court of Directors of the East India Company*, London, 1784.

—— *Memoirs Relative to the State of India*, 2nd edn., London, 1786.

HATTON, EDWARD, *Comes Commercii; or, the Trader's Companion*, 12th edn., London, 1722 (and later edns.).

HEY, RICHARD, *A Dissertation on the Pernicious Effects of Gaming: Published by Appointment as having gained a Prize (June 1783) in the University of Cambridge*, Cambridge, 1783.

HOOPER, S., *A Description of Vauxhall Gardens*, London, 1762.

HUDSON, JOSEPH, *Remarks Upon the History of the Landed and Commercial Policy of England, from the Invasion of the Romans to the Accession of James the First*, 2 vols., London, 1785.

HUME, DAVID, *Political Discourses*, Edinburgh, 1752.

HUTTON, WILLIAM, *An History of Birmingham to the End of the Year 1780*, Birmingham, 1781.

JENYNS, SOAMES, *A Free Inquiry into the Nature and Origin of Evil*, London, 1757.

[JONES, ERASMUS], *Luxury, Pride and Vanity, the Bane of the British Nation*, 3rd edn., London, 1737.

KAYE, F. B., ed., *The Fable of the Bees*, 2 vols., Oxford, 1924.

KNIGGE, BARON, *Practical Philosophy of Social Life*, 2 vols., London, 1799.

KNOX, JOHN, *A View of the British Empire*, London and Edinburgh, 1784.

LAW, WILLIAM, *Remarks upon . . . the Fable of the Bees*, London, 1723.

LOCKE, JOHN, *Some Thoughts Concerning Education*, London, 1693.

LODGE, THOMAS, trans., *The Workes of Lucius Annaeus Seneca, Morrall and Naturall*, London, 1614.

LUCAS, THEOPHILUS, *Memoirs of the Lives, Intrigues, and Comical Adventures of the Most Famous Gamesters and Celebrated Sharpers in the Reign of Charles II, James II, William III, and Queen Anne*, London, 1714.

M'FARLAN, REVD JOHN, *Tracts on Subjects of National Importance*, London and Edinburgh, 1786.

MAC PACKE, JOSÉ [James Peacock], Οἰκίδια, *or Nutshells: Being Ichnographic Distributions for Small Villas; Chiefly Upon Œconomical Principles*, London, 1785.

MACQUER, M. P., *A Chronological Abridgment of the Roman History, From the Foundation of the City to the Extinction of the Republic*, trans. Thomas Nugent, London, 1760.

MAITLAND, WILLIAM, *The History of London from its Foundation by the Romans to the Present Time*, London, 1738.

MANDEVILLE, BERNARD, *The Fable of the Bees, or Private Vices, Public Benefits*, London, 1714; rev. edn., London, 1723.

MILDMAY, W., *The Laws and Policy of England, Relating to Trade, Examined by the Maxims and Principles of Trade in General, and by the Laws and Policy of Other Trading Nations*, London, 1765.

MILLAR, *History of English Government*, 4 vols., London, 1787.

MONTAGU, EDWARD WORTLEY, *Reflections on the Rise and Fall of Antient Republicks*, 2nd edn., London, 1760.

MOORE, FRANCIS, *Considerations on the Exorbitant Price of Provisions*, London, 1773.

MORE, HANNAH, *Thoughts on the Importance of the Manners of the Great to General Society*, London, 1788.

MORTIMER, THOMAS, *The Elements of Commerce, Politics and Finances: In Three Treatises on Three Important Subjects*, London, 1772.

—— *Every Man his Own Broker; Or, A Guide to Exchange Alley*, 10th edn., London, 1785.

—— *A New History of England, From the Earliest Accounts of Britain, to the Ratification of the Peace of Versailles*, London, 1764.

NAISMITH, JOHN, *Thoughts on Various Objects of Industry Pursued in Scotland, with a View to Enquire by what Means the Labour of the People may be Directed to Promote the Public Prosperity*, Edinburgh, 1790.

NOORTHOUCK, JOHN, *A New History of London, Including Westminster and Southwark*, London, 1773.

OVERTON, THOMAS, *The Temple Builder's Most Useful Companion*, London, 1774.

PENNANT, THOMAS, *Of London*, London, 1790.

PORTEUS, BEILBY, and STINTON, GEORGE, eds., *Sermons on Several Subjects by Thomas Secker*, 7 vols. London, 1770–1.

POSTLETHWAYT, MALACHY, *Britain's Commercial Interest Explained and Improved; In a Series of Dissertations on Several Important Branches of her Trade and Police*, 2 vols., London, 1757.

—— *The Merchants' Public Counting House: or, New Mercantile Institutions: Wherein is shewn, the Necessity of young Merchants being bred to Trade with greater Advantages than they usually are*, London, 1750.

—— *The Universal Dictionary of Trade and Commerce*, 4th edn., 2 vols., London, 1774.

PRICE, JOSEPH, *The Saddle Put on the Right Horse; Or, An Enquiry into the Reasons why certain Persons have been denominated Nabobs; with an arrangement of these Gentlemen into their proper classes, of Real, Spurious, Reputed or Mushroom Nabobs*, London, 1783.

PRICE, SIR UVEDALE, *A Letter to H. Repton, Esq ... to which is Prefixed, Mr Repton's Letter to Mr Price*, 2nd edn., Hereford, 1798.

SANFORD, JAMES, trans., *The Manuell of Epictetus: Translated out of Greeke into French, and now into English*, London, 1567.

SCOTT, MAJOR JOHN, *Observations on Mr. Burke's Speech on Mr. Fox's India Bill*, London, 1784.

SINCLAIR, JOHN, *Hints; Addressed to the Public: Calculated to Dispel the Gloomy Ideas which have been lately entertained of the State of Our Finances*, London, 1783.

SMITH, ADAM, *Works and Correspondence*, 5 vols., Glasgow, 1978–84.

SMITH, SIR THOMAS, *The Commonwealth of England*, London, 1612.

SMOLLETT, TOBIAS, *The History of England*, new edn., 4 vols., London, 1830.

SPRAT, THOMAS, *The History of the Royal-Society of London*, London, 1667.

STAIR, JOHN DALRYMPLE, EARL OF, *An Attempt to Ballance the Income and Expenditure of the State*, London, 1783.

STEELE, RICHARD, *The Tradesman's Calling*, London, 1684.

STONE, THOMAS, *An Essay on Agriculture, with a View to Inform Gentlemen of Landed Property, whether their Estates are managed to the Greatest Advantage*, Lynn, 1785.

SULIVAN, RICHARD JOSEPH, *Letter to the Hon. the Court of Directors of the East-India Company*, London, 1784.

[TEMPLE, WILLIAM OF TROWBRIDGE], *An Essay on Trade and Commerce*, London, 1770 (sometimes attributed to J. Cunningham).

TEMPLE, WILLIAM, OF TROWBRIDGE, *A Vindication of Commerce and the Arts*, London, 1758.

THORESBY, RALPH, *Ducatus Leodiensis: or, The Topography of the Town and Parish of Leedes and Parts Adjacent*, London, 1715.

THOROLD, SIR JOHN, *A Short Examination of the Notions advanc'd in a book intituled The Fable of the Bees or Private Vices, Public Benefits*, London, 1726.

TOWNSHEND, CHARLES, 3rd VISCOUNT, *National Thoughts, Recommended to the Serious Attention of the Public*, London, 1751.

TRUSLER, JOHN, *Chronology; or, The Historian's Vade Mecum*, 7th edn., 2 vols., London, 1774.

—— *A Compendium of Sacred History*, 2 vols., London, 1797.

—— *The Country Lawyer: Containing, Not Only Large Abstracts of the Several Acts of Parliament, on the Following Heads But All the Doctrine and Adjudged Cases, and Every Thing relating to each Subject with Authorities*, London, 1786.

—— *The Habitable World Described, or, The Present State of the People in all Parts of the Globe*, 20 vols., London, 1788.

—— *The Historian's Guide*, Dublin, 1773.

—— *The London Adviser and Guide; Containing Every Instruction and Information Useful and Necessary to Persons Living in London, and Coming to Reside There*, London, 1786.

—— *Luxury No Political Evil, But Demonstratively Proved to be Necessary to the Preservation and Prosperity of States*, London, 1780.

—— *Monthly Communications; Being a Collection of Tracts on all Subjects*, London, 1793.

—— *The Progress of Man and Society*, 2nd edn., Bath, 1791.

—— *A Prospectus of a Work, Which the Author Proposes to Publish, under the title of Sententiae Variorum, and the Conditions*, Bath, 1800.

—— *Proverbs Exemplified*, Bath, 1790.

—— *Twelve Sermons by the Rev. John Trusler*, London, 1796.

—— *The Way to be Rich and Respectable, Addressed to Men of Small Fortune*, London, [?1775]; 4th edn., London, 1784.

TUCKER, JOSIAH, *Sermons on Luxury*, London, 1777.

VANDERLINT, JACOB, *Money Answers All Things; or An Essay to Make Money Plentiful Among all Ranks of People*, London, 1734.

WARBURTON, WILLIAM, *Faith working by Charity to Christian Edification: A Sermon*, London, 1738.

—— *A Sermon Preached at the Abbey-Church at Bath, for Promoting the Charity and Subscription Towards the General Hospital or Infirmary in that City*, London, 1742.

—— *The Works of the Rt. Revd. William Warburton*, 7 vols., London, 1788.

WHETSTONE, GEORGE, *A Mirour for Magestrates of Cyties*, London, 1584.

WHITWORTH, SIR CHARLES, ed., *The Political and Commercial Works of that Celebrated Writer Charles D'Avenant*, 5 vols., London, 1771.

WRIGHTE, WILLIAM, *Grotesque Architecture, or Rural Amusement; Consisting of Plans, Elevations, and Sections*, London, 1790.

VI. GRAMMARS, DICTIONARIES, AND ETIQUETTE BOOKS

The Complete Letter-Writer; or, New and Polite English Secretary, London, 1755.

The Gentleman's Companion and Tradesman's Delight, London, 1735.

ALLESTREE, RICHARD, *Gentleman's Calling*, 1717 edn., London.

ASCHAM, ROGER, *The Scholemaster*, London, 1570.

ASH, JOHN, *Grammatical Institutes*, London, 1769.

BAILEY, NATHAN, *An Universal Etymological English Dictionary*, London, 1721, and later edns.

BARCLAY, REVD JAMES, *A Complete and Universal English Dictionary on a New Plan*, London, 1779.

BICKNELL, ALEXANDER, *The Grammatical Wreath; or, A Complete System of English Grammar*, London, 1790.

BOYER, ABEL, *English Theophrastus: or, The Manners of the Age*, 2nd edn., London, 1706.

BRAHAM, H., *The Institucion of a Gentleman*, London, 1555.

BRATHWAIT, RICHARD, *The English Gentleman*, London, 1630.

DARRELL, WILLIAM, *A Gentleman Instructed in the Conduct of a Virtuous and Happy Life*, London, 1704; 9th edn., London, 1727.

DAY, ANGEL, *The English Secretarie*, London, 1586.

DYCHE, THOMAS, *A Guide to the English Tongue*, 2nd edn., London, 1710; 45th edn., London, 1764; 101st edn., Glasgow, 1797.

—— *The Spelling Dictionary; or, A Collection of all the Common Words and Proper Names*, 2nd edn., London, 1725.

—— and PARDON, WILLIAM, *A New General English Dictionary; Peculiarly Calculated for the Use and Improvement of Such as are Unacquainted with the Learned Languages*, London, 1735.

ELYOT, SIR THOMAS, *The Boke Named the Gouernour*, London, 1534.

ENTICK, JOHN, *New Spelling Dictionary, Teaching How to Write and Pronounce the English Tongue*, 2nd edn., London, 1766.

FISHER, GEORGE, *The Instructor, or the Family's Best Companion*, 5th edn., London, 1740.

FULWOOD, WILLIAM, *The Enimie of Idlenese*, London, 1568.

GAILHARD, JEAN, *The Compleat Gentleman; or, Directions for the Education of Youth as to their Breeding at Home and Travelling Abroad*, London, 1678.

Lowth, Robert, *Short Introduction to English Grammar*, London, 1762.

Moore, J. Hamilton, *Young Gentlemen and Ladies Monitor, And English Teacher's Assistant*, London, [178–].

Newbery, Francis, *Newbery's New Spelling Dictionary of the English Language*, London, 1788.

Peacham, Henry, *The Compleat Gentleman*, London, 1622.

Perry, W., *The Only Sure Guide to the English Tongue; or, New Pronouncing Spelling Book*, London, 1776.

Petrie, Adam, *Rules of Good Deportment or of Good Breeding For the Use of Youth*, Edinburgh, 1720.

Ramesey, William, *The Gentlemans Companion; or, A Companion of True Nobility, and Gentility*, London, 1672.

Rothwell, J., *A Comprehensive Grammar of the English Language for the Use of Youth*, London, 1788.

Shaw, Revd John, *A Methodical English Grammar: Containing Rules and Directions for speaking and writing the English Language with Propriety*, London, 1778.

Trusler, John, *The Difference Between Words, Esteemed Synonymous in the English Language*, London, 1766.

—— *The Distinction Between Words esteemed Synonymous in the English Language Pointed Out, and the Proper Choice of them Determined: Useful to all who would either write or speak with Propriety and Elegance*, 2nd edn. of *The Difference Between Words* with change in title, London, 1783.

—— *A System of Etiquette*, London, 1788.

Walker, Obadiah, *Of Education especially of Young Gentlemen*, Oxford, 1673.

Wilson, George, *Youth's Pocket Companion*, 3rd edn., London, 1777.

Woolgar, William, *Youth's Faithful Monitor: or, The Young Man's Companion*, London, 1761.

PRINTED SECONDARY WORKS

I. The book trade and readership

i. Books published before 1900

Ackermann, Rudolph, *Repository of Arts, Literature, Commerce, Manufactures, Fashion and Politics*, 14 vols., London, 1809–15.

Curwen, Henry, *A History of Booksellers, the Old and the New*, London, 1874.

Feltham, John, *A Picture of London*, London, 1804.

Knight, Charles, *The Old Printer and the Modern Press*, London, 1854.

[MARSHALL,——], *Catalogue of Five Hundred Celebrated Authors of Great Britain, Now Living*, London, 1788.

MOXON, JOSEPH, *Mechanick Exercises*, London, 1677–80.

NICHOLS, JOHN BOWYER, *Anecdotes, Biographical and Literary of the late Mr. William Bowyer*, London, 1778.

—— *Illustrations of the Literary History of the Eighteenth-Century Consisting of Authentic Memoirs and Original Letters of Eminent Persons*, 8 vols., London, 1817.

—— *Literary Anecdotes of the Eighteenth Century*, 9 vols., London, 1812–15, repr. edn., New York, 1966.

REES, THOMAS, and BRITTON, JOHN, *Reminiscences of Literary London from 1779 to 1853*, London, 1896.

RIVERS, DAVID, *Literary Memoirs of Living Authors of Great Britain*, 2 vols., London, 1798.

RIVINGTON, SEPTIMUS, ed., *The Publishing House of Rivington*, London, 1894.

ROBERTS, WILLIAM, *The Earlier History of English Bookselling*, London, 1889.

SMILES, SAMUEL, *A Publisher and his Friends: Memoir and Correspondence of the Late John Murray with an Account of the Origin and Progress of the House, 1768–1843*, 2 vols., London, 1891.

TIMPERLEY, C. H., *Encyclopaedia of Literary and Typographical Anecdote*, 2nd edn., London, 1842.

WELSH, CHARLES, *A Bookseller of the Last Century, Being some account of the Life of John Newbery and of the Books he Published, and a Notice of the Later Newberys*, London and New York, 1885.

WEST, WILLIAM, *Fifty Years Recollections of an Old Bookseller*, London, 1837.

WHEATLEY, HENRY B., *Prices of Books: An Inquiry into the Changes in the Price of Books which have occurred in England at different periods*, London, 1898.

ii. Books published after 1900

The English Provincial Printer, 1700–1800, London, 1983 BL exhibition notes.

ALSTON, R. C., ROBINSON, F. J. G., and WADHAM, C., *A Check-List of Eighteenth-Century Books Containing Lists of Subscribers*, Newcastle upon Tyne, 1983.

ALTICK, RICHARD D., *The English Common Reader: A Social History of the Mass Reading Public, 1800–1900*, Cambridge, 1957.

BALL, JOHNSON, *William Caslon, 1693–1766: The Ancestry, Life and Connections of England's Foremost Letter-Engraver and Type-Founder*, Kineton, 1973.

BARBER, GILES, and FABIAN, BERNHARD, eds., *Buch und Buchhandel in Europa im achtzehnten Jahrhundert*, Proceedings of the Fifth Wolfenbüttel Symposium, Nov. 1977, Hamburg, 1981.

BECKWITH, FRANK, *The Leeds Library, 1768–1968*, Dewsbury, 1968.

BENNETT, H. S., *English Books and Readers, 1603–1640*, Cambridge, 1970.

BERRY, W. T., and JOHNSON, A. F., *Catalogue of Specimens of Printing Types by English and Scottish Printers and Founders, 1665–1830*, London, 1935.

BESTERMAN, THEODORE, ed., *The Publishing Firm of Cadell and Davies: Select Correspondence and Accounts, 1793–1836*, London, 1938.

BIGSBY, C. W. E., ed., *Approaches to Popular Culture*, London, 1976.

BLAKEY, DOROTHY, *The Minerva Press, 1790–1810*, London, 1939.

BRENNI, VITO J., *Book Illustration and Decoration: A Guide to Research*, Westport, Conn., 1980.

BRISSENDEN, R. F., ed., *Studies in the Eighteenth Century*, Canberra, 1968.

CAPP, BERNARD, *Astrology and the Popular Press: English Almanacks, 1500–1800*, London, 1977.

CARLSON, C. LENNART, *The First Magazine: A History of the Gentleman's Magazine*, Providence, RI, 1938.

CARTER, JOHN, ed., *New Paths in Book Collecting: Essays by Various Hands*, London, 1934.

CHARTIER, ROGER, *The Cultural Uses of Print in Early Modern France*, trans. Lydia G. Cochrane, Princeton, NJ, 1987.

COCHRANE, J. A., *Dr. Johnson's Printer: The Life of William Strahan*, London, 1964.

COLE, RICHARD CARGILL, *Irish Booksellers and English Writers, 1740–1800*, Atlantic Highlands, NJ, 1986.

COLEMAN, D. C., *The British Paper Industry, 1495–1860*, Oxford, 1958.

CORBETT, MARGERY, and LIGHTBOWN, RONALD, *The Comely Frontispiece: The Emblematic Title-Page in England, 1550–1660*, London, 1979.

COUPER, W. J., *The Millers of Haddington, Dunbar and Dunfermline: A Record of Scottish Bookselling*, London and Leipzig, 1914.

CRANE, R. S., and KAYE, F. B., *A Census of British Newspapers and Periodicals, 1660–1800*, Chapel Hill, NC, 1927.

CRANFIELD, G. A., *The Development of the Provincial Newspaper, 1700–1760*, Oxford, 1962.

CRESSY, DAVID, *Literacy and the Social Order: Reading and Writing in Tudor and Stuart England*, Cambridge, 1980.

CRUMP, M., and HARRIS, M., eds., *Searching the Eighteenth Century*, London, 1984.

DARNTON, ROBERT, *The Business of Enlightenment*, Cambridge, Mass., 1979.
—— *The Literary Underground of the Old Regime*, Cambridge, Mass., 1982.

EISENSTEIN, ELIZABETH, *The Printing Press as an Agent of Change*, Cambridge, 1979.

ESCARPIT, ROBERT, *Sociologie de la Littérature*, Paris, 1958.

FEATHER, JOHN, *The Provincial Book Trade in Eighteenth-Century England*, Cambridge, 1985.

FRITZ, PAUL, and WILLIAMS, DAVID, eds., *The Triumph of Culture: Eighteenth-Century Perspectives*, Toronto, 1972.

GANS, HERBERT J., *Popular Culture and High Culture: An Analysis and Evaluation of Taste*, New York, 1974.

GASKELL, PHILIP, *A New Introduction to Bibliography*, 2nd edn., Oxford, 1974.

GEDIN, PER, *Literature in the Market Place*, trans. George Bisset, London, 1977.

GOODY, JACK, ed., *Literacy in Traditional Societies*, Cambridge, 1968.

GRIEDER, JOSEPHINE, *Translations of French Sentimental Prose Fiction in late Eighteenth-Century England: A History of a Literary Vogue*, Durham, NC, 1975.

HAIG, ROBERT L., *The Gazetteer, 1735-1797: A Study in the Eighteenth-century English Newspaper*, Carbondale, Ill., 1960.

HALL, JOHN, *The Sociology of Literature*, London and New York, 1979.

HAMMELMANN, HANNS, and BOASE, T. S. R., *Book Illustrators in Eighteenth-Century England*, New Haven, Conn., 1975.

HARDY, BARBARA, *Tellers and Listeners: The Narrative Imagination*, London, 1975.

HARRIS, MICHAEL, *London Newspapers in the Age of Walpole: A Study of the Origins of the Modern English Press*, London, 1987.

HAUSER, ARNOLD, *The Social History of Art*, 2nd edn., 4 vols., London, 1962.

HEAL, AMBROSE, *London Tradesman's Cards of the Eighteenth Century: An Account of their Origin and Use*, London, 1925.

HINDLE, WILFRED, *The Morning Post, 1772–1937: Portrait of a Newspaper*, London, 1937.

HODNETT, EDWARD, *Francis Barlow, First Master of English Book Illustration*, London, 1978.

HOWE, ELLIC, *A List of Bookbinders, 1648–1815*, London, 1950.

JEFFREYS, A., ed., *The Art of the Librarian*, Newcastle upon Tyne, 1973.

JUDGE, CYRIL BATHURST, *Elizabethan Book Pirates*, Cambridge 1934.

KAUFMAN, PAUL, *Borrowings from the Bristol Library, 1773–1784: A Unique Record of Reading Vogues*, Charlottesville, Va., 1960.

—— *Libraries and their Users*, London, 1969.

KELLY, THOMAS, *Early Public Libraries: A History of Public Libraries in Great Britain before 1850*, London, 1966.

KERNAN, ALVIN, *Printing Technology, Letters and Samuel Johnson*, Princeton, 1987.

KILGOUR, RAYMOND L., *Lee and Shepherd: Publishers for the People*, Boston, 1965.

KLANCHER, JON P., *The Making of English Reading Audiences*, 1790–1832, Madison, Wis., 1987.

KORSHIN, PAUL J., ed., *The Widening Circle: Essays on the Circulation of Literature in Eighteenth-Century Europe*, Philadelphia, 1976.

KUIST, JAMES M., *The Nichols' File of the* Gentleman's Magazine, Madison, Wis. 1982.

LANDON, RICHARD G., ed., *Book Selling and Book Buying: Aspects of the Nineteenth-Century British and North American Book Trade*, Chicago, 1978.

LAURENSON, DIANA, and SWINGEWOOD, ALAN, *The Sociology of Literature.*, London, 1972.

LEAVIS, Q. D., *Fiction and the Reading Public*, London, 1932.

LOWENTHAL, LEO, *Literature, Popular Culture and Society*, Palo Alto, Calif., 1968.

McKENZIE, D. F., *Stationers' Company Apprentices*, 1701–1800, Oxford Bibliographical Society Publications, 1978.

MANDROU, ROBERT, *De la culture populaire aux XVIIe et XVIIIe siècles: La Bibliothèque bleue de Troyes*, Paris, 1964.

MARSTON, E., *Sketches of Booksellers of Other Days*, London, 1901.

—— *Sketches of Some Booksellers of the Time of Dr. Samuel Johnson*, London, 1902.

MAXTED, IAN, *The London Book Trades*, 1775-1800, London, 1977.

MENHENNET, L., *Book Subscription Lists: Second Supplement*, Newcastle upon Tyne, 1977.

—— *Book Subscription Lists: Third Supplement*, Newcastle upon Tyne, 1980.

MINTO, JOHN, *A History of the Public Library Movement in Great Britain and Ireland*, London, 1932.

MORISON, STANLEY, *A Memoir of John Bell*, 1745–1831, Cambridge, privately printed, 1930.

MUMBY, FRANK ARTHUR, and NORRIE, IAN, *Publishing and Bookselling*, London, 1930.

MUNTER, ROBERT, *The History of the Irish Newspaper*, 1685–1760, Cambridge, 1967.

MYERS, ROBIN, and HARRIS, MICHAEL, eds., *Author/Publisher Relations During the Eighteenth and Nineteenth Centuries*, Oxford, 1983.

—— *The Development of the English Book Trade*, 1700–1899, Oxford, 1981.

—— *Economics of the British Booktrade*, 1605–1939, Cambridge, 1985.

—— *Maps and Prints: Aspects of the English Booktrade*, Oxford, 1984.

—— *Sale and Distribution of Books from 1700*, Oxford, 1982.

NEUBURG, VICTOR E., *Chapbooks: A Guide to Reference Material*, 2nd edn., London, 1972.

—— *Popular Literature: A History and Guide*, London, 1977.

PAILLER, ALBERT, *Edward Cave et le* Gentleman's Magazine, *1731–1754*, 2 vols., Lille and Paris, 1975.

PARDOE, F. E., *John Baskerville of Birmingham: Letter-Founder & Printer*, London, 1975.

PLANT, MARJORIE, *The English Book Trade*, London, 1939.

PLOMER, H. R., BUSHNELL, G. H., and McC. DIX, E. R., eds., *A Dictionary of the Printers and Booksellers who were at work in England, Scotland, and Ireland from 1726 to 1775*, Oxford, 1932.

POTTINGER, DAVID, *The French Book Trade in the Ancien Régime, 1500–1791*, Cambridge, Mass., 1958.

RAMSDEN, CHARLES, *Bookbinders of the United Kingdom (Outside London), 1780–1840*, London, 1954.

—— *London Bookbinders, 1780–1840*, London 1956.

RAVEN, JAMES, *The Commercialization of the Book, 1745–1814*, Cambridge, forthcoming.

RIVERS, ISABEL, ed., *Books and their Readers in Eighteenth-Century England*, Leicester, 1982.

ROBINSON, F. J. G., and WALLIS, P. J., *Book Subscription Lists: A Revised Guide*, Newcastle upon Tyne, 1975.

ROGERS, PAT, *Grub Street: Studies in a Subculture*, London, 1972.

ROPER, DEREK, *Reviewing Before the 'Edinburgh', 1788–1802*, London, 1978.

ROSCOE, SIDNEY, *John Newbery and his Successors, 1740–1814: A Bibliography*, Wormley, Hertfordshire, 1973.

ROUTH, JANE, and WOLFF, JANET, eds., *The Sociology of Literature: Theoretical Approaches*, Sociological Revue Monograph, 25–6. New York, 1977–8.

SADLEIR, MICHAEL, *The Evolution of Publishers' Binding-Styles, 1770–1900*, London and New York, 1930.

SCHÜCKING, LEVIN L., *The Sociology of Literary Taste*, trans. Brian Battershaw 2nd edn., London, 1966.

SHEPARD, LESLIE, *The History of Street Literature*, London, 1973.

SKINNER, ROBERT T., *A Notable Family of Scots Printers*, Edinburgh, 1928.

SPUFFORD, MARGARET, *The Great Reclothing of Rural England: Petty Chapmen and their Wares in Seventeenth-Century England*, London, 1984.

—— *Small Books and Pleasant Histories: Popular Fiction and its Readership in Seventeenth-Century England*, London, 1981.

STEPHENS, FREDERIC GEORGE, GEORGE, M. DOROTHY, *et al.*, eds., *Catalogue of Prints and Drawings in the British Museum*, 11 vols., London, 1870–1954.

SULLIVAN, ALVIN, ed., *British Literary Magazines: The Augustan Age and the Age of Johnson, 1698–1788*, Westport, Conn., and London, 1983.

—— *British Literary Magazines: The Romantic Age, 1789–1836*, Westport, Conn., 1983.

TAYLOR, JOHN TINNON, *Early Opposition to the English Novel: The Popular Reaction from 1780 to 1830*, New York, 1943.

VARMA, DEVENDRA P., *The Evergreen Tree of Diabolical Knowledge*, Washington, 1972.

WADHAM, C., *Book Subscription Lists: First Supplement*, Newcastle upon Tyne, 1976.

WALLIS, PHILIP, *At the Sign of the Ship: Notes on the House of Longman, 1724–1974*, London, 1974.

WERKMEISTER, LUCYLE, *The London Daily Press, 1772–1792*, Lincoln, Neb., 1963.

WILES, ROY McKEEN, *Freshest Advices: Early Provincial Newspapers in England*, Columbus, Ohio, 1965.

—— *Serial Publication in England before 1750*, Cambridge, 1957.

Williams, Raymond, *Culture*, London, 1981.

—— *Culture and Society, 1780–1950*, London, 1958.

—— *Key Words: A Vocabulary of Culture and Society*, London, 1976.

—— *The Long Revolution*, London, 1961.

WILSON, ROBERT N., ed., *The Arts in Society*, Englewood Cliffs, NJ, 1964.

WRIGHT, LOUIS B., *Middle-Class Culture in Elizabethan England*, Chapel Hill, NC, 1935.

iii. Articles

ALBRECHT, MILTON C., 'Does Literature Reflect Common Values?' *American Sociological Review*, 21/4 (Aug. 1956), 722–9.

ALDEN, JOHN, 'Pills and Publishing: Some Notes on the English Book Trade, 1660–1715', *Library*, 5th ser. 7/1 (Mar. 1952), 21–37.

BECKWITH, FRANK, 'The Beginnings of the Leeds Library', *Thoresby Miscellany*, 11 (1936–42), 145–65.

—— 'The Eighteenth-Century Proprietary Library in England', *Journal of Documentation*, 3 (1947–8), 81–98.

BELANGER, TERRY, 'Booksellers' Trade Sales, 1718–1768', *Library*, 5th ser. 30/4 (Dec. 1975), 281–302.

—— 'A Directory of the London Book Trade, 1766', *Publishing History*, 1 (1977), 7–48.

—— '100 Books on the 18th Century English Book Trade', *AB Bookman's Weekly*, 23 June 1975, 3020–50.

BERCH, VICTOR A., 'Notes on Some Unrecorded Circulating Libraries of Eighteenth-Century London', *Factotum*, 6 (Oct. 1979), 15–18.

BLAGDEN, CYPRIAN, 'Booksellers' Trade Sales, 1718–1768', *Library*, 5th ser. 5/4 (Mar. 1951), 243–57.

BUTTERFIELD, L. H., 'The American Interests of the Firm of E. and C. Dilly, with their Letters to Benjamin Rush, 1770–1795', *Papers of the Bibliographical Society of America*, 45 (1951), 283–332.

CAMERON, WILLIAM J., 'John Bell (1745–1831): A Case Study of the Use of Advertisement Lists as Evidence in Publishing History', *The Humanities Association Review*, 26/3 (Summer 1975), 196–216.

CLAPP, SARAH L. C., 'The Beginnings of Subscription Publication in the Seventeenth Century', *Modern Philology*, 19 (1931–2), 199–224.

CLARKE, ARCHIBALD, 'The Reputed First Circulating Subscription Library in London', *Library*, 2nd ser. 1 (1900), 274–88.

COLE, RICHARD C., 'Smollett and the Eighteenth-Century Irish Book Trade', *Papers of the Bibliographical Society of America*, 69 (1975), 345–63.

CRUMP, M. J., and GOULDEN, R. J., 'Four Library Catalogues of Note', *Factotum*, 3 (Oct. 1978), 9–13.

DARNTON, ROBERT, 'Reading, Writing, and Publishing in Eighteenth-Century France: A Case Study in the Sociology of Literature', *Daedalus*, 100/1 (Winter 1971), 214–56.

DURBRIDGE, L. G., 'Samuel Brown and George Miller: A Mystery', *Library Review*, 23/4 (Winter 1971), 131–4.

FEATHER, JOHN, 'British Publishing in the Eighteenth Century', *Library*, 6th ser. 8/1 (Mar. 1986), 32–46.

—— 'John Walter and the Logographic Press', *Publishing History*, 1 (1977), 92–134.

GALLAWAY, F. W., 'The Conservative Attitude Towards Fiction, 1770–1830', *PMLA* 55 (1940), 1041–59.

GARSIDE, PETER, 'Thomas Lockett's Catalogue of Novels', *Factotum*, Occasional Paper 3 (Oct. 1983), 8–13.

GOVE, PHILIP BABCOCK, 'Notes on Serialisations and Competitive Publishing: Johnson's and Bailey's Dictionaries, 1755', *Oxford Bibliographical Society: Proceedings and Papers*, 5 (1936–9), [305]–322.

HAMLYN, HILDA, 'Eighteenth-Century Circulating Libraries in England', *Library*, 5th ser. 1/3–4 (Dec. 1946, Mar. 1947), 197–218.

HARRIS, MICHAEL, 'Astrology, Almanacks and Booksellers', *Publishing History*, 8 (1980), 87–104.

—— 'The Management of the London Newspaper Press During the Eighteenth Century', *Publishing History*, 4 (1978), 95–112.

HARRISON, G. B., 'Books and their Readers, 1591–4', *Library*, 4th ser. 8/3 (Dec. 1927), 273–302.

HERNLUND, PATRICIA, 'Strahan's Ledgers: Standard Charges for Printing, 1738–1785', *Studies in Bibliography*, 20 (1967), 89–111.

—— 'William Strahan's Ledgers II: Charges for Paper, 1738–1785', *Studies in Bibliography*, 22 (1969), 179–95.

HOWE, E., 'London Booksellers—Masters and Men, 1780–1840', *Library*, 5th ser. 1/1 (June 1946), 28–38.

HUGHES, HELEN SARD, 'The Middle-Class Reader and the English Novel', *Journal of English and Germanic Philology*, 25 (1926), 362–78.

INGLIS, RUTH A., 'An Objective Approach to the Relationship between Fiction and Society', *American Sociological Review*, 3/3 (1938), 526–33.

JANNETTA, M. J., 'Footnotes on Circulating Libraries', *Factotum*, 5 (Apr. 1979), 15–16.

JOHNSON, FRANCIS R., 'Notes on English Retail Book-Prices, 1550–1640', *Library*, 5th ser. 5/2 (Sept. 1950), 83–112.

KAUFMAN, PAUL, 'The Community Library: A Chapter in English Social History', *Transactions of the American Philosophical Society*, NS 57/7 (1967), 1–65.

—— 'The Eighteenth-Century Forerunner of the London Library', *Papers of the Bibliographical Society of America*, 54 (1960), 89–100.

—— 'English Book Clubs and their Role in Social History', *Libri*, 14 (1964), 1–31.

KORSHIN, PAUL J., 'Book Subscription Lists', *TLS* 23 June 1972, 719.

LANDON, RICHARD G., 'Small Profits Do Great Things: James Lackington and Eighteenth-Century Bookselling', *Studies in Eighteenth-Century Culture*, 5 (1976), 387–99.

MASLAN, K. I. D., 'Book Subscription Lists' *TLS* 29 Sept. 1972, 1157.

MITCHELL, C. J., 'Provincial Printing in Eighteenth-Century Britain', *Publishing History*, 21 (1987), 5–24.

—— 'The Spread and Fluctuation of Eighteenth-Century Printing', *Studies on Voltaire and the Eighteenth Century*, 230 (1985), 305–21.

NOBLETT, WILLIAM, 'John Newbery, Publisher Extraordinary', *History Today*, 22 (Apr. 1972), 265–71.

PLAYFAIR, E. W., 'Book Subscription Lists', *TLS* 22 Dec. 1972, 1558.

POLLARD, GRAHAM, 'The English Market for Printed Books', *Publishing History*, 4 (1978), 8–48.

RAVEN, JAMES, 'The Noble Brothers and Popular Publishing, 1745–89', *Library*, 6th ser. 12/4 (Dec. 1990), 293–345.

ROGERS, PAT, 'Book Subscriptions Among the Augustans', *TLS* 15 Dec. 1972, 1539–40.

—— 'Pope and his Subscribers', *Publishing History*, 3 (1978), 7–36.

SHERBO, ARTHUR, 'Isaac Read and the European Magazine', *Studies in Bibliography*, 37 (1984), 210–27.

STUART, DANIEL, 'The Late Mr. Coleridge, Poet', *Gentlemen's Magazine*, NS 10/2 (1838), 25–6.

SWAIM, ELIZABETH A., 'The Auction as a Means of Book Distribution in Eighteenth-Century Yorkshire', *Publishing History*, 1 (1977), 49–91.

TREADWELL, J. M., 'Book Subscription Lists', *TLS* 7 July 1972.

WALLIS, P. J., 'Book Subscription Lists', *Library*, 5th ser., 29/3 (Sept. 1974), 255–86.

WARD, CATHERINE COGGAN AND ROBERT E., 'Literary Piracy in the

Eighteenth Century Book Trade: The Cases of George Faulkner and Alexander Donaldson', *Factotum*, 17 (Nov. 1983), 25–35.

WARNER, MICHAEL, 'Literary Studies and the History of the Book', *Book*, 12 (July 1987), 3–9.

WOOD, FREDERICK T., 'Pirate Printing in the XVIII Century', *N&Q* 159 (1930), 381–4, 400–4.

iv. Unpublished dissertations

BELANGER, TERRY, 'Booksellers' Sales of Copyright: Aspects of the London Book Trade, 1718–1768', Ph.D. thesis, Columbia University, 1970.

HAMLYN, HILDA M., 'The Circulating Libraries of the Eighteenth Century', MA thesis, London University, 1948.

HARLAN, ROBERT D., 'William Strahan: Eighteenth-Century Printer and Publisher', Ph.D. thesis, University of Michigan, 1960.

HUSBANDS, H. WINIFRED, 'The Lesser Novel, 1770–1800', MA thesis, London University, 1922.

THOMSON, ROBERT STARK, 'The Development of the Broadside Ballad Trade and its Influence upon the Transmission of English Folksongs', Ph.D. thesis, Cambridge University, 1974.

VARMA, DEVENDRA P., 'The Circulating Libraries of the Eighteenth Century', MA thesis, London University, 1948.

II. AUTHORSHIP, LITERATURE, AND DRAMA

i. Books

ADAMS, PERCY G., *Travellers and Travel-liars*, Los Angeles, 1962.

ALSTON, R. C., *A Bibliography of the English Language from the Invention of Printing to the Year 1800*, Ilkley, 1974.

BARRELL, JOHN, *English Literature in History, 1730–80; An Equal, Wide Survey*, London, 1983.

BEASLEY, JERRY C., *A Check List of Prose Fiction Published in England, 1740–1749*, Charlottesville, Va., 1972.

——— *Novels of the 1740s*, Athens, Ga., 1982.

BELJAME, ALEXANDER, *Men of Letters and the English Public in the Eighteenth Century, 1660–1774; Dryden, Addison, Pope*, trans. E. O. Lorimer, London, 1948.

BLACK, FRANK GEES, *The Epistolary Novel in the Late Eighteenth Century: A Descriptive and Bibliographical Study*, Eugene, Oreg., 1940.

BOEGE, FREDERICK W., *Smollett's Reputation as a Novelist*, Princeton, 1947.

BROOKS, DOUGLAS, *Number and Pattern in the Eighteenth-Century Novel: Defoe, Smollett and Sterne*, London, 1973.

BUTLER, MARILYN, *Jane Austen and the War of Ideas*, Oxford, 1975.

CHARTIER, ROGER, *Cultural History: Between Practices and Representations*, trans. Lydia G. Cochrane, Cambridge, 1988.

COLBY, ROBERT A., *Fiction with a Purpose*, Bloomington, Ind., 1967.

COLLINS, A. S., *Authorship in the Days of Johnson: Being a Study of the Relation Between Author, Patron, Publisher and Public, 1726–1780*, London, 1927.

—— *Profession of Letters: A Study of the Relation of Author to Patron, Publisher and Public, 1780–1832*, London, 1928.

CROSS, WILBUR L., *The History of Henry Fielding*, 3 vols., New Haven, Conn., 1918.

DAY, ROBERT A., *Told in Letters: Epistolary Fiction before Richardson*, Ann Arbor, Mich., 1966.

ESDAILE, A., *A List of English Tales and Prose Romances Printed Before 1740*, New York, 1912.

ERSKINE-HILL, HOWARD, *The Social Milieu of Alexander Pope: Lives, Example and the Poetic Response*, New Haven, Conn., and London, 1975.

ESHLEMANN, DOROTHY, *Elizabeth Griffith: A Biographical and Critical Study*, Philadelphia, 1949.

FORSYTH, WILLIAM, *The Novels and Novelists of the Eighteenth Century: In Illustration of the Manners and Morals of the Age*, London, 1871.

FOSTER, JAMES R., *History of the Pre-Romantic Novel in England*, New York and London, 1949.

FOXON, D. F., *English Verse, 1701–1750: A Catalogue of Separately Printed Poems with Notes on Contemporary Collected Editions*, 2 vols., Cambridge, 1975.

GALBRAITH, LOIS HALL, *The Established Clergy as Depicted in English Prose Fiction from 1740 to 1800*, Philadelphia, 1950.

GIGNILLIAT, GEORGE WARREN Jr., *The Author of 'Sandford and Merton': A Life of Thomas Day Esq*, New York, 1932.

GOVE, PHILIP B., *The Imaginary Voyage in Prose Fiction*, New York, 1941.

HELTZEL, VIRGIL B., *A Check List of Courtesy Books in the Newberry Library*, Chicago, 1942.

HEPBURN, JAMES, *The Author's Empty Purse and the Rise of the Literary Agent*, London, 1968.

HIGHET, GILBERT, *The Anatomy of Satire*, Princeton, NJ, 1962.

HILBISH, FLORENCE MAY ANNA, *Charlotte Smith, Poet and Novelist (1749–1806)*, Philadelphia, 1941.

HOGAN, C. B., ed., *The London Stage, 1660–1800: Part V, 1776–1800*, Carbondale, Ill., 1968.

HORNBEAK, KATHERINE GEE, *The Complete Letter Writer in English, 1568–1800*, Smith Studies in Modern Languages, 15/3–4; Northampton, Mass., 1934.

HUMM, PETER, STIGANT, PAUL, and WIDDOWSEN, PETER, eds., *Popular Fictions: Essays in Literature and History*, London and New York, 1986.

JAMES, LOUIS, *Fiction for the Working Man, 1830–50*, Oxford, 1963.

JOHNSON, JAMES WILLIAM, *The Formation of English Neo-Classical Thought*, Princeton, NJ, 1967.

KEATING, PETER, *The Victorian Prophets: A Reader from Carlyle to Wells*, London, 1981.

KELLY, GARY, *The English Jacobin Novel, 1780–1805*, Oxford, 1976.

KNAPP, LEWIS MANSFIELD, *Tobias Smollett, Doctor of Men and Manners*, Princeton, NJ, 1949.

KNIGHTS, L. C., *Drama and Society in the Age of Jonson*, London, 1937.

KOVAČEVIĆ, IVANKA, *Fact into Fiction: English Literature and the Industrial Scene, 1750–1850*, Leicester, 1975.

LEWIS, PETER, and WOOD, NIGEL, eds., *John Gay and the Scriblerians*, London and New York, 1988–9.

LOFTIS, JOHN, *Comedy and Society from Congreve to Fielding*, Stanford, Calif., 1959.

McBURNEY, W. H., *A Check List of English Prose Fiction, 1700–1739*, Cambridge, Mass., 1960.

MacCARTHY, B. G., *The Later Women Novelists, 1744–1818*, Oxford, 1947.

McKILLOP, A. D., *The Early Masters of English Fiction*, London, 1962.

MARGOLIOUTH, H. M., ed., *The Poems and Letters of Andrew Marvell*, Oxford, 1927.

MASON, JOHN EDWARD, *Gentlefolk in the Making: Studies in the History of English Courtesy Literature, 1531–1774*, Philadelphia, 1935.

MAYO, ROBERT D., *The English Novel in the Magazines, 1740–1815*, Evanston, Ill., 1962.

MILLER, EDWIN HAVILAND, *The Professional Writer in Elizabethan England: A Study of Nondramatic Literature*, Cambridge, Mass., 1959.

MISH, CHARLES C. *English Prose Fiction, 1600–1700: A Chronological Checklist*, Charlottesville, Va., 1967.

NORTHCOTE-PARKINSON, C., *Portsmouth Point: The Navy in Fiction, 1793–1815*, Liverpool and London, 1940.

O'DELL, STERG, *A Chronological List of Prose Fiction in English, 1475–1640*, Cambridge, Mass., 1954.

OLDFATHER, W. A., *Contributions Towards a Bibliography of Epictetus*, Urbana, 1927.

ONG, WALTER J., *Interfaces of the Word: Studies in the Evolution of Consciousness and Culture*, Ithaca, NY, and London, 1977.

—— *The Presence of the Word*, New Haven, Conn., 1967.

ORR, LEONARD, *A Catalogue Checklist of English Prose Fiction, 1750–1800*, Troy, NY, 1979.

PAULSON, RONALD, *Satire and the Novel in Eighteenth-Century England*, New Haven, Conn., 1967.

PITTOCK, JOAN, *The Ascendancy of Taste: The Achievement of Joseph and Thomas Warton*, London, 1973.

PRICE, MARTIN, *To the Palace of Wisdom: Studies in Order and Energy from Dryden to Blake*, Carbondale, Ill., 1970

PROPER, COENRAAD BART ANNE, *Social Elements in English Prose Fiction between 1700 and 1832*, 2nd edn., New York, 1965.

RADWAY, JANICE A., *Reading the Romance: Women, Patriarchy and Popular Literature*, Chapel Hill, NC, 1984.

RAVEN, JAMES, *British Fiction, 1750–1770: A Chronological Check-List of Prose Fiction Printed in Britain and Ireland*, London and Newark, NJ, 1987.

RAWSON, C. J., *Henry Fielding and the Augustan Ideal under Stress: 'Nature's Dance of Death' and Other Studies*, London, 1972.

ROGERS, PAT, *The Augustan Vision*, London, 1974.

SAMBROOK, JAMES, *The Eighteenth Century: The Intellectual and Cultural Context of English Literature, 1700–1789*, London, 1986.

SAUNDERS, J. W., *The Profession of English Letters*, London, 1904.

SCHNEIDER, BEN ROSS (comp.), *Index to the London Stage, 1660–1800*, Carbondale and Edwardsville, Ill., 1979.

SHEAVYN, PHOEBE, and SAUNDERS, J. W., *The Literary Profession in the Elizabethan Age*, Manchester, 1967.

SINGER, GODFREY F., *The Epistolary Novel: Its Origin, Development, Decline and Residuary Influence*, Philadelphia, 1933.

SLAGLE, KENNETH CHESTER, *The English Country Squire as Depicted in English Prose Fiction from 1740 to 1800*, Philadelphia, 1938.

SMITH, OLIVIA, *The Politics of Language*, Oxford, 1984.

SMYTHE-PALMER, A., *The Ideal of a Gentleman*, London, 1908.

SPEARMAN, DIANA, *The Novel and Society*, London, 1966.

STAUFFER, DONALD A., *The Art of Biography in Eighteenth-Century England*, New York, 1941.

STONE, G. W., ed., *The London Stage, 1660–1800: Part IV, 1747–76*, 3 vols., Carbondale, Ill., 1962.

TARR, MARY MURIEL, *Catholicism in Gothic Fiction: A Study of the Nature and Function of Catholic Materials in Gothic Fiction in England, 1762–1820*, Washington, DC, 1946.

TIEJE, ARTHUR JERROLD, *The Theory of Characterisation in Prose Fiction Prior to 1740*, Minneapolis, 1916.

TODD, JANET, ed., *A Dictionary of British and American Women Writers, 1660–1800*, London 1984.

TOMPKINS, JOYCE MARJORIE SANXTER, *Polite Marriage ... Eighteenth-Century Essays*, Cambridge, 1938.

—— *The Popular Novel in England*, 1770–1800, London, 1932.

TREFMAN, SIMON, *Sam. Foote, Comedian*, 1720–1777, New York, 1971.

UTTER, ROBERT PALFREY, and NEEDHAM, GWENDOLYN BRIDGES, *Pamela's Daughters*, London, 1937.

VICINUS, MARTHA, *The Industrial Muse—A Study of Nineteenth-Century Working Class Literature*, London, 1974.

WATSON, HAROLD FRANCIS, *The Sailor in English Fiction and Drama*, 1550–1800, New York, 1931.

WATSON, MELVIN R., *Magazine Serials and the Essay Tradition*, 1746–1820, Baton Rouge, La., 1956.

WATT, IAN, *The Rise of the Novel: Studies in Defoe, Richardson and Fielding*, London, 1957.

WHICHER, GEORGE F., *The Life and Romances of Mrs Eliza Haywood*, Columbia University Studies in English and Comparative Literature; New York, 1915.

WHITNEY, LOIS, *Primitivism and the Idea of Progress in English Popular Literature of the Eighteenth Century*, Baltimore, 1934.

WILLIAMS, RAYMOND, *The Country and the City*, London, 1975.

YUNCK, JOHN A., *The Lineage of Lady Meed*, Notre Dame, Ind., 1963.

ii. Articles

BEASLEY, J. C., 'Leonard Orr, *A Catalogue-checklist*', *Literary Research Newsletter*, 5/3 (Summer 1980), 140–7.

BLACK, F. G., 'A Lady Novelist of Colchester', *Essex Review*, 64 (1935), 180–5.

BROWN, WALLACE CABLE, 'The Near East in English Drama, 1775–1825', *Journal of English and Germanic Philology*, 46 (1947), 63–70.

CRANE, RONALD S., 'The Vogue of Guy of Warwick from the Close of the Middle Ages to the Romantic Revival', *PMLA*, 30/2 (1915), 125–94.

HIBBARD, G. R., 'The Country House Poem of the Seventeenth Century', *Journal of the Warburg and Courtauld Institutes*, 19/1–2 (1956), 156–74.

KNIGHT, CHARLES A., 'Bibliography and the Shape of the Literary Periodical in the Early Eighteenth Century', *Library*, 6th ser. 8/3 (Sept. 1986), 232–48.

MONKMAN, KENNETH, 'Bibliography of the Early Editions of Tristram Shandy' *Library*, 5th ser., 25/1 (Mar. 1970), 11–39.

PITCHER, EDWARD W., 'More Emendations and Facts', *Library*, 6th ser. 2/3 (Sept. 1980), 326–32.

—— 'A Reconsideration of Magazine Serials in the Town and Country Magazine', *Library*, 6th ser. 5/1 (Mar. 1983), 44–52.

—— 'Robert Mayo's "The English Novel in the Magazines, 1740–1815": New Facts', *Library*, 5th ser. 31/1 (Mar. 1976), 20–30.

PUNTER, DAVID, 'Smollett and the Realist Novel', *Literature and History*, 1/2 (Oct. 1975), 60–83.

RAVEN, JAMES, 'The Publication of Fiction in Britain and Ireland, 1750–1770', *Publishing History*, 24 (1988), 31–47.

SCANLON, PAUL A., 'A Checklist of Prose Romances in English, 1474–1603', *Library*, 5th ser. 23/2 (June 1978), 143–52.

iii. Unpublished dissertations

DALES, JOANNA CLARE, 'The Novel as Domestic Conduct-Book—Richardson to Jane Austen', Ph.D. thesis, Cambridge University, 1970.

DUTHIE, ELIZABETH J., 'Benevolence in English Poetry from the Seasons to the 1790s', Ph.D. thesis, Cambridge University, 1976.

McCLELLAND, E. M., 'The Novel, in Relation to the Dissemination of Liberal Ideas, 1790–1820', Ph.D. thesis, London University, 1952.

MEWS, H., 'Middle-Class Conduct Books of the Seventeenth Century', Ph.D. thesis, London University, 1934.

VAREY, SIMON ROBERTSON, 'The Craftsman, 1726–1752: An Historical and Critical Account', Ph.D. thesis, Cambridge University, 1976.

WOMERSLEY, DAVID JOHN, 'The Evolution of the Decline and Fall: A Study of Gibbon in his Historiographical Context', Ph.D. thesis, Cambridge University, 1983.

III. TRADE, SOCIETY, AND THE IMAGE OF BUSINESS

i. Books

The Long Debate on Poverty: Eight Essays on Industrialization and 'the condition of England', Institute of Economic Affairs, London, 1974.

The Topographer, 4 vols., London, 1789–91.

The United Kingdom in 1980, the Hudson Report, Associated Business Programmes, London, 1980.

ALLEN, ROBERT J., *The Clubs of Augustan London*, Hamden, Conn., 1967.

APPLEBY, JOYCE OLDHAM, *Economic Thought and Ideology in Seventeenth-Century England*, Princeton, NJ, 1979.

ASHTON, JOHN, *A History of English Lotteries: Now for the First Time Written*, London, 1893.

—— *The History of Gambling in England*, London, 1898.

ASHTON, T. S., *Economic Fluctuations in England, 1700–1800*, Oxford, 1959.

—— *An Economic History of England: The Eighteenth Century*, London, 1955.

AUSTIN, M. M., and VIDAL-NAQUET, P., *Economic and Social History of Ancient Greece: An Introduction*, London, 1977.

BECKERMANN, WILFRED, ed., *Slow Growth in Britain: Causes and Consequences*, Oxford, 1979.

BENNETT, G. V., and WALSH, J. D., eds., *Essays in Modern English Church History*, London, 1966.

BESTUL, THOMAS H., *Satire and Allegory in Wynnere and Westoure*, Lincoln, Nebr., 1974

BOND, E. A., ed., *Speeches of the Managers and Counsel in the Trial of Warren Hastings*, 4 vols., London, 1859–61.

BONFIELD, LLOYD, *Marriage Settlements, 1601–1710: The Adoption of the Strict Settlement*, Cambridge, 1983.

BOURKE, ALGERNON, ed., *The History of White's with the Betting Book from 1743 to 1878*, 2 vols., London, 1892.

BOWDEN, WITT, *Industrial Society in England Towards the End of the Eighteenth Century*, 2nd edn., London, 1965.

BRAUDEL, FERNAND, *Capitalism and Material Life, 1400–1800*, trans. M. Kochan, London, 1973.

BRIGHTFIELD, MYRON F., *Victorian England in its Novels*, 4 vols., Los Angeles, 1968.

BROMLEY, J. S., and KOSSMAN, E. H., eds., *Britain and the Netherlands*, London, 1960.

BRUNT, P. A., *Social Conflicts in the Roman Republic*, London, 1986.

BURTON, ANTHONY and PIP, *The Green Bag Travellers: Britain's First Tourists*, London, 1978.

CAIN, LOUIS P., and USELDING, PAUL J., eds., *Business Enterprise and Economic Change*, Kent, Ohio, 1973.

CHAUDHURI, NIRAD C., *Clive of India: A Political and Psychological Essay*, London, 1975.

CHURCH, ROY, *Herbert Austin: The British Motor Car Industry to 1941*, London, 1979.

CLARK, J. C. D., *English Society, 1688–1832: Ideology, Social Structure and Political Practice during the Ancien Regime*, Cambridge, 1985.

——— *Revolution and Rebellion: State and Society in England in the Seventeenth and Eighteenth Centuries*, Cambridge, 1986.

CLARK, PETER, ed., *The Transformation of English Provincial Towns,* . *1600–1800*, London, 1984.

——— and SLACK, PAUL, *English Towns in Transition, 1500–1700*, Oxford, 1976.

CLARK, WALTER ERNEST, *Josiah Tucker, Economist: A Study in the History of Economics*, Studies in History, Economics and Public Law, 19/1; New York, 1903.

CLAYRE, ALASDAIR, ed., *Nature and Industrialization: An Anthology*, Oxford, 1977.

COATES, DAVID, and HILLARD, JOHN, eds., *The Economic Decline of Modern Britain: The Debate between Left and Right*, Brighton, 1986.

COGGIN, PHILIP, *Education for the Future: The Case for Radical Change*, London, 1979.

COLEMAN, D. C., *What Has Happened to Economic History? An Inaugural Lecture*, Cambridge, 1973.

CORFIELD, P. J., *The Impact of English Towns, 1700–1800*, Oxford, 1982.

COSGROVE, DENIS, and DANIELS, STEPHEN, eds., *The Iconography of Landscape: Essays on the Symbolic Representation, Design and Use of Past Environments*, Cambridge, 1988.

CROUZET, FRANÇOIS, *The First Industrialists: The Problem of Origins*, Cambridge, 1985.

CRUMP, THOMAS, *The Phenomenon of Money*, London and Boston, 1981.

DAVIDOFF, LEONORE, and HALL, CATHERINE, *Family Fortunes: Men and Women of the English Middle-Class, 1780-1850*, London, 1987.

DAVIES, C. COLLIN, *Warren Hastings and Oudh*, Oxford, 1939.

DAVIES, P. N., *Sir Alfred Jones: Shipping Entrepreneur Par Excellence*, London, 1978.

DEANE, P. and COLE, W. A., *British Economic Growth, 1688–1959*, Cambridge, 1962.

DODWELL, HENRY, ed., *Warren Hastings' Letters to Sir John Macpherson*, London, 1927.

DORE, RONALD, *British Factory Japanese Factory: The Origins of National Diversity in Industrial Relations*, Berkeley, Calif., and London, 1972.

DOUGHTY, W. L., *John Wesley, Preacher*, London, 1955.

DOUGLAS, MARY, and BARON, ISHERWOOD, *The World of Goods: Towards an Anthropology of Consumption*, London, 1979.

DOWNEY, JAMES, *The Eighteenth Century Pulpit*, Oxford, 1969.

EDWARDES, MICHAEL, *Warren Hastings: King of the Nabobs*, London, 1976.

ELIAS, NORBERT, *The Court Society*, trans. Edmund Jephcott, London, 1983.

ELLIS, AYTOUN, *The Penny Universities: A History of the Coffee-Houses*, London, 1956.

L'ESTRANGE EWEN, C., *Lotteries and Sweepstakes*, London, 1932.

FAWCETT, C. B. ed., *General Handbook of the British Association: Leeds Meeting 1927*, Leeds 1927.

FEILING, KEITH, *Warren Hastings*, 2nd edn., London, 1966.

FLOUD, RODERICK, and McCLOSKEY, DONALD, eds., *The Economic History of Britain since 1700*, 2 vols., Cambridge, 1981.

FORREST, G. W., ed., *Selections from the State Papers of the Governors-General of India*, 2 vols., London, 1910.

FOSTER, WILLIAM, *East India House: Its History and Associations*, London, 1924.

FRASER, DEREK, ed., *A History of Modern Leeds*, Manchester, 1980.

FURNISS, E. S., *The Position of the Labourer in a System of Nationalism*, New York, 1920.

GALAMBOS, LOUIS, *The Public Image of Big Business in America, 1880–1940*, Baltimore and London, 1975.

GEORGE, M. DOROTHY, *English Political Caricature to 1792: A Study of Opinion and Propaganda*, Oxford, 1959.

—— *London Life in the Eighteenth Century*, 2nd edn., London, 1979.

GILMOUR, ROBIN, *The Idea of the Gentleman in the Victorian Novel*, London, 1981.

GOODWIN, A., ed., *The European Nobility in the Eighteenth Century: Studies of the Nobilities of the Major European States in the Pre-Reform Era*, London, 1953.

GOUGH, W., *The Rise of the Entrepreneur*, London, 1969.

GRAND, G. F., *Narrative of the Life of a Gentleman Long Resident in India*, Cape of Good Hope, 1814.

GRANNICK, DAVID, *Managerial Comparisons of Four Developed Countries: France, Britain, United States and Russia*, Cambridge, Mass., 1972.

GRIER, SYDNEY C., ed., *The Letters of Warren Hastings to his Wife*, London and Edinburgh, 1905.

GWYN, WILLIAM B., and ROSE, RICHARD, eds., *Britain: Progress and Decline*, London, 1980.

HAMPSON, R. T., *Origines Patriciae*, London, 1846.

HANSON, L. W., *Contemporary Printed Sources for British and Irish Economic History, 1701–1750*, Cambridge, 1963.

HARLOW, VINCENT T., *The Founding of the Second British Empire, 1763–1793*, 2 vols., London, 1952.

HARTE, N. B., and PONTING, K. G., eds., *Textile History and Economic History*, Manchester, 1973.

HEATH, ANTHONY, *Social Mobility*, London, 1981.

HIGGS, HENRY, *Bibliography of Economics, 1751–1775*, Cambridge, 1935.

HIRSCHMAN, ALBERT O., *The Passions and the Interests: Political Argument for Capitalism before its Triumph*, Princeton, NJ, 1977.

HOFFMANN, WALTHER G., *British Industry, 1700–1950*, trans. W. O. Henderson and W. H. Chaloner, Oxford, 1955.

HOLZMAN, JAMES M., *The Nabobs in England: A Study of the Returned Anglo-Indian, 1760–1785*, New York, 1926.

HONEYMAN, KATRINA, *The origins of Enterprise: Business Leadership in the Industrial Revolution*, Manchester, 1982.

HONT, ISTVAN, and IGNATIEFF, MICHAEL, eds., *Wealth and Virtue: The Shaping of Political Economy in the Scottish Enlightenment*, Cambridge, 1983.

HOPPIT, JULIAN, *Risk and Failure in English Business*, 1700–1800, Cambridge, 1987.

HUDSON, PAT, *The Genesis of Industrial Capitalism: A Study of the West Riding Wool Textile Industry*, c.1750–1800, Cambridge, 1986.

HUGHES, PETER, and WILLIAMS, DAVID, eds., *The Varied Pattern: Studies in the Eighteenth Century*, Toronto, 1971.

HUTBER, PATRICK, ed., *What's Wrong with Britain?*, London, 1978.

IMPEY, ELIJAH BARWELL, *Memoirs of Sir Elijah Impey, Knt*, London, 1846.

JACKSON, G., *Hull in the Eighteenth Century*, Oxford, 1972.

JONES, BARBARA, *Follies and Grottoes*, 2nd edn., London, 1974.

JONES, E. L., and MINGAY, G. E., eds., *Land, Labour and Population in the Industrial Revolution*, London, 1967.

KAELBLE, HARTMUT, *Historical Research on Social Mobility: Western Europe and the United States of America in the Nineteenth and Twentieth Centuries*, trans. Ingrid Nokes, London, 1981.

KLINGENDER, FRANCIS D., *Art and the Industrial Revolution*, rev. and extended edn., London, 1968.

KRAMNICK, ISAAC, ed., *Is Britain Dying?*, Ithaca, NY, 1979.

LANDES, DAVID S., *The Unbound Prometheus*, Cambridge, 1969.

LARKIN, PASCHAL, *Property in the Eighteenth Century with Special Reference to England and Locke*, London, 1930.

LAWFORD, JAMES PHILIP, *Clive: Preconsul of India: A Biography*, London, 1976.

LECKY, EDWARD HARTPOLE, *A History of England in the Eighteenth Century*, 8 vols., London, 1887.

LETWIN, SHIRLEY ROBIN, *The Gentleman in Trollope: Individuality and Moral Conduct*, London, 1982.

LETWIN, WILLIAM, *The Origins of Scientific Economics: English Economic Thought*, 1660–1776. London, 1963.

LIPPINCOTT, LOUISE, *Selling Art in Georgian London: The Rise of Arthur Pond*, New Haven, Conn., 1983.

McALMON, ROBERT, *Being Geniuses Together*, London, 1933.

MACAULAY, THOMAS BABINGTON, *Critical and Historical Essays, Contributed to the Edinburgh Review*, 3 vols., London, 1843.

McCLOSKEY, DONALD N., *Enterprise and Trade in Victorian Britain: Essays in Historical Economics*, London, 1981.

McGEE, J. SEARS, *The Godly Man in Stuart England: Anglicans, Puritans and the Two Tables*, 1620–1670, New Haven, Conn., 1976.

McKENDRICK, N., ed., *Historical Perspectives: Studies in English Thought and Society*, London, 1975.

—— and OUTHWAITE, R. B., eds., *Business Life and Public Policy*, Cambridge, 1986.

—— Brewer, John, and Plumb, H. H., *The Birth of a Consumer Society: The Commercialization of Eighteenth-Century England*, London, 1982.

McVeagh, John, *Tradefull Merchants: The Portrayal of the Capitalist in Literature*, London, 1981.

Mangan, J. A., *Athleticism in the Victorian and Edwardian Public School*, Cambridge, 1981.

Marshall, P. J., *East India Fortunes: The British in Bengal in the Eighteenth Century*, Oxford, 1976.

—— *The Impeachment of Warren Hastings*, Oxford, 1965.

Mathias, Peter, *The First Industrial Nation: An Economic History of Britain, 1700–1914*, London, 1969.

—— *The Transformation of England*, London, 1979.

Mayhall, John, *The Annals of York, Leeds, Sheffield*, Leeds, 1861.

Meek, Ronald L., *Social Science and the Ignoble Savage*, Cambridge, 1976.

Melada, Ivan, *The Captain of Industry in English Fiction, 1821–1871*, Albuquerque, N. Mex., 1970.

Meteyard, Eliza, *The Life of J. Wedgwood*, London, 1865.

Miller, Henry Knight, Rothstein, Eric, and Rousseau, G. S., eds., *The Augustan Milieu: Essays Presented to Louis A. Landa*, Oxford, 1971.

Minchinton, W. E., ed., *Essays in Agrarian History*, 2 vols., Newton Abbot, 1968.

Mingay, G. E., *English Landed Society in the Eighteenth Century*, London, 1963.

Minney, R. J., *Clive of India*, 2nd edn., London, 1757.

Mitchell, B. R. *British Historical Statistics*, Cambridge, 1988.

—— and Deane, P., *An Abstract of British Historical Statistics*, Cambridge, 1962.

Money, John, *Experience and Identity: Birmingham and the West Midlands, 1760–1800*, Manchester, 1977.

Monro, Hector, *The Ambivalence of Bernard Mandeville*, Oxford, 1975.

Moore, John Scott, ed., *The Goods and Chattels of our Forefathers: Frampton Cottrell and District Probate Inventories, 1539–1804*, London, 1976.

Morize, André, *L'Apologie du luxe au XVIIIe siècle et 'Le Mondain' de Voltaire*, [1909]; 2nd edn., Geneva, 1970.

Morris, William, *News from Nowhere*, London, 1890.

Mossner, Ernest, *Bishop Butler and the Age of Reason: A Study in the History of Thought*, New York, 1936.

Mui, Hoh-Cheung and Lorna H., *Shops and Shopkeeping in Eighteenth-Century England*, London, 1989.

Musson, A. E., and Robinson, E., *Science and Technology in the Industrial Revolution*, Manchester, 1969.

Namier, Lewis, *England in the Age of the American Revolution*, 2nd edn., London and New York, 1961.

—— *The Structure of Politics at the Accession of George III*, 2nd edn., London, 1957

OUTHWAITE, R. B., ed., *Marriage in Society*, London, 1981.

OVERY, R. J., *William Morris, Viscount Nuffield*, London, 1976.

PAGNAMENTA, PETER, and OVERY, R. J., *All Our Working Lives*, London, 1984.

PARES, RICHARD, *A West-India Fortune*, London, 1950.

PARSONS, E., *The Civil, Ecclesiastical, Literary, Commercial and Mercantile History of Leeds ... and the Manufacturing Districts of Yorkshire*, 2 vols., Leeds, 1834.

PAYNE, P. L., *British Entrepreneurship in the Nineteenth Century*, London, 1974.

PEMBERTON, J. and J., *The University College at Buckingham: A First Account of its Conception, Foundation and Early Years*, Buckingham, 1979.

PERKIN, HAROLD, *The Origins of Modern English Society, 1780–1880*, London, 1969.

PHILIPS, C. H., *The East India Company, 1784–1834*, 2nd edn., Manchester, 1961.

PLUMB, J. H., *In the Light of History*, London, 1972.

POCOCK, J. G. A., *The Machiavellian Moment: Florentine Political Thought and the Atlantic Republican Tradition*, Princeton, NJ, 1975.

—— *Virtue, Commerce and History: Essays on Political Thought and History, Chiefly in the Eighteenth Century*, Cambridge, 1985.

PORTER, ROY, *English Society in the Eighteenth Century*, London, 1982.

PRESSNELL, L. S., *Country Banking in the Industrial Revolution*, Oxford 1956.

PRICE, JACOB M., ed., *Joshua Johnson's Letterbook, 1771–1774: Letters from a Merchant in London to his Partners in Maryland*, London, 1979.

RAGATZ, J., *Absentee Land Lordism in the British Caribbean*, London, 1929.

READ, DONALD, *The English Provinces, c.1760–1960: A Study in Influence*, London, 1964.

REID, JOHN, *Illustration of Social Depravity*, 2 vols., London, 1834.

RIMMER, W. G., *Marshalls of Leeds: Flax-Spinners, 1788–1886.*, Cambridge, 1960.

ROBBINS, CAROLINE, *The Eighteenth-Century Commonwealthman: Studies in the Transmission, Development and Circumstance of English Liberal Thought from the Restoration of Charles II until the War with the Thirteen Colonies*, Cambridge, Mass., 1959.

RODERICK, G. W., and STEPHENS, M. D., *Education and Industry in the Nineteenth Century: The English Disease?*, London, 1978.

ROLL, ERICH, *An Early Experiment in Industrial Organisation*, London, 1930.

RUBINSTEIN, W. D., *Men of Property: The Very Wealthy in Britain since the Industrial Revolution*, London, 1981.

—— ed., *Wealth and the Wealthy in the Modern World*, London, 1980.

RUDÉ, GEORGE, *Hanoverian London, 1714–1808*, London 1971.

RUSSELL, NORMAN, *The Novelist and Mammon: Literary Responses to the World of Commerce in the Nineteenth Century*, Oxford, 1986.

SCATTERGOOD, V. J., *Politics and Poetry in the Fifteenth Century*, London, 1971.

SCHLATTER, RICHARD B., *The Social Ideas of Religious Leaders, 1660–1688*, London, 1940.

SCHOFIELD, R. S., and WRIGLEY, E. A., *The Population History of England, 1541–1871: A Reconstruction*, London, 1981.

SCHOFIELD, ROBERT E., *The Lunar Society of Birmingham: A Social History of Provincial Science and Industry in Eighteenth-Century England*, Oxford, 1963.

SCHUMACHER, ERNEST FRIEDRICH, *Small is Beautiful: A Study of Economics as if the People Mattered*, London, 1973.

SCHUMPETER, E. B., *English Overseas Trade Statistics, 1697–1808*, Oxford, 1960.

SEKORA, JOHN, *Luxury: The Concept in Western Thought, Eden to Smollett*, Baltimore and London, 1977.

SEMMEL, BERNARD, *The Rise of Free Trade Imperialism: Classical Economy and the Empire of Free Trade and Imperialism, 1750–1850*, Cambridge, 1970.

SHINAGEL, MICHAEL, *Daniel Defoe and Middle-Class Gentility*, Cambridge, Mass., 1968.

SIMON, BRIAN, and BRADLEY, IAN, eds., *The Victorian Public School: Studies in the Development of an Educational Institution*, Dublin, 1975.

SKINNER, ANDREW S., and WILSON, THOMAS, eds., *Essays on Adam Smith*, Oxford, 1975.

SMILES, SAMUEL, *The Life of George Stephenson*, London, 1857.

—— *Lives of the Engineers*, 3 vols., London, 1861.

SMITH, R. ANGUS, *A Centenary of Science in Manchester*, London, 1883.

SPEAR, PERCIVAL, *Master of Bengal: Clive and his India*, London, 1975.

—— *The Nabobs: A Study of the Social Life of the English in Eighteenth-Century India*, London, 1963.

STANWORTH, PHILIP, and GIDDENS, ANTHONY, eds., *Elites and Power in British Society*, Cambridge, 1974.

STEPHEN, SIR JAMES FITZJAMES, *The Story of Nuncomar and the Impeachment of Sir Elijah Impey*, 2 vols., London, 1885.

STEVENSON, LAURA CAROLINE, *Praise and Paradox: Merchants and Craftsmen in Elizabethan Popular Literature*, Cambridge, 1984.

STONE, LAWRENCE and JEANNE C. FAWTIER, *An Open Elite? England, 1540–1880*, Oxford, 1984.

STREATFIELD, DAVID C., and DUCKWORTH, ALISTAIR M., eds., *Landscape in the Gardens and the Literature of Eighteenth-Century England*, Los Angeles, 1981.

STRICKLAND, MARY, ed., *A Memoir of the Life, Writings and Mechanical Inventions of Edmund Cartwright*, London, 1843.

STURT, GEORGE, *The Wheelwright's Shop*, London, 1928.

SUMMERSON, SIR JOHN, *Georgian London*, rev. edn., London, 1970.

SUTHERLAND, LUCY S., *The East India Company in Eighteenth-Century Politics*, Oxford, 1952.

TANN, JENNIFER, ed., *The Selected Papers of Boulton and Watt: The Engine Partnership, 1775–1825*, 2 vols., London and Cambridge, Mass., 1981.

TAWNEY, R. H., *The Acquisitive Society*, London, 1920.

TAYLOR, R. V., *Biographia Leodiensis*, London, 1865.

TEGG, THOMAS, *A Present for an Apprentice*, 2nd edn., London, 1848.

THATCHER, MARGARET, *Let our Children Grow Tall: Selected Speeches, 1975–1977*, London, 1977.

THIRSK, JOAN, *Economic Policy and Projects: The Development of a Consumer Society in Early Modern England*, Oxford, 1978.

THOMAS, KEITH, *Man and the Natural World: Changing Attitudes in England, 1500–1800*, London, 1983.

THOMIS, MALCOLM I., *Responses to Industrialism: The British Experience, 1780–1850*, Newton Abbot and Vancouver, 1965.

TREBILCOCK, CLIVE, *The Vickers Brothers: Armaments and Enterprise, 1854–1914*, London, 1977.

TURBERVILLE, A. S., *English Men and Manners in the Eighteenth Century: An Illustrated Narrative*, 2nd edn., New York, 1957.

TURNBULL, PATRICK, *Warren Hastings*, London, 1975.

VEBLEN, THORSTEIN, *The Theory of the Leisure Classes*, ed. J. K. Galbraith, Boston, 1973.

VEEN, HARM REIJNDERD SIENTJO VAN DER, *Jewish Characters in Eighteenth-Century English Fiction and Drama*, Groningen, 1935.

VINER, JACOB, *Studies in the Theory of International Trade*, New York and London, 1937.

WARD, J. T., and WILSON, R. G., eds., *Land and Industry: The Landed Estate and the Industrial Revolution*, Newton Abbot, 1971.

WEATHERILL, LORNA, *Consumer Behaviour and Material Culture in Britain, 1660–1760*, London, 1988.

WEBB, IGOR, *From Custom to Capital: The English Novel and the Industrial Revolution*, Ithaca, NY, 1981.

WESTERFIELD, RAY BERT, *Middlemen in English Business Particularly between 1660 and 1760*, New Haven, Conn., 1915.

WHITEMAN, ANNE, BROMLEY, J. S., and Dickson, P. G. M., eds., *Statesmen, Scholars and Merchants*, Oxford, 1973.

WIENER, MARTIN J., *English Culture and the Decline of the Industrial Spirit, 1850–1980*, Cambridge, 1981.

WILLAN, T. S., *An Eighteenth-Century Shopkeeper: Abraham Dent of Kirkby Stephen*, Manchester, 1970.

WILLIAMS, JUDITH BLOW, *British Commercial Policy and Trade Expansion,* 1750–1850, London, 1972.

WILSON, R. G., *Gentleman Merchants: The Merchant Community in Leeds,* 1700–1830, Manchester 1971.

WOODHOUSELEE, A. FRASER TYTLER of, *Memoirs of the Life and Writings of Hon. Henry Homes of Kames,* 2nd edn., 3 vols., Edinburgh, 1814.

WRIGHT, PHILIP, *Monumental Inscriptions of Jamaica,* London, 1956.

WRIGLEY, E. A., *People, Cities and Wealth: The Transformation of Traditional Society,* Oxford, 1987.

WROTH, WARWICK, *The London Pleasure Gardens of the Eighteenth Century,* London, 1896.

ii. Articles

ALLISON, LINCOLN, 'The English Cultural Movement', *New Society,* 43 (Jan.–Mar. 1978), 358–60.

ANDERSON, B. L., 'Provincial Aspects of the Financial Revolution of the Eighteenth Century', *Business History,* 11/1 (Jan. 1969), 11–22.

ANDERSON, PERRY, 'Origins of the Present Crisis', *New Left Review,* 23 (Jan.–Feb. 1964), 26–53.

APPLEBY, JOYCE, 'Ideology and Theory: The Tension Between Political and Economic Liberalism in Seventeenth-Century England', *The American Historical Review,* 81/3 (June 1976), 499–515.

BARNETT, CORRELLI, 'Obsolescence and Dr. Arnold', *Sunday Telegraph,* 26 Jan. 1975, 23.

BECKETT, J. V., 'English Landownership in the Later Seventeenth and Eighteenth Centuries: The Debate and the Problems', *Ec.HR* 2nd ser. 30/4 (1977), 567–81.

BENSON, LEE, 'An Approach to the Scientific Study of Past Public Opinion', *Public Opinion Quarterly,* 31/4 (Winter 1967), 522–67.

BERRILL, K., 'International Trade and the Rate of Economic Growth', *Ec.HR* 2nd ser. 12/3 (1960), 351–9.

BONFIELD, LLOYD, 'Marriage Settlements and the "Rise of Great Estates": The Demographic Aspect', *Ec.HR* 2nd ser. 32/4 (1979), 483–93.

BORSAY, PETER, 'The English Urban Renaissance: The Development of Provincial Urban Culture, *c.*1680–*c.*1760', *Social History,* 2/5 (May 1977), 581–603.

BRITTAN, SAMUEL, 'A Very English Status System', *Financial Times,* 7 Mar. 1983, 15.

CLAY, CHRISTOPHER, 'Marriage, Inheritance, and the Rise of Large Estates in England, 1660–1815', *Ec.HR* 2nd ser. 21/3 (1968), 503–18.

COATS, A. W., 'Changing Attitudes to Labour in the Mid-Eighteenth Century', *Ec.HR* 2nd ser. 11/1 (1958), 35–51.

—— 'Economic Thought and Poor Law Policy in the Eighteenth Century', *Ec.HR* 2nd ser. 13/1 (1960), 39–51.

—— 'The Relief of Poverty: Attitudes to Labour and Economic Change in England, 1660–1782', *International Review of Social History*, 21/1 (1976), 98–115.

COHEN, JACOB, 'The Element of Lottery in British Government Bonds, 1694–1919', *Economica*, NS 20 (1953), 237–46.

COLEMAN, D. C., 'Adam Smith, Businessmen, and the Mercantile System in England', *History of European Ideas*, 9/2 (1988), 161–70.

—— 'Gentlemen and Players', *Ec.HR* 2nd ser. 26/1 (1973), 92–116.

—— and MACLEOD, CHRISTINE, 'Attitudes to New Techniques: British Businessmen, 1800–1950', *Ec.HR* 2nd ser. 39/4 (1986), 588–611.

COLLEY, LINDA, 'The Apotheosis of George III: Loyalty, Royalty and the British Nation, 1760–1820', *Past and Present*, 102 (Feb. 1984), 94–129.

CRAFTS, N. F. R., 'English Economic Growth in the Eighteenth Century: A Re-Examination of Deane and Cole's Estimates', *Ec.HR* 2nd ser. 29/2 (1976), 226–35.

CULE, J. E., 'Finance and Industry in the Eighteenth Century: The Firm of Boulton and Watt', *Economic History*, 4 (1940), 319–25.

DAVIES, K. S., 'Joint Stock Investment in the Later Seventeenth Century', *Ec.HR* 2nd ser. 4/3 (1952), 283–301.

FARRANT, SUE, 'The Development of Landscape Parks and Gardens in Eastern Sussex, *c.*1700 to 1820–a Guide and Gazetteer', *Garden History*, 17 (1989), 166–80.

FREUDENBERGER, HERMAN, 'Fashion, Sumptuary Laws, and Business', *Business History Review*, 37/1–2 (1963), 37–48.

GOLDSMITH, M. M., 'Mandeville and the Spirit of Capitalism', *Journal of British Studies*, 17/1 (Fall 1977), 63–81.

HABAKKUK, H. J., 'English Landownership, 1680–1740', *Ec.HR* 1st ser. 9/1 (1940), 2–17.

—— 'The Long-Term Rate of Interest and the Price of Land in the Seventeenth Century', *Ec.HR* 2nd ser. 5/1 (1952), 26–45.

—— 'The Rise and Fall of English Landed Families, 1600–1800', Part I, *TRHS* 5th ser. 29 (1979), 187–207, Part II, 30 (1980), 199–221, Part III, 31 (1981), 195–217.

HEAL, FELICITY, 'The Idea of Hospitality in Early Modern England', *Past and Present*, 102 (Feb. 1984), 66–93.

HOLDERNESS, B. A., 'Credit in a Rural Community, 1660–1800: Some Neglected Aspects of Probate Inventories', *Midland History*, 3/2 (Autumn 1975), 94–115.

—— 'The English Land Market in the Eighteenth Century: The Case of Lincolnshire', *Ec.HR* 2nd ser. 27/4 (1974), 557–76.

Horwitz, Henry, ' "The Mess of the Middle Class" Revisited: The Case of the "Big Bourgeoisie" of Augustan London', *Continuity and Change*, 2/2 (Aug. 1987), 263–96.

INNES, JOANNA, 'Jonathan Clark, Social History and England's "Ancien Regime"', *Past and Present*, 115 (May 1987), 165–200.

JOHN, A. H., 'Agricultural Productivity and Economic Growth in England, 1700–1760', *Journal of Economic History*, 25/1 (Mar. 1965), 19–34.

KAIN, RICHARD M., 'The Problem of Civilization in English Abolition Literature, 1772–1808', *Philological Quarterly*, 15/2 (Apr. 1936), 103–29.

KELSO, RUTH, 'The Doctrine of the English Gentleman in the Sixteenth Century', *University of Illinois Studies in Language and Literature*, 14/1–2 (Feb.–May 1929), 1–288.

—— 'Sixteenth-Century Definitions of the Gentleman in England', *Journal of English and Germanic Philology*, 24 (1935), 370–82.

KITCHIN, LAURENCE, 'North is North and South is South ... and Ne'er the Twain shall Meet', *THES* 21 Aug. 1981, 10–11.

KLEIN, ADOLPH I., 'Fashion: Its Sense of History—Its Selling Power', *Business History Review*, 37/1–2 (1963), 2–5.

LANG, R. G., 'Social Origins and Social Aspirations of Jacobean London Merchants', *Ec.HR* 2nd ser. 27/1 (1974), 28–47.

LAWSON, PHILIP, and PHILIPS, JIM, ' "Our Execrable Banditti": Perceptions of Nabobs in Mid-Eighteenth-Century Britain', *Albion*, 16/3 (Fall 1984), 225–41.

LEIBENSTEIN, H., 'Bandwagon, Snob, and Veblen Effects in the Theory of Consumers' Demand', *Quarterly Journal of Economics*, 44/2 (May 1950), 183–207.

McCLOSKEY, DONALD N., 'Did Victorian Britain Fail?', *Ec.HR* 2nd ser. 23/3 (1970), 446–59.

McINNES, ANGUS, 'The Emergence of a Leisure Town: Shrewsbury, 1660–1760', *Past and Present*, 120 (Aug. 1988), 52–87.

MARWICK, ARTHUR, 'Getting Down To It', *TLS* 7 Sept. 1984, 991.

MOKYR J., 'Demand vs. Supply in the Industrial Revolution', *Journal of Economic History*, 37/4 (Dec. 1977), 981–1000.

NORRIS, J. M., 'Samuel Garbett and the Early Development of Industrial Lobbying in Great Britain', *Ec.HR* 2nd ser. 10/3 (1958), 450–60.

PUMPHREY, RALPH E., 'The Introduction of Industrialists into the British Peerage: A Study in the Adaptation of a Social Institution', *American Historical Review*, 65 (1959), 1–16.

RAGATZ, L. J., 'Absentee Landlordism in the British Caribbean, 1750–1833', *Agricultural History*, 5/1 (Jan. 1931), 7–24.

RAPP, DEAN, 'Social Mobility in the Eighteenth Century: The Whitbreads of Bedfordshire, 1720–1815', *Ec.HR* 2nd ser. 27/3 (1974), 380–94.

RAVEN, JAMES, 'The Abolition of the English State Lotteries', *Historical Journal*, 34/2 (June 1991), 371–89.

—— 'British History and the Enterprise Culture', *Past and Present*, 123 (May 1989), 178–204.

RICHARDS, R. D., 'The Lottery in the History of English Government Finance', *Economic History*, 3 (1934–7), 57–76.

ROBINSON, DWIGHT E., 'The Importance of Fashions in Taste to Business History: An Introductory Essay', *Business History Review*, 37/1–2 (1963), 5–36.

—— 'The Styling and Transmission of Fashions Historically Considered', *Journal of Economic History*, 20/4 (Mar. 1960) 576–87.

ROBINSON, E., 'Eighteenth-Century Commerce and Fashion: Matthew Boulton's Marketing Techniques', *Ec.HR* 2nd ser. 16/1 (1963), 39–60.

ROGERS, NICHOLAS, 'Money, Land and Lineage: The Big Bourgeoisie of Hanoverian London', *Social History*, 4/3 (Oct. 1979), 437–54.

ROTHSTEIN, JOHN, 'Famous Leeds Artists and Scientists', *Yorkshire Post*, 21 May 1938.

RUBINSTEIN, W. D., 'New Men of Wealth and the Purchase of Land in Nineteenth-Century England', *Past and Present*, 92 (Aug. 1981), 125–47.

—— 'Wealth, Elites and the Class Structure of Modern Britain', *Past and Present*, 76 (Aug. 1977), 99–126.

SINKO, GRZEGORZ, 'Samuel Foote: The Satirist of Rising Capitalism', *Prace Wrocawskiego Towarzystwa Naukowego*, ser. A., 47/2 (1950), 5–72.

STEELE, E. D., 'The Leeds Patriciate and the Cultivation of Learning, 1819–1905: A Study of the Leeds Philosophical and Literary Society', *Proceedings of Leeds Philosophical and Literary Society*, 16/9 (Jan. 1978), 183–202.

SYPHER, WYLIE, 'The West-Indian as a "Character" in the Eighteenth Century', *Studies in Philology*, 36/3 (July 1939), 503–20.

THOMPSON, E. P., 'Eighteenth-Century English Society: Class Struggle without Class?', *Social History*, 3/2 (May 1978), 133–65.

TROMP, HEIMERICK, 'A Dutchman's Visits to Some English Gardens in 1791', *Journal of Garden History*, 2 (1982), 41–58.

USTICK, W. Lee, 'Advice to a Son: A Type of Seventeenth-Century Conduct Book', *Studies in Philology*, 29/3 (July 1932), 409–41.

—— 'Changing Ideals of Aristocratic Character and Conduct in Seventeenth-Century England', *Modern Philology*, 30/2 (Nov. 1932), 147–66.

WARWICK, PAUL, 'Did Britain Change? An Inquiry into the Causes of National Decline', *Journal of Contemporary History*, 20/1 (Jan. 1985), 99–133.

WEATHERILL, LORNA, 'Consumer Behaviour and Social Status in England, 1660–1750', *Continuity and Change*, 1/2 (Aug. 1986), 191–216.

WILCOCKSON, COLIN, 'A Note on Riflynge in *Piers Plowman*', *Medium Ævum*, 52/2 (1983), 302–5.

WILSON, C. H., 'Twenty Years After', *Journal of European Economic History*, 1/2 (1972), 449–58.

WILSON, R. G., 'The Fortunes of a Leeds Merchant House, 1780–1820', *Business History*, 9 (1967), 70–86.

—— 'Three Brothers: A Study of the Fortunes of a Landed Family in the Mid-Eighteenth Century', *Bradford Textile Society Journal* (1964–5), III–21.

WRIGLEY, E. A., 'A Simple Model of London's Importance in Changing English Society and Economy, 1650–1750', *Past and Present*, 37 (July 1967), 44–70.

iii. Unpublished dissertations

ALLAN, DAVID G. C., 'The Society for the Encouragement of Arts, Manufacture and Commerce: Organization, Membership and Objectives in the First Three Decades, 1755–1784: An Example of Voluntary Economic and Social Policy in the Eighteenth Century', Ph.D. thesis, London University, 1977.

BENDING, STEPHEN, 'Politics, Morality, and History: The Literature of the Later Eighteenth-Century Landscape Garden', Ph.D. thesis, Cambridge University, 1991.

DICKENSON, M. J., 'The West Riding Woollen and Worsted Industries, 1689–1770', Ph.D. thesis, Nottingham University, 1974.

KENT, RICHARD, 'Home Demand as a Factor in Eighteenth-Century English Economic Growth: The Literary Evidence', M.Litt. diss. Cambridge University, 1969.

MONEY, J., 'Public Opinion in the West Midlands, 1760–1795', Ph.D. thesis, Cambridge university, 1967.

RAVEN, J. R., 'English Popular Literature and the Image of Business, 1760–1790', Ph.D. thesis, Cambridge University, 1985.

SALES, ROGER BEADON, 'The Literature of Labour and the Condition of England Question, 1730–1860', Ph.D. thesis, Cambridge University, 1975.

SYPHER, WYLIE, 'The Anti-Slavery Movement to 1800 in English Literature', Ph.D. thesis, Harvard University, 1937.

WILSON, R. G., 'Leeds Woollen Merchants, 1700–1830', Ph.D. thesis, Leeds University, 1964.

INDEX

Printed in the United Kingdom
by Lightning Source UK Ltd.
109334UKS00001B/6